MANY ROADS,
ONE JOURNEY

ALSO BY THE AUTHOR

Women, Sex, and Addiction:
A Search for Love and Power

MANY ROADS, ONE JOURNEY

MOVING BEYOND THE TWELVE STEPS

Charlotte Davis Kasl, Ph.D.

HarperPerennial
A Division of HarperCollins*Publishers*

Copyright acknowledgments appear on page 417.

Pages 327–330 contain versions of the twelve steps by various people. The reader is free to copy these pages for *personal use* as long as credit is given to the person who wrote them. They are not copyrighted except for reproduction in publications.

The reader is also free to copy pages 336–339 for personal use as long as credit is given to *Many Roads, One Journey,* copyright © 1992 by Charlotte Kasl, published by HarperCollins Publishers. For reprints in publications please contact Harper-Collins Publishers.

HarperCollins books may be purchased for educational, business, or sales promotional use. For information, please call or write: Special Markets Department, HarperCollins Publishers, Inc., 10 East 53rd Street, New York, NY 10022. Telephone: (212) 207-7528; Fax: (212) 207-7222.

First edition

Designed by Alma Orenstein

Library of Congress Cataloging-in-Publication Data

Kasl, Charlotte Davis.
    Many roads, one journey: moving beyond the twelve steps /
Charlotte Davis Kasl.—1st HarperPerennial ed.
      p.   cm.
    Includes bibliographical references and index.
    ISBN 0-06-055263-8   —ISBN 0-06-096518-5 (pbk.)
    1. Compulsive behavior—Alternative treatment.   2. Substance
abuse—Alternative treatment.   3. Codependency (Psychology)—
Alternative treatment.   4. Self-help groups. 5. Twelve-step
programs.   I. Title
RC533.K365 1992
616.86′06—dc20   90-56435

92 93 94 95 96 CC/HC 10 9 8 7 6 5 4 3 2 1
92 93 94 95 96 CC/HC 10 9 8 7 6 5 4 3 2 1 (pbk.)

Written in the hope that people will adopt a life-loving spirituality that is passionate, powerful, loving, creative, and joyful, a spirituality that embraces all life as interrelated and sacred.

The following Quaker quote embodies the spirit of this book.

"Dearly beloved Friends, these things we do not lay upon you as a rule or form to walk by; but that all, with a measure of the light, which is pure and holy may be guided . . . and so in the light walking and abiding, these things may be fulfilled in the Spirit, not in the letter: for *the letter killeth but the Spirit giveth life.*" (emphasis, the author's)

Postscript to an epistle to "the brethren in the north" issued by a meeting of elders at Balby, 1656.

Contents

Illustrations

Acknowledgments

This book was written through the voices of many people who contributed time, wisdom, and energy.

My heartfelt thanks to the ninety people who completed lengthy questionnaires bringing a personal voice to this subject. I am also grateful to over one hundred people who attended group and individual interviews bringing a diverse perspective in terms of background, race, class, gender, and experience in working with or healing from addiction. I send warm appreciation to the nearly four hundred people who responded to the Ms. magazine article on the twelve steps. Your encouragement kept me going when the going wasn't easy.

To the Society of Friends in the Twin Cities I am grateful for the title, Many Roads, One Journey, which you created for the Friends General Conference in 1986. I loved the sound and feeling of the words from the first time I heard them.

Heartfelt appreciation and wishes for a long vacation to Janet Goldstein, my editor, for guidance and insightful input. A bouquet of roses for Edith Kroll, my agent, for invaluable input, support, and friendship. I also appreciate the creative input, humor, support, and editing throughout the process by Barbara Miller. To Linda Taber, who has managed my office with great efficiency and creativity and helped bring organization to my life, blessings and best wishes. Even though I'm moving away, you will be with me always in spirit. Thanks to Peternelle van Arsdale, at HarperCollins, for coordinating much of this project.

To my dear sister, Lenore Davis, who did the illustrations—it was great fun to collaborate. It's magical to watch you work, and I look forward to our next venture together. Also, to Pat Rouse who did the graphics, many thanks for your patience and creative work.

I appreciate the interviews given by numerous pioneers in the field of addiction recovery—Jean Kirkpatrick, James Christopher, James Milam, Jack Trimpey, Joan Matthews Larson, P. Joseph Frawley, M.D., Joanne Detweiler, Antiga, Martha Boesing, Anodea Judith, and members of the Upper Midwest Sexual Abuse Consortium. The views of these people represent a broad range of perspectives validating that there are indeed many different roads on the journey. I did my utmost to quote precisely from our interviews but take responsibility for the presentation of their ideas.

Special thanks to Mary Daly who helped me bring my thoughts together on the notion of a Life-Loving/Creative spirituality and for support to be creative and speak my truths. Also thanks to Gloria Steinem for support in writing an article on the twelve steps for Ms.

To others who helped edit, gave wonderful support, sent articles of interest, and made helpful suggestions, thank you so much: This list includes Gail Derrick, Gail Lewellan, Faye Heille, Virginia Jacobson, Marjory Singher, Aaron Perry, Paul Victor Kirschman, and Fred Johnson.

And to those of you who helped me through my own healing journey this past year, with Reiki healing, love, care, tenderness, and humor, I send you gratitude and bright blessings: Denise Wakefield Dearly, Mary Lee Hardenbergh, Adair Soderholm, Barbara Simmonds, Laurie Savran, Kristie Houser, Yvonne Barrett, Jerry Dearly, Bea Liu, and Aya de León.

To my father, Kenneth Pickett Davis, who had an inquisitive, logical mind and supported me questioning everything (except him, of course), thanks for paving the way. Finally, I thank my grandma, Charlotte Pickett Davis, who read to me, told me stories, loved me, and taught me to question. Your spirit is very much with me.

CHARLOTTE KASL

January 1992
Minneapolis, Minnesota

Introduction

S ometime in 1985, in a grubby church basement lounge, I did what
seemed like a small personal act. I said to the women in my small
twelve-step recovery group, "I can no longer say these steps as written
because they don't feel right to me. Either I have to say them in a way
that feels good, or I have to leave. I'm not asking anyone else to change
or agree with me, but I'm violating myself to say them this way."

Making this statement in my group was scary—like going up
against some immutable force of tradition that for many was beyond
question. I didn't want to lose my connection with the group, but the
conflict was exhausting me; I was getting a knot in my gut and an urge
to sleep before every group meeting. I also felt caught in the loneliness
of self-betrayal, knowing in my heart that my silence violated my
deeply cherished Quaker belief that the highest spiritual value is to
speak the truth, even if it means taking a risk.

Many of the women in my group responded positively to my
request, while a few remained silent. What the silence masked I'll never
know, but I was greatly relieved that no one suggested I should leave.
I stayed, and said the steps my way. Some of the other women did
likewise, which brought an aliveness and spontaneity to the group that
I came to treasure.

As it turned out, my small personal act was not an isolated event.
In many twelve-step meetings across the country people were saying (or
wanting to say) they were dissatisfied with aspects of the twelve-step

model. Others had left groups, feeling alienated or discouraged, and still others had attended one or two meetings but were unable to relate to the whole approach. As a result of networking and talking with many people, in 1986 I put together a monograph on the subject: "A Quaker Feminist Perspective on the 12 Steps."

Over a period of years I gave talks and presented several workshops for organizations such as the Association of Women in Psychology and the National Women's Studies Association to get a broad feel for what women were saying about the twelve-step programs. In addition, I was asked to participate in a Minnesota state-funded project to develop a treatment manual that took into account all relevant concerns of women seeking sobriety and that empowered women to think for themselves. My chapter was to be a spin-off of my article, "A Quaker Feminist Perspective," presenting different models of recovery and encouraging women to reword and rewrite the twelve steps based on their own internal wisdom, or to adopt new steps that fit for them.

The strong positive response to the chapter by women and men supported my belief that a massive movement for change was well underway. I felt excited by the prospect of exploring the subject more deeply and putting together a book. It was like starting on an adventure with a general idea in mind, but not really knowing what I would find.

To gather information for the book, I distributed lengthy questionnaires and held numerous group and individual interviews with richly diverse groups of people. Of the 80 completed questionnaires, 76 were from women. The personal interviews with over 100 people included a more even proportion of men to women. I have also interviewed therapists and psychologists who work with clients who are dealing with addictions as well as childhood abuse.

My journey in writing this book has taken me to inner-city treatment programs for African Americans, to a healing center on a Native American reservation in Montana, to a rural woman's treatment program in Ohio, and to an ashram in Massachusetts where people combine meditation, service, and yoga with twelve-step programs. If there was anything I learned and relearned, it is that people heal and grow in immensely different ways and that there is a great deal to be learned through listening to others tell their stories and share their beliefs.

The willingness of so many people to tell me their stories and give of their time by filling out questionnaires reinforced my belief that there are many voices with strong opinions on this subject, eager for change.

While writing the book I had a brief excerpt of my empowerment version of the twelve steps in the December 1990 *Ms.* magazine called "The Twelve Step Controversy." Nearly four hundred people (all but four were women) wrote to me and many others to *Ms.* The responses varied immensely, ranging from people's being extremely relieved to their being upset and angry, as if I were committing heresy to question the twelve-step model.

This led me to ponder the whole notion of fear and its pervasiveness in our culture, particularly when people start to deviate from traditional forms, be creative, and speak from the heart. Even people who willingly came for interviews expressed fear of discussing this subject. This led me to devote a whole chapter to exploring people's fear of questioning institutions along with an affirmation of the need for people to question, struggle, and internalize a personal set of values that feel grounded and rooted within.

As with many projects, the initial subject broadened. The question, "How do people best heal from addiction?" became, "Why is addiction so pervasive in our culture? What are the roots and what has to happen to create systemic change?" Thus looking at the functioning of twelve-step groups became a mirror for looking at our social system, our approaches to healing, and the many ways we are affected by societal conditioning.

Many Roads, One Journey is for all people, but it is essentially positioned from the perspective of women and minorities, for it is their reality which has so often been omitted in approaches to overcoming addiction and dependency. Thus it gives support to people who want to follow or create new models for healing, and can be used to increase everyone's sensitivity to the beliefs and perspectives of others.

The subtitle *Moving Beyond the Twelve Steps* can be understood in different ways. Some people are moving beyond the specific twelve steps by rewording them, others are moving beyond the model and using other approaches, and still others are feeling healed from addiction and no longer attend support groups of any kind. If I could sum up my hopes for this book in writing, this is what they would be:

That people come to believe that healing from addiction and dependency can involve all of a person's potential—the rational mind, creativity, passion, power, internal wisdom, and social conscience.

That the form for models of healing should follow individual's needs, not imprison a person in a system that remains an external authority as a parent is to a child.

That people become healthy and empowered by learning to think for themselves, listening to the signals of their bodies, and trusting what they hear.

That people move beyond the concept of being an addicted person to that of being a sacred person who is an integral and important part of society at large.

At a societal level, I hope:

That we come to realize that addiction and dependency are societal problems rooted in the sexism, racism, and poverty that result from hierarchy and patriarchy. Even if an addiction such as alcoholism has a genetic factor, the will to abstain and the availability of help is tied to our social system.

That for many the seeds of addiction and dependency are planted in the first years of life and reinforced through social inequities that pervade our culture.

That prevention is possible and must start with a vast shift in consciousness concerning the importance of childhood development, including the need for bonding, stability, food, shelter, protection, and mental stimulation.

That prevention must include a deep examination of racism, sexism, and homophobia, and take steps to help people and institutions operate from the stance that all life is sacred.

Although many of the chapters are self-contained and need not be read sequentially, the book takes the reader on a journey leading up to an empowerment/discovery model. I start by looking at the need to understand different people's needs, and then look at fear as a block to developing a healthy, aware sense of self and define what it is to be a fully functioning human being. I then define all forms of addiction and dependency at physical, psychological, and spiritual levels, and suggest there is great diversity in the forms addiction takes and thus a need for diverse approaches to healing.

In the next section, I describe some specific models of recovery, including Women for Sobriety, Rational Recovery, the Secular Organization for Sobriety, and aversion therapy. I devote several chapters to people's reactions, both positive and negative, to twelve-step groups, along with an exploration of their "approved" literature and of the sexual and emotional abuse that sometimes takes place in groups.

I am not advocating that we throw the baby out with the bath water in regard to the twelve steps. Rather, I hope to explore the wisdom inherent in this and other models of recovery, to reach for their essence and encourage people to think for themselves and create a path that flows from their internal wisdom. Thus healing from addiction becomes a process of trial and error, experimentation and search, rather than adherence to a fixed external form.

Another question I explore is the adaptation of the steps for survivors of abuse or those with "codependent" traits, which I will explore as a euphemism for characteristics of internalized oppression. I suggest that applying the twelve-step model—intended to break down an inflated ego—to people lacking ego strength further perpetuates many people's victimization.

In the last section, I suggest ways to make twelve-step groups more flexible and then propose a sixteen-step form for empowerment and discovery. It is not proposed as a rigid model but rather as a springboard; I urge people to take a leap into their own wisdom and find the words that speak powerfully for them. Finally I suggest a massive shift in consciousness along with social action to stop the escalation of addiction, which is a symptom of our declining culture.

As a feminist, Quaker, psychologist, healer, peace and social justice activist, and a woman on my own spiritual journey, I bring a wide range of perspectives to this book.

The feminist in me seeks a model that fully reflects the needs of women and minorities in recovery, a model that affirms all people's wellspring of personal power and creativity and promotes understanding between diverse groups of people.

The Quaker part of me believes in a spirituality that is life-loving and creative rather than the traditional Christian belief in original sin which one must redeem throughout life—a philosophy which is the source of much child abuse, violence, and low self-esteem. A basic Quaker belief, also embodied in other religions, is that God or Goddess or Spirit resides in all people and that we are born blessed.

I bring my perspective as a psychologist who has worked for fifteen years with women and men healing from addiction which was often directly connected to childhood abuse and neglect. A large part of my practice has been with groups. I have heard numerous accounts of experiences with regard to twelve-step groups, from extremely positive to extremely negative. Seeing people get stuck in the self-defined role of addict, which limits their thinking and expansiveness, has led me to an approach that moves beyond "getting over" abuse and addiction to becoming an empowered human being—self-aware, self-protective, wise, lively, passionate, and creative. Also, in response to people who define themselves as codependent and focus on staying *detached* from partners and friends who are abusive or neglectful, I shift the focus to finding healthy *attachments* with people who are emotionally available.

As a healer working with energy systems in the body at the physical, psychological, and spiritual levels, I am interested in going to the core of addiction and dependency. Energy work is done at the level of transformation and transmutation rather than control or management of problems. The goal is to truly release a person from negative core beliefs, fear, the sting of painful memories, and the urge to self-destruct. This creates internal balance, which leads to a sense of inner security and freedom. As a result of inner healing, some people transcend addictions and, while the body may be physically unable to tolerate a substance throughout life, the addictive impulse dissolves, removing the need to attend addiction recovery groups.

The peace and social justice activist in me seeks a model that helps people move beyond a self-contained identity as an "addict" or "codependent" and become identified with all people living perfectly imperfect lives in a world both troubled and beautiful. It is important that personal healing extend to include an exploration of our relationship to our community and to society that eventually results in social action; otherwise we are still living in denial, cut off from a part of ourselves and others.

From a personal perspective, I write this book as a woman on my own spiritual journey who has attended three different twelve-step groups, and who appreciated the support, but reached a point when it felt right to move on. I have a passionate interest in finding approaches that are expansive, exciting, creative, and empowering, both for myself and others.

Now I invite you to come on this journey into the lives of people who are moving beyond addiction, each in their own special way. To get an idea of the diversity of people's healing journeys, imagine a road map of the United States or another country where everyone is heading toward their favorite place. For some, it would be the mountains to go hiking; for others, a beach; for others, a nightclub in the city. Some would just stay home and relax. Some would go by air, others in cars or by trains, buses, or bicycles, or on foot. The important point is that people go where their heart and wisdom leads them, using the means that fit for them. There are truly many roads on the journey.

PART I

A Time for Change

1

Naming the Controversy:
Different People, Different Needs

In 1935, when Bill Wilson, cofounder of Alcoholics Anonymous, stopped drinking alcohol, he went home to a loyal, dedicated wife, a warm home with enough food, and a circle of people who cared about him. He had a law degree, was an experienced stockbroker, and had all the privileges accorded an upper-middle-class white man from an old New England family. Most of the men who were instrumental in putting together the AA program and whose experiences were to be recorded in *Alcoholics Anonymous*, the AA "Big Book," came from similar backgrounds.

Fifty-two years later, in 1987, when a woman named Cathy sobered up at age thirty-two, she went home to a small apartment in a poor neighborhood in Cleveland, two difficult children, and an abusive boyfriend. Two weeks into her newfound sobriety, long-repressed memories of incest—no longer shielded by alcohol and drugs—began to surface, plunging her into anxiety and depression. A psychiatrist put her on antidepressants. Not trusting the system to give her help, she didn't reveal to anyone that she was being battered by her partner. A physician prescribed pain killers for a back problem that resulted from the abuse. She began eating compulsively and eventually relapsed into substance addiction. A year later she was admitted to a hospital for severe depression and drug addiction. Eventually, she was able to maintain sobriety—after attending an all-women's treatment program and an incest survivors' group where she could also talk about the violence in her relationship.

Joseph, a Native American, started to drink in the Army, where it was considered "manly." He had been through World War II, the Korean War, and what he called the "worst war of all"—being emotionally, physically, and sexually abused in a Catholic boarding school where he had been taken against his will as part of a government-ordered program to "assimilate" Native Americans into white culture. Thirty-four years later, after a vision of a relative came to him, he quit drinking. For the first month he had hallucinations and the shakes, couldn't sleep, and was afraid he would die. He couldn't imagine what he would do with his life. He felt it was over and that he was condemned. Living in Butte, Montana, separated from his Native American culture, Joseph worked in a mine with mostly white people and knew only one other sober person—his sister. He never drank again and eventually returned to his native reservation, where he reconnected with his people's rituals and customs and worked at a healing center for alcoholism.

Madge was an upper-middle-class woman of thirty-seven when she first went through a women's treatment program for addiction to alcohol and prescription medications. After she completed the program, she ate compulsively and eventually returned to drinking. For years she had lived in the shadow of her professionally successful husband, medicating her resentments. She also had a well-kept secret that fueled her desire to escape. She went through treatment three times before a counselor helped her open up the buried subject of her attraction to women. Only then was she able to maintain her sobriety, which cleared the way to begin the process of giving up the security, stability, and status of her home and heterosexual privilege to "come out" as a lesbian.

Alan, a history teacher, joined AA after an intervention by family and friends. While he appreciated the support from other people recovering in the group, he felt increasingly negative about the AA belief in setting aside logic and reason and surrendering to God or a Higher Power. He left the group, tried a program for controlled use of alcohol, and started drinking again. He then realized that abstinence was the only way for him. He eventually decided to use Antabuse, a substance that makes you violently ill if you drink, to keep from drinking. Since then, he's never attended a support group and has been sober for many years.

Cathy, Madge, and Alan could be any race or color. Their stories reflect many people's experiences. There are many other stories I could tell. In 1948, my Uncle Ron overcame alcoholism with the help of an aversion treatment program in Seattle called Shadel. He never attended AA, and he helped more than four hundred people find sobriety through aversion therapy, an approach still available but not widely understood or used. Danny, a young Native American/Caucasian from the South, told me he quit drinking at eighteen "because I get crazy from that stuff." He never had treatment and he never joined a support group. His life has been chaotic, but he doesn't drink.

Whatever your feelings about the different ways these people sobered up, the fact is that they are all sober today. Some used twelve-step support groups and some didn't. Some found life after sobriety a great improvement over their using days; for others, sobriety opened the door to new problems and old pain that had been buried under alcohol and drugs.

LOOKING BACK

Bill Wilson's imagination, determination, and creativity in putting together the twelve-step program that worked for him and many others does not change the fact that he was influenced by white, male, middle-class Christian values of the 1930s. Bill Wilson could not have known about issues that would become central in the ensuing decades—sexism, racism, homophobia, drug abuse, homelessness, and child sexual abuse—that are interwoven with addiction. He could not have known that, fifty years later, the steps he wrote would be used internationally for men and women struggling with all types of addictions—from narcotics to food, sex, dependent relationships, medication, smoking, gambling, and spending, as well as incest and emotional problems.

It is important to remember that Bill Wilson based the steps and the Big Book on experiences of a hundred white men and one woman. He also based his definition of an alcoholic personality—egocentric, arrogant, resentful, controlling, or violent—on these people. I think this is a mistaken personality syndrome that frequently describes traits of white, upper-middle-class men who have power in the system. There are many men with these personality traits who are not alcoholic or drug addicted, and there are countless people who are passive, afraid, and lacking a sense of self who are alcoholic and drug addicted.

When Bill Wilson put together the twelve steps, he wasn't trying to stop smoking (he died of emphysema), he wasn't concerned with addictive sexual impulses, and he was not interested in examining his dependency on his wife, Lois. He was thinking about *not drinking*, primarily as it applied to people like himself. His goal was to stay sober in order to stay alive, and it worked for him and for many others like him. It was an incredible breakthrough in finding a way to stop drinking.

But that doesn't mean it always works for everyone or every form of addiction or dependency. Can we really say that compulsive eating, so prevalent among women, comes from the same source as alcoholism and needs the same approach for healing? If, as many people suggest, compulsive eating stems more from lack of power in society, incest and childhood abuse, and the media's portrayal of beautiful women as inordinately thin, the twelve steps do not address these core issues.

THROUGH THE VOICES OF MANY PEOPLE

For several years I gathered information for this book simply by talking about the subject and observing and pondering people's responses. At a presentation I gave in 1987 in which I presented alternative empowerment steps particularly designed for codependency, I had sixty-three requests for copies of the steps—all but one from women. I observed my clients trying twelve-step groups, sometimes with success, but sometimes leaving because they couldn't relate to the God-language, or the intense reverence for the model, or the male domination in the groups.

The thirty-one page questionnaire that was filled out, primarily by women from around the United States, gave me a broader view. In both interviews and questionnaires I asked what was helpful and what was harmful or limiting about recovery groups, treatment programs, psychotherapy, literature, nutritional counseling, sponsors, same-sex groups, and same-ethnic groups. I asked numerous questions on dating, flirting, and sexual exploitation in groups as well as major turning points in recovery. Then I presented a sixteen-step empowerment/discovery model and asked for people's input. Although not everyone was enthusiastic, many were. One woman wrote, "Very beautiful. Let's get going on these." Others wrote, "What a relief it is to read these steps. Something always felt wrong to me, but I didn't know what it was." Many wrote to say they had adopted the steps in their groups, and several counselors from treatment programs said they were integrating the ideas.

The interviews included privileged white males who came from a background similar to Bill Wilson's, Native American men and women, psychotherapists who work with addiction, treatment counselors who are also recovering from addiction, people from an African-American treatment program, and groups of lesbian and heterosexual women who have attended twelve-step groups for myriad addiction and dependency problems: drugs, food, sexually dependent relationships, and more.

While collecting stories for this book or presenting workshops and talks on the subject, or in response to my writing, I have encountered some strongly felt resistance. "Who do you think you are to raise these questions?" "You can't change the steps—you haven't been a down-and-out drunk like Bill Wilson." "It saved my life." "The traditions say that AA shouldn't be brought into public controversy." "The alternative to Alcoholics Anonymous is death, prison, and insanity." The underlying message was that there is only one road, one way to sobriety.

And there were some very convincing stories.

I interviewed a taxi driver who said he owed his life to "the program." He was battered as a child, educated through the eighth grade, and hospitalized several times with mental illness. His pride in his sobriety and his gratitude to AA were heartrending. The AA slogans and belief system had become his language, his recipe for life. "Yep, if I went to a new city I'd go to ninety meetings in ninety days. That's what you have to do to stay sober." He had found a prescription for survival—free of charge—that no doctor or hospital had been able to give him.

That was one end of the spectrum. On the other end was Andrea, who came to therapy deeply scarred from her AA experience. Her trust in herself was totally shattered and she had all the symptoms of a person brainwashed by a cult. She had been taught to believe that the group kept her sober, that it was the best AA group, and that people who questioned AA were deluded, lacked humility, were on a "dry drunk," or hadn't accepted their powerlessness.

Her particular group was dominated by a charismatic man who attracted dependent, vulnerable women whom he advised, controlled, and shamed without mercy. If they so much as questioned the program, he would yell, "You must turn your life and your will over to this group." Members of this group were taught to carry the "Big Book" with them, read nothing but program literature, and look with scorn on those who didn't. The leader was sexually abusive, requiring women to stand before the group and hear how seductive, disgusting, and disloyal they were. The other men in the group, often lacking identity or assurance, copied his approach.

Although Andrea mustered the strength to leave the group, has never again attended AA, and is still sober, the leader's constant, righteous threats that she would surely use drugs again have rumbled in her brain, waking her at night and penetrating her with fear for a long, long time. Several years later she still felt nervous whenever she knew I was giving a talk suggesting changes in the twelve steps, because it triggered the unconscious fear that something terrible would happen to me for questioning the twelve steps.

In the past fourteen years of working with women and men "recovering" from addiction, along with the enthusiastic responses to and horror stories about twelve-step programs, I have heard many mixed reviews. Many people appreciate the support they get there, but find the steps oppressive and dislike the rigid approach or the custom of reading the Lord's Prayer. It is time to examine AA and the twelve steps, viewing it as *one* approach with strengths and limitations—a program that works for some but not for everyone; a program that may provide one part of healing from addiction and dependency, but, for many, is not a cure-all.

NOTES ON LANGUAGE

You might notice I put the word "recovery" in quotes. Because the power of language so strongly affects our unconscious beliefs, and this book is about a new understanding of addiction, I am changing some terms. The idea for this comes from Mary Daly, the author of *Gyn/Ecology* and other important books in which she explores the use of these terms and many others. The implication of *re-covery* is to cover something over. I am interested in helping people *un-cover* all the programming and beliefs that keep them mired down, depressed, impoverished in mind and spirit. My image is of people casting off the blanket of addiction that holds them down, keeps their senses numbed, and perpetuates isolation. Thus we start the process by un-covering our thoughts and beliefs that perpetuate addiction, and then dis-covering our true selves.

Throughout the book, when I use the word recovery, I refer to people having their minds and spirits covered over. I will use *un-covery* to connote "getting out from under" addiction, and I will use *dis-covery* to mean opening up, learning, growing, and exercising free choice. Another definition I want to make clear is that of substance abuse or chemical dependency. I use this term for alcohol, drugs, medication, and foods used compulsively or addictively.

WHAT ABOUT CODEPENDENCY AND ADULT CHILDREN OF ALCOHOLICS?

So far I have focused primarily on groups for addiction. The twelve steps have been taken as written for addiction groups and used for "codependency" groups—partners and children of addicted people. These codependency groups have expanded by the thousands and include anyone from a "dysfunctional family," the definition of which has broadened to include not only families with alcoholic parents but also families where there is incest, physical abuse, or where parents looked to their children to meet their emotional needs.

I believe the term "dysfunctional family," which became so prevalent in the eighties has too often led people to have a one-dimensional perspective on their families. While some are extremely abusive, most families are a mixed bag with numerous strengths and weaknesses. Instead of flatly describing a family as "dysfunctional" it would be more useful for people to recognize the traits that were harmful, along with the legacy of strengths that were passed on. It would also be more accurate to move beyond the term *dysfunctional* and understand families as *sexist*. This more accurately describes the power imbalance inherent in traditional heterosexual families which naturally leads to dysfunction.

Many people attend both addiction and codependency groups. Codependency has many definitions. In essence, it describes people who lack a defined inner self, feel defective, and, as a result, look outside themselves for self-esteem and self-definition. This often results in their constantly performing and striving to "do it right" to please parents, teachers, spouses, children, friends, and partners. Other codependent traits are passivity; docility; the inability to act out or express anger directly; staying in painful, destructive relationships; controlling others; and setting one's own needs aside to please others.

In chapter 11, "Moving Beyond Codependency," I discuss the adaptation of the original twelve steps for "codependency" because they were designed to break down an inflated ego. People who have been victimized and oppressed need to build a sense of ego and affirm their power in order to take charge of their lives. Reminding people of their faults and reinforcing humility hardly seems the remedy for a person who has little sense of self, feels ashamed of being alive, and self-blames for just about everything that goes wrong. I also question using the codependency concept without a cultural framework that looks at domination, subordination, and oppression. I suggest that the traits of "codependency" are synonymous with the traits of internalized oppression.

For people who are both addicted and have traits of codependency/oppression, it is important to discern core problems and use a model of healing that is appropriate. Even though a person may be alcoholic or drug addicted, if these addictions are symptomatic of a deeper sense of dependency and lack of self, then the model used should help build up the self and support empowerment. For example, while Andrea, who was abused in her twelve-step group, had a drug and alcohol addiction and presented a tough exterior, it was clearly a fragile cover for childhood battering, incest, and neglect, and she needed understanding, tenderness, affirmation of self, and alleviation from shame. These were the core problems that needed to be un-covered. Both her "codependent" behavior and her addiction started as survival behaviors used in an attempt to escape pain, feel pleasure, or find meaning. The positive intention was to take care of herself, feel a sense of control, to be loved or avoid being abused. In general, traits of codependency/oppression and addiction both are ways people attempt to gain power, feel pleasure, find security, protect themselves, and anesthetize pain. Thus when I refer to addiction in a general way, I also include people who suffer from debilitating dependent behavior.

WOMEN'S FEAR OF QUESTIONING THE TWELVE STEPS

While both women and men are questioning the twelve steps, the preponderance of discontent appears among women. It is not surprising that it has taken women nearly fifty years to start questioning the AA twelve-step model en masse. As women we are socialized to be loyal to male institutions and protect male egos. The punishment for doing otherwise is being called bitches, dykes, and man-haters, and being physically assaulted and sometimes losing jobs, partners, and friends. Thus many women self-protect by keeping their doubts to themselves.

Many women reported negative reactions in their attempts to question twelve-step groups or treatment approaches, especially in settings dominated by men or women who are rigidly attached to the model. One woman in a training program for chemical dependency counselors questioned the program's male God-language, only to be told that if she "kept that up," she would be asked to leave the training program. One woman who took the empowerment steps I wrote to her treatment counselor was told, "off the record," that the counselor preferred this model and hadn't attended AA for two years, but if she said anything she might lose her job. Thus the program perpetuated oppression—dutiful obedience at the cost of honesty and self-affirmation. Another woman described an AA meeting where several women suggested they refer to God without using the pronoun "he." Several men got up and walked out.

The doubts of men who are independent thinkers and of agnostics who question the twelve-step approach are also countered with similar patronizing statements that suggest something is wrong with them for not accepting the program with complete loyalty. The most common responses of these independent thinkers are that the program feels too religious or too rigid, and that they feel too much like a bunch of sheep.

Many people have confided to me that they personally change the steps, omit the word God, inventory their strengths rather than their shortcomings, and don't read the program literature. Until recently, few have said so openly for fear of recrimination and rejection. But the hunger for something that is positive, empowering, and nonshaming is growing.

GRASS-ROOTS MOVEMENTS FOR CHANGE

Different kinds of people with different needs have given birth to a ground swell of activity leading to revisions and expansion of the twelve-step model and a shift in focus on what is important to uncovering from addiction. Treatment programs by and for women, lesbians and gays, teenagers, African Americans, and Native Americans are recognizing the multitude of problems underlying or coupled with substance abuse or repeated relapses.

It is not surprising that minority groups are forming their own support groups or creating their own treatment programs. Drug and alcohol treatment has a narrow focus and was created by and for white, upper-middle-class men who have been insensitive to the needs of minority peoples. In interviews with numerous minority groups, people mentioned two common themes: first, that there is great comfort, safety, and trust in being with a homogeneous group whose members understand and accept each other at a cultural, racial, or sexual preference level; second, that part of discovery is linking the addiction to oppression of their particular group and understanding the impact it has on their addiction and attempts to un-cover.

As an African-American man said, "In an all Black group, I don't have to sit and wonder what that white person is really thinking about me—if he jokes about me behind my back or if he would be loyal to me outside of the group." Likewise, other minority groups talk about sharing common concerns and being understood in their support groups: "coming out" for gay and lesbian people; being working class in a culture that ignores class differences; growing up on a Native American reservation; or simply being a woman in patriarchy. Another theme was that minority people felt more comfortable talking about battering and violence in their own reference groups because they did not want to expose these problems to people who held a dominant position over them in the culture. Some of these treatment programs and support groups use the twelve-step model; some de-emphasize the steps, some suggest rewording them, and some don't use them at all. But, most important, these groups seek a wholistic approach to healing for chemical dependency that fits their needs.

Existing models besides AA are Women for Sobriety (WFS), started by Jean Kirkpatrick in 1976, which has about three hundred fifty groups nationwide. There is also Rational Recovery, described by Jack Trimpey in a book by that name. James Christopher has pioneered Save Our Selves, or the Secular Organization for Sobriety (SOS). I will describe these programs in chapter 7.

Founders of the three above-mentioned models all stated that they were not in competition with AA; rather, they were creating models that worked for them and provided choices for other people like themselves who did not like twelve-step groups.

OTHER PATHS ON THE JOURNEY

There is considerable research that links healing from chemical dependency to repairing the body ecology in order to relieve cravings and alleviate emotional problems that are exacerbated by a depleted body. Health Recovery Associates in Minneapolis takes a more physical approach, advertising "physical healing for a physical disease."

In the Minneapolis-St. Paul area there are at least three programs that address women's special needs. One woman's treatment program no longer uses the twelve steps at all; it uses instead an empowerment model that raises consciousness on how the culture impacts women and urges women to realize they have choices. Because this program recognizes the importance of support groups, women are required to attend either AA or WFS weekly, but the program is open to new models that are empowering for women.

The most important goal is to have many roads that lead to un-covery from addiction. The more people move beyond addiction and dis-cover their inherent power and capacity for joy, the better for everyone. The important words are choice and support for people to do what feels best for them.

Because of individual, cultural, and religious differences and the numerous types of addiction and dependency problems, it follows that no one model or set of words will work for all people at all times. Some people need to shore up a shaky, guilt-ridden ego. Others need to deflate their arrogance. Some people need to do both. Others want their own ethnic group, or a gender-specific group, while some want a diverse mixture.

I have spoken of ethnic, racial, and specific gender groups' wanting to be separate. This wasn't true for everyone. If I learned one thing through my interviews, it is that one cannot generalize about any group of people. There are always individual differences. While many women prefer women-only groups, several spoke of the warmth and support they appreciated receiving from men in a mixed meeting. Some lesbian women preferred groups mixed with heterosexual women and some with men as well. One Native American said he really learned how a good step meeting went in a primarily white group. One Native Ameri-can center in Montana used Native American rituals, psychotherapy, advocacy, AA, and even Catholicism, taking their wisdom in spirit without becoming lost in rhetoric or dogma.

"THE LETTER KILLETH AND THE SPIRIT GIVETH LIFE"

Like many models or forms of healing that started out working better than anything else available, AA attracts grateful disciples who forget the model is just a model—a form and words put together by a human being. They forget that it is health, un-covery, dis-covery, and healing that are sacred, not the words we use to get us there.

Words are words. They are not truths. They are not holy. Words are mechanisms that connect us to existing truths. As with universal symbols, we do not create truths, we discover them. They have always existed. Language is simply a vehicle to get us from mind to spirit, from unconsciousness to awareness—to our internal, spiritual center, which could be called the living God, Goddess, or Great Spirit that resides within.

Yet words are extremely important. What we say conditions our perceptions and thoughts. The words we use can condition our minds to think in a certain way often resulting in rigid, narrow perceptions. When we are flexible with words and continually seek those that feel right and affirm our beliefs, we come to know ourselves more deeply because we stay tuned into our inner world. Also, by hearing people use different words to describe a situation, our minds can expand: "Aha! When you say it that way, it all makes sense."

Words carry a vibration that can penetrate and heal when they feel right. Many people have a favorite poem or saying that helps bring a sense of calm when they are feeling upset. One of my favorites is, "The Lord is my shepherd, I shall not want." Or the line from Kabir's ecstatic poem #43: "The Universe is shot through in all parts by a single sort of love." Just saying these phrases brings a feeling of calm. I don't need to know why. I just feel it. A favorite group experience of mine is to have everyone say the phrases that help them get back on center and feel good. At the end of doing this, the feeling of the group is often lighter and more calm. That's how powerful words can be in shifting energy in the body and in groups of people.

In many patriarchal religious practices, the words and rituals become the core, and the essence of the religion becomes buried under rigid rhetoric, dogma, and the beliefs and prejudices of the dominant few. As a result, the spirit of love, compassion, and acceptance gets lost. The same thing sometimes happens with the twelve-step model.

It is a symptom of our addictive society's dysfunction for us to want quick fixes and simple answers, a neat and tidy path uncluttered by differences. Thus, like adolescents clinging to their peer group, people cling to the twelve-step model and are defensive when others suggest it has limitations or is not effective for everyone. "If it has worked for so many people, don't question it. And if it doesn't work for you, then it is *your* resistance, *your* unwillingness to change, *your* problem." This is not what Bill Wilson intended.

A RETURN TO THE SPIRIT OF BILL W.

I have been fascinated by accounts of Bill W.'s creativity, flexibility, and willingness to change. He observed people, asked questions, listened to their ideas. His searching mind was always open to new possibilities. He sought to understand alcoholism both as a physical and spiritual problem. He was interested in the concept of alcohol as an "allergy," or as somehow related to hypoglycemia. He explored psychic phenomena, experimented with LSD, and used a Ouija board. In contrast, talking to some current AA loyalists tends to surface pat answers, closed minds, and dreary rhetoric.

Bill was flexible when he talked with others affected by alcoholism. As described in *Bill W.*, by Robert Thomsen, his heartfelt desire was to reach "other drunks" who were suffering, and draw them closer to each other. In this biography, there are touching references to those moments of an I-Thou connection—seeing the hope ignite in a fellow drunk's eyes as they talked, one drunk to another. "In talking with others, he would say higher power, life force, or any words the listener might be comfortable with." For him the program was not etched in stone. It was deeply centered in fellowship and service to others.

Bill constantly reminded people that AA was a "suggested program of recovery." "You can't tell addicts what to do," he said. "You just bang up against their defenses. They have to come to it themselves." In responding to mail, and throughout AA history, he would say things like: "Of course you are at liberty to handle this matter any way you choose, but the bulk of our experience does seem to suggest . . ."

As described in *Pass It On*, Bill Wilson eventually decided to step down from his leadership role with AA because he felt too many people looked to him as a father figure. In a letter attempting to clarify his thoughts, he wrote, "I understand that the father symbol will always be hitched to me. Therefore, the problem is not how to get rid of parenthood; it is how to discharge mature parenthood properly.

"A dictatorship always refuses to do this and so do the hierarchical churches. . . . They sincerely feel that their several families can never be enough educated (or spiritualized) to properly guide their own destinies. Therefore, people who have to live within the structure of dictatorships and hierarchies must lose, to a greater or lesser degree, the opportunity of really growing up. I think AA can avoid this temptation to concentrate its power, and I truly believe that it is going to be intelligent enough and spiritualized enough to rely on our group conscience."

Let's suppose that Bill Wilson were still alive. What would he do in the face of mounting doubt about the program's effectiveness as it is currently practiced? What would his response be to people saying they don't like the male God-language or that the notion of a moral inventory is shaming or an inappropriate starting place for abuse survivors? Would he dismiss people who call themselves rational thinkers who don't believe their sobriety comes from a higher power? What would his response be to people attending Secular Sobriety or Women for Sobriety groups, or to reading data about people who aren't helped by AA? What would he say about the fact that African Americans, women, gays and lesbians have felt the sharp pangs of discrimination in groups, or that Native Americans want a form of healing that honors their customs?

I think Bill Wilson would sit down and talk with them, taking seriously what they have to say. After all, that is what happened during the formation of the steps. He didn't just write all twelve steps in one day. He drew from the Oxford Group, an organization that predated AA groups, where people had achieved sobriety, and reflected on five years of his uncovery, asking himself, "What worked for me and for others?" He took the six steps the Oxford Group had used, expanded them to twelve steps, and submitted them to the scrutiny of other recovering people. There was plenty of heated debate and strong emotion expressed before something resembling consensus was reached.

I believe Bill Wilson would listen openly and expand his vision. If he were still alive, he might greatly revise the Big Book or be moved to greater social activism. We are left to guess, but creative pioneers like Bill Wilson seldom stop changing and looking for deeper answers to life's questions.

LEARNING FROM THOSE WHO KNOW

So what roads do we take in this age of diversity in order to help people seeking uncovery from addictions and dependency? We can distill the wisdom of the twelve-step model and bring it into harmony with our current knowledge. We can also open our minds to totally separate roads. I suggest we stop looking for one answer and start looking for many.

It is common for second- and third-generation followers of a school of thought or a model for healing to become rigid about its application and often to get caught up in the letter of the model while forgetting the spirit. That's how we've ended up with rigid, defensive thinking about AA that leads treatment programs to tell their clients only about AA when other models exist. When people are threatened with statements like, "If you leave the program, you'll surely use again" and "Don't make any major decisions for a year after you sober up" regardless of their personal situation, we are sliding into a dangerous one-size-fits-all mode that is sure to be wrong for many people. In many

situations the spirit of Bill Wilson's suggested model got lost somewhere as the program was handed down through the years. Many times
the model was controlled by white males who dominated the recovery
groups, women who blindly accepted their leadership, and treatment
programs often run by people new to recovery who projected many of
their unresolved conflicts on their clients.

My intention is to open discussion reflecting the spirit of Bill
Wilson and to take stock of individual and minority group differences.
Instead of a you-versus-me stance, we can accord equal respect to loyal
followers of the program as well as to those who say "This isn't for
me" or "I want some changes." If we remember that the overall goal
is to alleviate human suffering, we can put our rigid egos aside and ask,
"What works? What doesn't work? Does it work or not work for
certain people at certain times? Are there ways support groups could
be more effective, possibly for different groups of people? What are the
ways other people have recovered/uncovered from addiction?"

We also need to sort out the problems in groups that stem from the
model and those that reflect the sexism and racism so pervasive in our
culture. In other words, how are the problems of patriarchy getting
played out in groups?

THE ROLE OF EGO: DEFLATED OR AWARE?

Bill Wilson was constantly concerned with the need to deflate a rigid,
over-blown ego as a requisite to admitting one has a problem with
alcohol. Generally, this worked for the white, upper-middle-class, alcoholic men he knew. But it does not always fit the needs of most women
and many underprivileged people.

I could appreciate the power of the twelve steps when interviewing
a group of men similar to Bill Wilson, men of status and wealth. Their
stories of denial about their drinking and drug problems were mind-
boggling—stories of crashed boats and cars, loss of marriages, wealth,
and health. One man, Jack, said, "I needed the steps just the way they
were. I knew I was good, I was smart." Another man explained, "I had
a hundred and twenty employees under me. I was used to running
anything. It was beyond my belief that I couldn't control something as
simple as my drinking. I needed to be brought down to size . . .
(laughing) I still do."

The twelve steps contain words like humility, character defects,
shortcomings, and moral inventory, which follow traditional Christian
teachings of sin and redemption. One must constantly atone and be

brought down to size. Because a rigid, over-inflated ego thinks it is right and others are wrong, Bill Wilson's attempt to deflate the ego was certainly relevant for the men he knew, and for many it worked.

Even so, I would like to suggest a totally different approach toward understanding the role of the ego that is nonviolent and nonshaming. If we take Bill Wilson's idea of deflating the ego to its extreme we would have a crushed, nonexistent ego. That's what lots of women and minorities already have, which is not functional.

My image is to move toward a balanced, aware ego, not a battered one. It is unfortunate that so much spiritual literature talks about the ego needing to die, to be broken down. That is a violent, dualistic approach—if it's too big, beat on it, crush it, and demolish it. I suggest we think in terms of a healthy ego as one that is porous, flowing, and flexible—an ego infused with compassion, awareness, and wisdom. *Thus the ideal is an ego, or a sense of self, continually merging with awareness and compassion. Ultimately ego, self, and compassion become an integrated whole.*

A strong ego is not necessarily a bad thing. For example, I need ego to sit here and write. I need a sense of self in order to bring my thoughts together or to believe I have something worth saying. The question to ask is, "Who does the ego serve? The self? Or society and a greater good?" It needs to be a combination of both. People who have been instrumental in social change have had strong egos. Thus, the mitigating factor is compassion and awareness, not size of ego.

If the ego is totally self-serving, the inner voice, which speaks from the heart, gets muffled or one becomes righteous or lost in sentiment without substance. But if one lacks an ego or sense of self, they have no voice at all or lack the strength to write with conviction and say what they believe, no matter what. A person can have a strong ego yet realize one is playing a part in the greater scheme of things. For example, I can feel a strong conviction about what I am writing, yet realize it filters through my personal experience and is but one voice among many.

The other aspect of ego important for a healthy, empowered person is to have choices over one's ego boundaries. We can have strong, firm boundaries, or relax them in order to merge with people and nature. For example, if I'm confronting a hostile system, I put up a strong ego boundary so I won't get thrown off center or conned. I stay wary and alert.

By contrast, when being intimate, attending a spiritual ritual, or being in nature, I want my boundary to become porous and soft so I can feel a sense of unity and openness that takes me beyond my self.

The important words in regard to ego/self boundaries are choice, consciousness, and control.

Many women, minorities, and some men need their egos built up through celebration, validation, and a system that is responsive to their needs. My goal in writing the sixteen steps in chapter 14 is to move toward a healthy ego in balance. For many people, this has to do with reinforcing intelligence, creativity, power, and strength. An underinflated ego thinks it is wrong all the time and doesn't trust its own intelligence.

My goal is not terribly different from the spirit of Bill Wilson's. We are just looking at the ego from different directions with a different perspective. The goal in both cases is simply to find ways to help people find the path that leads to balance of self and ego in a way that promotes healing from addiction.

COMING TOGETHER: LIFE-LOVING/CREATIVE SPIRITUALITY

I believe the greatest challenge of the 1990s and the early twenty-first century is to learn the art of bridging differences and developing respect for all people, all life. In order to make treaties, to keep them, to keep the world from eventual disaster, we need to get rid of the concept of "the other" and realize we are all in the same boat together. My pollution is your pollution, your pain is my pain. Seeing things from this perspective is a sign of an aware ego.

It also reflects the movement back toward a spirituality that is life-loving, creative, and open; one that is sometimes described as feminine, Goddess, or creation-centered spirituality, which is similar to the views held by indigenous peoples such as Native Americans. All these approaches believe that all life is interconnected and sacred. We are not here to transcend life or conquer the earth; rather, we are to merge with each other and our environment and live in harmony, using our resources wisely and unselfishly.

I spoke with Mary Daly about language to describe this kind of spirituality. She talked about the term *biophilic*, which literally means to love life. It is listed in her *Wickedary* as meaning "the Original Lust for Life that is at the core of all Elemental E-motion; Pure Lust, which is the Nemesis of patriarchy, the Necrophilic State . . . N.B. Biophilia is not in ordinary dictionaries, although the word necrophilia is."

To the term life-loving I add the word creative, as derived from creation spirituality. Mary Daly suggested this as a way to move from a noun to an active word. A life-loving spirituality fosters creativity for when our senses are open to take in the natural wonders of the earth, and we live without fear of abuse, our playfulness and creativity are free to grow throughout our lives.

Moving toward a life-loving/creative spirituality involves bridging differences by increasing our capacity to accept, understand, and be empathic to different people, their cultures, traditions, and values, and to stop thinking that anyone has a corner on truth or anyone has the right to exploit others. Like the earth, people are not objects to be exploited; rather, we are all part of an interrelated whole. When we think we are right or we exploit others, we become alienated and miss the richness of human love.

Twelve-step programs are based on many principles congruent with notions of equality and empathy for a broad range of people. There are no leaders (only trusted servants); groups are free or operate on voluntary donations; tremendous value is placed on helping one another with a nonjudgmental, empathic understanding of all people sincerely seeking recovery.

A landmark aspect of the AA model was the tradition of putting "principles before personalities" in the groups, the idea being that you set aside some of your own personal prejudices and opinions in the interest of maintaining group cohesiveness. I suggest we take that principle and apply it more broadly to all people and to the earth.

My mind keeps going back to Joseph, the Native American man I quoted in the introduction. I asked him what he thought about the title *Many Roads, One Journey*, and what was important to say in the book. He paused for a moment, reflected, and then said, "Tell people that when we understand the journeys of each other, it strengthens our own."

If understanding others' journeys strengthens our own, then why are so many people closed to other people's ways? Why are people defensive about the twelve-step model or afraid to engage in open discussion about their reservations? Symptoms of addiction and codependency are rigidity, righteousness, projection, all-or-nothing thinking, and oversimplification—all of which are based in fear. Perhaps that is why people in recovery sometimes get rigid about their program for recovery.

In order to move beyond these limitations, we must first look at our fears of differences, fears of change, and our fears of questioning. To heal is to move beyond irrational fear.

2

The Fear of Questioning, the Need for Questioning

A core question we can ask ourselves on our journey is whether we choose a path based on fear or a path that leads toward love and a life-loving, creative spirituality. While fear can be an important signal of danger that a wise and wary person needs to recognize, for the moment I am referring to the fear of growing, expanding, and feeling the discomfort that accompanies breaking through our limitations.

FEAR OR LOVE

People may give up addiction out of fear, but they heal out of love. Fear is the ego wanting facts, guarantees, recipes, security. Fear is righteous, tight, restricted, breathless, paralyzing. Fear requires logic and proof. Fear argues and attacks. Fear fears change: "We've always done it this way, so why try anything new?" Fear is future-oriented: "If I do this, then . . ." Fear leads us to avoid the unknown because it might get our shoes muddy, bring tears, or stir up conflict. Fear leads to lives of inner alienation and separateness from others, as hopes and dreams are obscured by demands for constant security. *Fear may motivate us but it does not heal.*

Love is in the moment, a state of being where the awakening heart

21

is both receptive and giving. Love sings without the words and dances without the music. Love creates trust and helps us expand and enter the unknown with curiosity and fascination. Love leads to laughter and good wishes for others. Love leads to a state of openness grounded in faith, a knowingness that we exist on this planet as a miracle of life. Love leads us to look within, to listen to the beating of our heart and accept all that we are—frail, scared, strong, bright. Love leads to the knowledge that under the surface of our human differences we share a common pulse—a desire for love, purpose, and connectedness.

Fear blocks love. Therefore, any form of genuine healing will go beyond fear. It's an ongoing process. As we find our truths, speak our truths, stay in harmony with our wisdom, and connect with other people, we walk through fear again and again. It involves struggle because fear is deeply programmed within us, and taking steps toward love and connectedness often feels like breaking a colossal rule, which will lead to some terrible disaster or punishment.

Paradoxically, one of the first steps in moving through fear is to know when we are afraid, and simply to say "I am afraid" instead of masking our fear with rigidity and control. We can be with our fear, feel it, and ask what it is about.

Many people I interviewed described twelve-step groups that perpetuated fear. Fear was expressed through control and a robot-like adherence to the model. In many cases the fear stemmed from a belief that people were completely under the power of some outside force and lacked personal choice and will. It paralleled the threatening, all powerful God-image—from you'd better be good or you'll be punished, to you'd better follow the program right, or you'll fall into your addiction.

One woman said, "They kept telling me if I ever used again I would die. It was like this big terrifying threat hanging over my head. Then when I did use again, I thought, well, that's it, I might as well keep going, so I drank and drank and drank. Then it occurred to me, I could stop again. I had stopped before and I didn't have to die. I went to friends and asked for help and I've been sober ever since—without going to AA."

Other groups expressed fear of changing the wording of the twelve-step meetings in any way, as if it were the words that kept them sober. Jeanette wrote in her questionnaire, "In one group there were *adamant* feelings about not changing a word of the steps. The rigidity was hard for me . . . I almost felt defiant and wanted to say, 'Then I just won't try.'" Other people said that being told what to do triggered their defiance, which made them want to go out and drink after the meetings.

The most common complaint from women was that men in addiction groups were afraid of feelings being expressed, especially sadness. One woman wrote, "I never admitted I was in therapy because the 'strong-willed old timers' in the group were against therapy and against any display of feelings. While I believe in twelve-step work, I have noticed in some groups it may be used as a way to not deal with feelings and to subtly threaten others to not bring feelings up either. It was as if everyone was afraid of feelings."

A number of people mentioned that ARIA and ACA or ACOA (Adult Children of Alcoholics) groups tended to be less afraid of open expression of feelings, although some women from these groups said the opposite: "Everyone was trying to do it right, look good, and be above human feelings."

A group permeated by fear has a profound effect on its members. It leads people to tighten up, hold back feelings, and stick to the form. It also triggers defiance in people who maintained a sense of identity as children by acting defiant toward authoritarian, rigid caregivers.

One woman said, when I was told I had to admit I was "codependent" in order to "recover," my first impulse was to say, "No way! I won't label myself that way. You can't tell me what to say!"

Rigidity double-binds people. I remember wanting to be in a group but wanting to be true to myself as well. I started thinking, "Maybe I should go along." But that gave me a stomach ache. In other words, the *external* rule created an *internal* duality, resulting in a physical reaction. Many people I interviewed described situations where they experienced this inner conflict.

GRABBING THE LIFELINE OF RECOVERY

When people desperate to stay sober or heal from dependent relationships come to a recovery group, the group may seem like a lifeline, and people are often quick to grab hold. One woman said, "I wanted sobriety so bad I would have done anything. If they had said crawl through hot coals, I would have asked, 'How many and how long?'"

People become attached to the program with differing degrees of intensity, depending on their sense of self-identity and their desperation for recovery. At one end of the spectrum, Kristie, who had had several years of therapy had developed a strong inner sense of her values, was able to take what she liked and ignore the rest when she went to a twelve-step group. When a group didn't feel right to her, she left and found another one.

For someone lacking internal ego development, it is not so easy. Andrea, a survivor of profound abuse and years in a fundamentalist, hellfire-and-damnation religion, initially accepted the words of her twelve-step group program and the advice of other group members without question. It was familiar and nothing in her background encouraged her to do otherwise. Only with the support of women friends and a counselor did she develop a new frame of reference that said groups could be nonshaming and caring and still help you stay sober. She thought the only way to grow was through pain, suffering and rigid rules.

When I have given talks on abuse in recovery groups, I am often met with remarks such as, "They should have left" or "It's everyone's responsibility to take care of themselves." This is a blame-the-victim stance that creates separateness among people. I believe these righteous, one-up statements come from fear—fear of knowing about the abuse and exploitation that sometimes happens, and fear of hearing someone's feelings. It also comes from not understanding the difference between care taking and a sense of community responsibility for each other.

We need to get away from blame, understand the profound effects of victimization and child-rearing practices that teach strict adherence to authority, and find ways to create safety in recovery groups so there are fewer instances of alienation and exploitation.

THE ROLE OF FEAR IN RECOVERY

People who get into recovery/discovery are usually motivated by survival fear—fear of dying, losing friends, jobs, loved ones, or feeling miserable the rest of their lives. In the early stages of the uncovering process, it is often fear of horrible consequences that keeps people coming back to their twelve-step or other support group.

Using fear as a motivator is all right for a short while. It's an emergency measure, sort of like jump-starting a car with a dead battery. But when that fear is reinforced and we continue for long periods of time to operate from unexamined external rules based on fear, the healing power remains outside us, limiting our growth and fostering a *new* dependency on our recovery group. In other words, recovery grounded in fear does not lead to development of a healthy, aware ego.

We remain as children with the program cast as the paternalistic authority.

WHAT WOMEN ARE SAYING

In 1986, I presented a workshop titled "A Quaker Feminist Perspective on Twelve-Step Groups" at a National Association of Women in Psychology meeting. I remember sitting in my room the night before, feeling both a sense of excitement and a tremor of fear. At that time, addiction and codependency were rarely mentioned at these meetings. Would anyone come? Would they be hostile? Would I be called arrogant? TV images reducing feminists to crazy bra-burners or thoughts of being called a trouble-maker jabbed at my mind.

The deeper fear was that I was the only person who felt so uncomfortable about twelve-step programs. I was afraid people would say I was crazy and I would feel terribly alone.

I arrived at the workshop about ten minutes early. To my surprise, there were already twenty women in the room, generating a strong feeling of excitement. By the time I started, there were easily fifty. While a few were staunch defenders of twelve-step programs, the majority of women voiced discomfort with the model. Some had been deeply involved with and then left the program, some had moved on to other types of groups (Native American spirituality, witchcraft, Buddhism), and some had never been involved with twelve-step programs.

One woman said, "I am so glad you are talking about this. I knew I had a problem with drinking so I went to one of those groups. They went around in a circle reading those steps and when it got to my turn, I asked, 'What's all this male God stuff?' They were shocked and told me if I stayed, I'd come to understand, but I should just sit down, be quiet, and listen. They acted as if just because I was new, I didn't have any brains. So I got up and left. I tried to talk with other people about it later, but no one understood. I felt crazy."

Other women poured out similar stories. There was a sense of excitement amid this burst of woman-energy, of truths finding their voice. One woman, responding to the excitement, said with relish, "I feel like we're in some underground meeting of rebels, a conspiracy—and we could get in trouble for this."

Some women in the workshop reacted differently. "How could you question something that helped me so much? I could have died without the program." Going deeper, one woman said, "I'm afraid you'll take

something away from me." This statement, which I encountered repeatedly in interviews, questionnaires, and in response to the Ms.
article, speaks to an underlying lack of internal power. It is this lack of
self or personal power that this book seeks to address and heal.

Neither I nor anyone else can take away someone's program by
speaking of other ways. When someone thinks I can, it is because they
have not internalized their own belief system and are giving their power
to another person. They have not yet given birth to the concept that
they are the authority in their own life, and can choose whatever model
of recovery/discovery they like.

After the workshop, I found myself asking, Why do women who
like the program get so angry at others who question it? Why have so
many women sat silently alone with their discomfort in recovery
groups? Some obvious answers flickered through my mind, but I
wanted a deeper understanding.

FAITH DEVELOPMENT

While pondering this on a cold winter night, I went to a talk by Anne
Thomas, a Quaker biblical scholar visiting from Montreal. She talked
about stages of faith development and referred to a book, *Faith Is a
Verb: Dynamics of Adult Faith Development*, by Kenneth Stokes. He had
drawn his ideas from James Fowler's *Stages of Faith*. As I listened to
her, a light went on. The stages of "faithing" she described fit into my
exploration of twelve-step programs.

Anne spoke of the differences among people in different stages of
faith development. "Stage two people adhere to words literally. People
at stage four question and become disillusioned. People at stage two of
faithing are threatened by people at stage four. People don't usually get
along well with people two stages apart."

Faith Is a Verb has taken James Fowler's model and made it more
accessible. Fowler draws on Wilfred Cantell Smith's writing in *The
Meaning and End of Religion*. It is to Smith's definition of faith that I
refer throughout this chapter. It reflects a person who lives by their
own internal authority.

> Faith, then, is a quality of human living. At its best, it has taken
> the form of serenity and courage and loyalty and service; a quiet
> confidence and joy which enable one to feel at home in the
> universe, and to find meaning in the world and in one's own
> life, a meaning that is profound and ultimate, and is stable no

matter what may happen to oneself at the level of the immediate event.

Smith speaks of "a *quiet* confidence," as opposed to people who manipulate, preach, and impose their will. He says people with a highly developed faith feel "at home in the universe," not just in their own back yards; they are able to see a broad perspective. He also speaks of alignment of the heart and the will—in other words, the believing and the living becoming one. This, then, is our context for the following discussion on faith.

In *Faith Is a Verb*, Stokes argues that faith is not fixed. Rather, faith grows and changes with age and experience. Thus he uses the term "faithing." I have taken the stages as he adapts them from James Fowler and adapted them once again to fit our discussion.

I have also made additional changes related to male and female differences in development. This is influenced by the work of Carol Gilligan, author of *In a Different Voice*, who explored moral development of girls and boys from a female perspective.

The stages follow a linear pattern that parallels human development, starting with early childhood. Like all linear models, it's difficult to accurately portray a steady process of growth, since the phases often overlap and there is a tendency to return to earlier stages under stress or new circumstances. These stages are also cumulative, each new stage building on the ones that came before. I will first review the stages of faith, giving a brief description of each. (I have put my labels of the stages first, followed by Stokes's terms in italics.) Then I will go through the stages again in greater detail, applying them to people's experiences in twelve-step groups.

Stages give us a clear picture that is necessarily oversimplified. They are only a starting point.

STAGES OF FAITH AND APPROXIMATE AGES
1. Early Childhood, *The Innocent*: Age one–six
2. Late Childhood, *The Literalist*: Age six–eleven/twelve
3. Early Adolescence, *The Loyalist*: Ages eleven/twelve–fifteen/sixteen
4. Late Adolescence and Early Adulthood, *The Critic*: Ages sixteen–twenties and thirties
5. Integrated Expansive Faith, *The Seer*: Usually not before age thirty
6. Wisdom, *Universalizing Faith*

I have put together a list of traits that typify growth toward maturity and an internalized faith. They are:

1. People move from reliance on external authority in defining their beliefs to reliance on their internal experience and wisdom.
2. People become increasingly comfortable with and interested in differences—ethnic, religious, cultural.
3. People expand their concept of community, eventually including all people on the planet.
4. Connectedness to people and quality of human relationships becomes, increasingly, more important than unneeded possessions and status.
5. Nonviolence becomes a stronger value as people feel more connected to others.
6. People come to see the universality in seemingly different belief systems and cultures.
7. People's lives increasingly reflect their beliefs, eventually merging into an integrated whole.
8. People detach their ego from labels, realizing that at their center they are spiritual beings, worthwhile no matter what their external circumstances.
9. Fear gives way to excitement, fascination, wonder, and awe as people gain a broad perspective in life and their place in the cosmic scheme of things.
10. People create a balance between self-nurture and reaching out to others.

You may want to keep these in mind as we proceed through these overlapping stages.

1. Early Childhood (The Innocent)

This is primarily the level/stage of faith of preschool children, who echo what their parents say and do: "I go to Sunday school because Mommy and Daddy go there." The child does not grasp concepts in a personal way. Thus practices like prayer before dinner, hearing the Nativity story, or celebrating Passover are filled with fantasy and imagination. Children at that age simply mouth the words as best they can. Imitating parents indicates bonding to the parents. (I am attached to you, so I become like you.)

MALE-FEMALE DIFFERENCES. An important part of male development that affects future development of faith is that around the ages of three to six, little boys are encouraged to separate from their mothers, submerge their need for nurture and tenderness, and adopt a model of maleness that includes the Marlboro man, Superman, war heroes, conquerers, and dominators. Little boys are not helped to grieve this terrible loss.

Because boys are called weak, queer, or sissy if they cry, the grief often turns to anger, violence, or simply an inner numbness or sense of detachment. This profound separation from the heart—the ability to give and receive love—takes a terrible toll and later makes it a struggle for men to move beyond levels three and four of faithing, because level five requires love, compassion, and connectedness to others. If one is programmed not to experience one's heartaches, one has difficulty developing compassion for others.

2. Late Childhood (The Literalist)

This stage of development occurs approximately between ages six to eleven or twelve, and is characterized by concrete, literal thinking. When the child hears that the earth was created in seven days, the child takes that to mean seven twenty-four hour days as opposed to a process of seven phases. If challenged, the child will retort, "My Sunday school teacher told me so," or "The Bible says so." The authority still rests almost entirely outside the child, but the reference group now includes teachers, religious leaders, older friends and relatives, and media images of men and women. There is a security in this phase because one believes, so simply, that this is the only way and the right way.

MALE-FEMALE DIFFERENCES. By age eleven, girls and boys show a marked difference in approach to moral dilemmas. Girls tend to place more emphasis on relationships and finding ways to work things out among people, while boys approach problems more mathematically or from a right-wrong, legalistic perspective.

A second major change occurs at this period, which Carol Gilligan describes in *Making Connections*. Between the ages of eleven and thirteen, girls undergo a profound change in sense of self-confidence. At eleven, girls are often very forthright and strong-minded, and express their opinions and their anger. However, faced with a culture that puts women in a one-down position in relation to boys and men and rewards females for submissiveness and passivity, girls slowly start learning to hold back their feelings, opinions, and desires, and move toward an "I don't know, whatever you want" stance, which is often apparent by age thirteen. This makes it difficult later on to move to the questioning level, the critic, without something such as the feminist movement for support.

3. Early Adolescence (The Loyalist)

In this stage of development, *belonging, loyalty, harmony* and *conformity* are key words. In adolescence, fitting in and having close bonds with peers become paramount. This is where we see adolescents hanging out together, often dressed the same, and talking alike, with the current "in-group" expressions. There are words associated with those who fit in—cool, hip—as well as words for those who don't—nerd or dork. These words change over time.

This is a stage of development when people shift their loyalty ties from parents and teachers to their peers, which brings comfort in a time of dramatic change, both physically and emotionally. Belonging and acceptance help build a sense of security. If adolescents succeed at this stage and find a fit somewhere, they are then laying the groundwork for moving to adult autonomy where, ideally, people are interdependent, cooperative, and maintain their own secure identity.

The differences between males and females in this phase are in the nature of conformity and bonding. Girls often bond together more intimately, highly valuing relationships and cooperation, while boys are more likely to bond together in goal-oriented teamwork, competition, and domination. They are less likely to tell their peers about their feelings and disappointments. An important point is that both young adolescent males and females are given roles that limit a part of their personal development.

According to Fowler's study of faith development, a majority of church members in the United States fit this level of faithing. They are most comfortable belonging to a like-minded group of believers. They say things such as "*We* Episcopalians believe" or "*We* Jews believe." In Ken Stokes's words, "It places a strong emphasis on those creeds and doctrines and traditions that are the expected norms for membership in that particular group." This builds community and is important to cohesiveness. Yet, the authority still rests largely outside of people and in the doctrine of their particular belief system.

In stages one, two, and three, people have difficulty realizing that what they believe are simply learned beliefs, as opposed to concrete truths, or the one and only truth. It is from this sense of rightness that they may come to feel convinced they have a right to impose their beliefs on others, who are obviously wrong if they disagree. It is from this stance that war, violence, and oppression take place, because differences are feared and there is no concept of many roads on the journey.

4. Late Adolescence and Early Adulthood (The Critic)

This phase includes observation, experimentation, and growing inner awareness, which often lead to disillusionment, struggle, doubt, and difficult questions that go against the established order. It can be a shattering time, as people discover that much of what they have been taught wasn't really in their best interest. As one loyal Catholic woman wrote, "I realized I'd been lied to all of my life. I did everything they said I should, and I ended up miserable and suicidal."

This stage of questioning may start in late adolescence, and can be repeated throughout one's lifetime as new situations arise.

Developmentally, the late teens and early twenties are a time when idealism and concerns for social justice are often deeply felt, which is why college students often lead or become active in movements for social change. Some people never get to this phase. They adopt the teachings from parents, church, and culture, and never question or examine them or attempt to integrate other belief systems.

Stokes writes about this stage as being both uncomfortable and necessary.

> Fullness of maturity in one's faith *must include* some dissonance of doubt and the facing of hard questions that often move against the current of popular belief. It is unfortunate that so many people—clergy and laity alike—view the questioning stance from the negative perspective of "losing one's faith" rather than the positive affirmation of a person who is truly taking charge of her or his faithing and seeking answers that will provide the fullest possible dimension of a meaningful personal faith.

At this level, people start paying attention to their inner experience and observations. People start developing the ability to reflect, understand paradox, and look within. The question shifts from "What do *they* think?" to "What do *I* think? What do *I* observe? What do *I* see? What is *my* place in the bigger picture?"

The admission ticket to this stage of personal development is a willingness to feel internal discomfort and doubt, to acknowledge uncertainty, to be able to say "I don't know," and to experience periods of emptiness when the old beliefs fade away and new ones are not yet in place. It is a time to listen to a broad range of other people's experiences and learn that they are as valid as one's own. My way was just one way that represents only a fraction of belief systems on the planet. It was influenced by my culture, ethnic background, and family. It's not absolute truth, it's programming.

This questioning period is a crucial time in faith development that sets the stage for an internalized, secure faith. The external authority is giving way to internal integration.

It can be be difficult for women or minorities to move into this stage as individuals, because society so strongly punishes them from talking back, questioning, and defining their own experience. It often takes a huge social movement such as the civil rights, feminist, or gay liberation movement to help groups coalesce, organize, and move en masse into the critic phase.

Once women move to this phase of faithing, it is generally easier for them than men to move on to phase five, because this phase centers on bonding together with cooperation, compassion, and empathy, traits females developed in the early adolescent loyalist phase. It is also likely that minority or oppressed people who have gone through the fourth phase might move to this phase more easily if they grew up in communities that valued cooperation or they took part in cooperative social action.

Because adolescent boys are programmed to grow up to be heroes and rugged individualists, it is often more difficult for them to get past the questioning phase. They don't have the same experience with empathy and compassion that girls and oppressed minority groups develop.

5. Integrated Expansive Faith (The Seer)

At this stage we find people whose faith is an integration of the four previous stages. They have taken in their experience, mulled it over, questioned, synthesized, and integrated it until they arrived at values that ring true for them. There is a deep sense of internal rightness, or what Quakers call the "clearness" one feels when they reach their inner truths.

This is, of course, not a finite stage. People can be part loyalist, part critic, and yet have certain aspects of their lives clearly embedded in stage five. And things that are clear for a while—such as relationships, career, and so on—may shift. But values such as honesty, responsibility, service, and honoring the spirit within others become deeply embedded in the person, providing a foundation for human relationships and decision-making.

A nun I know who works in a shelter and very much lives by her faith as described in the fifth and sixth levels said to me in an interview, "I seldom think about why I do this. I just know this is what I'm meant to be doing." Another person said, "I don't even like talking about this—as if I'm some sort of special person. I shy away from intellectual debate and discussion." People talk of a sense of body integration and peacefulness. It simply feels like their faith is "what's true and natural." Giving and receiving merge as one experience. You don't give to be "good" or be admired, you give and serve because it is natural, rewarding, and personally satisfying.

In this stage, according to Stokes, people "are able to identify with people of different races, socioeconomic status, or ideological convictions." One is able to reach beneath external forms to the underlying truths, which often have a common thread. People find connecting threads among Quaker meetings, social action, psychotherapy, Buddhist retreats, yoga, meditation retreats, juice fasts, and Native American sweat lodges.

People in this phase more rapidly move beyond reacting to people based on external appearance, status, and color, and see human beings, individual souls. With an integrated faith common to both stages five and six, the principle of treating others as you would treat yourself and vice versa, is deeply felt. One can no longer stand back passively in the face of starvation and pain. One's quality of life is experienced in the context of the quality of our life as a community. One no longer has a concept of "the enemy" because all people are seen as sacred, as children of the creator. Ignorance, suffering, and poverty become the forces to be overcome, not people. To be in this level of faith is to move away from our hierarchical system, as we will discuss in the next chapter.

People at this level are rarely threatened by differences because they rest comfortably on their own personal sense of identity, which feels harmonious within. When they have judgments of others, they also realize that judgments are just a superficial, programmed reaction, and that underneath there is a common connection.

6. Wisdom (Universalizing Faith)

According to Stokes, this group includes the small percentage of people "whose faith is more than beliefs or even a way of life, but is one of total commitment to the ongoing, guiding presence of God or whatever the person recognizes as Ultimate Authority." I think of this as living at one with the spirit. Values, beliefs, and the actions become one. One doesn't think about values so much as simply living them.

Judgments slip away even further as one becomes deeply connected with all humanity and ceases to experience oneself as separate. People who have integrated aspects of this level of faith may be well known, as in the case of Mother Teresa or Gandhi, but they can also be ordinary people. When we are around people who are deeply integrated with their purpose and humanity, we may experience peacefulness as well as a sense of lightness and humor. We may also feel fear and want to criticize or attack them, because their sense of internal values threatens our buried anger and lack of self. People with a universalizing faith see beyond the moment and have a broad perspective on life and death and their place in the scheme of things.

I was deeply moved by the PBS special "Warriors of the Spirit." It was about Christian rural, farming people in Southern France who risked their lives by sheltering Jews throughout World War II. This story is also told in *Lest Innocent Blood Be Shed: The Story of the Village of Le Chambon and How Goodness Happened There*, by Philip Hallie. When asked why they risked their lives, their words had a disarming simplicity. "I had to do it." "The Bible says to love one's neighbor as oneself." Several indicated that they didn't understand what all the fuss was about. They were simply helping other people. Typical of people with a universalizing faith is the ability to hold strong beliefs or defy a system they consider unjust, but without malice in their hearts toward individuals.

TWELVE-STEP GROUPS AND STAGES OF FAITHING

How do these stages of faithing apply to twelve-step groups and other models for recovery from addiction and dependency? The twelve-step model operates primarily at levels two and three of faithing—the literalist and the loyalist. Following the form and staying loyal to the group are highly encouraged. Critical examination of the form is not encouraged, although people are encouraged to be critical of themselves. Encouraging people to pray for God's will and the power to carry it out does relate to the fifth stage of an integrated faith, but there is no bridge through the critic phase to help us get there.

Individuals I interviewed were at many levels of faithing. Some were very loyal to the groups and followed their guidance literally; others used twelve-step groups for support but did not adhere rigidly to the form in any way and had an integrated sense of faith.

In group interviews and from the questionnaires it appeared that there were tremendous differences among groups—some are very rigid and some very flexible, reflecting different stages of faithing. The groups tend to develop a personality or a norm. Some indicators of the norms of groups were statements such as, "A lot of people give advice and pat phrases in that group"; "That group is very warm and supportive and people really listen"; "People get really uptight if you want to change one word of anything or question anything"; "People reword the steps, seldom read program literature, and say things their way."

The Stages of Faithing and Human Development

Earlier I mentioned that the stages of faithing follow human developmental stages to some degree. For example, the literalist phase that occurs between ages six and eleven relates to brain development. A child at that age simply cannot deal with abstractions, a skill that develops in early adolescence.

Because the stages move on a continuum from an external locus of control to an internal locus of control, authoritarian parenting and childhood abuse and neglect will leave some people stuck in the early stages. Generally, the greater and earlier the abuse, the more a person is stuck in the earlier stages of maturity or faithing.

When parents squelch or punish autonomy and critical thinking, children internalize a belief that questioning is dangerous. Another block to development is the addiction itself, which slows or thwarts human development. Thus many people who enter twelve-step groups are developmentally in the first three levels of faithing and afraid of questioning.

A healthy group where people are supportive, flexible, and caring can help a person fill in some missing pieces from childhood and move forward. If, however, the group norm is rigid and dogmatic, it may only reinforce the rigid, authoritarian family of origin. And while a person may maintain sobriety, they may do so at cost to their human development, staying locked in a rigid box of rules and authority.

Stage 1: Early Childhood (The Innocent)

People who are essentially at stage one, the innocent, are easily victimized in groups. They do what they are told and it doesn't have to make sense to them. The most common scenario is when an older member—usually a man—takes on a fledgling member, purporting to be helpful while actually feeding his own ego-need to be superior and distanced from his own feelings. People who are in the innocent phase often hunger for any sort of positive parent figure and are easily taken in by someone who appears warm and supportive. Not infrequently women have been emotionally used or sexually abused in twelve-step groups; I will discuss this at length in chapter 10.

Let's take a look at Ella, a woman who was developmentally centered in stage one when she entered a twelve-step group. She got stuck at stage one because of sexual abuse and her parents' thwarting any development toward autonomy. They rewarded dependency and helplessness and pressured her into conforming to society's stereotype of a little girl, dressing her in cute outfits and teaching her to smile and be charming. Her authentic self had been submerged at a very early age. As a result, she looked to the older men in her group for guidance and approval, and they readily gave it to her. Ella told me, "I was like a child seeking a parent, and when they told me what to do I simply did it. It never occurred to me to question anything they told me." Thus Ella stayed developmentally in stage one. Sadly, one of the men came on to her sexually, which triggered overwhelming feelings resulting from her father's molesting her and which resulted in her self-abusing and being hospitalized. Her counselor at the hospital suggested she join a women's group and supported her in starting to listen to her own inner voice.

In this group, which was warm and caring and in which the women clearly supported Ella in thinking for herself, Ella started slowly to form a trusting bond that helped her heal at a very deep level.

Many women wrote of similar positive experiences. Many group experiences filled early needs for understanding and care. One woman in an Adult Children of Alcoholics group wrote, "I learned what love is. . . . People listened while I cried, and cried, and cried. Their listening without interruption was my first understanding of love. . . . I saw compassion, humility, kindness . . . they knew that somewhere deep down, I had something good in me." This is exactly what children need in the first years of life and what Ella was still needing in order to develop a basic sense of security.

Ella's being sexually abused in the group is not solely the fault of the twelve-step form per se—it is a common result of our sexually exploitive society. But the twelve-step model plays a part. Because twelve-step programs are treated as hallowed ground and people are told they are the only road to recovery, women sometimes blindly trust everyone, forgetting that no one magically changes just because they walk in the door of a twelve-step meeting. Some people are trustworthy and others are not. There are predatory and abusive people in twelve-step groups, just like anywhere else.

Another common scenario was epitomized by Jeanette's situation, which did not involve sexual abuse but kept her locked in the innocent phase. She grew up in a fundamentalist family where she was repeatedly told by her parents to "do it my way or else." She was struck for talking back (having opinions) and praised for being "good," that is, silent, emotionless, unquestioning. Any opinions she might venture were seen as arrogant, and she was told that God punished little girls for thinking evil thoughts. She submerged her will, learned to please everyone, and did not develop a "center" of her own. She was frozen in stage one development.

She took her "good girl" survival role into AA and desperately tried to please everyone, as if they were her parents or a vengeful God.

When she told group members she was continually depressed, they told her to inventory her faults. When her depression did not lift after several such inventories, she berated herself: "I haven't done them well enough. I should do more. I've done it wrong." It never crossed her mind that she might have been given bad advice.

When she was upset with her husband, people told her to "turn it over to God," give up her resentments and look at her part. Every problem had a "program" solution, and no one suggested that she look for solutions that felt right for her. The group re-enacted her family of origin's behavior by discounting her feelings, telling her what to do, and reinforcing her belief that her suffering was due to her inadequacies.

Another trap of being stuck in this innocent phase is that people focus more on being good and doing what they are told than on absorbing what they are reading or hearing. Jeanette did all the suggested readings, but she could hardly remember the content. She was doing the assignment so she could check in as a "good girl." She followed suggestions to the letter. "You should read two pages a day of the Big Book" meant just that. Don't get carried away and read six pages. Don't take a day off and skip it altogether. Jeanette did not translate the suggestion to mean it might be a *good idea* to read the Big Book, or that reading related literature might be helpful. She also adopted the teaching that addicts can't afford to get angry, which then served as an excuse to not confront her abusive husband.

Because she placed her self-esteem totally in the hands of others, Jeanette's mind was like an endless tape recording: "Am I doing it right? What do they think of me? Will they accept me? I'll be kicked out if I make a mistake." Underneath this was a buried rage that could kill, because her spirit was buried and no one was helping her retrieve it.

Only when a friend convinced her to find a good therapist did she start addressing her abusive marriage, her depression, and her rage.

Most important, she started on the arduous path toward developing a self-identity, a healthy ego that would help her say, "I'm angry. I'm being violated. This isn't working, and I think I should try something else." Looking back on her experience, she said, "I now see that group as very abusive to me because they did not help me grow up. I stayed sober but I never stopped feeling afraid."

So far we've talked about people being victimized in groups. The perpetrators of abuse are often frozen in very early stages of development as well. They become stuck in a narcissistic view typical of two- and three-year-old children who believe the world revolves around them. Translated in terms of their role in groups, this view becomes "It worked for me, so it must work for you." Instead of playing a victim role, they assume a domineering or perpetrator role. Their sense of powerlessness is expressed by turning their anger outward and blaming and controlling others. These are the people who take over and dominate groups, often attracting people like Jeanette or Ella. Thus, everyone's childhood gets replayed in the group, with people projecting their fears and anger onto other people.

2. Late Childhood (The Literalist)

In the second phase, people connect intensely with "the program" format and adhere to it literally. There is little room for questioning, and, well . . . if it saved me, it must be the way for everyone. Thus, recovery, the literal wording of the steps, and the program rituals become synonymous with growth. People tend to believe it was the steps and the program that saved them, not their own hard work. Adults who are primarily at this stage still have an underdeveloped sense of ego and thus fear anyone's changing the program because that structure is holding them together. In other words, without an inside structure, they depend on an external one.

On the positive side, a person might enter a group and, because they accept the program uncritically, spend their energy working the steps, which helps them grow. On the negative side, people at this stage become righteous about "the program" and discount people with differing beliefs.

As Jane wrote, "Working the twelve steps has saved my life. I cannot see any other way I or anyone else can live a full life apart from the twelve steps." Jane, who wrote this literalist statement, is making incredible recovery from numerous addictions as well as moving beyond a childhood of poverty, racism, and abuse. The positive side is that the twelve-step program provided Jane a lifeline to hang onto, an external structure, and a sense of direction to quell the inner chaos.

The negative part is her complete allegiance to the twelve steps and her separating belief that no one could live a full life without them. She was not alone.

In response to my question, "How do you feel about people rewording the steps in their own way?" people wrote, "I don't think it should be done. If it works, don't fix it." Another woman wrote, "I would never come to such a group." Still another response was, "They wouldn't dare with me around!" And at the greatest extreme, a woman wrote, "Why would you change something that works so well? We *fight* to keep Al-Anon and the Steps *pure*" (emphasis mine). These remarks echo statements by conservatives when social change to benefit the disempowered segments of society is suggested. And the phrase keeping the steps "pure" has chilling parallels to racist beliefs that have resulted in massive violence toward individuals and groups of people.

Because the belief system at this phase of development is literal as opposed to internalized and integrated, any threat of changing the words, the format, or the belief system feels to participants like taking their sobriety away. Many twelve-step groups operate at this level. Any attempt to vary the established order is met with huge resistance. People in this phase think concretely, and rarely understand words symbolically or as metaphor. They are, in a very real sense, dependent on the structure of the program.

For people who come into a recovery program in the throes of a life-and-death struggle, a certain amount of rigidity may be useful, like a foster child having caretakers who impose clear limits and rules that bring a sense of order where there has been chaos. On the other hand, many people who enter the program at more mature levels of faithing become convinced that they must revert to this childlike stage in order to become well. The effect of this is to instill fear—fear of thinking, questioning, and using one's mind. Thus their journey takes a backward turn as they trade in personal identity and attach to "the program." People I interviewed would often say, "Oh yes, in the beginning I resisted and my big ego got in the way, but now I see they were right and I was wrong." There isn't room for shades of gray.

I don't see it as all or nothing. A steady ritual, a predictable group is helpful. A person needs a clear path to follow and human role models. But it can be healing and strengthening to be asked from the beginning, "What seems to help you the most? What do you think?" The twelve steps form a *suggested* program of recovery, and *you* are the one in charge. Instead of giving people pat answers, asking these questions suggests that the individual has it within him or her to find the answers they need. It also leads people away from seeking addictive quick-fix answers.

The dangers of having adults and group leaders frozen in the literalist phase are reflected in history, where literalist despots can see only one way and attempt to eliminate those who differ. Groups with a literalist norm often adopt a we-versus-the-world stance that is very appealing for people who have always felt left out or who have been abused as children. They can bond together, often propelled by a charismatic leader, and project their buried anger against a common enemy, that is, anyone who doesn't do it their way. But they are bonding in fear and dependency, which is ultimately destructive. Treatment programs routinely bring in AA people to talk to newly sober people about "the program," which is often presented as the *only* way to stay sober.

THE LITERALIST AND CHEMICAL DEPENDENCY COUNSELORS.   Some people who become chemical dependency counselors operate at the literalist phase. So do some of the people who teach courses in chemical dependency. They perpetuate a robot-like adherence to the beliefs, myths, and dogma of the program. When I was taking a course in chemical dependency counseling as part of my doctoral program, we were taught that people couldn't recover without AA. Period. About that time, I visited a local salvage store and struck up a conversation with a man from a working-class community in the area. Eventually I told him I was taking a class on alcoholism. "Oh yeah?" he said. "That stuff can be terrible for you. I had to quit, it was wrecking my life."

"Did you go to AA?" I asked.

"Nah," he said. "I just stopped, haven't had a drink since."

"Really."

"It was wrecking my family, my marriage, everything. My wife was about to leave me."

"So you just quit?"

"I had to. It would have killed me if I didn't."

"Wow! How long ago was that?"

"About five years."

When I brought this information back to class, I was told that either he wasn't truly alcoholic or he would probably relapse some day. No one was interested in the fact that he *had* stopped of his own free will or wanted to find out what his drinking habits had been, what he did to keep himself sober, or how long he had been sober. This rigidity and lack of believing that you can learn from other people's experiences is typical of the literalist phase of development.

This incident stayed etched in my mind over the years as I listened to people repeat the same phrases almost verbatim in the same automatic way without reflection. "If they stopped on their own they couldn't have been alcoholic." It always had a "party line" ring. Yet over the years I have met many people who quit drinking on their own after some devastating consequences. And from everything I could discern, they were definitely addicted.

3. Early Adolescence (The Loyalist)

Being accepted by a group of loyal peers can be a healing balm, particularly for people who never had a healthy peer group as children or adolescents. Twelve-step groups often provide a place where people experience their first supportive bonds.

In describing how twelve-step groups had helped her, Helen wrote, "TRUST—for the first time in my life, I could show a little of my real self. I didn't have to be strong and together every minute—and people liked me. In fact, they seemed to like me even more the more I opened up and showed my real self." This typified the responses of many people who said they were understood, accepted, and cared about as never before when they joined a twelve-step or other forms of support groups.

Groups have an immense capacity for healing, but it is important that we not attribute this healing capacity solely to twelve-step programs. Women have had support groups and participated in rituals through the ages. Many men, unaccustomed to bonding outside of work and sports, may associate closeness and support with twelve-step programs because it is the only group they've ever attended that fosters this kind of care and bonding.

In stage three faith development, people often become more secure in their sobriety as they replace their dependency on alcohol with a healthy dependency on their group. Members phone each other for support, and some members' entire social circle consists of people in "the program." The ego becomes more secure as people internalize the messages: I belong, I am lovable, I am accepted.

But the dependency can go too far. The words associated with this stage—*conformity*, *harmony*, and *agreement*—may also lead to group symbiosis and dependency. Instead of *growing* from having a community of like believers, a person's security becomes *dependent* on belonging to the group, and they fail to honor their own wisdom and internal strength. This leads us back to fear.

Acting Out Family Patterns in Groups

Very often individuals transfer childhood longings for a caring parent onto their twelve-step group. Again, this may be useful for a while, but when people unconsciously attach to the group as child to parent and do not develop true peer relationships, they do not open the door to healing the underlying wounds from childhood. It can be useful for a limited period of time to *consciously* relate to people as surrogate care-givers, but one also needs to grieve losses from childhood. If one *unconsciously* relates to the group as the longed-for family, he or she will often make unhealthy adaptations to the group that parallel those they made to their parents.

Kelly, whom you will meet throughout this book, had been shuffled around as a child, taught to be seen and not heard, and was often slapped for "talking back" (having opinions). As a result she continually suppressed her deep inner misgivings about her twelve-step group. It was the same adaptation she made in her family, where she contained her hurt and anger to avoid abandonment and physical abuse. She was unconsciously using the group to fill the emptiness from childhood, which kept her from grieving the sorrows of the past. Ideally, members will be healed through the group's support and eventually move to more peer-interdependent relationships, rather than stay locked into parent-child transference.

Twelve-step programs and their approved literature tend to reinforce conformity, typical of the loyalist stage. They also give numerous contradictory messages. On the one hand, they say it is a suggested program of recovery, yet assertions that one cannot recover without a spiritual experience and a belief in God abound. Nearly all the program material, including the Big Book of Alcoholics Anonymous, uses the word "we." "*We* never apologize for God. . . . *We* have a way out on which we can absolutely agree." The implication is that "*we* alcoholics" are all alike. This creates considerable internal distress for many people attending the group who feel different.

To lump everyone into "we" reinforces people's staying locked into the third level of development, and doesn't open a door to move on and explore differences. While basking in we-ness for a while can be wonderfully healing, one doesn't need to stay in an amorphous mass to experience the joy of connecting with kindred spirits. "We addicts, we codependents, we Quakers, we psychologists." Those are just labels. There's no "we." Each one of us is unique.

The huge problem of using the "we" approach to recovery from addiction is that recovery/discovery is a process and people have different needs. Let me return to the story of Kelly. I met her five years ago when she came to clean house for me. She is very attractive, slender, rides a motorcycle, and has an amazing ability to dress in incredible outfits she finds at thrift shops. When she first came, I remember thinking to myself, "What is a bright woman like this doing cleaning my house?"

She told me she had recently sobered up, left a destructive relationship, and was bringing up a young child on her own. Over the following weeks I learned she had been left alone much of her childhood and shifted from one place to another, and that her parents had died of alcoholism. She had abused cocaine, heroin, and alcohol for nearly eighteen years. She rattled off standard AA talk: "You can't get well without AA. You have to really work hard at the program. If you don't attend AA, you will surely drink again. Having a Higher Power is the only way to recovery. You must read twelve-step literature every day."

So for a few years she appeared to be at stages two and three of faithing with regard to her group. Though Kelly stayed sober, she was depressed and stayed in a dependent relationship that had her in tears some days. She often spoke of feeling empty. We weren't very close those first couple of years. I observed that she was terribly afraid of doing something wrong, and it was only after a couple of years that she would say to me, "I'm getting worried, I can't get everything done, please tell me your priorities." She started getting interested in what I was writing, my relationships, and my spiritual journey. She asserted her autonomous self by starting training at a vocational school and saw a therapist. She started to have misgivings about AA and its stress on conformity, which was counter to her developmental needs.

AA often becomes one's community and one's faith at the literalist and loyalist stages. There is in-group language and a shared belief system, the rightness of which is repeatedly reinforced by the dominant group members and program practices and literature. There is an assuredness that is very comforting and very seductive to someone who has been experiencing loneliness and pain and who has never had a secure family.

Because people want to maintain group cohesiveness, they are somewhat more tolerant of differences in the loyalist phase, although any genuine differences may be met with kindly coercion in an attempt to bring people back into the fold. While people in the literalist phase use authoritarian tactics of shame, humiliation, and threats to keep people loyal to a group, at level three it is more the kindly father/ mother, benevolent dictator approach.

One problem with staying at this stage is the continued dependency on the group and adherence to external authority, which blocks progress toward a deeper level of maturity and integration.

Reflections on Stages One, Two, and Three and the Culture

My concern with twelve-step groups reflects my concern with our culture, which operates primarily at the first three levels of faithing. The stress on group conformity and allegiance to authority figures creates fear and a sheep-like mentality that can be very dangerous. That's why I propose a model of healing from addiction that encourages and supports people moving beyond these first three stages of development toward an internalized, integrated faith.

An extreme consequence of creating loyal, unquestioning children and adults was the situation in Nazi Germany that led to the Holocaust. In *For Your Own Good*, Alice Miller explores the allegiance of German people to Hitler and the question of why people could so easily be influenced to pull the gas levers that killed so many. Essentially people went along with the violence because they were not brought up to have a will of their own. They were taught complete obedience and compliance—their will was the will of the parent, or the authority figure. What was the lesson needed to avoid another Holocaust and bring people closer together? To teach children to think for themselves, to have a social conscience, and to value all life.

What are we doing in the United States to help this happen? We make heroes of people who rebeled in the past, but call pacifists and social justice activists unpatriotic troublemakers. And while some teachers are attempting to teach values and good communication, the predominant values taught in our system center on competition, winning, and success—as measured by status, money, and sexual conquest.

Maintaining conformity at all costs leaves people without the ability to appreciate and bridge differences. Thus it locks us into racism, sexism, homophobia, violence, war, and unsatisfactory or shallow relationships. To move in the direction of social justice, we need to create educational and spiritual institutions that help people reach for levels four and five, that help them grapple with the complexities of our inner and outer worlds. When people do not develop a secure center, a mature, integrated faith, they are easily led by benevolent friends and therapists, as well as by despots, perpetrators, and those who would do them harm or lead them to harm others. Maintaining conformity leads to institutions full of the dutiful people who defend their harmful actions, saying, "It's my job; I'm just doing what I'm told."

* * *

My hope is to validate people seeking a deeply felt internal faith that is alive and fluid, open and receptive, grounded and secure. We need to develop the art of having cohesive, supportive communities that embrace differences instead of suppressing them. Our approach to addiction recovery/uncovery will be strengthened if these communities learn to respond to input from the vastly different people seeking to move beyond addiction and "codependency."

Whether a child moves beyond the first three stages depends on his or her family and as well as school, religious institutions, and cultural norms. The norms of our child-rearing practices and education are aimed at keeping children in these obedient, conforming, dependent roles, which train people to work in factories, be loyal wives, to turn the other cheek to abuse, to be violent, to fight wars, and to give one's will to authorities, bosses, and religious leaders without question. They also train some people to be authoritarian bosses and leaders.

In *Thou Shalt Not Be Aware*, Alice Miller writes, "It will depend on a person's earliest experiences whether he will be able to deal creatively with new theories and ultimately find his own point of view or whether he will cling anxiously to the orthodoxy of a school. If this person was raised to be absolutely obedient, without ever being able to escape his parents' watchful eyes, he will run the risk as an adult of making theories into absolutes and becoming a slave to them." (The paradox in this wise passage is that Miller uses the male pronoun instead of inclusive language, itself a form of obedience to the patriarchal system.)

To set the stage for moving beyond the third phase, children need respect, security, safety, autonomy balanced with interdependency, and encouragement to *choose* the beliefs and practices that feel right for them.

People in twelve-step groups need the same. A person may abstain from drugs and chemicals by staying at levels two and three, but personal development is thwarted. Thus groups need to encourage questioning and respect different roads to recovery.

In twelve-step circles, questioning is often met with attempts to pull people back to unquestioning loyalty. It's as if the stages are reversed and the stage two and three people look on the dissenters—stage four people—as children who will get over this silly phase and come back into the fold. Underneath the subtle pressures people exert to bring back the wandering sheep lies fear—fear of change, fear of differences, and fear of people's leaving. These fears may actually hark back to long-forgotten fears of childhood that the loyal member wants to avoid. The childhood fear of a father's leaving gets translated into fear of anyone leaving the group. The fear that Dad will blow up and start hitting if his authority is questioned gets translated to fearing anyone who questions the status quo and shows anger or resists conformity.

For groups to help people heal, we need to become aware of the underlying family dynamics we are playing out. This will happen when we go on an inner journey of awareness that will lead us to question not only our families but the culture that creates the norms.

4. Late Adolescence and Early Adulthood (The Critic)

At this level people stop accepting the status quo, start to ask questions, and often get angry at the deceptions they've been handed in their families and in our cultural institutions. Fear starts to slip away as an internal sense of self is born.

One day when Kelly was cleaning, I heard her banging the pots and pans around the kitchen.

"What's up?" I asked her, feeling excited by this explosion of energy in this woman who had been so afraid and depressed.

"I'm so mad at my AA group. Every time I bring up a problem, they give me these pat answers. Do this step, do that step. No one wants to just sit and listen to the way I feel. I just want to be upset sometimes and have people listen. You'd think emotions were this terrible thing to get rid of. I just want to be angry for a while!"

I could relate to Kelly. I have spent a lot of my life at the critic stage, asking questions, feeling angry, and wanting to be understood. Many people admire spirited people from a distance, but when passionate people get close others often move away, afraid of igniting their own inner feelings or stirring up discomfort. When someone's passion or beliefs make us uncomfortable, either we move through the feelings they raise in us or we distance ourselves.

Questioning can be painful, confusing, relieving, exhilarating—but it helps us move beyond fear. For most people it opens up the energy flow in the body because it connects us with our inner truths, often our anger. Tapping into one's anger can be very healthy for women such as Kelly because it helps connect her with knowledge of her abuse and neglect. "I was hurt and I'm mad about it." That's a lot better than remaining in pain and chronically depressed.

James Christopher, in *How to Stay Sober*, a book on finding sobriety without a belief in God, writes, "I remember questioning things at AA meetings in my early sobriety: 'What is "God's will?" How do nontheists, Jews, and Buddhists feel about saying the Lord's Prayer?' One longtime AA member simply said, 'Shut up.' Another answered, 'Your best thinking got you here,' meaning if you 'think'—that is, if you question the AA dogma, it really means that you want to drink."

Christopher goes on to ask, "What about free thinkers? Must we give up our identities and our free-thought processes and develop faith in a higher power to stay sober? Obviously not. Obvious to me now, several years after gaining a less-robotic foothold on my sobriety. But not so obvious in the beginning—especially during the first few days, weeks, months, and through the first year of my sobriety."

When people who have moved into level four enter traditional twelve-step groups, they are likely to experience some form of conflict with the rigidity. In level four, the disillusionment, confusion, discomfort, and anger often lead to upheaval in relationships. Friends leave or we lose interest in the people who cannot understand our inner yearning, confusion, and disillusionment. Alienation from the norm leaves an ache some days. "I want to fit in." Yet something precious is waking up inside, feeling alive, making music, learning to love. Most of all, fear starts to subside. To question the unquestionable—a metaphor for developing autonomy from parents—is to give birth to the self.

Sometimes amid the churning and the change one flashes on the thought, "I wish things were simple and clear like they used to be." But you can't go back, because you know too much, and deep inside, most people don't really want to. Sometimes you just want it to be easier.

Overall, people in twelve-step programs do not encourage this type of exploration, which paradoxically might lead a person to a level of transformation and maturity where they no longer need a twelve-step group identity. People at this questioning stage of faith who remain in twelve-step programs often become part of renegade meetings—meetings that encourage members to reword the steps, take a less literal view of the program, and absorb information on healing and recovery from many other sources.

Rather than "program people," they identify themselves as individuals on a healing path or a spiritual journey. They may use twelve-step groups but they don't pledge allegiance to them. There is a sense of learning from each other's individual experiences. Differences are better tolerated, and platitudes and jargon diminish. Various types of literature are welcomed into the group library and, for many, the twelve-step group becomes only one means of support in their lives. They have friends who are not "program people," and they are not invested in pushing the program onto others.

Some people who enter this questioning period leave twelve-step programs and experiment with other support groups, communities, or

activities that resonate with their beliefs. Throughout life, as new problems and situations arise, people may return to this phase of questioning over and over. Because it brings discomfort, people tend to want
resolution. Some people find communities or groups that are accepting
of their beliefs. Others, overwhelmed by the conflict and not offered
alternatives, return to level three.

Several weeks after Kelly expressed her unhappiness with her AA
group, she found a solution.

"I've found a great new group," she said to me one day with a lot
of enthusiasm.

"Great!" I said.

"It is so wonderful. It uses sixteen steps and they are all positive
and I can relate to them." She had read an ad in a local recovery
newsletter for an all-women's Narcotics Anonymous group started by
a woman named Suzee.

"Can I see the steps?" I asked, hoping to find some more good
quotes for this book.

"Sure."

I sat down and started reading them, then I looked up at Kelly and
smiled. "Do you know where these come from?"

"No, why?"

"I wrote them—they were in my questionnaire."

"No kidding!"

"Did the women know where they came from?"

"No, I don't think so. Someone in an ARIA (incest recovery) group
had them and was passing them around."

Kelly and I were amazed at the coincidence. Out of thousands of
women in recovery/uncovery groups in the Twin Cities, she was one
of a handful who had joined the first group that used the steps I had
written. (You will find them in chapter 14, where I present an empow-
erment/discovery model.)

By joining a group that expressed her inner beliefs and felt instinctively right, Kelly had moved at least one aspect of her life—her uncovery program—to level five of faithing, an integrated expansive faith.
Her group was now at one with her beliefs and her needs.

5. Integrated Expansive Faith (The Seer)

We can look at this level of faith on a continuum. People touch it
the way Suzee and Kelly did. They resolve inner conflict about a given
situation by finding a form that feels respectful to their inner beliefs.
As we move along the continuum, people become more centered as
they take all parts of their life—work, friendships, eating habits, educa-

tion, sexual relationships, living situations, spiritual communities—and bring them into alignment with their beliefs. It becomes a faith to call one's own. It is intensely personal, deeply felt, not easily shaken and rarely a subject for intellectual debate. It has a deep, inner, resonating quality. "I know this is what is right for me." To be untrue to oneself at this level is painful. One is immediately aware of the internal dissonance.

People at this level have a well-developed inner core, and are not suddenly changed by a passionate speech or slick propaganda. They can see through rhetoric and hype and are strongly grounded in their values, which were formed over a long period of time.

When one has an integrated expansive faith, situations rarely have a do-or-die intensity, because people have a broad perspective on life. Paradoxically, people may express their emotions strongly because they do not censor themselves. Thus they feel genuinely alive and allow themselves to be passionate about their beliefs. At the same time they can witness their behavior with acceptance and humor, relishing the paradoxes of life and feeling compassion for their own inconsistencies and foibles.

According to Fowler, this stage is rarely attained before the age of thirty, if at all, because reflection, working through values, and casting off the teachings of religion, education, and social custom takes time and effort. It can't be done intellectually. It is part of a journey where the living and the believing become one.

Many people leave twelve-step programs as they become more deeply embedded in this harmonious level of faith. If they do attend, their twelve-step meeting is but one part of a greater personal faith that is central to their lives. They have reached deeply beneath the words to the underlying wisdom, which they are likely to integrate with numerous other models that support their faith and spiritual journey. They draw support, give to others, but do not see "the program" as a panacea or as being without fault. Their healing journey evolves into a personal spiritual journey. At this point people are less likely to consider themselves "in recovery"; rather, they see themselves as growing, stretching human beings not separate from other people.

One of the primary characteristics of an integrated faith is the ability to draw from different belief systems and integrate their wisdom. This brings to mind an experience I had while visiting a celebration of the second anniversary of a Native American healing center in Montana. I arrived to hear the end of a very informal Catholic mass that integrated Native American wisdom. This was followed by an AA meeting. Some people attended the meeting while others stayed outside to talk.

As the AA meeting went on, I sat outside and spoke with several people. I asked one woman, Jean, a teacher at a Native American college, how it worked, combining so many forms. "Very well, thank you." She laughed. It was obvious, simple. "I do what feels helpful," she added. Many of the people who had stayed sober rarely attended AA meetings for a variety of reasons. The community spirit that supported their recovery went far deeper than a given form. It was rooted in Native American culture and a deeply felt commitment to bring sobriety and dignity to their Native American brothers and sisters.

At stage five, people experience much less fear, and the need to argue or prove a point dissipates. Different opinions and shifts in thinking are accepted as part of being alive. Fear is replaced by curiosity and interest. There is increased empathy or warmth toward people who are at other stages of faith, and indeed recognition that there are stages of development of faith.

6. Wisdom (Universalizing Faith)

I know of no one at this level who belongs to an AA or a twelve-step group. My hunch is that people at this phase have so transcended duality, and live so much at one with their faith, that their addictive qualities have melted away. They are at one with spirit. The ego, awareness, and compassion are merged together.

Because it is difficult to put this level of faith into words I would like to tell a story of a man who was at this level who worked with addiction. The beautifully articulated story appeared in *How Can I Help*, by Ram Dass and Paul Gorman. A man, having heard of monks who through meditation had gained great powers, wondered if the stories were true. He then visited a monastery in Thailand in which heroin and opium addicts were allegedly cured in ten days . . . for fifteen dollars.

> The monk had previously been a Thai "narc" . . . something like our federal drug enforcement agency. He had an aunt who I was told was a Buddhist saint, whatever that means. One day she apparently said to him, while he was still a narc, "What are you doing? If you don't watch out you're going to end up killing people in this job. Why don't you help these people instead of hurting them?" He said that he didn't know how. She apparently told him to clean up his act and she'd show him.
>
> So he left government service and became a monk. Now the

Buddhists monks in Thailand are part of the Theravadin tradition which requires very severe renunciation in order to purify your mind so that you can do deep meditation. There are some two hundred eighteen prohibitions, all of which he adopted. Then he even added ten more on his own, such as never driving in automobiles. This meant that when he had business in Bangkok, about a hundred and fifty miles away, he'd just pick up his walking stick and start walking.

This rigorous training prepared him to do very intensive meditation practice which allowed him to tune to the deeper and more powerful parts of his mind. When his aunt felt he was ready, she instructed him in the preparation of an herbal diuretic which she instructed him to give to the addicts, and he started his monastery.

When we met him my most immediate reaction was that I was shaking hands with an oak tree. His presence was immensely powerful and solid. He had us shown through the monastery where some three hundred addicts were undergoing treatment.

You could really see who was which. The first day arrivals all looked like strung-out junkies. They were in one room. Then further on, by the time they had been there for four days, you could really see a change. And by eight days they seemed cheerful, were bumming cigarettes from me, and seemed really friendly—not particularly like addicts at all. And then after ten days they were gone. And their statistics showed seventy percent remained free of addiction afterwards. Amazing.

When I interviewed the monk, I asked him, "How do you do it?" He said, "Well, it's simple. I tell them that they can only come for ten days and they may never come again, and that the cure will work." I asked him if a lot of religious indoctrination was included in the ten-day program. "No," he said, "none of that. These people aren't suitable for that."

I had heard that many drug experts, media people, and even some congressmen had come from the West but that none of them could figure out why what he did worked. The herbal brew clearly wasn't the whole ballgame. As I hung out with him longer, I began to realize that his mind was so centered and one-pointed that his being was stronger than their addiction. Somehow he conveyed to those addicts a sense of their non-addiction that was stronger than their addiction. And I saw that his commitment was so total that he wasn't just someone using a skill. He had died into his work. He *was* the cure. . . .

While few of us reach this level, its existence—evidence of which includes the Mother Teresas and Gandhis of the world—gives us inspiration. I believe we all have potential to be at this stage in some way. I think of people in this stage as living in the ecstasy people are seeking through addiction. They are at one with their spirit, their love, and their purpose. They live by faith and without fear.

The question remains, do twelve-step programs help people move toward a highly integrated faith or do they somehow block the way? Before we reach the answer we need to explore the role of patriarchy, hierarchy, and capitalism in addiction.

3

Is Addiction Inevitable?
Patriarchy, Hierarchy, and Capitalism

In this chapter, I am questioning our patriarchal system, not individual people. I subscribe to Ghandi's explanation of *ahimsa*, the love for all people. He writes in his autobiography, "It is quite proper to resist and attack a system, but to resist and attack its author is tantamount to resisting and attacking oneself. For we are all tarred with the same brush, and are children of one and the same Creator. . . . To slight a single human being is to . . . harm not only that being but with him the whole world."

Having said this, I proceed to the tenet of this chapter, namely that *patriarchy, hierarchy, and capitalism create, encourage, maintain, and perpetuate addiction and dependency.* Patriarchy and hierarchy are based on domination and subordination, which result in fear. This fear is expressed by the dominators through control and violence, and in the subordinated people through passivity and repression of anger. The external conflict of hierarchy between dominants and subordinates becomes internalized in individuals, creating personal inner chaos, anxiety, and duality. To quell the inner conflict people resort to addictive substances and behavior.

53

* * *

"I was born to be addicted, and it's a miracle I'm alive," Suzee Rivers told me in a group interview. Her statement echoes that of many people I interviewed or who completed questionnaires. Given the nature of patriarchy, hierarchy, and capitalism, and the prejudice, incest, violence, and poverty that so often result from this sometimes merciless system, millions of people in the United States are indeed *born to be addicted*.

Before I tell you Suzee's story and that of others who were "born to be addicted," I would like to draw some connections among patriarchy, hierarchy, capitalism, and addiction. In the last chapter I suggested that moving toward levels four, five, and six of faithing—questioning, integrating our beliefs, and feeling a compassionate connection to all people—is the antidote to addiction. Here we will see how patriarchy resists movement in this direction and thus promotes addiction by encouraging people to fill up their empty places with substances and things, not wisdom, love, and connectedness to others.

PATRIARCHY

According to Mary Daly, feminist, theologian, and author of *Gyn/ Ecology*, "Patriarchy is itself the prevailing religion of the entire planet, and its essential message is necrophilia ["An obsessive fascination with death and corpses," according to the *American Heritage Dictionary*]." If we read the newspaper or popular magazines, go to movies, look at how we allocate money for military spending as opposed to social programs and how we treat our life-giving natural resources such as air and water, it is clear to see that our system is more enamored of death and destruction than life. *Thus addiction, which leads to death—either physically or spiritually—is a natural outgrowth of patriarchy.*

Mary Daly continues. "All of the so-called religions legitimating patriarchy are mere sects subsumed under its vast umbrella/canopy. They are essentially similar, despite the variations. All—from buddhism and hinduism to islam, judaism, christianity, to secular derivatives such as freudianism, jungianism, marxism, and maoism—are infrastructures of the edifice of patriarchy. And the symbolic message of all the sects of the religion which is patriarchy is this: Women are the dreaded anomie. Consequently, women are the objects of male terror, the projected personifications of 'The Enemy,' the real objects under attack in all the wars of patriarchy."

Because patriarchy assigns a secondary position to women, it creates a hierarchy, in which human value is determined by gender, race, class, position, religion, age, appearance, ethnic background, and physical ability. Thus hierarchy promotes the death of spirit, because people are rendered as objects. Most of all, patriarchy maintains the subordination of women, which it has done for five thousand years through manipulation, violence, exclusion from decision-making groups, and economic deprivation—all of which create shame, exhaustion, fear, and pain, the fuel of addiction.

Patriarchy is invested in keeping women and minorities immersed in self-hatred and apathy. Thus it makes sense that as women have bonded together to assume self-determination and equal rights in the past three decades, there has been a terrible backlash—a virtual guerilla war on women, including rape, incest, battering, control of reproductive rights, pornography, and the feminization of poverty. The same is true in the reaction to the civil rights movement where the eighties reflect an increasing decline in the gains African Americans made in the seventies.

Whether this warfare against minorities is done consciously or not is beside the point. That oppression is a function of patriarchy is what is relevant to our discussion of addiction, because oppression creates the emptiness and fear that lead toward addictive behavior. The desire to live gets turned into a struggle to survive the pain of our system. Instead of affirming life, we are taught to medicate ourselves in order to cope with it. This is, again, the theme of necrophilia—going toward death and destruction rather than openness and love.

Patriarchy is defined in the *American Heritage Dictionary* as "1. A system of social organization in which descent and succession are traced through the male line. 2. The rule of a tribe or family by men when lineage is passed down through the men who are seen as dominant."

It is a system derived from Greek and Roman law "in which the male head of the household had absolute legal and economic power over his dependent female and male family members."

The *practice* of patriarchy is defined by Gerda Lerner in *The Creation of Patriarchy* as "the manifestation and institutionalization of male dominance over women and children in the family and the extension of male dominance over women in society in general. It implies that men hold power in all the important institutions of society and that women are deprived of access to such power."

If we understand patriarchy as a prevailing religion then we see violence, control, and domination as the objects of worship. This has resulted in seeing the earth and less powerful people as resources to be exploited; the pairing of sex with violence, control, and power; the desecration of women's sexuality and the sacred ability to nurture life; the worship of war, winning, competition, death, and destruction; the worship of the rational mind and linear thinking as opposed to intuition and wisdom that connects thinking with caring and love; the dualities of right-wrong, and good-bad, and as opposed to seeing all things as an integral part of a whole, with each part having an important function.

HIERARCHY AND OUR PHYSICAL BODIES

Our hierarchical system, which objectifies and uses people, is reflected in the ways we treat our bodies. We use and exploit the earth as an inanimate resource, without regard for the delicate balance of the ecological system. Instead of accepting what the earth will produce by natural means, we use fertilizers and insecticides that give short-term gains and in the long term poison the earth and the food we eat.

We are taught to do the same with our bodies. Instead of being guided by the natural capabilities of our bodies and being tuned into our personal ecosystems—resting when we are tired, eating natural food when we are hungry—we get short-term highs by using caffeine, sugar, highly processed food, nicotine, and alcohol to force our bodies to do more than is natural, ultimately leaving us stressed, tired, and out of balance both emotionally and physically. This mirrors the control and force, and lack of harmony with nature that prevails in every aspect of our culture.

Our insensitivity to our bodies, our inability to live in tune with them, leads to chronic types of substance addiction—the constant use of stimulants or depressants to keep a person functioning as their adrenal glands become increasingly exhausted from all the intense highs and lows. People become more and more exhausted, needing more and more stimulants to keep going as they slowly weaken their immune system. This constitutes ecological destruction at the personal level. Thus we have the highs and lows of hierarchy, the highs and lows in the body, and the highs and lows of addiction—which is often a search for a high to escape the inner low.

Forcing our bodies beyond their natural capacities also affects the intricately interwoven web of the energy centers of the body associated with security, passions, power, love, communication, and wisdom. In other words, it keeps people chronically off balance and out of touch with the wonder and strength of our incredible physical bodies. I will talk about these energy centers, known as the chakras, later in this chapter.

PATRIARCHY AND OBEDIENCE

Another aspect of patriarchy that attempts to block our development beyond the loyalist level of faithing and thus leads to addiction is the strong value placed on obedience. In *The Chalice and the Blade*, Riane Eisler writes, "As we have seen in the Genesis account of how Adam and Eve are eternally punished for defying Jehova's order to stay away from the tree of knowledge, any rebellion against the authority of the ruling male priesthood . . . was made a heinous sin." The dictum that follows was: "Don't think, accept what is, accept what authority says is true. Above all, do not use your own intelligence, your own powers of mind, to question us or to seek independent knowledge."

This dictum still exists in hierarchy. Translated to our model of faith development, the message is, Don't develop beyond the loyalist phase into a mature adult with an expansive, searching mind.

PATRIARCHY AND COMPARTMENTALIZATION

Another of the primary traits of patriarchy is to compartmentalize and segment our knowledge instead of seeing connections. To do this, we are taught at all levels of our society to dissociate from what we see, think, believe, and experience. Women and minorities are taught to dissociate from their pain and anger at being abused and exploited. The perpetrators of exploitation are taught not to empathize with the people they exploit; thus they dissociate from love and compassion.

Addiction is a natural cover-up for both victim and perpetrator. It helps anesthetize knowledge of the truth. "I don't want to know I'm being exploited by people who say they care." "I don't want to know I'm abusing others for my own selfish gains." So, forget. Have a drink, eat more ice cream, spend money, go to the race track, or work until you drop.

AN EPIDEMIC OF PSYCHIC NUMBING
AND DISSOCIATION

Helen Caldicott talks about *psychic numbing* in *Missile Envy*. Psychic numbing is when we detach and dissociate from parts of ourselves in response to overwhelming or terrifying situations. Another related term is *anhedonia*, the inability to feel. Anhedonia is common among the homeless, people who live in extreme poverty, and people who exploit or abuse others.

We are creating more and more of this type of dissociation through increased childhood abuse. Abuse survivors talk about leaving their bodies, going to another place, disconnecting from the physical and emotional pain of assault and rape. Then, to keep the dreaded memories at bay, they expend tremendous energy repressing these parts of themselves, often with the use of addictive substances. Much of my work as a therapist is to help people reconnect with memories of abuse and violence and face the painful feelings they have exhausted themselves avoiding.

Reading the newspaper, one sees constant evidence of psychic numbing or dissociation on the part of our leaders. Some examples: A recent article reported that authorities at coal mines had been charged with tampering with air samples so they would pass pollution requirements. They were psychically numbed against the ramifications of their act, which would result in countless cases of black lung disease and upper respiratory problems; another talked about the severe, long-term negative effects of childhood sexual abuse; on a recent episode of the TV program *20/20* on medical care for children, it was reported that many children no longer have access to basic immunizations for childhood diseases and many will die of measles and other diseases because the funding for rural health clinics has been cut. It takes a lot of psychic numbing to deprive children of basic immunizations.

Meanwhile, we read that the United States had a $5 million party to celebrate (I choke on the word) the victory (choke again) in the Persian Gulf, although we killed nearly 200,000 people and an estimated 170,000 children will die as a direct result of our bombing raids. It must have taken a lot of psychic numbing to attend the "party" without thinking about all the children who will grow up without fathers, women left without husbands or providers, or what it is like to die from starvation or to hold your dying child and be powerless to keep him or her alive. As a backdrop to these happenings, we have the exhumed Watergate tapes revealing that Nixon replied approvingly to H. R. Haldeman's suggestion that "hardhats and Legionnaires" and "teamster union thugs" be used to "beat the shit out of some of these people," referring to demonstrators against the war. It continues.

These stories that require psychic numbing could be from 1991 or 1971. They all require dissociation from compassion and from a sense of oneness with all peoples—a dissociation that appears increasingly pervasive in the United States.

Psychic numbing is another term for denial, something most addicted people are familiar with. Your life can be falling apart and you still maintain drugs aren't causing any problem. The same thing is true in our society when it comes to violence toward women and children. We hear political speeches condemning the taking of hostages in the Middle East, but I'm still waiting for the presidential speech that says, "We won't stand for these bullies who rape our women and children. We won't tolerate prejudice and assault on people of color. We won't stand for women being held hostage by violent and abusing men."

Like addicted people, our leaders blind themselves to seeing what is in their own back yard. And the masses follow suit with mass psychic numbing, often using addictive substances to ensure the denial.

As if in a trance, addicted people set aside their alleged values and sometimes ruthlessly pursue their addiction. The military-industrial complex does the same, maintaining their addiction to control and violence. The nation's food money gets spent on weapons and millions of people starve or go without homes.

CULTURE AS A MULTIPLE PERSONALITY

In extreme cases of torture and abuse, people's dissociating results in multiple personalities, which therapists are seeing in increasing numbers. In a multiple-personality system, one personality might be competent and hold a job but experience no feelings, another part might retain memories of childhood torture, while another might carry the fear and yet another feel the rage. One part might compulsively eat and another become alcoholic. There is often a personality that self-abuses. It sees itself in a protective role, stopping other parts from telling the secrets, fearing they will be killed if they do so.

Some of the personalities have co-consciousness with other parts; like looking through a one-way mirror, they are aware of what the other is doing, but feel powerless to control it. If the person cuts or burns himself some parts will feel the pain but others will experience nothing. There are also personalities who see many parts of the system and are able to explain how it all works together, and the reason for seemingly harmful or puzzling behavior. These are called the helper personalities. Many people with multiple personalities function, but life is often chaotic, unpredictable, and highly stressful. The person is still one whole person, but the various parts are cut off from knowledge of the other parts.

Our society, which has become fractured and compartmentalized, has become like a multiple personality in order to cope with and deny the profound pain that exists among us. We have groups of people in one section making decisions for others with no consciousness of the devastating effects of those decisions on others. For example, one segment of our system, the government, passes laws limiting women's reproductive rights, while being walled off with absolutely no experience of what it is to be poor and alone with an unwanted child, or to be an unwanted child, growing up hungry or neglected.

In another example of our multiple-personality system, we have white men of privilege isolated in the Pentagon and the White House declaring war with little or no consciousness and compassion for the underprivileged or people of color who will die or be emotionally maimed in the war—not to mention the people they will kill or maim in some foreign country.

Like a multiple-personality system, some people or organizations have co-consciousness—they see beyond the isolated section they were trained to occupy and they work to break down the walls and connect and bring social justice. These are the people feared by the government, because the survival of patriarchy, like addiction, depends on compartmentalization, denial, and lack of vision.

Thus segmenting, separating, and isolating people are the weapons of patriarchy. All of this relates to addiction, which is itself a dissociative process where one part wanting escape from pain, isolation, or hopelessness overwhelms the wisdom of another part and engages in behavior that is ultimately self-destructive. Short-term relief from pain is exchanged for long-term destruction. This follows the model of patriarchy and capitalism, which is short-term economic gain at the price of long-term destruction of the ecosystem and people's spirits.

THE PATRIARCHAL SWITCH

A concept important to understanding the deceptions of patriarchy is *the patriarchal switch*. Mary Daly initially referred to this in *Gyn-Ecology* as a reversal, or a male method of mystification. Historically, between 10,000 and 3,000 BC there is considerable evidence that we moved gradually from a Goddess-worshiping culture that revered life, nature, creation, and harmony to patriarchy. Part of the change involved desecrating and redefining the Goddess myths and beliefs. A major foundation of the patriarchal switch affecting us today was the book of Genesis, which forever proclaimed women inferior to men, along with providing the Garden of Eden story. In the book of Genesis, the Goddess image of the tree of life, symbolizing the cosmic energy, the serpent as a sacred symbol of wisdom, and the fruit as a source of knowledge were changed to the serpent as evil and apple as something forbidden. If we think back to our levels of faith development, this set the stage for people's becoming locked into the first three levels of faithing, because taking from the tree of knowledge resulted in banishment.

Another form of the patriarchal switch was defining traits of nurture, intuition, and emotional expression as weak, and saying they were the natural traits of women. Cooperation was replaced with a conquest mentality, and the ability to maim and kill became the measure of the conquerer's worth. Menstruation, once seen as a sacred time for quiet reflection, was renamed "the curse" and was regarded as unclean. Bearing children, a natural, sacred act usually attended by women, became a sickness ultimately needing hospitalization, drugs, male doctors, and eventually the extensive use of high-tech machines for a normal birth. Aging, especially for women, has been redefined as a malady to be overcome with makeup, liposuction, and estrogen (we even have the term "untreated menopause." We don't have a term for untreated aging for men).

A basic foundation of the patriarchal switch is a blame-the-victim stance that pervades our culture. Instead of focusing on people who perpetrate violence, indifference, exploitation, and abuse, we blame people for being poor, abused, and raped. In an article by Kay Hagan titled "Codependency and the Myth of Recovery," Hagan comments that having a book called *Women Who Love Too Much* instead of one called *Men Who Love Too Little* is another example of the patriarchal switch.

CAPITALISM

Mixing capitalism with patriarchy is like combining barbiturates with alcohol—a lethal brew. Capitalism creates addiction because it rests on making people feel insecure, unlovable, and ashamed in order to have them purchase all kinds of things to make them—allegedly—attractive, lovable, and powerful. To function optimally, the capitalist system needs people to stay in the first three levels of faithing where they can be easily seduced by advertising propaganda that appeals to their low self-esteem.

The system is self-perpetuating because all this stuff doesn't make people feel happy or loved. When people don't know that happiness comes from love, purpose, and connectedness, they keep seeking the right partner, job, whatever, to make themselves happy. It is totally unsurprising that one of the primary results of this system is incredible stress. Many people are working terribly hard to buy things and then reaching for the medicine bottle, food, or drugs to ease the distress. The other result of capitalism is that while some people are drowning in their junk, other people can't afford even minimal survival needs, which also causes stress.

This takes us back to where I began this chapter, with Suzee Rivers' saying "I was born to be addicted and it's a miracle I'm alive."

"I WAS BORN TO BE ADDICTED"

I met Suzee through Kelly, whom I talked about in the last chapter. I was interested in meeting Suzee and members of the newly formed sixteen-step group, so I asked Kelly if she might help arrange an interview.

Suzee, Kelly, and two other women in the group, Kim and Eleanor, consented. The four women arrived together. They were all quite young and from working-class backgrounds. When they arrived, I felt their initial uneasiness and sensed that everyone was picking up the cues, testing out the situation, asking questions, creating safety for themselves. Suzee was in her late twenties, outspoken, strong-minded, yet gentle. I was glad to meet this pioneer woman who had started a women's NA group, and she was curious to meet me, the woman who wrote the sixteen steps they had adopted for their group.

After we introduced ourselves, the women told some of their childhood histories, which echoed the theme, "I was born to be addicted."

"I was born addicted to phenobarbital. My father fed me alcohol when he incested me. No one ever took care of me."

"I, too, was born to be alcoholic and stick needles in my arm. My parents were both alcoholic. I was shuffled around. I felt invisible most of my life."

"I was unprotected. I seldom knew what love and care meant. All

I ever learned was to grow up and find a man to take care of me."

These addictions to drugs, food, sex, and dependent relationships were the all-too-common results of our system. The women had used drugs and food for comfort, and sex to gain relationships or for economic security, and often lived in fear of losing a man who they hoped would bring safety and security. And it's not just a working-class woman's story. It can be a Black male in a Black ghetto, a Native American, a middle-class woman from an abusive household, or a white middle-class man who was sexually abused or physically battered and neglected.

Thus we see the system of hierarchy being played out in a recovery group and having a negative effect on women. The women described their dissatisfaction with their mixed Narcotics Anonymous group. They said the men dominated, and that they didn't regard their concerns and problems as important or make serious attempts to listen and understand. Thus, while trying to maintain sobriety, they had the added stress of a nonsupportive group.

Part of comprehending the destructive aspects of hierarchy is understanding the dynamics of what Jean Baker Miller termed the roles of the dominants and subordinates.

Miller lucidly explains the intricacies of domination and subordination in *Toward a New Psychology of Women*, a book I recommend to everyone. Here are a few quotes that relate to our discussion:

A dominant group inevitably has the greatest influence in determining a culture's overall outlook—its philosophy, morality, social theory, and even its science. The dominant group thus legitimized the unequal relationships and incorporated it into society's guiding concepts. . . . Inevitably the dominant group is the model for "normal human relationships." . . . It follows from this that dominant groups generally do not like to be told about or even quietly reminded of the existence of inequality. Dominants prefer to avoid conflict—open conflict that might call into question the whole situation. . . . Dominants are usually convinced that the way things are is right and good, not only for them but especially for the subordinates. All morality confirms this view, and all social structure sustains it."

This echoes the complaints Suzee, Kelly, and many others had about their experiences with AA and NA, which were dominated by men.

Kelly spoke. "I felt really brainwashed by AA, starting with treatment. It was offered as the only way, and if you wanted to stay sober, you had to go. People came into my treatment program daily from AA telling how wonderful it was. All the time in my AA meeting something felt fake. The connections didn't feel real, but I wanted to stay sober, so I mouthed the words and acted like they did."

Suzee continued the discussion. "I felt like a renegade for saying what was true for me. It was supposed to be all grand and wonderful that we were all together in recovery. Being in pain meant I constantly felt like a failure. If I mentioned being abused by a man, I was told to give up resentments."

Because our hierarchical system often "obscures the truth of what it is doing"—which is to maintain inequality—men and women are carefully and subtly programmed from childhood to maintain the status quo. It is not surprising that this carries over into treatment programs.

Suzee continued. "When I was in an outpatient therapy group for addiction, I came in really upset because my partner had battered and raped me the night before. The male counselor rolled his eyes and said, sarcastically, 'Are we going to hear that girl shit again?' "

Another woman, Kim, said, "When I was in treatment, they announced we were going to have family week and I had to bring my family. I told them I didn't want to see my family—they had been too abusive to me. I didn't have the strength to argue further. I was never given a choice and no one took seriously what I said. My family came and I got abused all over again. My father started screaming at me and blaming me for the incest. After the family session, the counselor said she could see what I meant. But they should have believed me in the first place. Just because I go for treatment doesn't mean I have no brains and don't know anything. Even after that, they started talking to me about the need to forgive him. Again they were telling me what to do."

This kind of re-victimization of women and minorities goes on repeatedly in systems set up and run by white males at the top of hierarchy.

THE NEED TO LOOK BEYOND FAMILY SYSTEMS

You might be wondering at this point whatever happened to the role of the family in addiction. Rather than *causing* addiction, I see the family as the *transmitter* of cultural values that result in addiction and dependency. It can be subtle—such as parents' laughing at sexist and racist treatment of people on TV programs—or overt as with violence and incest. But the fundamental values communicated to children in families are those of domination and subordination—people are valued by external measures, giving some people the right to use and exploit others. That's where the concept of shame fits into the picture.

Shame is often considered a root cause of addiction. Shame is the feeling of being defective or unloved that leads people to anesthetize themselves with addictive behavior. It's not that you *made* a mistake that makes you feel guilty, you *are* the mistake; there is something intrinsically wrong with you. Feeling shameful is attributed to dysfunctional families where there is alcoholism, incest, emotional role reversals, and neglect. But I believe the incest, violence, and neglect are a direct result of the values and practices of our system. Thus the real culprit is a shame-based hierarchical social system that does not value life.

Limiting our view to the family as source of addiction actually perpetuates addiction, because the true source remains invisible and people remain steeped in denial. Thus we have people say, "Oh yes, I get incredibly afraid because I'm an adult child of an alcoholic," or "I'm addicted because I come from a shame-based family." While these statements are partially true, they mask another deeper reality that Suzee voiced in our interview. "I'm addicted because I was born into a culture that allowed me to be a victim of incest, abuse, violence, poverty, and sexism. There was never care and protection for me. There was never access to higher education for me."

Staying overly focused on family as *the* source of addiction creates a negative cycle that works like this: people explore the family as the source of addiction and codependency problems. They analyze, investigate, draw conclusions, and dig up reasons for their behavior. This first step in healing takes us to our personal pain and gives us an understanding of our family system and the ways we were wounded as children. But if one doesn't eventually stop pointing a finger at the family and start looking at the culture, an important source of the problem is missed. This makes it hard to forgive or let go of the negative behaviors of our parents or others. As a result people don't feel healed or whole, and are often encouraged by therapists and others "in recovery" to have more therapy, go to more groups, and continue to analyze their family. *Thus we have the perpetual "adult child" or dysfunctional family, as opposed to a healed adult living an imperfect life in an imperfect world.* It is convenient for the system that we continue to focus on shame-based "dysfunctional" families, because the system is let off the hook.

I was never able to let go of my hurt or forgive my mother for suppressing my passion, talent, and mind until I could tune in to her predicament as a woman growing up in patriarchy in the early 1900s—a woman who was taught to believe with every inch of her being that marriage and motherhood were the only respectable, satisfying roles for a woman. Her responses to my strong beliefs and feelings stemmed from her belief that she had to control me so I could "catch" a man. Given her socialization, it is not surprising she shamed me for my strong views: they were too bold . . . for attracting a man. My passion for piano was too intense . . . for attracting a man. And yes, I hid my pain with drugs, depression, and food. I needed to be angry at her, to drop into the angry child and rage at my losses, but I also needed to feel my rage at the female socialization that set us up against each other and robbed us of the kind of mother-daughter bond we both yearned for and never had. How could she love the power in me when she had so deeply buried her own to be a "good" wife and mother?

Ultimately, we will heal more deeply when we understand that we grew up as wounded children in a culture that wounds all children by not teaching values that support life.

"EVERYONE'S LOOKING FOR SOME KIND OF LOVE": A TRIP THROUGH HIERARCHY

My sister, Lenore Davis, collaborated with me to create an image of hierarchy and patriarchy in the United States.

If we look at our illustration of hierarchy and patriarchy, we see people of different genders, ages, colors, races, classes, educations, or economic situations. To survive this system, all of them have been conditioned to lose, bury, or not develop parts of themselves. It could be their ability to love, cry, show tenderness, feel pain, express anger, experience their fear, be assertive, or pursue their personal hopes and dreams. The part that gets lost or buried or never developed depends on where they are in the hierarchy, their particular childhood circumstances, and their personal empowerment. This ties in with our discussions of the human energy system—chakras—that follows.

For example, the white males at the top get to set the rules, but are cut off from their sensitivity and love because they must blind themselves to the fact that they are living off the backs of the people below them. The people who live below the chain-link fence spend a lot of time figuring out the rules of the people who live above them because they have to survive in their world. Thus they may have insight into the

Hierarchy Patriarchy

workings of the people above them, but they may not have a lot of time left to understand themselves. And the ones on the very bottom are exhausted simply trying to survive. This hinders them from experiencing the luxury of self-exploration and personal growth.

When we have parts of ourselves buried or undeveloped, we feel out of harmony, empty, or off-center, and often experience a sense of alienation that results in an inner void fueling both compulsive and addictive behavior as well as codependency. Gotta fill up the emptiness, gotta get rid of the pain and desperation. Give me money, sex, drugs, food, status, a wife, a husband. *We engage in compulsive or addictive behavior so we don't have to feel what's inside. Patriarchy/hierarchy maintains and perpetuates addictive and dependent behavior in order to cover up the incredible losses of self and separateness created by our system.*

The White, Privileged Male Club

Let's start with the triangle above the chain link fence. Admittance to this segment of our hierarchy requires being white, privileged, and male, with money and status. Lawyers, doctors, businessmen, and politicians abound here. Typical addictions in this club are work, money, status, sex, drugs, and alcohol. Codependent traits exist but are not acknowledged because vulnerability, particularly to those below them, is forbidden. Codependent behavior includes corporate dress conformity, pleasing the boss, and working whatever hours you are told to work, which often results in pressure, heart attacks, and broken promises about spending time with the family. Another trait rarely acknowledged by privileged men is their dependency on women for emotional support.

Not all professional men elect to be in this club, but the ones who do often pay the price of losing their compassion and empathy for anyone or anything below them. Let's take the man at the top with the money bags. His name is Ronald. He's addicted to money, status, and sexy, "pretty" women who pet his ego and don't talk back. We have the man Ted sitting at his desk reading pornography and drinking alcohol. He also uses cocaine. He has been in charge of so many people in his corporation, all of whom jump at his command, as well as his family and his many sexual partners, that he can't believe that he couldn't control his drinking and drug use. So he's still drinking and saying, "I can control it."

We also have Dr. Pill, who was pressured by his upwardly mobile family from early childhood to become a doctor. As he hands the prescription for tranquilizers over the fence, he flashes on a nearly forgotten memory of a tragedy during his residency. When tired, at the end of a thirty-five hour shift (a typical macho male initiation right), he made a mistake that cost a person's life. He and two others covered up the mistake by changing the records. The fear of being found out and the feelings of remorse have never been spoken. Instead they chew away at him inside. Slowly, over time, he has become addicted to alcohol and drugs, which he also hands out liberally to his patients.

Underneath the surface, these men at the top are often afraid and lonely—afraid of losing their status, afraid they're only loved for their money, and lonely for honest, noncompetitive human bonds. Yet this king-of-the-mountain status is presented in our culture as the ultimate goal.

Below the Exclusive Club

Moving below the fence, we see women playing cards. They are the wives of the men above the chain-link fence. Take the dark-haired woman on the right, Sally. She came from a working-class family. As a child, she felt unloved and rejected and her dream was to live out the image in *Better Homes and Gardens*. She attained her goal of moving up in the system by "marrying up."

To mold herself into the privileged-wife image, she spent countless hours throughout high school and college trying to look pretty, stay thin, wear the right clothes, and be charming. She dropped out of college to support her husband in medical school. To fit the role of the perfect wife, she has been a compulsive dieter, and was at one time bulimic. She turns her head the other way when her husband flirts with nurses, comes home late, breaks commitments, or rages at the children. She is addicted to cigarettes and endless efforts to quit have failed.

She still feels remorse and guilt, because her inability to quit smoking during her second pregnancy was a likely cause of her daughter's being born three months prematurely. Her buried resentments are stacking up inside. She started taking tranquilizers just last year and she is gradually escalating her use of alcohol.

Moving down the left side of the drawing, we come to the woman couple where the one on the right is carrying the basketball. That's Andrea, whom you met in chapter 1, who came to therapy to heal from her twelve-step group. For the last ten years, she's been working to uncover from abuse, bulimia, addiction, and codependency—and to pay the bills.

As a child, her father beat her and made sexually derogatory remarks about women. Her mother leaned on Andrea for support. Although her father is rich, he won't give her any money for college. He doesn't say why, but she suspects it's because of her lesbianism and because her father's second wife is terribly jealous of her. Andrea's twenties have been consumed with surviving an abusive relationship, maintaining abstinence from drugs and alcohol, getting treatment for sex addiction, and, with years of therapy, to help release the pain of childhood and shore up her fragile self-esteem. She is also grappling with the cultural bind of wanting to find a career where she can be "out" as a lesbian, because keeping secrets feels like a way to perpetu- ate her inner shame. And finally, at thirty-one, for the first time since high school she is doing something she loves by being on a community basketball team.

Moving to your right, notice the figures of two Black adult men being admired by a little boy. By the age of eight, this inner-city boy realizes that he is unlikely to have access to the mainstream United States privileges of education and respect, so he is finding his heroes. Who are they? The local drug dealers. Like every child everywhere, he is looking for some way to fit in, to feel important and powerful.

Moving to the lower right corner, we see a Native American man with a broken treaty. He has suffered from alcoholism, compulsive eating, and depression. The federal government is trying to take back the land he is pointing to, but a group of Native Americans have plans to build a treatment center to be run by Native Americans—*their* way, with *their* rituals.

Choose someone in the illustration. Ask yourself how they got to their particular place in the system. Is the homeless man in the bottom left a Vietnam vet with post-traumatic stress syndrome who got hooked on pain killers in a VA hospital? Was he a sexual abuse victim who became drug addicted? Or was he one of the many people with mental disorders who were turned out of the mental hospital where they had lived for many years, and instructed to get his medication at a neighborhood clinic?

Moving to the right, was the young woman engaged in prostitution an incest victim? Did her pimp manipulate her to be addicted to drugs to have control over her? Did she ever know safety in her childhood home?

Going back to the chain fence: Did the white woman trying to climb over it who ignored her children, left a marriage, and worked to the point of exhaustion really think a woman could be accepted in the exclusive club or that money and status would make her happy?

Moving to the middle right, we find Kelly, whom you've met in previous chapters; the mother of a five-year-old who, at forty, is cleaning houses because her drug and alcohol addiction took over her life in early adolescence to mask her deeper sense of being unworthy and unwanted. Since sobering up, she has been stuck on welfare because her earnings don't cover child care. This led to severe depression and only now that her son is in school can she get vocational training and some relief from the welfare system and the demands of child care. She says her biggest problem now is giving up the dream that someone will come and take care of her. In her words, "Caring for myself when no one else did is much harder to overcome than my drug addiction."

Now meet Rhoda, standing at the bottom center of the picture holding the hands of two children. She has gained and lost hundreds of pounds, always gaining back more than she lost. She is a victim of the addictive system's simplistic, outside solutions for insider problems—solutions that have taken the form of diet pills, diet drinks, and a multitude of wonder diets that have slowly damaged her metabolic system. Her food use is related to stress, to sexual abuse, and to loneliness. It is the something sweet in her otherwise bleak life. What she needs is much more than a new wonder diet. She needs good therapy for her childhood abuse, work she likes, affordable child care and medical benefits if she gets off welfare—all things she has little access to, being at the bottom of the hierarchy.

The Drug Pushers Aren't Always on the Streets

Return to the top of our drawing. The men studying the War on Drugs map don't notice one of the biggest sources of drugs we have, namely, the white male doctor representing the patriarchal medical profession. Of course, there are wonderful people in the profession, but the nature of the medical philosophy is typically to focus on isolated pathology. Instead of prevention or a natural healing process or seeing problems part of an ecological system requiring a wholistic form of healing, they often respond to the symptoms, not the source. Thus the medical system frequently promotes removing the symptom while harming the body's ecosystem. They are also imbued with top-of-hierarchy thinking, which locks them into a perspective that says their way is the only way, in spite of the "patients' " (an interesting word) intuition about their own bodies.

Let's talk about Dr. Pill, who is passing the prescription for tranquilizers over the fence to a depressed woman. Limited by his white male socialization, he doesn't realize that she is depressed because her life is depressing and she doesn't have a sense of identity. Adhering to the rule of hierarchy—that is, the people on top know what's best for those below—he has no awareness about other approaches to depression for women—like getting mad, talking back, getting education, having therapy, reading feminist books, or joining women's support groups, to name a few.

Also, given the narrow focus of his medical training, it doesn't occur to him to check for other possible sources of her depression, such as abuse, loneliness, exhaustion, bad diet, or allergies. And even if he did, he might not realize that the five cups of coffee, three bottles of cola, and her sugar-laden diet feed her depression. So she eventually gets hooked on pain pills which, combined with the synergistic effect of alcohol, gives us the Kitty Dukakis or the Elizabeth Taylor story.

Scanning our hierarchy, we might ask who else is addicted to prescription medication. The man in the wheelchair at a nursing home is totally doped up on them. The woman at the computer terminal was prescribed medication to lower stress from eye strain and her time-pressured job. So was the corporate woman who works sixty hours a week at the desk below the chain-link fence. The baseball player is addicted to cocaine, which he started using back when he was given massive doses of painkillers so he didn't have to miss a game when he had an injury. And on it goes—alienation, separateness, and stress blocking so many people from even remotely tapping into their creative source, their joy and potential.

HOW HAS THIS SYSTEM PERPETUATED DRUG ADDICTION?

One social issue that is being used in the United States as a political issue is drug addiction. The way our government is approaching this problem exemplifies the way our leaders purport to help those below them while actually perpetuating their oppression—which, of course, maintains the status quo.

Notice the men in the top part of the illustration looking at a map of Central America, attempting to find "solutions" to the drug problem. Why are they suddenly concerned with drug addiction in this country? Does it come from a sudden, heartfelt concern for people dying from drugs and related violence? Or has the drug problem started to threaten their personal safety or the odds for re-election? It is highly likely that even men at the top who feel some genuine care have at least some ambivalence about drug prevention for "those people down there." After all, so long as women, African Americans, or Native Americans are sick, poor, and hooked on drugs and alcohol, they can't threaten the status quo or stage a very effective revolution. (Remember that the motivating force behind the white men at the top is often fear of losing their control over others.)

Even if some of the white men on top sincerely hope to alleviate the drug problem, they are limited by their white male thinking. Because it doesn't occur to them to ask for the input of those below the fence or include them in the decision-making, the ones on top have very little understanding of the broad range of drug abuse problems for different people.

How does the thinking go?

What's the problem? Drug addiction.

What do you do? Get rid of the drugs.

How do you do it? Have a *war* on drugs; name a drug czar and get out the *guns*.

But who do we aim at? You can't shoot poverty or racism. So . . . well . . . cut off the source of the drugs. Spend millions of dollars blocking drugs from entering the country, invade Panama (and then do a massive cover-up about the civilians killed there), and so on . . .

It's absurd, of course, because the male conquest approach ignores the fact that people use drugs often as a result of hopelessness and despair resulting from poverty, hunger, racism, sexism, and homophobia. The problem is *inside* people's minds and hearts, not in Central or South America. *Outside solutions don't work for inside problems. That's totally addictive thinking.* But the white male illusion of power and authority leads to the delusion that by cutting off the supply you stop the problem. You need to stop the *desire* or *need* to self-obliterate with drugs.

In a fascinating article on the drug war that appeared in the *Village Voice* of January 22, 1990, Daniel Lazare writes:

> After 20 years of troop sweeps, police actions and military rhetoric, the evidence is all around us. The war on drugs has flopped. It's been more than ineffective—it's actually made things worse. It has caused street crime to mushroom and the murder rate to soar. It has intoxicated ghetto kids with visions of gold chains, black Mercedes, and other fruits of an underground economy. Rather than stopping drugs, it has ensured a flow of harder and harder substances onto the street.
>
> "When I first started in the early '80s a big coke seizure was 70 pounds," mused a former federal prosecutor in Miami. In 1981, federal drug agents confiscated 4,263 pounds of cocaine. By late 1989, the haul was approaching 171,000 kilos—40 times

as much—not because the Drug Enforcement Administration has gotten better at its job, but because smugglers have gotten better at theirs.

This story parallels how addicted people operate internally. The addicted part gets increasingly clever at outwitting the part of the person that says, "You shouldn't do that." To try and outsmart an addict is folly. Yet the government persists in this approach because it is all they know. *The use of force to keep addicted people from "using" never works, never has, and never will. Addressing social issues, and getting input from the populations most affected by addiction, is far more likely to help the situation.*

Some questions we need to ask are:

- What population groups use drugs?
- Which drugs do they use and how do they get them?
- What would be a way to create situations where these groups of people don't want to use drugs?
- How do we access information from the people in need and give them power over their lives?

We need to ask the same questions about "codependency" and other addictions, particularly to food, which has led to a terrible epidemic of bulimia and anorexia.

So, why doesn't it occur to even the best-intentioned folks on top to seek inside solutions or gain input from those affected by drug addiction? As mentioned before, it's not in the nature of an authoritarian system for the ones in the dominant role to ask subordinates' input. It would take humility and would risk implying that there is equality among people. Another reason is that it takes time and energy to listen to others, and it is a long, slow process that inevitably involves the human heart. Imagine the people in charge of the war on drugs sitting down and quietly listening to African Americans, Native Americans, gay and lesbian people, women on welfare, homeless people, women in prostitution, and old people in nursing homes talk about their childhood, their drug abuse, and their painful living conditions and frustrations in getting help from the system. This goes against the very core of white male power, which seeks out quick solutions, avoids inner discomfort, and above all does not want to openly acknowledge the inequities they perpetuate in the system.

EVERYONE LOSES IN PATRIARCHY

As a therapist, I have had clients from every level of this hierarchy—all of whom have complaints about the situation. One of the common complaints from every sector is exhaustion and stress. It's interesting that capitalism, which is supposed to give us comforts, has made many people exhausted either caring for what they have, striving to have more, or simply trying to survive.

In workshops, I often hand out this hierarchy illustration and have people meet in small groups to explore the core beliefs and addictions people might have. Then people explore where they fit into the picture. Once, when I asked the group to brainstorm ways this system creates and perpetuates addiction, one woman said, "Is there any way it doesn't?"

PATRIARCHY, HIERARCHY, AND LEVELS OF FAITHING

Patriarchy adamantly discourages people's going beyond the loyalist level of faithing. To explore this for yourself, you might make a list of all the ways people and institutions have taught and encouraged you to conform to the patriarchal viewpoint on sex roles, history, spirituality, education, religion, and race relations. Then make a list of the people or institutions that have encouraged you to think for yourself, to determine your own values even if they fly in the face of traditional thought. Who has encouraged you to take risks, appreciate your strengths, be passionately alive and speak against authority if authority violates your beliefs?

Some questions you might include are: Where are women and minorities taught to explore their socialization and norms? Where are girls and minority children taught to know and appreciate their heritage? Where are white males taught that history is more than a series of wars—of power and conquest and discovery? Where are people taught cooperation instead of competition? Where are people taught to value differences, to embrace inner struggle, and to accept that solutions come as a process of exploration, experimentation, and compromise?

The many individuals—creative teachers, clergy, parents, and social leaders—who do attempt to go beyond the narrow limits of stage three of faithing have to do so on their own, and as most of them will tell you, it is exhausting, because they are bucking a system that thwarts this level of development. A typical comment of social service workers or teachers is, "It's not the work that gets me, it's dealing with the politics of the system."

The same thing happens when women and minorities start treatment programs and explore the needs of their people. They have to struggle for funding, work for low pay, and develop the strength to fend off the negativity of the society which doesn't like such a clear statement that racism and sexism exist. Yet we see over and over again that when committed people communicate self-respect and hope to those they serve in agencies or schools, profound change can occur.

Still, when people decide to move beyond rote loyalty or start openly showing pride in themselves they may encounter not only inner discomfort that comes from shaking up long-held beliefs, but also a system that tries to bring them back into the fold with the use of shame, exclusion, intimidation or outright violence. That is why it is crucial people bond together to support one another in making change.

PATRIARCHY AND HIERARCHY: EFFECTS ON BODY, MIND, AND SPIRIT

We have been talking about our system's effect on groups of people. But that's just one piece of the picture. I will now go inward and explore how patriarchy and hierarchy affect our bodies, our thinking, our emotions, and our access to inner wisdom, which guides us in making self-affirming decisions and living at one with each other. To give us a starting point, I will present my image of a whole, integrated person using the concept of chakras. (Now, don't run away if this sounds weird to you; remember, it's just a word.)

Remember, the more integrated, balanced, and alive we are, the higher our level of faithing and the lower our impulse for addiction. When we talk about chakras, we are talking about the energy body as opposed to the physical body. The body emanates vibrations that we often describe using the term *vibes*—"She has good (or bad) vibes." We also use natural elements when describing people's energy. For example, when someone emanates a sense of inner power or brilliance we say they have a lot of fire or spark—the third chakra. People who are grounded and straightforward are sometimes called "earthy." When we say "That person has guts," we are talking about their energy that emanates from the second and third chakras. When we are around a person with an open heart chakra we often say they are "warm." Someone with a sense of humor seems "light." If someone seems ungrounded and spaced out, we might use the term "air-head."

We are constantly transmitting and receiving energy from people whenever we are around them. We radiate fear, joy, peacefulness, anger, whether we intend to or not. In a literal sense, we exchange energy with people around us as we all inhale and exhale the air in the room. Most of us have had the experience of being tired and then being with someone or a group of people who are vital and caring and becoming energized. We picked up some of their energy, which sparks our own. On the other hand, in the presence of a person who has heavy or "dead" energy we sometimes start feeling depleted, possibly because they are siphoning off our energy or we are breathing in their dense or negative energy. In *Women, Sex, and Addiction*, I have an entire section on tuning in to energy and using it to make your life lighter.

UNDERSTANDING THE CHAKRA SYSTEM

Chakra is a Sanskrit word meaning *wheel* or *disk*. In her excellent book *Wheels of Life*, Anodea Judith defines chakra as "a *spinning vortex of energy* created within ourselves by the interpenetration of consciousness and the physical body. Through this combination, chakras become *centers of activity for the reception, assimilation, and transmission of life energies.*"

The different chakras are concerned with different emotional and physical functions. There are seven chakras moving up the body from the base of the spine. They all play an important role in our development toward being a fully integrated human being. They are:

1. Security (base of spine)
2. Passion and sensation (genitals, lower abdomen, digestive system)
3. Power/will (solar plexus)
4. Love (heart)
5. Communication (throat)
6. Perception/knowing (third-eye area)
7. Wisdom/connectedness (crown of the head)

My image of a whole, functioning person is someone with all chakras functioning in an integrated way. For example, if your second chakra is all charged up and you are very sexually attracted to someone, instead of rushing off to follow the desire of this one chakra, you check in with your heart chakra to see if it would be loving, and your mind chakra to see if it would be wise. I think of the chakras as a committee,

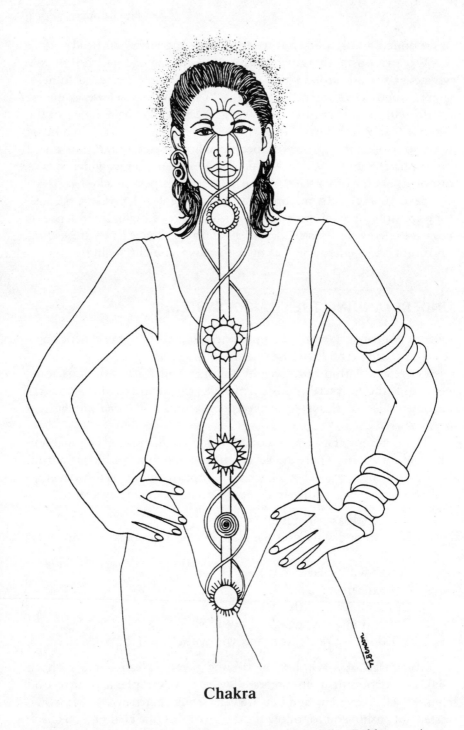

Chakra

Taken from *Wheels of Life*, by Anodea Judith (Llewellyn Publications), © 1987.

and life goes best when you don't act on one without consulting the rest. It doesn't mean a person has to be all clear and perfectly function-ing, but it does mean a person knows when an energy center is shut down, off center, and out of touch. They can go inside and say, "Hmmm; I wonder what that's about. I'm feeling out of touch with my gut." They can take steps to open up chakras that may be blocked.

When we are out of touch or have not opened certain chakras, we tend to reach for other people who have access to those energy centers, thinking we can get from them the energy center we haven't developed in ourselves. The following section draws from Judith's book, personal conversations with her, as well as my own perspective.

Take a look at the chakra system. Which ones are men encouraged to develop in the culture? Which ones are women encouraged to de-velop? Essentially, men are encouraged to develop 1, 3, 5, and the rational part of 7—security, power, communication, and the rational mind. Women are allowed to develop 2, 4, 6, and the intuitive half of 7—emotion/passion, heart, perception, and intuition. In other words, our institutions train men and women to develop only half of their potential.

Of course there are personal differences depending on our families, but, overall, our institutions have a strong effect on which parts of our energy systems we develop. This is what creates enmeshed, dependent relationships, particularly with heterosexual couples. Each person brings half the chakra energy and when merged the couple becomes one person. The thought of separating then feels like losing half your life. It is not surprising that lesbian women, who often develop both their power and love, often report higher levels of satisfaction in rela-tionships than heterosexuals, according to Shere Hite in *Women and Love*. There is more potential for an integrated self, that is, an inte-grated relationship.

Recently when I asked at a workshop which energy centers are well developed in an extremely codependent woman, the room went still. "None," one woman whispered. Eventually someone suggested that the heart and throat might be doing a lot but without wisdom or the power to say no or give wisely, she would become depleted.

The answer to the question, "Which chakras does our political system use when making decisions?" was security for themselves, power, and the rational mind. The heart was most notably missing.

As you read through the descriptions of the seven energy centers and the verb associated with each one, you might want to tune in to your body. In any chakra, do you feel dense, light, afraid, shut down, flowing? Just allow yourself to feel without judgment. You could also ask yourself how you were helped to develop or repress the different energy centers.

1. The Root Chakra/Security

VERB: I have
ELEMENT: Earth

This chakra is found below the base of the spine at the central, lowest part of the torso. It is the foundation for the whole energy system. According to Judith, "Its function is to respond to any issues concerned with survival: eating, sleeping, exercising, recovering from illness, making a living, or simply feeling safe and secure. If our survival needs are properly taken care of, then we can safely focus on other levels such as learning, creativity, or relationships. If there is some damage to the chakra, then we find ourselves repeatedly coping with threats to our survival, which keeps us from accomplishing other things."

Part of developing this chakra is to feel grounded to the earth. We let our energy flow down through our legs, sinking into the earth. As Judith says, "Grounding involves opening the lower chakras, merging with gravity and feeling ourselves as an integrated flow of energy. Without grounding we are unstable, we lose our center, fly off the handle . . . we lose the ability to contain, to have or to hold. When we lose our ground, our attention wanders from the present moment, and we appear to be 'not all here.'" Grounding is what is missing in addictive relationships. When people believe they are unable to meet their own security needs, or feels unstable, they attach to someone else.

Because we are taught that bodily functions are dirty, people often hold their energy very tightly in this area. You can check this out for yourself by putting your focus on your first chakra, breathe deeply and think, Let go. Another way to tune into the grounding aspects of this chakra (especially for women) is to focus your consciousness on the security chakra as you are walking with very comfortable shoes, rocking from heel to toe, thinking of your energy going down your legs into the ground. Then do the same with other types of shoes. Feel the difference in the energy flow? When we feel more grounded and secure we are more able to find ways to meet our security needs. When we make bargains for our security, particularly through dependent relationships, we disable our ability to ground, which affects all the other chakras.

2. The Seat of Life

VERB: I feel
ELEMENT: Water

The second chakra is in the lower abdomen. It is a center of motion for the body. It is often called the "seat of life." As Judith says, "Classically, this chakra is the center of sexuality, emotions, sensation, pleasure, movement, and nurturance. Its element is water and its Sanskrit name, Svadisthana, means sweetness, corresponding to the sweetening of desire, pleasure, and sexuality."

When this chakra is open and people are comfortable with touch, sexual feelings, nurturance and emotion, the energy flows upward helping open the other chakras. Unfortunately, patriarchal Christianity has shamed women about this chakra by asserting that women's sexuality is associated with evil or duty. Patriarchy has negatively affected men by teaching them that sexuality is connected to power and conquest, and thus separate from love.

Patriarchal Christianity also conveys the fear that if you express your feelings with passion or let yourself openly enjoy pleasure you'll get lost in it. Actually people who get lost in pleasure through food or sex are usually extremely conflicted about these things, often associating them with shame, loss of control, or power. It is far more likely that *unambivalent* pleasure, eating, sexuality, and open expression of feelings helps people feel alive, filled up, and enables us to direct our attention to other aspects of our lives.

The repression of the sexual energy that is a fundamental part of the second chakra is also associated with violence. By repression I mean that sex is considered shameful, feared, or done in a dissociated or detached way (you don't feel love for the person you are with). In a cultural study by James Prescott relating sexual taboos to the incidence of violence, the more stringent the taboos on sex, the higher the violence rate. When people associate pleasure, nurturance, and positive feelings with sexuality, they are less likely to become violent.

Related to twelve-step programs, the typical approach to addiction is often fear of this chakra. If your desire, eating, or passions are getting out of control, we are taught to limit them, cut them off, or control them. From the approach of integrating all the chakras, rather than fear your addictions, you explore them—even though you may use abstinence, you still ask what desires are longing for expression. Is the food a substitute for love, or the sex a desire for power or nurture? You also learn that it is safe to feel passion, to derive pleasure from food or sex. In fact, when one partakes consciously, without shame or fear, one often starts feeling filled up and one comes to realize one is not a bottomless pit with endless needs.

3. The Power Chakra

VERB: I can
ELEMENT: Fire

This energy center is the seat of the will. When it is strong and functioning well, we experience a sense of "I can" that we need in order to face adversity, make changes, and take care of ourselves. When the will is disabled or not developed, we are vulnerable to people who manipulate our will, using it for their own selfish purposes. Because we all need a sense of personal power to feel whole, when we are deprived of it, we tend to attach to people who have power. This creates dependent relationships and results in victimization.

Patriarchy/hierarchy systematically disables the wills of all but the privileged few in an attempt to maintain power over others. Women are taught to repress this chakra so basic to taking charge of their lives. "Don't be too strong, bright, angry, energetic, observant, or honest because you might offend someone, get battered, or scare away a man." Thus it is crucial that women and minorities examine their feelings and beliefs about power, and learn to ignite this chakra so they can take action.

People defined as minorities or those from disadvantaged families are also discouraged from using their power in positive, self-affirming ways. Sanctions against open expression of anger are a huge block to the functioning of the power chakra. It is important to remember that when people are violated, they feel angry. When they are told not to feel angry, the energy has no place to go.

When the power chakra is energized and has no outlet, it becomes like an electrical current, undirected and chaotic, pulsing through the body and creating a sense of pressure. People often attempt to relieve this pressure with addictive or compulsive behavior. Instead of expressing rage, you eat, drink, or beat someone up. To feel power and repress it creates tremendous inner conflict, and the energy often turns on itself like a negative force in the body.

When the power chakra is aligned with our goals, we are able to say, "I am going to do this task today," and then do it. When the will is weak, we experience ourselves wanting to do something but we can't seem to get started and end up feeling exhausted, which makes it more difficult to get started. I have experienced this lack of energy when I get stalled and put off my writing. The amazing thing is that once I sit down and get going, my energy immediately picks up. That's because my will becomes energized and in harmony with my purpose.

Addiction is often an attempt to activate an undeveloped will and feel powerful. I don't feel loved, but I can seduce someone, get drugs, or eat a box of cookies. Addiction typically creates an imbalance in this chakra. Instead of using our will for positive acts it is used as the servant of the addiction. Thus power is associated with negative energy. On the positive side, one can learn to redirect energy for positive purposes. Rechanneling energy is sometimes easier than igniting the power in someone who has repressed theirs for a lifetime.

According to Judith, "On the physical plane, the third chakra rules metabolism, the process whereby we turn food (matter) into energy and action. Digestion troubles, stomach troubles, hypoglycemia, diabetes, ulcers, or addictions to stimulants such as caffeine are all related to malfunctioning of the third chakra."

The sin-and-redemption theme of Christianity that is carried over into the twelve steps focuses on deflating and humbling the ego and does little to activate the will and internal sense of power. That's why I am proposing an empowerment model in this book. Women typically feel far more comfortable bonding through pain, sadness, and victimization than through success and accomplishment.

To energize the will—the power chakra—it is important that women bond through power and cheer for each other. Because many women are afraid of power—they're afraid if they let loose they will explode with rage, or they have seen power used to over-power and wound people—they put down women who are powerful. It is important to understand that power can be used for positive acts. Power does not corrupt people if it is aligned with their hearts and their wisdom.

4. The Heart Chakra

VERB: I love
ELEMENT: Air

The attributes of the fourth chakra are love, balance, relationships, and compassion. The element is air—formless, invisible and necessary, just like love. Judith writes, "The fourth chakra, located over the heart, is the balance point between the 'lower' physical chakras and the upper centers which relate to our mental world. The operating force in this chakra is *equilibrium*."

When people have power but use it without love we have exploitation and abuse of others. This predominates in our patriarchal institutions, where power is primarily about over-powering others. When we talk about a mass consciousness change on the planet, we are talking about opening the heart chakra so that people cannot coldly detach from the suffering of others, whether seen or unseen.

According to Judith, "In entering the fourth chakra, there is a transcendence of ego that allows us to lose our self-defined boundaries and merge with the world around us. As we escape the constriction of the lower chakras, we break through into a sense of the infinite. The experience of love as an infinite source is the joyous opening and abundance of the heart chakra."

What Judith describes here echoes what happens as people move to levels four and five of faithing. Their reference group expands greatly and they open themselves. Judith talks about people transcending the ego and merging with the world around us, whereas I see it as an ego merging with love and with the world around us.

The twelve steps, with their focus on faults and shortcomings and surrender, keep people's energy directed inward, which does not lead to a merger with the world around us. While people gain support in meetings and have loving experiences and are encouraged to help other addicted people, the basic construct of the program does not provide a path toward a transcendent kind of love embracing all people.

5. The Throat Chakra

VERB: I speak
ELEMENT: Sound

The attributes of the throat chakra are sound, vibration, communication, and creativity. This chakra is located in the center of the neck and shoulders. Communication is the creative art of transmitting and receiving information. Good communication that is honest, simple, and direct incorporates the integration of all the other chakras.

A symptom of lack of integration, particularly with the security chakra, is compulsive talking and chattering, which seem more to fill up space than to actually communicate with another person. We have the expression of someone talking "off the wall." What we are referring to is a person who is ungrounded, the function of the first chakra. Sometimes, if the person lacks integration with the power chakra, the voice is dissonant, flat, shallow, lacking vitality. In these cases, it is extremely hard to follow the meaning of what someone is saying because it feels like "just words."

When one is grounded and the other chakras are open, the voice resonates with a vibrant tone that comes from within the person.

6. Perception and Knowing

VERB: I see
ELEMENT: Light

This chakra is located at the level of the forehead, just above the eyes. Judith writes, "the place where we store our memories, perceive our dreams, and imagine our future." In my empowerment steps, I talk about people learning to see what they see, know what they know, and believe themselves. I think of this as a place where we perceive and "see" truth through dreams and through a combination of all of our senses associated with the other chakras. For example, if our security chakra is not developed, we often don't let ourselves see what we see because we are too afraid.

Related to our levels of faithing, from this chakra we see through the teachings and programming we have been handed, to a deeper reality and a sense of knowing that is internal and universal. Thus, development of this chakra is associated with the fourth, fifth, and sixth levels of faithing—a universal, expansive, integrated faith.

Judith makes a connection between this chakra and our culture. "As each chakra corresponds to a gland, chakra six is related to the pineal gland . . . located in the geometric center of the head at approximately eye level. . . . The pineal gland, often called the 'seat of the soul' by René Descartes and others . . . reaches the height of its development at the age of seven." Judith poses the question, "Is the immaturity of our culture at this sixth chakra level relevant to the atrophy of the pineal gland?" This is congruent with viewing patriarchy and capitalism as an addictive system. In other words, have we chosen denial over seeing "what is." We program children at an early age to stop seeing what they see and knowing what they know in order to squeeze them into the patriarchal mold.

7. The Crown

VERB: I know
ELEMENT: Thought

The attributes are information, understanding, awareness, consciousness, seeing patterns, and ability to meditate. This is the chakra that takes us beyond time and space to knowledge, wisdom, and interconnectedness with all we are, and with other people.

It mirrors our sixth level of faithing—an integrated universalizing faith. Judith writes, "It is through the crown chakra that we reach into the infinite body of 'information' and run it through our own chakras to bring it to recognition and manifestation. This is the process of knowing—the active function of the seventh chakra.''

FINDING A BALANCE

Becoming a whole, integrated person through opening up and integrating all the chakras parallels the concept of moving through the levels of faithing toward wholeness. It's like approaching the same idea from two different perspectives. The progression of personal evolution associated with levels of faithing described in chapter 2—developing an internal set of values, increased compassion and connectedness to others—happens on both paths. For example, the fourth level of faithing, which includes questioning the status quo, helps open up the power (solar plexus) and communication (throat) chakras. Compassion for all people, which evolves in the fourth and fifth levels of faithing, opens the second and fourth chakras—feelings and love.

We see the depth of patriarchy's damage to us as individuals when we think about the ways our social system discourages development of our energy centers/chakras. Addiction is often the result of the second and third chakras operating in isolation, leading to passion, desire, hunger, feelings, and power going out of control. If the second and third chakras are balanced by the other chakras—love, security, and wisdom—fulfilling our hungers and feeling our emotions will bring sweetness to us and will not lead to addiction.

Dependency includes a lack of development at the security center, our root chakra that helps us feel grounded. If we lack a sense of security we tend to seek material possessions, partners who take care of us, follow external rules, and engage in compulsive behavior. Paradoxically, the more we try to overcome insecurity with possessions and other people, the more insecure we feel.

The more we inhibit our energy and block development of human potential, the more we have despair, violence, and addiction. Or, said more positively, the more we encourage and free people to open up all their energy centers, celebrate the wonderful body they have been given, and feel awe and wonder for life, the less violence and addiction we will have.

This takes us to the concept of life-loving/creative spirituality, which will be incorporated into the model/process for healing from addiction

I propose in chapter 14. The concept is similar to feminine, creation-centered, or Goddess spirituality, which I will talk about in the last chapter.

Whereas the traditional Christian sin-and-redemption model sees us as born sinful and in need of salvation—baptism, confession, deflation of self—a life-loving spirituality sees us as born holy. Thus life is not a sin to be conquered and controlled, but a blessing to be received. Instead of fearing that our passions and desires will go out of control, we consider them part of the whole, to be enjoyed in balance with responsibility and love. Thus life-loving spirituality takes us beyond fear, control, and duality toward harmony and integration.

This takes us beyond "recovery narcissism," where people become obsessed with recovery perfection, ridding themselves of character defects and shortcomings, and constantly analyzing their behavior. They lose perspective of the external world, the naturalness of imperfection and the wonder and mystery of life. What is needed is a balance between inner understanding and outer connectedness.

Understanding life-loving/creative spirituality can lead us to perceive addiction in a new way—not as a sin, a defect, or something to fear, but rather as a painful sign of imbalance in individuals that reflects a tremendous imbalance in our social system. We have traditionally approached addiction with the patriarchal conquest mentality—it's bad and painful, so get rid of it. This creates duality and violence and keeps the focus on individuals.

Thus we need to go beyond the question of how we control addiction and ask, What is missing in our lives? Where is the sweetness and connectedness that can fill our spirits? What perpetuates the violence, greed, abuse, and prejudice that weaken our links to each other? What in our social system blocks so many people from feeling security and joy in their lives?

In a life-loving spirituality, sin is seen as separateness, separateness from compassion for oneself and others as well as nature. The intricate balance of our personal energy system is the microcosm of the balance of our planetary ecosystem. As we develop consciousness for one, we will develop consciousness for the other, because ultimately we are part of an integrated whole. Just as people need to integrate feelings, passions, intelligence, wisdom, and power, we need to live integrated with the earth—not as conquerers or stewards of the earth, but rather as intrinsically interwoven with it.

A reverence for life is the antidote to addiction. This will come about with a mass consciousness change that takes us away from hierarchy to a circle image where we feel ourselves connected to one another and to all life. In chapter 16 I will talk about what it means to return to the circle.

PART II

The Many Aspects of Addiction

4

Defining Addiction:
Patterns of Chemical and Psychological Addictions

In Part I, I talked about the role of patriarchy and hierarchy in fostering addictions and the need to create models for uncovering and discovering that help people grow toward integration and wholeness. Now I will turn to the personal experience of addiction, exploring how it operates at the psychological, physiological, and spiritual levels.

Just as hierarchy and patriarchy lead toward dis-integration and splitting, so does addiction, which is experienced individually as an inner duality—a split where a person lives with two parts pulling at each other. One part is the child survivor who started using substances or behaviors as a way to find pleasure or as a flight from pain, abuse, or stress. The other part is the new survivor/wise self who has access to the rational mind and says, Hey, this stuff is messing up my life and I'd better stop. The new survivor/wise self is like our rational, wise, adult self, who can reflect on a situation and see what's going on and make self-caring decisions on our behalf.

The conflict between the two parts often escalates, resulting in a binge-and-starve, teeter-totter pattern leading to inner devastation, broken promises, harmful consequences, and a diminished capacity to be sustained from the natural pleasures in life.

The old-survivor-versus-new-survivor/wise self conflict gets set in place because the brain gets misprogrammed in the following way: If a child is hurt, lonely, sexually abused, neglected, or unhappy, the survival self seeks ways to feel comforted. Through trial and error, using whatever is available, the child finds the means that works best. It could be food, sugar, caffeine, masturbation, fantasies of being rescued, hero fantasies, violent sexual fantasies, and so on. Over time the emotional connection between the wish to feel good and the substance or behavior is reinforced, resulting in a powerful pairing in the brain or unconscious mind. It creates what feels like an automatic reflex: Need comfort? Eat. Feeling pain? Take drugs. Feeling one-down? Have a conquest fantasy. Feel like a nobody? Try winning at bingo.

The other way a paired response gets set in place is through associations made with abuse. For example, if a child was given money as a bribe to be sexual, then money and sex get paired. If a child is beaten with a belt on her bare behind while the father has sexual feelings, the child too may have sexual feelings. This can result in a pairing between belts and sexual arousal, violence and sexual arousal, and partners who are sexually violent. This is why pornography is so often linked with sexual abuse; it sets off a paired response creating tension and sexual arousal, and then the person using pornography seeks an outlet.

Sometimes this learned pairing starts in a serendipitous way and not as a result of direct abuse or pain. A person is given a drug that gives them a strong pleasure sensation, and the brain records this, leaving the person to want more of the same.

The stimulation that creates a paired response can also happen at a cultural level. In the United States, children from an early age are given sexual stimulation through commercials, ads, songs, rock videos, magazines, cartoons, MTV, and on and on, all of which have paired sex with both power and popularity, male dominance and female victimization. It is not surprising that the teenage incidence of sexual relationships, pregnancy, and abuse toward smaller children has mushroomed in our country. You can't expect to program young people to feel that pleasure and power is associated with sexual arousal and conquest and not expect them to act on it. Paired survival responses are extremely strong and when reinforced with repetition can become addictive or compulsive, particularly if there has been abuse or neglect one wishes to bury.

In adulthood when situations create feelings of loneliness, shame, or rejection, the old survivor reflex reaches for a substance or behavior that brings relief. Afterwards, the person, realizing it was a harmful thing to do, asks, What happened to me? That's the cunning, baffling nature of addiction. After the euphoria of the addictive substance or behavior wears off, the new survivor/wise self sees the harmful consequences and often proclaims convincingly, "I'll never do that again. This time I really mean it." And that part does mean it, but often it's no match for the deeply entrenched old survivor. This explains why a person can wake up in the morning with the rational mind saying, I'm not going to overeat today, and at 10 AM is gobbling down donuts and chocolate eclairs, and why a person who was sexually abused can say, I'm not going to pick up any more strangers to sleep with, it's dangerous, but that night have the survival belief that loneliness can be filled up by sex result in a trip to the singles bar to pick up a partner.

With repetition, the paired responses that were often started in early childhood get locked into place and become extremely powerful. That's why addictions are so hard to break. You have to give up what once felt like survival and retrain the brain to believe survival comes from new behavior that often feels uncomfortable or boring. It's like shifting from hot fudge sundaes to lentil soup and brown rice for pleasure. It takes a while to retrain the pleasure messages sent to the brain.

INDIVIDUAL VARIATIONS

The interactive physiological, social, psychological, and genetic components of addiction vary from individual to individual. In order to make progress in guiding the treatment of addiction we need some clear definitions and distinctions between different addictions and their root causes. In other words, to find the best cure, we must make an accurate diagnosis.

Physical and Psychological Addictions

1. Physical Addiction

A physical addiction is when the body makes a physical adaptation to cope with a substance it was not created to handle. This can be alcohol, medications, caffeine, sugar, nicotine, heroin, drugs, cocaine, and more. Once the body has adapted to the substance, it goes into physical withdrawal when the substance is not available.

With physical dependencies, the intensity of withdrawal typically increases as the body becomes more dependent on the substance to feel normal or to function. In other words, a person wants more and more of the substance—or something else that produces the same effect—just to feel normal, or, eventually, to function at all. The one drink to relax after work escalates into three or four; a person needs three sleeping pills to sleep four hours, and the food binge increases from two thousand calories to four thousand calories to get the same sense of relief. Ultimately, the withdrawal symptoms exceed the body's physical tolerance for the substance, which means the addicted person lives in a constant state of withdrawal.

Within the realm of physical addiction there are three predisposing factors determining whether a person will become addicted to a substance:

—the availability of the substance,

—the addictive qualities of the substance, and

—the person's individual physical constitution or predisposition.

AVAILABILITY.   In terms of availability, repeated exposure to a drug or substance increases the chances of using that substance. For example, if people in your social circle do not drink or serve alcohol, you will probably drink less than if alcohol is served at social gatherings and appears to be the norm—given that you are not alcoholic. Most of us have had the experience of saying no to food because we were full, but then as the chocolate goodies are offered to us for the third time, our sensory response system takes over, our resolve dissolves and there we are, munching away again on food we don't really want.

And while people see the Prohibition era as folly, in reality, people drank less. In *Addiction, Who Is in Control?* P. Joseph Frawley, M.D., cites a study of medical records at a Los Angeles County hospital where the percent of liver cirrhosis dropped to almost nothing during Prohibition and rose dramatically afterward. I don't advocate a return to Prohibition, but we need to recognize that exposing children and young people repeatedly to alcohol and alcohol ads that equate alcohol with being sexy, glamorous, cool, and watching sports may make it harder for the people with alcoholic chemistry to abstain because they keep getting presented with a trigger to their unconscious pleasure center.

Availability is also relevant to psychological addictions. For example, the sexual stimulation from listening to pornographic messages on the phone was cited by a teenager as the reason he sexually abused a neighbor child. Without the phone messages, it is doubtful he ever would have gotten the idea.

ADDICTIVE PROPERTIES OF THE SUBSTANCE.   We can look at the addictive properties of various substances on a continuum. Crack and cocaine, for example, are highly addictive, usually creating a physical
dependency in a short time for almost anyone. Heroin, nicotine, sleeping pills, and tranquilizers create an escalating dependency that may
happen in weeks, months, or years. Marijuana and caffeine create
physical dependency, and may take a long time to feel debilitating for
some but be extremely addictive in a short time for others.

The level of physical dependency can be measured in part by the
duration and intensity of physical withdrawal symptoms and the difficulty a person has in quitting. Withdrawal can include headaches,
heart palpitations, sweating, nervousness, inability to concentrate,
cravings for other substances, fatigue, irritability, and an overall sense
of feeling lousy.

PHYSICAL PREDISPOSITION.   A person's physical constitution is the
third predetermining factor in developing a substance dependency. A
person's physiological makeup leads to preferring particular substances because they bring an especially pleasurable high—in the beginning. This is where the term "drug of choice" fits in. For some people,
the best high is with alcohol; others gravitate toward marijuana, and
still others crave sugar, heroin, nicotine, or caffeine. The tolerance level
of different people for different substances varies tremendously, with
some people being able to use ten times the amount someone else can.

Similarly, people have different experiences in quitting addictive
substances. I had a client who withdrew comfortably from antidepressants in three weeks after ten years of use. Someone else took a year.
I know a person who quit a twenty-year, two-pack-a-day cigarette habit
with one hypnosis session, while another friend went through program
after program, trying desparately to quit, and only after being hospitalized with emphysema did she stop. I had a fairly easy time quitting
cigarettes, but going off caffeine was a nightmare with terrible withdrawal symptoms.

Alcohol differs to the extent that approximately 10 percent of the
population has a genetic predisposition to become addicted no matter
how hard they try to control it, while others, even if they abuse alcohol, are very unlikely to get into a progressive physical alcohol dependency unless they combine it with other addictive substances. I will go
into different types of alcoholism as well as the progression of alcohol
dependency in chapter 5, "The Many Faces of Alcoholism."

2. Psychological/Process Addictions

Psychological or process addictions include relationships, sex, gambling, shopping, spending, workaholism, and other behavior that is not directly related to chemical use. "Codependency" also falls under this category. I prefer to call these psychological rather than process addictions because the belief systems underlying these addictions are rooted in the brain and psychological makeup of a person. For example, people who get into "fatal attraction"-type relationships usually lacked sufficient bonding as an infant and their desperate clinging to a lover is an unconscious re-enactment of a tiny child's craving a loving parent. With psychological addictions, people are typically trying to fill empty spaces, hide from pain, or find solace through behavioral activities rather than substances.

IS THERE SUCH A THING AS A "TRUE" ADDICTION?

There is considerable debate between people who believe substance abuse—that of drugs and alcohol—is the only "true" addiction, and that so-called process or psychological addictions are not "true" addictions. It has been argued that classifying sex, food, relationships, and gambling as addictions rather than as psychological compulsions trivializes the seriousness of drug and alcohol addiction. This kind of thinking is symptomatic of our hierarchical approach to understanding the world. It shows a lack of understanding of the intricate interwoven nature of the body and the mind.

For years this kind of thinking has resulted in rehabilitation programs for substance abuse treating a person's addiction to the substance without relating to the whole person, whose history may include incest, violence and neglect, and multiple addictions. Thus many people leave treatment and either resort to other addictions or eventually relapse because the underlying pain is so great. I have interviewed people who went through treatment for substance abuse up to fourteen times because the core problems of abuse, dependency, and neglect were not addressed.

My stance is that both substances and psychologically motivated behavior can become addictions because they follow the same progression of escalation and harmful consequences that can lead to personal destruction and death. Relationship and sexual addictions are sometimes associated with homicide, suicide, rape, incest, and violence. Food addictions lead to early death in the form of self-starvation, bulimia, or a myriad of associated diseases. One woman I worked with desperately wanted to quit her sexual acting out, but the unconscious message that she didn't deserve to live led her to act out sexually, risking AIDS, venereal disease, and the loss of her partner. And, as discussed earlier, both psychological and physical addictions are related to an emotional survival response system set up in the brain and the unconscious mind.

I don't believe we can quantify human suffering, and even if we could, the point is to address and help alleviate all human suffering. The question I prefer to ask is, *"What is the best mode of treatment for each individual, given their addiction, dependency, or compulsive patterns?"* The second question is, "What is the learned survival response that triggers the addictive behavior?" This gets us to the source.

I also believe we should honor the individual decisions people make about their own behavior. In other words, if someone says, "I define myself as sexually addicted," we should listen to them and not immediately discount what they are saying. People know when something is driving them to self-destruct. An important step to empowerment for people is to help them define their own experience by giving them ample information on the subject, so they make an informed "diagnosis."

Physical and Psychological Addictions Combined

It is difficult to make separations between physical and psychological addictions because we operate as an integrated whole—body, mind, and spirit. An addiction may be motivated by a physical predisposition or by an unconscious belief that is a result of childhood abuse or cultural socialization.

Food brings forth an exquisite combination of emotional and physical responses in the body. The learned paired responses may go back to infancy and result in all sorts of emotional experiences—pleasure, pain, pleasing others, reward and punishment. And remember that the emotional experience is often stronger than the rational mind. My mother was obsessed with food and food preparation. You pleased her by eating what she cooked. To this day, I feel guilty saying no to someone offering me food they prepared, because I got stuck with the learned response that I would hurt my mother if I didn't eat what she cooked. The difference is that now I simply know it's a learned response going off in my brain and that I get to take care of myself.

Food may start as a psychological addiction and become a physical addiction, the two operating simultaneously with one reinforcing the other. A person starts out by consuming food because they were emotionally abandoned; then, as a result of bingeing and starving, they develop food allergies and physical addictions, which create stronger desires for certain substances, which result in greater feelings of despair, which in turn lead to more compulsive eating and other desperate behavior. So is it a psychological or physical addiction? I believe it has aspects of both.

When we have a combination like this, do we address the dependency on food or do we focus on grieving the loss of a caring parent? Once again, instead of an either-or solution, we need a wholistic approach. The body needs to be balanced with healthy food, and the loss of a mother needs to be grieved.

In some cases, people have intense food cravings that result from physical states in the body and are not psychologically rooted. Many women are besieged with food and sugar cravings a few days before their periods, which has to do with brain physiology—a fact ignored by medical professionals for years. Compulsive eating can also be triggered by a systemic yeast condition called *Candida albicans* that creates outrageous cravings for sugar and carbohydrates. I know many people who started having tremendous food cravings and were told it was emotional, or to see a therapist, or go to Overeaters Anonymous, when the source of the problem was a physical imbalance. We are so indoctrinated at present to see compulsive behavior as psychological that we miss the boat with many people who need physical help.

When substance abuse treatment programs take the rigid stance that substance abuse is the only true addiction they often overlook other addictions or psychological concerns and fail to guide people toward appropriate resources for help. On the other hand, when psychologists ignore physiological or substance abuse problems and label everything as emotionally based, they also miss half the picture. That's why it is crucial that we take a wholistic approach to defining addiction and be open to the notion of multiple addictions and addiction as symptomatic of deeper problems.

The important thing to remember is that the brain is involved in all addictions. Learned responses that started as survival skills operate unseen in the body or psyche as driving forces that feel out of control, leading a person toward addictive behavior.

In my experience working with people healing from addiction, breaking a paired learned response (sex equals love, food equals nurture) closely parallels people facing withdrawal from a physical substance. In fact, the learned response can be far more difficult to break because it is so deeply embedded in the unconscious and is associated with powerful emotions often stemming from abuse and early childhood experiences.

IS THERE AN ADDICTIVE PERSONALITY?

It has become common to speak of an addictive personality. Some people who work with alcoholism say there is no such thing. A distinction needs to be made between an *addictive* personality, which does exist, and an *alcoholic* personality, for which there is no substantial evidence.

If we accept the preponderance of research that suggests that alcoholism involves a physical predisposition, then alcoholism could not be about one's personality. We don't say a person has a diabetic personality. We say a person has the disease of diabetes and make no other assumptions about their personality.

In *The Natural History of Alcoholism: Causes, Patterns, and Paths to Recovery*, George Vaillant writes, "Most future alcoholics do not appear different from future asymptomatic drinkers in terms of premorbid psychological stability. However, not until several prospective studies were available could such a hypothesis be seriously entertained. It was difficult to conceive that the 'alcoholic personality' might be secondary to the disorder, alcoholism. . . . Subjects with an alcoholic parent but with an otherwise stable family were five times as likely to develop alcoholism as were subjects from clearly multiproblem families without an alcoholic parent."

The case is strong and supported by numerous studies, but it leaves us with a lot of unanswered questions relating to social issues, such as: Why are such a disproportionate number of lesbian and gay people diagnosed as alcoholic? Were these people actually abusing alcohol and mistakenly diagnosed alcoholic? Likewise, why do we find that upwards of 70 percent of incest survivors are also chemically dependent? Is there more incest in families where one or both parents have a genetic predisposition toward alcoholism? Were many incest survivors misdiagnosed as chemically dependent because counselors based their evaluation on psychological reasons for drinking and did not accurately evaluate the physical dependency? Or had the synergistic effects of using alcohol with other mind-altering substances resulted in an addiction to alcohol? The answers are not simple and there needs to be more research.

When most people talk about an "addictive personality," they are referring to a person who attempts to fill an inner emptiness or assuage inner pain with substances, relationships, sex, things, and other compulsive behavior. It's as if the natural longing for human ties, purpose, and self-expression were blocked and rechanneled into ties with substances and compulsive behavior. If the person gives up one addiction or dependency without healing the wounds, they will switch to another.

This was very evident in my study for *Women, Sex, and Addiction,* where a high percentage of women with sexual addiction and sexual codependency problems had struggled with numerous compulsions and addictions that at one time or another had been active. People would give up addictive sex and eat compulsively; they would starve themselves and then shop addictively. Anything would do to fill up the emptiness and displace feelings of pain and unhappiness.

ADDICTIVE VERSUS ADDICTED

In terms of finding accurate definitions that lead us toward workable solutions for addiction, it is important to distinguish between *addictive* and *addicted.* Addictive is when we substitute a substance or behavior for the genuine underlying need, but it does not become an escalating pattern. If we are angry and have sex to get rid of the anger, if we feel sad and eat a candy bar for comfort instead of crying, we are using sex and candy addictively. Some people can lead very addictive lives without any one substance or behavior becoming a full-fledged addiction.

Some people develop what I call a generalized addiction. They chronically medicate themselves throughout the day with addictive use of food, work, caffeine, nicotine, fantasies, sex, whatever. No single addictive behavior takes on a life of its own and becomes a full-fledged addiction but life is hazy and off center most of the time. The person with a generalized addiction is always struggling, not quite happy, often with a chronic mild depression and has difficulty staying present with people or being comfortable with feelings.

Habits, Compulsions, and Addiction

I have heard numerous arguments in the addiction field about compulsion versus addiction, particularly in regard to sex and food. In my workshops, in a section I call "Lighten Up," I talk about a phrase I learned at the Ken Keyes College: "It matters but it's not serious." I would like to apply this notion to the compulsion versus addiction controversy.

It is nice to be precise and have definitions that are clear, but in the cosmic picture, it is simply not a big deal whether we call it a compulsion or an addiction. The important thing is to help relieve human suffering. However, in the interest of our discussion, it matters simply as a means of communication so we can understand each other. I have put together a continuum on habits, compulsions, and addiction adapted from a lengthier section in *Women, Sex, and Addiction*. The idea came originally from Craig Nakken, Minneapolis psychologist and author of *The Addictive Personality*. Here, in brief, are the distinctions among habits, compulsions, and addictions. While I list them in distinct sections, they are best viewed on an overlapping continuum. Something that starts as a habit—drugs, nicotine, sex, food—may or may not progress to a compulsion and eventually an addiction.

Habits

The words *usually, prefer,* and *like to* accompany habits. I *like to* have a beer when I watch football. I *usually* have sex a couple of times a week. I *usually* eat chocolate every day. I *prefer* to have a new car every two years. The person *prefers* these things, but if they aren't available, the desire soon passes and the person can enjoy life without the beer, sex, chocolate, or new car. Habits can be broken with a bit of determination and will. It doesn't necessarily take a lot of insight or inner work.

As habits become more deeply entrenched and a person lives at odds with him or herself—"I should stop doing this but I just can't seem to"—we are moving into the realm of compulsive behavior.

Compulsions

"Compulsive behavior is rooted in a need to reduce tension, often caused by inner feelings a person wants to avoid or control." *The Diagnostic and Statistical Manual of Mental Disorders* (DSM III), used by psychologists and psychiatrists to make diagnoses, describes a compulsion as "repetitive and seemingly purposeful behaviors that are performed according to certain rules or in a stereotyped fashion." This can involve sex, food, caffeine, nicotine, gambling, spending, TV watching, violent outbursts, cleaning, washing, drugs, or alcohol. "The activity is not connected in a realistic way with what it is designed to produce or prevent, or may be clearly excessive."

Thus we have someone who never had enough love filling up on a gallon of ice cream; abused children washing their hands six times a day to get rid of the shame; someone who was never touched or helped to feel joy masturbating two or three times a day to stimulate a good feeling. With relationships, we find a person who is afraid of bonding with a partner zoning out with TV or a woman who hates her father having outbursts of rage at her husband for no apparent reason.

Like addictive behavior, compulsive behavior often starts as a protective way to detach from the terror of betrayal originating in childhood abuse, neglect, or broken bonds. One girl counts while being sexually abused; another leaves her body for a fantasy land, and both run for the cookie jar when the abuse is over. A little boy imagines being Superman or a war hero after his father bangs his head against the wall. A young adolescent girl dreams of becoming a movie star or finding a Prince Charming to carry her off after she is repeatedly told she is incompetent and stupid. Food, sweets, fantasies, dreams of finding the all-loving, perfect person, being extra good or extra bad—all are used to quell the inner ache. But sadly, what starts as a protective childhood device often becomes destructive compulsion in adulthood.

Can't, must, and *I've got to* are words associated with compulsions. I *can't* get sexually aroused without a violent fantasy. I *must* have caffeine to get through the day. I *can't* feel good without exercising every day. *I've got to* get the house cleaned before I go out or sit down and take it easy. The feeling is much more intense than with a habit.

If you ask why a person has to, they can't always give you a reason beyond, "If I don't, I can't relax," or, more strongly, "If I don't, I go nuts." Most people don't realize it stems from a paired response pattern that got set up unconsciously in the brain. They just think, "That's the way I am," as if it were etched in stone. When the person doesn't have their compulsive ritual, substance, thing, or person, they often experience feelings of agitation and distress, which may continue for hours or days until the compulsive urge is met. The discomfort can be caused by physical withdrawal or it can be a psychological build-up of inner tension.

Compulsive behavior limits life and can create harmful consequences. A mother is unable to be present and friendly with a partner or children until the house is clean. A man interrupts an intimate conversation because he *needs* to get a cola to stave off withdrawal symptoms; a person *can't* stop spending money and is always behind with the bills.

In general, compulsions *limit* life and intimacy in relationships, but they do not necessarily destroy them. People are more likely to admit to a compulsion than an addiction. Compulsive behavior does not necessarily escalate. Compulsive behavior sometimes involves shame, but less than with addiction. "I wasn't going to do that again and I did. What's wrong with me?" Having a lot of compulsions breaks the flow in life. It's like traveling in a broken-down car that barely gets you there as opposed to a reliable car that provides a comfortable, relaxing ride.

Giving up compulsive behavior is difficult to do alone and generally requires that a person develop new insights, thought patterns, or undergo a process of growth. Very often the process results in the discomfort of having buried feelings and memories come to one's consciousness. A crucial part, as with addiction, is to recognize and then break the unconscious connection between a survival belief and the compulsive behavior. While it's tough to do this, breaking an unconscious paired response feels like liberation from a hidden tyrant and helps people feel more energy, harmony, and control over their lives.

When we cross that invisible line between compulsion and addiction, we board a brakeless train that is careening down the tracks. What was once a limiting part of life becomes life-threatening. Nearly any compulsive behavior I have described can become an addiction.

Addictions

Addiction is a process that involves a split in the personality where the life-affirming side and the addictive part become increasingly separated. It's as if a person has two sets of dreams warring away inside, which leads to a life-and-death struggle. While the following traits are usually present, the degree varies tremendously as well as the form.

1. Feeling powerless to quit by will; feeling out of control.
2. Unmanageability in other aspects of life.
3. Harmful consequences.
4. Escalation of the behavior.
5. Withdrawal upon quitting.

This progression spans months, years, or decades. Some people use alcohol, drugs, or food addictively, yet are able to function at work and manage to hang on to some semblance of family life for years before the cracks start to split open. While compulsion may stay constant, an addiction inevitably escalates—more drugs, sex, shopping, food, gambling—as part of a desperate attempt to cover up inner turmoil or placate a body becoming increasingly dependent on a substance.

In most cases, the web of deceit, cover-ups, and detachment from one's authentic self also escalate. Harmful consequences can be external—fights, loss of job or family, crashed-up cars—or they can be internal—headaches, detachment, depression, lack of ability to feel or concentrate. Consequences can also be physical, including sickness, memory loss, lack of concentration, depression, hypertension, high blood pressure, and a numbing of senses or ability to care for others.

A person lost in an addiction sometimes appears crazy to an outside observer. That's because the misprogrammed survivor part takes charge and the rational mind or healthy survivor sinks into oblivion. A man leaves the hospital after having liver surgery and goes to the bar. A woman fixes dinner for her partner the day after he or she breaks her arm. A part of the person may see the craziness of what they are doing, but all willpower collapses in the desire to stave off the pangs of physical or psychological withdrawal. This is where the term *denial* becomes relevant. Many people will admit to compulsions, but people generally deny addiction, even though it may be killing them.

Another way to separate addiction from compulsion is that addiction often involves people in one's social network colluding in the denial. This can be family, friends, or work colleagues. A common image counselors use is that it's like having an elephant in the living room and no one says a word. Everyone tiptoes around it. In real-life situations, collusion takes the form of no one mentioning that Mom just passed out again, that Dad is raging, or that the daughter is starving herself.

On the flip side, in some situations there is overinvolvement; everyone focuses on changing the addictive person, often to avoid looking at their own feelings. The crucial factor is that the addiction usually has profound effects on people in the immediate network.

To tie this discussion into the notion of patriarchy and addiction, read through the above description of addiction and think of our culture. We have two factions warring with each other: those who would channel resources into life-affirming programs for people and our natural resources versus those whose addiction for money and power causes them to continue to ignore the demise of our planet. The harmful consequences are the homeless, the poor, the battered, people with cancer from the toxic air and waste, and the damage to our earth. The escalation is the federal deficit, increased military spending, the increase in sexist and racist legislation, the savings and loan scandals and decreased spending for social programs. And the withdrawal . . . well, unfortunately, as a culture we haven't gotten there yet, although lots of people are individually feeling withdrawal as they attempt to heal from addiction and live with life-affirming values. As a culture, withdrawal will include people learning to live more simply, giving up excessive possessions, and slowing down the pace of their lives. It will mean many people managing with less so everyone has enough and the ecosystem of the earth can be brought back into balance.

FIVE-STAGE ADDICTIVE EPISODE: RELAPSE PREVENTION

Alcoholics Anonymous describes addiction as "cunning and baffling." What is really cunning and baffling are the ways our minds can get sneaky and lead us to relapse. Very often someone is committed to abstinence but doesn't understand the signs of the addictive mind trying to get them to use again, and are caught off guard. In many ways an addictive episode is parallel to going into a hypnotic trance; the addictive side that stems from the old survivor induces the trance so it can have its way.

To prevent relapse, we need to understand the thought processes that often lead to addiction. Thoughts enter the mind as if from some alien force, seeming to take over. Learning to recognize the early stages of an addictive episode can help dramatically in preventing the addictive urge from overwhelming a person. Essentially, the new survivor/wise person learns to recognize the symptoms of addiction and get help before the old survivor reflexes take over.

An addictive episode can be broken down into five parts: fleeting idea, mental attention (inviting the fantasy in), planning/obsession, acting it out, and the hangover involving shame, guilt, remorse, or physical withdrawal.

1. *FLEETING IDEA.* A thought or image of the addictive behavior pops into the mind. It is the hypnotic cue. It could be a thought such as "Wouldn't a drink/sex/hot fudge sundae feel good?" It seems as if the thought or desire enters from outside oneself. This fleeting thought can be triggered from either physical withdrawal—headaches, cravings, restlessness, and so on—or psychological withdrawal—emptiness, sadness, or anger the person may want to avoid getting close to consciousness. In terms of relapse prevention, it is important to know one's personal cues—those things that are likely to trigger the addiction—and either avoid them or eventually break the associations.

A person can be cued into sexual acting out by a picture, a song, music, smell, or anything that is associated with the pleasure that got paired in their brain with sex. Food addictions can get triggered by smell, sight, pictures, or commercials, as well as sadness, rejection, or feelings of shame.

Sometimes the thoughts seem to appear out of nowhere when everything is going well. People in recovery often notice addictive urges ganging up on them just when they are feeling good or having a new success. One woman in therapy went through a repeated cycle of being assertive with her family and then had a tremendous urge to use drugs. Another woman abstaining from sugar said she was walking down the street thinking, "You've been doing well; it's been a long time since you've had sugar," and that these thoughts were followed shortly by a sugar craving.

Having an addictive impulse after feeling good for a while is especially common for people becoming psychologically healed or recovering from childhood abuse. As the person becomes happier and more in control of life, or as the sense of self expands, the "You don't deserve to be happy" side wants to jump in and mess things up. For some, the urge for sedative addictive substances (sugar, alcohol, some drugs) comes when they are feeling high or intense, and the desire for stimulants (caffeine, nicotine, sex, alcohol) comes when they feel low.

In terms of relapse prevention, the best time to intervene in the cycle is the minute the fleeting idea enters one's mind. One can call a friend or use "self talk." "No, I don't want to do that, it will cause pain, I have a choice. I can take a walk, meditate, read, pray, whatever." These statements energize the new wise survivor and help derail the addictive process. People learn that they can have an addictive thought roaming around and can still maintain control by taking action. The important step is not to invite it in and start to savor the idea.

2. MENTAL ATTENTION: *INVITING THE FANTASY IN.* In the next stage the person gives willing attention to the fleeting idea, playing with the fantasy, savoring the feelings of the addiction. "Ummm." The person imagines the sensation a drink/hot fudge sundae/romantic dinner/sex/more money/shopping spree would bring. Toying with the addictive idea and creating an image triggers a chemical response in the body, a pleasant feeling. The hypnotic trance deepens, allowing the addicted part of the system to take hold. It often takes just one permission-giving statement to activate the addiction: "Just once won't hurt. Maybe it will be different this time. I get to do what I want."

The high is underway as the person slides into the euphoria of an addictive state. Pain, tension, or boredom ease away. A person may keep this image and the chemical high going all through the afternoon at work, or for days and weeks, imagining a romantic encounter, sex, food, or drugs. Someone who is chemically dependent and trying to get through the day of work before having the five o'clock drink might use substitute stimulants such as sugar or coffee or learn to trigger physical feelings simply by having a fantasy of drinking alcohol. For some people, the addiction *is* to float off in a fantasy world of euphoric recall of past encounters with the substance of the behavior of choice.

People in uncovery soon learn that when you start playing with thoughts and images of your favorite addiction/compulsion you are playing with fire. The old survivor part who thinks of the addiction as relief from pain is gathering power and the rational mind has more difficulty doing "self-talk" or calling someone to break the cycle. Making a connection with another human being is often the antidote to addiction because the bond or bondage to the addictive substance is then replaced by the longed-for bond of a caring, understanding human being.

Other ways to intervene on the cycle are movies, exercise, reading, TV (if it's not an addiction itself) and, again, the power of the mind. "I don't want to do this to myself." "This isn't good for me. NO. NO. NO! I'm going to take a walk, go swim, and not pay any attention to it."

If a person does not interrupt the addictive trance, the body continues to create the chemical response in anticipation of the euphoria to follow. In this preoccupied state, concentration fades, and people lose touch with the present—forgetting, spilling things, running red lights, or getting irritated with anyone who intrudes on the addictive trance. "Oh, my God, what did they just say to me?" "Oh, I forgot to pick up the children/buy groceries." We have lots of phrases for this—"out in the ozone" or "spaced out," to name two. This is where we see children pulling at their parents, desperately trying to get their attention as they feel their lifeline slipping away.

3. MAKING PLANS.   In the third stage, a person makes plans for the addictive acting out. They call someone to get together for sex, walk into the store to buy the food, plan when and where to get the drugs or the drink. They are in an addictive trance. The adrenaline is pumping, the euphoric state is getting stronger. People talk about the "click" into the world of addiction, where pain falls away and one feels a sense of peace or calm.

It is more difficult to intervene at this stage, because the addictive side has gathered momentum. Depending on the severity of the withdrawal, some people can still make choices. A person on the way to a bar can turn the car around and go back home and phone someone, or go to a friend's house, or find a meeting. A person starting to have hallucinations or going into delirium tremens, however, won't have enough left of the will, or the rational side, left to intervene. Every cell in the body is crying out for alcohol. They need a hospital setting with medical and nutritional intervention. This is also true with psychological addictions. When the old survivor feels that life depends on the addictive behavior, it is likely one will act addictively.

4. ADDICTIVE ENCOUNTER. In this stage, an individual acts out the addiction for alcohol, substances, food, money, sex, or buying something. There is an orgasmic quality to it, a release. It may break the tension of the physical withdrawal from an addictive substance that has gone on for hours or days. Or it may be a psychological release. A chemical or drug high may continue for a long time. With sex or food, the high may be momentary. Often the high includes a combination of substances and behavior—alcohol and sex, drugs and gambling.

5. HANGOVER: SHAME/GUILT/REMORSE/PHYSICAL WITHDRAWAL. In this last stage of an addictive episode, a person either snaps back into reality or slowly wakes up to reality. The euphoria is gone and one is back to life, faced with all they wished to escape. The hangover takes many forms. After the sexual encounter, an emptiness engulfs a person, and they may create distance from their partner, feel disgust, remorse, or shame. After eating three thousand calories of food, one converts feelings of emptiness to the pain of a stomachache and self-loathing. After the consumption of alcohol or other substances, the withdrawal symptoms subside for a while and then the cycle begins again. If the person is attempting to stop the addictive behavior, they might feel ashamed and say things like, "Dammit, I've done it again. What's wrong with me?"

The cycle is now completed and the person is back to the world—the physically dependent body or the emptiness, shame, and unhappiness that triggered the addiction in the first place.

As the overall addiction cycle escalates, people spend more and more time in the trance state of addiction. Their life is increasingly centered on drugs, alcohol, food, sex, relationships, or gambling. The physical and psychological deterioration progresses. In the final stages, they are in that state most or all of the time. A harmful consequence will sometimes jolt a person out of the addictive cycle. A death, loss, rejection, intervention, or accident might sound an alarm to the mis-programmed survival part—a warning that a new form of survival is necessary in order to live. This is called bottoming out. The person finally gets it: what they are doing will destroy them.

What I describe in this chapter are common patterns. There is no definitive way all people "do addictions." This is how many people seem to do them much of the time. The important point is for each person to have a clear understanding of their own addictive process and for counselors and therapists to see people as unique individuals. When we are willing to cope with the complexities and interwoven nature of the physical, psychological, and social aspects of addiction, we will be able to make more effective interventions into addiction.

5

The Many Faces of Alcoholism:

Use, Abuse, and Addiction

I am including a separate chapter on alcohol use, abuse, and addiction for several reasons. First, there is a persistent tendency in this country to use a single description of alcoholism that leaves much alcohol abuse and addiction unrecognized or improperly treated.

Second, while other types of drug abuse are currently in the political spotlight, alcoholism and alcohol abuse are still far more prevalent problems in our country and are associated with more violence, car accidents, childhood abuse, physical battering, and illness than other drug abuse. Yet, alcoholism is the number-one drug problem for whites, African Americans, Native Americans, and Hispanics. It is the number-one drug problem for all classes of people. According to the Hazelden *News* (May 1991), alcoholism and related problems cost the nation an estimated $85.8 billion in 1988, $27.5 billion more than the illicit use of other drugs. Fetal alcohol syndrome is one of the three known causes of birth defects and the only preventable one. Yet the government shuns including the drug of alcohol in its war on drugs and puts little emphasis on prevention. Of the $11.65 billion budget request for the "War on Drugs," which has been a complete failure, 70

percent was earmarked for "supply reduction measures (law enforcement, interdiction, and international initiatives), as opposed to 30
percent for demand reduction (treatment, prevention, and education).
It's difficult to expect changes in the harmful use of alcohol and drugs,
when the government itself models a totally addictive approach—go
for the dramatic authoritarian approach, ignore the causes, and skip
forms of prevention that require true change in policy and belief system.

I believe we need to stress alcohol use and abuse and increase
public education, putting the emphasis on informed understanding
that leads to conscious choices and strategies for the prevention of
alcoholism and alcohol-related accidents. In the Twin Cities on New
Year's Eve, for example, there was a big publicity campaign to have
people take free taxis and not drive under the influence. That was great,
but what about the other 364 days of the year?

Alcohol is the first drug most people use, and while it does not
necessarily lead to other drugs or addictive use, it is usually part of the
picture for many people who become chemically dependent. According to the National Council on Alcoholism and Drug Dependency
(NCADD), "Alcohol users—particularly women and younger drinkers—frequently use other drugs. Close to half (46%) of Alcoholics
Anonymous members, up from 38% in 1986, reported addiction to
other drugs as well as alcohol."

The third reason is that information on the synergistic effects of
alcohol and other substances that can lead to numerous physical problems and death is not made readily available to the public and continues to be largely ignored in the medical profession. For example, did
you know that alcohol in combination with medications commonly
used for fungal or vaginal infections can result in intense flushing,
severe headache, nausea, vomiting, heart palpitations, and chest pain?
If you are taking any type of medication it could be worth your while
to write to the National Clearinghouse for Alcohol and Drug Information for their article on synergistic effects of alcohol and medications.
(Write them at P.O. Box 2345, Rockville, MD 20852—request article
number MS 363).

A third reason I am putting the spotlight on alcoholism is that the
physical effects of alcohol use and abuse are still being treated primarily
with family therapy, psychological insight, and with the twelve steps,
which have to do with sin and redemption. Treatment programs and
literature on alcoholism discuss the physical causes and consequences
of drinking and then ignore them except to say, "Stop drinking."
That's like treating a person who accidentally drank poison with in-

sight psychotherapy and confession, ignoring the physical body.

It doesn't make sense, and it feeds into the revolving-door syndrome: people repeatedly going through treatment programs and then using again because the physical ecology of the body is so far out of balance that the craving to drink overpowers the will to abstain. In addition, the paired response in the brain between alcohol and pleasure or relief needs to be broken. So long as the paired response remains, feelings of powerlessness can emerge, particularly under stress. Once the paired association is truly broken, the person will feel a tremendous inner freedom because the urge to use is no longer lurking around the corner, needing to be kept at bay. We will explore this in more depth in chapter 8, "The Physical Connection."

Most of the above problems in dealing with the complexities of alcohol abuse and addiction hark back to our second and third levels of faithing, where patriarchal thinking leads people to want clear, uncomplicated definitions rather than encouraging people to deal with the complexities of making individual decisions based on an integrated understanding of a situation. It's the *one* road, one journey approach that usually leaves out a majority of the people.

If we want to make progress in dealing with alcohol abuse and addiction, we have to be willing to enter the realm of confusion, differences, and "gray area" so typical of the fourth level of faithing. Through a willingness to see differences, we will move to a more integrated understanding of alcohol abuse and addiction (levels five and six of faithing) that will help us to be more sensitive to the needs of all individuals.

ALCOHOL-RELATED PROBLEMS

Here is some data from the NCADD and the National Clearinghouse for Alcohol and Drug Information (NCADI):

- "As many as 10.5 million Americans show signs of alcoholism or alcohol dependence, and another 7.2 million show persistent heavy drinking patterns associated with impaired health and/or social functioning."
- "An alcohol-related problem strikes one of every four American homes."
- "Over a ten-year period, 250,000 Americans lost their lives in alcohol-related traffic accidents."
- "Nearly half of all fatal highway crashes are alcohol-related."

- "In 1988 1.8 million arrests were made for drinking and driving, nearly double the number in 1975."
- "Alcohol-involved motor vehicle accidents are the leading cause of death for teenagers (15–19)."
- "A high percentage of offenders convicted of violent crimes used alcohol before the offense: 68% convicted on manslaughter charges, 62% on assault, 49% on murder or attempted murder, and 52% of rape or other sexual assault."
- "Fetal alcohol syndrome is one of the top three known causes of birth defects with accompanying mental retardation."
- "Alcoholism and related problems cost the nation an estimated $85.8 billion in 1988, $27.5 billion more than illicit use of other drugs."

Stop and think about these numbers for a while. Seventeen million people addicted to or abusing alcohol—that's more than the population of New York City and Chicago combined, and seventeen times the population of the state of Montana. Think of all the children in school right now—one in four of them goes home to problems related to alcoholism. When you are in a crowd, keep the figure of one in four in your mind to get an idea of how many people are affected by alcoholism.

Then think of all the people whose lives have been damaged by alcohol-related abuse, assault, or neglect. Think of the millions of children who will face the terror of sexual abuse today—half of the perpetrators under the influence of alcohol. Think of all the women who will be battered today (one every 18 seconds), more than half of them by a man under the influence of alcohol.

Think of the millions of people undergoing psychotherapy to heal from the abuse and battering. The human cost is staggering. And while we cannot lay all the reasons for battering and sexual abuse at the feet of alcohol, we can see it as an integral part of the picture.

MANY TYPES OF ALCOHOLISM, MANY TYPES OF EVALUATIONS

Along with many types of alcohol use and abuse we have many approaches to evaluating people. Some approaches reflect the literalist stage of faithing by having concrete checklists based on the "classic" definition of alcoholism typically discussed in AA as well as many treatment programs. Such simple evaluations are usually brief. One agency I worked with took from forty-five minutes to an hour to perform one.

At another extreme, one evaluation process had the client bring in family or friends for numerous meetings, discussed every aspect of their life and used a checklist so broad that just about anyone who had ever abused alcohol would be considered to have a chemical dependency problem—and be referred to their treatment programs.

In a third case, a woman counselor scheduled as many appointments as needed, hoping to help a person reach their own conclusion. She also took into account patterns of drinking related to psychological problems, symptoms of physical dependency, and gender. I asked her about the objectivity of the evaluations. She said, "It is very subjective whether someone is using or abusing. You can't just punch individuals into a computer. It's a judgment call, but over the years, I've learned to trust the judgment. The patterns are very diverse, but you learn to recognize them. I look for the impact on their life. They may be psychologically or physically addicted, or a combination of both. *The important question is whether alcohol is harming them emotionally, physically, or spiritually.* Doing an evaluation is a combination of experience and intuition based on data, and eventually it boils down to the person deciding if their alcohol use/abuse is harming them."

Her description of an evaluation parallels the traits of the integrated level of faithing, level five. She has learned through experience, and is able to use her own intuition along with data. She recognizes that people are different and doesn't make snap decisions. She also tries to lead people to internalizing the decision, thus helping them move toward greater sense of self.

If we think of evaluating alcohol use from a life-loving spirituality approach, then whenever alcohol is harmful to a person or the community they live in, there is an alcohol problem. In *Understanding Alcoholism*, the Christopher D. Smithers Foundation concludes that alcoholism may be defined as "any use of alcoholic beverages that causes any damage to the individual or society or both." Thus we move beyond the patriarchal duality that asks, Are you alcoholic or are you not? in order to set aside debate and ask questions such as:

- What are your drinking habits?
- How is alcohol affecting your mind, relationships, finances, health, work, and energy levels?
- What's your first reaction when you think of not drinking for a while?

- Do you ever feel uncomfortable about your alcohol use, or worry that it might be harming you?
- Are you aware of the physical effects alcohol has on the body?
- Do you feel the need to drink to relax, when you're upset or to feel comfortable being sexual?
- Is your alcohol use associated with violence or dishonesty toward others?
- Do you ever try to quit to prove you do not have a problem with alcohol, or set limits on your drinking?

It is also important to ascertain whether a person has had blackouts, whether they lose control or not, and the quantity of alcohol they consume, but these should not be seen as the only important questions.

Only when we ascertain the nature of the abuse or addiction can we look for the best remedy.

A WORD TO THERAPISTS, PSYCHOLOGISTS, AND PSYCHIATRISTS

Because therapists, psychologists, psychiatrists usually learn only about "classic" alcoholism as described by AA—powerlessness, loss of control, and withdrawal symptoms—they often miss the fact that their client's alcohol use may be blocking them from making changes. A typical symptom is that the client just never seems to push through a problem and get to a new place. Another sign is what I call the sieve phenomenon. The emotional work of one week that may appear very significant is totally forgotten and the client arrives the next week as if nothing important happened. I remember a typical case when a woman did her first intense emotional work one week and then when I asked how she felt about it the next week she looked at me blankly. She had forgotten. This is typical of the denial and segmenting that accompany addiction.

Another sign of addiction in hiding is that the person never lands in one place for long or carries through on assignments. Each week the person brings up a new topic. On any individual day you may think you are getting somewhere but when you look at the big picture you realize there have been no fundamental changes.

Another symptom is that the person has surprising behavior that seems out of character. Someone who is usually honest shoplifts or steals, for example, or is suddenly very mean to another person. The other overall symptom is that the person never seems to grow up—they seem immature, often like adolescents or even younger. These symptoms are true with any addiction, but alcohol and drug use and abuse is the place where I start asking questions.

I think it is extremely important that therapists ask clients about drug and alcohol use—when, where, how much, and about all the effects. I also suggest they ask for a period of abstinence from mind-altering drugs, including alcohol, even if the person says they use very little or it is not a problem. Many people are unaware that they use alcohol as an escape hatch every time life gets a bit uncomfortable. They may not use much, but their use has profound psychological impact. Suggesting that people stop also stimulates a lot of reactions that get the conversation going. Some people agree, saying "No problem," and find they can't keep their contract to abstain. Others argue and agree to abstain only when they see it as an experiment to help them gain self-awareness. Others leave and go to another therapist.

Asking clients to abstain may seem like an authoritarian approach. I see it as setting a bottom line for myself. I have had too many experiences with people dabbling in therapy, getting nowhere, and my eventually finding out they were using alcohol to anesthetize themselves every time they started to get close to feelings or memories. I want to work with people who are committed to their growth. The therapy commitment needs to be on both sides.

In my doctoral dissertation on psychotherapy with lesbian women, numerous respondents reported years of useless therapy prior to realizing they were chemically dependent. Typically, the therapist never asked about their use, and on some occasions the therapist minimized the effects of the use even when the client brought it up or even when they asked for help.

I tell a person something to the effect that they need to close the back door on their emotional escape hatches and that drinking can be a hindrance to making progress in therapy. Basically I try to get people to see that they are doing it for themselves. Do they really want to pay me all this money and have nothing happen? A medical doctor checks for blood pressure and pulse—I want to check if there are any problems with alcohol or drugs.

ALCOHOLISM AS A PHYSICAL DISEASE

So far in this book I have talked about addiction as an outgrowth of our patriarchal, hierarchal society. Now I will apparently contradict myself by saying that much alcohol addiction appears to come from an inherited physical predisposition that affects about 10 percent of the United States' population.

To integrate the two concepts: While becoming alcoholic often has a genetic factor, the will to give it up, having treatment programs available to help people quit, and the motivation to stay sober are social concerns. If treatment programs are not accessible, if someone feels hopeless, or if existing programs are unresponsive to particular groups of people—women or African Americans, for example—many will go without help.

ETHNIC DIFFERENCES

We have talked about a genetic physical predisposition for alcoholism. One might ask why are some people more susceptible than others. Certain ethnic groups appear to have different susceptibility. In *Under the Influence*, Dr. James Milam describes a study by Bert Vallee at Harvard Medical School on susceptibility differences among ethnic groups. He found that the longer the time an ethnic group has had access to alcohol, the lower their susceptibility to alcohol and subsequent rates of alcoholism. This relates in part to the ability of the body to oxidize and eliminate alcohol.

Ethnic Differences and Susceptibility to Alcoholism

Ethnic Group	Length of Exposure	Rates of Alcoholism
Mediterranean Jews	7,000 years	Low susceptibility Low rates of alcoholism
Scandinavians, Irish, and French	1,500 years	Medium susceptibility Medium rates of alcoholism
North American Native Americans and Inuits (Eskimos)	300 years	High susceptibility High rates of alcoholism—approximately 80–90%

These differences are attributed to the principle of natural selection. Those who adapted to and survived the use of alcohol over the generations passed on their susceptibility level.

Within ethnic groups, there are individual variations that prevent any oversimplification of the problem. In Milam's words,

> The scientific evidence clearly indicates an interplay of various hereditary, physiological factors—metabolic, hormonal, and neurological—which work together and in tandem to determine the individual's susceptibility to alcoholism. It would be a mistake to simplify the interactions in the body, making it appear that one specific gene, one enzyme, or one hormone is solely responsible for a chain of events leading in a straight line to physical dependency and addiction. Even a slight difference in the number or types of liver enzymes, for example, could alter a person's drinking patterns, preference, and problems. Yet, while additional predisposing factors to alcoholism will undoubtedly be discovered, abundant knowledge already exists to confirm that alcoholism is a hereditary, physiological disease and to account fully for its onset and progression.

DIFFERENT FACES OF ALCOHOL ABUSE AND DEPENDENCY

While categories are imperfect because people usually fit into them only to a degree, they can give us useful guidelines. The important thing is for people to observe alcohol use in light of the questions posed earlier in this chapter. Some people attempt to fit alcohol use patterns into the habit, compulsive, or addictive categories. Again, while this can work to a degree, ultimately there is a subjective element in evaluating alcohol problems and the ultimate answer rests with the individual.

In *Understanding Alcoholism*, published in 1968 by the Christopher D. Smithers Foundation, different types of alcoholism are listed as Alpha, Beta, Gamma, and Delta alcoholism. Gamma alcoholism is the classic type we hear about most of the time, and the type referred to in AA with terms such as powerlessness, loss of control, and so on. While these categories are no longer in common use, it is significant that various types of alcoholism were recognized as far back as the 1960s. Before describing gamma or "classic" alcoholism, I will describe some other forms of alcohol abuse-addiction. While I draw from the

Smithers Foundation definitions, the descriptions and categories come from my own observations and research.

These types are not finite, definite, or absolute; they are tendencies.

1. Robot Drinking

This is the use of alcohol on a daily basis, often to escape the world. It can be heavy use or as little as one glass of wine a day or a couple of beers. Some people use this much alcohol with no particular effects, while others consume on a daily basis for physical and psychological reasons. This person drinks regularly but does not build up a high tolerance for the substance or necessarily lose control. The degree of withdrawal symptoms vary, but the person seems to require a certain amount every day to feel all right. The harmful consequences are physical (heart and liver damage); to relationships (robot drinkers put up a wall around themselves); and to the brain (memory and concentration are impaired), and emotional state (depression, moodiness, irritability are often present). A more insidious consequence is that the person never seems to fully mature and often blames external forces for their problems.

A typical case of fairly heavy use was Lenny. Along with a smoking addiction, he came home and drank four to six beers every night, often while watching television. If he just had one beer he felt uncomfortable and craved more. It was as if he drank a quota to get a desired feeling. One harmful consequence was that it created extreme distance with his wife, who described him as a robot when he drank. Another was that he didn't get his carpentry work done on time for his customers because his evenings were dedicated to drinking. This led to financial problems. He also maintained a hostile stance toward the world, often blaming people and situations for his loneliness and difficulties making a sufficient living.

His wife finally persuaded him to go with her for couples counseling. After a family therapist made abstinence a criterion for therapy, he quit drinking and experienced almost no emotional withdrawal, although physically he developed a desire for chocolate and sweets. Almost immediately he felt physically better, was more energetic, and felt clearer in his work. While his hostile or victim stance toward the world did not disappear overnight, because he felt better and became more successful in his work, his mental outlook became more positive. His relationship to his wife also improved. He never went to a support group and has maintained sobriety for nearly two years.

An example of light robot drinking that was nonetheless harmful can be seen in the case of Emily, who was in a therapy group. Although she had periods of abstinence, when she started using, it was typically on a daily basis and led to profound isolation and psychological problems.

At age fifty-seven, Emily was going through a difficult time waiting for the outcome of a lawsuit that affected her financial future. She started smoking cigarettes, a habit she had given up for two years, and having one or two little glasses of wine as soon as she got home from work at night. A tip-off that an addiction was taking over her life was that she didn't tell the group (even though she had agreed not to use alcohol). She became distant, righteous—and emotionally shut down, except for intense hostile outbursts toward people in her group, the primary source of her support.

Although the group cared about her, she accused them of not understanding her, and she never revealed her feelings of fear and pain. Whenever I see a sudden defensiveness or a wall like this go up around a person, I look for addictive behavior. I asked her if she was smoking. Yes. Was she drinking? Yes. How much and how often? One or two glasses of wine as soon as she got home from work. Was she calling friends? No.

Emily has transferred her source of comfort from human ties to alcohol ties. Previously she had made great strides in breaking through her isolation and getting support from people, but when the stress went up she regressed to old patterns, a fairly universal response. Whether she was physically addicted wasn't clear—although two of her children had been diagnosed alcoholic—but the spiritual and emotional cost to her was deadly.

Sitting alone night after night, she got angrier, more scared, and more desperate. She was extremely sensitive and short-tempered at work and started lashing out at people, jeopardizing her relationships there. It was as if her fear paralyzed her heart, causing her to sever the ties with people that made care and comfort possible. This is a very common pattern.

It is extremely hard to get robot drinkers—especially those who use very little—to realize that they are living one step outside of life and will not grow and mature until they give up drinking. It is important that "robot" drinkers abstain completely, because once they start, they crave alcohol on a daily basis, which suggests that there could be a metabolic adaptation to alcohol.

2. Escape-hatch Drinking

These are people who use alcohol as a psychological escape hatch. In contrast with robot drinkers, they may not use alcohol daily, but they never quite face life. They keep alcohol in their hip pocket, so to speak, giving themselves a psychological out when the going gets rough. They can reach for alcohol to reduce tension or muffle their fears and feelings. It may be a quick drink before seeing a friend, before sex, at a party, or when one has a hard day. It is often part of social ritual—an elegant glass of wine before dinner. Very often escape-hatch drinkers also drink to please others, sometimes a chemically dependent partner who is still using.

I have had many such people in my therapy practice. I'll tell you about Sophie. Both her parents were using alcoholics and her husband liked to drink. Thus she might have had a chemical predisposition, but it was difficult to tell because she did not lose control, and her life was not externally unmanageable, just numbed out. There had been a period of heavy use during her early twenties, but at thirty-five she did not consume large quantities of alcohol. She could keep up a corporate exterior in her work and appeared extremely competent, but when it came to authentic relationships, she felt blank inside and acted out a role reflecting her upper-class upbringing. She didn't know how to talk honestly or be genuine, and was disconnected from her feelings.

When she visited her parents she would drink to fit in and not make waves, thus blinding herself to their destructive, dishonest relationship. She did the same with her husband, drinking with him at business gatherings so he would feel comfortable. Thus her alcohol use was a combination of psychological escape, drinking to please others (codependent drinking), and possibly a physical addiction that created cravings, particularly under stress. Sophie fell through the cracks of a chemical dependency evaluation because she did not drink heavily, did not lose control drinking, and could abstain for periods of time.

Two telltale clues that alcohol was having a negative effect were evident. First, Sophie could not keep an agreement not to drink for a week. Moreover, she would not tell the therapy group about her drinking unless someone brought it up. Usually after weeks of her being distant and detached in group, I would ask her about her drinking. She would look like a guilty kid confessing to some great transgression. It became an important part of the therapy to assure her that her drinking was *her* problem, not mine, and to separate me from her authoritarian parents.

She would occasionally go to AA and then quit and drink again, but she did not make the connection that alcohol was related to her emotional problems, especially problems with intimacy. The other sign that the alcohol was getting in the way was that after two years of therapy she was emotionally stuck, detached from her feelings; nothing in her life was changing, and she was not becoming more authentic and honest with group members.

As an aside, I may seem to contradict myself by first saying that I don't work with people who will not abstain from alcohol, and then tell a story about keeping a client for two years who apparently had an alcohol problem. Some therapists immediately cease working with people whom they consider chemically dependent and who still use. I make a judgment call. If the person is not willing to look at their use, I will usually not work with them. If there seems to be hope, the person is not destructive to the therapy group, and it feels right to hang in, then I will. I ask people to abstain, and then have them observe their behavior. It is crucial for their overall development that they reach their own internalized conclusion at levels four and five of faithing. I keep bringing home the point that abstinence is an experiment to help them to learn about themselves, and that the important thing is to stay awake and stay aware of the effects of alcohol.

Getting back to Sophie: After nearly three years of group therapy, she was finally fed up being emotionally stuck, living with so much fear related to pleasing others, and getting feedback in group that she said a lot of prepackaged words that did not seem real or genuine. While she didn't really believe the alcohol was the problem, she decided to try quitting for a while. For the first time it was her decision, from inside. The effect was gradual but dramatic nonetheless.

After a few weeks she became aware of a greater clarity and a growing sense of self. Over a period of several months, she talked back to her husband when he intimidated her, she got mad at someone in group, she broke down in tears one night and asked someone to hold her, and she started to genuinely laugh with the group. It was like seeing a birth. More exciting was that Sophie made the internal connection between alcohol, confusion, emotional detachment, and lack of clarity. Abstinence was then something she *chose* in order to feel better and be more connected to her feelings and to other people.

Because she didn't drink when she visited her alcoholic parents, she was able to see how abusive they were to her children, and she was more able to take a stand. Likewise she was more honest about her problems with her husband.

If you didn't see the impressive changes it would be hard to believe that so little alcohol could make such a huge difference in someone's life.

A possible reason for such a dramatic change is that someone like Sophie is physically prone to alcoholism and is trying desperately to control it, which is draining their physical and psychic energy. Another possibility is that when a person knows deep down inside or even in their unconscious that they have an addiction, keeping the secret or not talking about it is a tremendous block to their ability to function genuinely with other people. They are always protecting the secret by not getting close to anyone.

Ultimately, I can only guess at the reasons, but I have seen numerous people like Sophie, who feel emotionally trapped and distant from others, who quit alcohol and experience enormous changes in their lives.

To summarize common traits I have seen in escape-hatch drinkers and, very often, in robot drinkers:

THEY DRINK:
1. to take the edge off emotions and to keep distance from family members;
2. to go along with other people and fit in socially.

PERSONALITY TRAITS/BEHAVIORS OFTEN INCLUDE:
1. difficulty connecting genuinely or committing to other people;
2. complaining about situations but taking no action to make changes;
3. a strong need to please others, or fear of displeasing others;
4. fear of saying "no" to others and of setting limits;
5. keeping up a good front on the outside but often feeling afraid, empty, or uneasy on the inside;
6. repressed anger, often from repressed childhood abuse or neglect (they often deny or minimize childhood abuse or neglect);
7. the person wants to make changes in their life but they don't want to feel emotional discomfort;
8. their diet often includes lots of caffeine, sugar, nicotine, and junk food—or, if they are trying to appear healthy, it includes fruit yogurt, honey-coated granola, and lots of dairy products and salty foods, which I discuss more in the description of stimulant addiction.

In addition, the family of origin often includes an alcoholic parent or sibling.

Many escape-hatch drinkers will drive after drinking because they are in so much denial about their drinking and its effects. My experience in being with escape-hatch drinkers is that when we talk, it is pleasant, but I am left with an emptiness because conversation is either superficial or ungrounded which results in the lack of a genuine connection.

3. Stimulant addiction for low blood sugar

People with low blood sugar often use alcohol in conjunction with other stimulants to keep going. Because their blood sugar level continually drops they are always in search of a stimulant to pick themselves up and get their adrenaline going. These substances do stimulate the adrenal glands momentarily, but when the insulin comes in to bring down the adrenaline level it often sinks lower than the previous level causing tiredness and the feeling you need some sort of pick-me-up. This results in grazing at the fridge, trying to figure out what will bring that nice little pick-me-up.

In spending time with people who have low blood sugar the day goes something like this. Coffee with caffeine first thing in the morning, maybe a cigarette, toast with jam, or some form of cereal with sugar, or a leftover piece of pie. Maybe some orange juice (which is high in natural sugar). By midmorning a sweet roll or candy bar along with more coffee or a cola. Then by late morning a beer (maybe only on weekends). For lunch lots of pasta, chips, bread, or cold cuts and cheese with mayonnaise and mustard, and something sweet for dessert, maybe another beer as well. More coffee (or beer, or cigarettes) to get through the afternoon, another piece of that leftover pie at 3:00 PM, or a candy bar, salty chips, or a sweet roll. If they do have some token vegetables or a salad at dinnertime, they will usually want a creamy dressing that has sugar in it. If they use fruit it will often be bananas which have a high starch content. And on it goes, their bodies are never stable, and these people are exhausting their immune systems.

A person may not use all of these substances, but if they give up one, they will usually start using more of another. For example, if a person gives up cigarettes, their use of sugar or caffeine skyrockets.

If people try to get into healthier foods they will often gravitate toward cheese and dairy products that are naturally sweet, yogurt with fruit (which has about six teaspoons of sugar), fruit juices, granola coated with honey, pasta, and sweet or starchy fruits such as grapes and bananas. And well, let's have a little chocolate around . . . just for special occasions.

When I spent some time with a person who was on such a totally stimulant-centered diet, it was as if he could never quite relax, focus, or pay attention for long. We would take walks, but by the time we got home he had to have coffee or a sweetened juice drink. (Was he preoccupied with needing a blood sugar fix while we were walking?) We would be talking and he had to get up and get a beer. We would be traveling and he would carry his Snickers bars with him. He was trying to quit smoking, but when we had a mad rush at an airport because of a mixup, he quickly grabbed a cigarette and took a couple of heavy puffs before we got on the plane, nearly making us late. If someone crossed his path he could be suddenly very mean or sharp. He had lots of hopes and dreams in his life, but he could never seem to follow through with them. His concentration was good short term, but didn't last long and he had a lot of mood swings.

Other people I have known may have follow-through but have difficulty ever getting close to someone. This may be for psychological reasons, but is also because they are constantly walking the line of regulating their blood sugar so that they are fundamentally preoccupied and hardly even know it.

The more the person uses stimulants, the more the body creates insulin to counteract the sharp rise in sugar. This can be related to adult onset of diabetes and a number of health problems that a doctor may or may not associate with a long-term stimulant diet, which has left the adrenal glands exhausted, thus affecting the immune system.

For some people, alcohol is a small part of the story, but for others, beer and other forms of alcohol are used in small doses virtually nonstop from the time they get home from work and throughout the weekend. This form of alcohol use may combine with all forms of alcohol use and abuse, but for some it is a generalized stimulant addiction that affects both health and emotional well-being, often in vague, disguised ways.

4. Heavy Drinkers

Understanding Alcoholism refers to this as Beta Alcoholism. Here people may drink to the extent that it damages their liver or heart, causes gastritis and other physical problems, shortens their life span, and causes family problems, but they do not have a clear psychological or physical dependency because they do not experience withdrawal symptoms when they quit. In some cases, their heavy drinking is a cultural norm that is accepted by the family.

This type of drinking may create profound harm to others in that the person may batter, abuse, or rape while under the influence. Children and partners often live in fear of the heavy drinker's returning home drunk, having a rage, and beating or sexually abusing the children or partner. This type of abuse and violence is also associated with alcohol addiction.

5. *"Classic" Alcoholism*

This is called gamma alcoholism by the Smithers Foundation. This is the form of alcoholism most prevalent in the United States and Canada, as well as other Anglo-Saxon dominated countries. It is also the type of alcoholism common among Native Americans. *Understanding Alcoholism* gives the following definition:

1. acquired increased tissue tolerance to alcohol
2. adaptive cell metabolism
3. withdrawal symptoms and
4. loss of control.

I would include (5), harmful consequences. In classic alcoholism there is a definite, escalating progression that includes behavior changes and psychological problems. This is the type of alcoholism most generally recognized by AA and treatment programs, because they use loss of control, unmanageability, withdrawal, and cravings as common criteria, although AA welcomes anyone with a desire to cease using alcohol. I have drawn from Milam's book and from personal conversations with the author in putting together this description of the process of alcoholsm.

Here are some myths and realities about "classic (gamma)" alcoholism listed by James Milam in his excellent book, *Under the Influence*.

MYTH: *Alcohol has the same chemical and physiological effect on everyone who drinks.*

REALITY: Alcohol, like every other food we take into our bodies, affects different people in different ways.

MYTH: *Alcohol is an addictive drug, and anyone who drinks long and hard enough will become addicted.*

REALITY: Alcohol is a selectively addictive drug; it is addictive for only a minority of its users, namely alcoholics. Most people can drink occasionally, daily, even heavily, without becoming addicted to alcohol. Others (alcoholics) will become addicted no matter how much they drink.

MYTH: *Alcohol is harmful and poisonous to the alcoholic.*

REALITY: Alcohol is a normalizing agent and the best medicine for the pain it creates, giving the alcoholic energy, stimulation, and relief from the pain of withdrawal. Its harmful and poisonous after-effects are most evident when the alcoholic stops drinking.

MYTH: *Addiction to alcohol is often psychological.*

REALITY: Addiction to alcohol is primarily physiological. Alcoholics become addicted because their bodies are physiologically incapable of processing alcohol normally.

MYTH: *People become alcoholics because they have psychological or emotional problems which they try to relieve by drinking.*

REALITY: Alcoholics had the same psychological and emotional problems as everyone else before they started drinking. These problems are aggravated, however, by their addiction to alcohol. Alcoholism undermines and weakens the alcoholic's ability to cope with the normal problems of living. Furthermore, the alcoholic's emotions become inflamed both when they drink excessively and when they stop drinking. Thus, when they are drinking and when they are abstinent, alcoholics will feel angry, fearful, and depressed in exaggerated degrees.

MYTH: *Craving for alcohol can be offset by eating high-sugar foods.*

REALITY: Foods with a high sugar content will increase the alcoholic's depression, irritability, and tension, intensifying the desire for a drink to relieve these symptoms.

MYTH: *If people would only drink responsibly, they would not become alcoholics.*

REALITY: Many responsible drinkers become alcoholics. Then, because it is the nature of the *disease* (not the *person*), they begin to drink irresponsibly.

MYTH: *Some alcoholics can learn to drink normally and can continue to drink with no ill effects as long as they limit the amount.*

REALITY: Alcoholics can never safely return to drinking because drinking in any amount will sooner or later reactivate their addiction.

MYTH: *Psychotherapy can help many alcoholics achieve sobriety through self-understanding.*

REALITY: Psychotherapy diverts attention from the physical causes of the disease, compounds the alcoholic's guilt and shame, and aggravates rather than alleviates the problems.

MYTH: *Tranquilizers and sedatives are sometimes useful in treating alcoholics.*

REALITY: Tranquilizers and sedatives are useful only during the acute withdrawal period. Behond that, these substitute drugs are destructive and in many cases deadly for alcoholics.

STAGES OF "CLASSIC" OR GAMMA ALCOHOLISM

> *"The man takes a drink, the drink takes a drink, the drink takes the man [or woman]."*
>
> —CHINESE PROVERB ON A FORTUNE COOKIE

1. *Early Adaptive Stage:* "The man or woman takes a drink." Drinking for a high, pleasure, relaxation, escape.
2. *Middle Stage:* "The drink takes a drink." Drinking as medicine to maintain functioning and stave off withdrawal.
3. *Late Deteriorative Stage:* The drink takes the man—or woman. Less tolerance, more toxicity, and physical damage as the person's body, mind, and spirit degenerate owing to the toxic effects of alcohol.

Stage One: The Man or Woman Takes a Drink

Let me tell you the story of a friend of mine named Ed who typifies the form of alcoholism most commonly recognized. Toward the end of high school, I hung out with a group of people who were on the margin of the mainstream. We were involved in music, arts, writing, and theater. We partied a lot and one night someone slipped a bottle of vodka in the punch. It was fun. We got silly, high, made up songs together, joked, and then got sleepy. Spiking the punch got to be a habit.

Ed, a wonderful singer and actor, got especially funny, creative, and energetic when he drank. We all marveled at his enormous tolerance for alcohol and said things like, "He can really hold his liquor."

Ed was demonstrating the early symptoms of alcoholism. For him, alcohol acted as a stimulant, putting him in a euphoric state, and he developed a high capacity for it—a "hollow leg," as it is often called. He could drink large quantities because of the way his body processed alcohol.

This is the paradox of alcoholism and why it is difficult to recognize it without public education. The disease is masked in the early stages. The alcoholic looks as if he or she can handle their liquor very well. Their performance is improved, and they can walk a straight line after many drinks and talk without slurring their words, while the nonalcoholic can't handle anywhere near as much alcohol. While early high tolerance is a symptom of alcoholism, the alcoholic finds no apparent reason to stop because the alcohol feels particularly good and the person functions better than normal *because* of their alcoholic chemistry.

Even so, the body cells suffer severely because they are going to great lengths to adapt to the high intake of alcohol. According to Milam:

> Their enzymes, hormones, and numerous chemical processes are thrown out of balance by alcohol and the normal ebb and flow of materials into and out of the cells is upset. To counteract this confusion, the cells make certain changes in their structures. These adaptations gradually allow the cells to work smoothly and efficiently even when alcohol is present in the body in large quantities. In fact, the alcoholic's cells become so competent at using alcohol for energy that they choose alcohol over other energy, or food, sources. This phase of the disease process can go on for months or years.

Stage Two: The Drink Takes a Drink

Our little group of friends got together two years after we had graduated from high school. I remember smelling alcohol on Ed's breath when we arrived at his parents' home. Things started out much as before. We drank a bit, got high, and had fun singing and dancing together. But something about Ed was different. He drank a lot more than before, and seemed upset after a while. Then he suddenly picked up a vase and threw it at a large ship's model that he had built as a child. He was both crying and laughing. He picked up other things and threw them around the room, smashing five or six beautiful models. It felt like he had switched from Dr. Jekyll to Mr. Hyde.

What was wrong with our friend Ed? The rest of us stood by, silent, upset, and having no idea what to do. Ed's father, bleary-eyed and with drink in hand, came downstairs, and I was deeply saddened by the look of hurt and sadness on his face when he saw all the smashed models strewn around the room. He looked around at all of us and said, "We like to have you kids come and have a good time. Why do you do this?" We stood there, frozen. None of us knew. We thought Ed must be having emotional problems.

Ed was moving from the first to the second stage of alcoholism—the maintenance stage of drinking. Instead of drinking for a high, he was drinking daily to avoid the disastrous effects of a drop in his blood alcohol level. His emotional and psychological functioning were impaired and his friendships and work abilities were deeply affected by his drinking.

At this stage, there is a shift from drinking to feel good to drinking in order to stave off symptoms of withdrawal. In spite of harmful consequencess, the survival programming in the brain remembers only the original euphoria of drinking. At this point in the process, billions of cells of the central nervous system change their functioning to accommodate alcohol. According to Milam,

> As he [the alcoholic] drinks more and more often to get the desired effect, the cells of his body are soaked in alcohol for long periods of time. The cell membranes become increasingly resistant to alcohol's effects, and the mitochondria within the cells increase in size and shift functions in order to accommodate the alcohol. With these changes, the adapted cells are able to live and thrive in an environment where alcohol is continually present in large amounts. The situation continues as long as the alcoholic does not drink more than his cells can process—in other words, as long as he drinks within his tolerance—and as long as he continues drinking. If the alcoholic overdrinks his tolerance, the cells will be overwhelmed, and he will get drunk. If he stops drinking, the addicted cells will suddenly be thrown into a state of acute distress. They have become unable to function normally without alcohol.

Dr. Milam describes the physical impact of *not* drinking:

> All hell breaks loose. Blood vessels constrict, cutting down on the flow of blood and oxygen to the cells. The blood glucose level drops sharply and remains unstable. The brain amines, serotonin and norephinephrine, decrease dramatically. Hormones, enzymes, and body fluid levels fluctuate erratically. The body's cells are malnourished and toxic from long exposure to large doses of alcohol and acetaldehyde. . . . The brain cells, or neurons, become excited and agitated . . . and send out highly disorganized and chaotic distress signals. The acute withdrawal at the early stages can include memory loss, anxiety, nervousness, agitation, sleep disturbances, and nausea, although the person may function throughout the day. More extreme withdrawal symptoms include mental confusion, memory defects, lack of muscular coordination, convulsions, hallucinations, paranoia, violent or fearful behavior, and

delirium tremens (DT's), and the person increasingly is unable to function without alcohol throughout the day.

Over time, hangovers become excruciating, exceeding anything a non-alcoholic is likely to experience.

Sadly, the shame and remorse an alcoholic person often feels when he takes stock of the harm he has done to himself and others is attached to thoughts of being weak-willed or somehow a bad person, as opposed to a person whose body is physically dependent on a substance. This is where the double message of AA, with its focus on faults and moral inventories, can keep a person from understanding the need for physical help. Operating in a continuous, negative cycle, the shame and lack of knowledge often prevent a person from getting needed help. The person may want to quit, but the hunger of the cells for alcohol to stave off withdrawal easily overwhelms all willpower. Underlying all of this is an increasing sense of hopelessness and despair that is seldom recognized as a response to the physical double bind of alcoholism.

This period may also go on for months or years, with the alcoholic person becoming increasingly preoccupied with walking the fine line between drinking enough to placate the addicted cells and not drinking so much they get drunk, which is extremely unpleasant at this stage. Typically, there is a loss of control at this stage, which happens gradually and with varying intensity, but the bottom line is that *the tolerance for alcohol decreases and the withdrawal increases.*

To an observer of someone losing control to alcohol, it seems as if the person is gradually disappearing behind an ever-growing wall. They talk and are physically present, but something is missing. At worst, the Dr. Jekyll and Mr. Hyde fluctuations become more extreme and there are angry outbursts, lies, yelling, violence, and fighting.

Another symptom of this maintenance stage is that people start making sure they have a stash. If they are going to visit a friend who doesn't drink, they bring their booze with them. They may keep some hidden in the house, if they are trying not to have others know how much they drink. Inside they feel uneasy if alcohol is not available. The important point to remember is that the person is regulating their body with the use of alcohol because they *believe* they *like* and *need* alcohol. In reality, the brain, feeling the symptoms of withdrawal, sends a message to the mind that says, "A drink will help you feel better." They feel out of balance *without* alcohol—just the opposite of how the nonalcoholic experiences excessive alcohol.

Many people, aware of their increased and constant use, try to prove they don't have a problem. They might stop drinking for a week or several days or rationalize their drinking by saying, "I run three miles a day, so I'm not alcoholic. I get to work each day, so I'm not alcoholic. I don't get drunk, so I'm not alcoholic. I only drink after 5 PM or on weekends, so I'm not alcoholic." This is more likely to be a *symptom* of alcoholism than proof it doesn't exist. Typically, we obsess about things that feel out of our control.

If a person goes to a psychologist or psychiatrist at this point, the symptoms may be treated as psychological or the person may even be put on Valium or other antidepressants, which further mask the true problem of alcoholism and can be physically disastrous to the body. To this day, I get many clients who are taking medication who were never warned of the harmful effects of using the medication in conjunction with alcohol. This can have a tragic outcome.

Many years ago, I had a client named Joan who was diagnosed as schizophrenic and who had been in and out of hospitals for a ten-year period. During one hospitalization, she was given up to 100 milligrams of Thorazine every hour—a very heavy dosage. When I asked her about her alcohol use, she said she had often wondered about it, but since no one said anything, she continued drinking up to a bottle of wine or more each day, along with the Thorazine she was taking. When I told her this could fry her brain cells and cause terrible emotional and physical damage, she looked surprised but relieved. She said that in all her therapy and hospital stays for ten years, only I and one occupational therapist had ever asked about her alcohol use. Fortunately, my sense of alarm reached her and she stopped using immediately. I knew to ask about her alcohol use only because the counseling program I attended had a course on alcoholism.

The psychological changes that followed were remarkable. While there were still problems from childhood, many of Joan's symptoms of disorientation, hallucinations, paranoia, and so on started to fade away. Within six months, she got off Thorazine and worked on her childhood abuse. She started taking karate classes and began to expand her social network. When I spoke to her six years later, she was free of all symptoms of schizophrenia and had a black belt in Karate, a master's degree, and was doing very well.

One cannot assess exactly how much her difficulties stemmed from the synergistic effects of alcohol and Thorazine, but the alleviation in symptoms once she stopped drinking was dramatic. It is highly likely that much of the pain this woman suffered, the indignity of endless hospital stays, and the diagnosis of schizophrenia would have been avoidable had medical schools, nursing schools, and psychology and counseling departments taught a correct understanding of alcoholism and the synergistic effect of coupling alcohol with other medication. As I write this I feel a sadness wondering how many other people are suffering terrible symptoms of paranoia, hallucinations, fear, and depression because the people in the medical and therapeutic community are not asking questions about alcohol use with medications.

Stage Three: The Drink Takes the Man . . . or Woman

I saw Ed off and on during college, but our visits got further apart in the years to follow. At one point I heard that he had been hospitalized to "get his body back in shape" from drinking and diabetes and life on the road as an actor. One summer, when he was acting in a summer stock theater, several of us went up to see him. He acted well, but his sparkle was gone. There was a tired look about him. Afterwards, we went back to his motel room, where several bottles of vodka and gin were on the table. He smoked and drank, and, although he joked, he seemed terribly remote.

At one point I reached over and took his arm and asked, "Ed, if you have diabetes, why do you keep drinking?" He looked at me in a gentle way, and I at him, making a momentary connection. I could feel his deep sense of hopelessness. I don't think he really knew why he kept drinking. We resumed our superficial conversation and I left a couple of hours later.

In this third, deteriorative stage, for which there is no clear demarcation from the previous stage, the toxicity of the body and the damage to the organs, including the liver, brain, and central nervous system, lead to a decreased tolerance and increased severity of withdrawal symptoms. There is more mental confusion and physical weakening, and the immune system breaks down. Now the disease that actually got underway months, years, or decades ago, when the cells started adapting to alcohol to survive, becomes visible. It seems that the only relief comes from drinking more alcohol—but this will lead to death if not interrupted. The physical dependency is so great at this point that it is excruciating *not* to drink. Although life is falling apart, alcohol offers quick, brief relief from the physical symptoms of withdrawal. Paradoxically, while alcohol is experienced as relief from pain, it is poisoning the system.

Many people who are alcoholic die of other diseases before their alcoholism is diagnosed. According to Milam, in two-thirds of these cases, death is attributed to medical consequences, and in one-third of the cases it is attributed to suicides, accidents, or drownings. The most prevalent physical causes are cardiovascular disease, cirrhosis of the liver, gastrointestinal disease, and lung cancer.

I never saw Ed again. A few years later a friend sent me the newspaper clipping of his obituary. I still miss him and continue to wonder what might have made a difference.

PART III

The Way Out

6

An Introduction to Twelve-Step Programs

The fundamental question when considering this or any model of recovery/discovery is, Does this program help people achieve sobriety? And, in the case of the twelve-step approach which purports to be spiritually based, does it help people develop a mature level of faith, one that includes a strong internal sense of self, spirit, passion, compassion, and the ability to reflect on oneself and the system one lives in? Or, simply, does it empower people?

In Alcoholics Anonymous literature we find two contradictory statements that underlie the frequent double message communicated by twelve-step programs. One is humble and suggests there is choice: "Our book is meant to be suggestive only. . . . We realize we know only a little." And the other makes an unconditional assertion: "As soon as a man can say that he does believe or is willing to believe [in a Power greater than oneself] we emphatically assure him that he is on his way." Unfortunately, the "we realize we know only a little" has been largely forgotten in recovery circles, while the claim of needing a belief in God has been widely accepted.

As we have seen, addiction has many faces, and for every person who is addicted to a substance or a behavior, there is a unique personal story, physiological makeup, and set of cultural and family influences at work. While the twelve steps were originally designed for alcohol addiction of the gamma or classic type, they are now recommended for all people with all sorts of problems. They have been adopted, usually with few changes, for numerous spinoff groups numbering upward of two hundred. Most people attending these groups have virtually no idea of why the twelve steps are being used for their problems; for example, incest, dependent relationships, or mental health problems.

All of this gives us an idea of the powerful mystique accorded to AA, or twelve-step groups, and while I honor all people who have found it useful, I also want to bring a rational look at the effectiveness of this particular program using these particular steps.

An exploration on outcome studies affirms this need. According to Charles Bufe, author of *Alcoholism, Cult or Cure?*, "It has also been noted by two prominent alcoholism treatment researchers, William R. Miller and Nick Heather, that there is virtually no overlap between alcoholism treatments known to be effective and those which are widely employed. Treatment which they list as currently supported by controlled outcome research are 'aversion therapies, behavioral self-control training, community reinforcement approach, marital and family therapy, social skills training, and stress management. The treatment methods which they list as currently employed as standard practice in alcoholism programs, but which are not supported by controlled research, are Alcoholics Anonymous, alcoholism education, confrontation, disulfiram (antabuse), group therapy, and individual counseling.' " While this doesn't mean that the latter are never effective, it does mean there is no systematic research showing that they are.

It is also important to continually make a distinction between what helpful characteristics are specific to twelve-step programs and what aspects of twelve-step programs are universal, such as the healing power of telling one's story, being with an unshaming group of peers who have similar problems, getting group support, and receiving unconditional care. These age-old practices did not start with twelve-step groups, although Bill Wilson did a very creative job of pulling together this universal wisdom and making it accessible.

Another important distinction is to separate the problems that arise from the use of the steps per se and the problems people have in groups because they are imperfect people in patriarchy—sometimes rigid, abusive, or acquiescent. While abuse and oppression that happen in groups cannot be attributed totally to twelve-step format, the sacrosanct nature of the twelve-step institution, which echoes patriarchy's self-righteous stance, has often led people to mute their inner wisdom and surrender to external control such as group "rules" which are counter to the goal of empowerment.

Another thing to keep in mind as we discuss this grandfather of recovery programs is our understanding that addictive impulses are programmed into the survival part of the brain. Thus the goal is to break the link between thoughts of addiction and pleasure and relief. I think Bill Wilson was describing this phenomenon when he referred to the alcoholic mind—wanting to quit, then totally forgetting the harmful consequences and using again. Thus another important question is, How does this program help break that programming and help create new survival behavior?

Lastly, we have looked at substance abuse as having a strong physical component that affects the cells, central nervous system, and major organs. Does this program address the need for physical healing that leads to a lessening of physical cravings and thus to a more relaxed, secure sobriety? In other words, is it wholistic?

A HISTORY OF TWELVE-STEP PROGRAMS

To give us a backdrop for Bill Wilson and Dr. Bob Smith's formulation of the twelve-step programs we need to spend a minute talking about the Oxford Group.

Preceding the formation of twelve-step programs was the Oxford Group, a nondenominational evangelical movement that was in many ways the parent group of AA. It dates back to 1908 but was primarily active in the 1920s and 1930s It started as a small group of people—mostly men—who came from a strong Christian background and who hoped to create a human chain of good relationships based on honesty and moral principles that would change the world. Unfortunately, the relationships were locked into sex-role stereotypes, so that women were taught to "serve" and take a secondary role.

The Oxford Group stressed principles that became essential parts of the twelve-step approach—deflation of the ego, humility, confessing one's defects, and being willing to make restitution; again, traits important for men with inflated egos, but not always helpful for women who had been trained to block development of self and ego.

The other four principles the Oxford Group espoused—*absolute* honesty, *absolute* purity, *absolute* unselfishness, and *absolute* love—were not directly adopted in AA because they were seen as too rigid. Oxford Groups operated throughout the country in the 1930s, and used the practice of "witnessing" to help alcoholics become sober, although recovery from alcoholism was not the primary purpose of many of the groups. Eventually the Oxford Groups expanded from small intimate groups into large groups who took the name Moral Rearmament, the goal being to reform "drunken" countries rather than drunken individuals.

Bill Wilson's connection to the Oxford Group was part of a chain of events that led him to form twelve-step programs.* In December of 1934, he was in desperate straits with his drinking, which he had tried in vain to stop. He had been hospitalized on several occasions and was in the late deteriorative stages of alcoholism. One day, Ebby, an old drinking buddy he hadn't seen in five years, showed up at his door. While Bill Wilson sat and drank at the kitchen table, he listened intently to Ebby, who had joined the Oxford Group, tell how he had found sobriety through religion. He couldn't get over how Ebby had changed. In *Alcoholics Anonymous*, he writes that "The door opened and he stood there, fresh-skinned and glowing. There was something about his eyes. He was inexplicably different."

Ebby told him he had "got religion" and that "God had done for him what he could not do for himself."

"Ebby especially emphasized the idea that he had been hopeless. He told me how he had got honest about himself and his defects, how he'd been making restitution where it was owed, how he'd tried to practice a brand of giving that demanded no return for himself. . . . He touched upon the subject of prayer and God. He claimed that prayer had released him from his desire to drink and that he had found peace of mind and happiness as a result."

Although Bill, who believed more in a universal wisdom rather than an all-powerful God, was skeptical, over the following days he was unable to forget the words of his friend who had at one time been pronounced incurable. He writes, "The good of what he said stuck so well that in no waking moment thereafter could I get that man and his message out of my head."

Shortly after that, when Bill Wilson was hospitalized with delirium tremems, facing possible death or madness, he cried out, "I'll do anything. . . . If there be a God, let Him show Himself." He recounts, "What happened next was electric. Suddenly my room blazed with an indescribably white light. I was seized with an ecstasy beyond description . . ."

"There I humbly offered myself to God, as I then understood Him,

---

*In recounting this story I am drawing from the books, *Pass It On: The Story of Bill Wilson and How the AA Message Reached the World*, a fascinating historical account published by AA world services; *Bill W.*, by Robert Thomsen, another compelling book; "Bill's Story," from *Alcoholics Anonymous*; and *Alcoholics Anonymous: Cult or Cure?* by Charles Bufe.

to do with me as He would. . . . I admitted for the first time that of myself I was nothing; that without Him I was lost. I ruthlessly faced my sins and became willing to have my new-found Friend take them away, root and branch. I have not had a drink since.''

Many aspects of this conversion experience became intrinsic to twelve-step philosophy: One must have a spiritual awakening, completely surrender to God, confess one's sins, and be willing to live a life of high integrity in order to be sober. Wilson's conversion experience led him to believe that religious people, whom he had once doubted, must be right after all—a point frequently made in *Alcoholics Anonymous.*

Bill Wilson and his wife Lois attended Oxford Group meetings for a few years, but he saw a need for changes in the program, such as less evangelism, no coercion, no religious requirements, no exclusion, alcoholics working with other alcoholics in small groups, and more stress on practicing tolerance and love. He wisely changed the notion of *absolute* honesty and purity to progress, not perfection. He also differed with the belief that one must give the group total credit for one's personal changes.

It is also paradoxical that Bill Wilson's dislikes of the Oxford Group parallel what hundreds of women and men are currently saying they don't like about AA and other twelve-step groups: they get rigid, righteous, self-centered, sometimes intolerant, and demand unswerving loyalty. And while the intent of Bill Wilson was to have tolerance for all, we will see that in his writings and those of AA there is tremendous vacillation between saying, on the one hand, Find your own way, and on the other, Complete surrender to God is the only way.

The original six steps used by Bill Wilson and the groups were similar to the Oxford Group beliefs:

1. Complete deflation.
2. Dependence and guidance from a Higher Power.
3. Moral inventory.
4. Confession.
5. Restitution.
6. Continued work with other alcoholics.

Bill Wilson formulated the current twelve steps from 1938 to 1939, several years after meeting Dr. Bob Smith, who joined him in working toward the creation of anonymous support meetings. The steps and the format for meetings are included in *Alcoholics Anonymous*, which is generally referred to as the "Big Book."

The popular image that Bill Wilson sat down one night and through divine inspiration wrote the twelve steps mixes Hollywood with history. The steps are a direct spin-off of the Oxford Group beliefs, with which he had been familiar for some time. This is not to underestimate the importance of what he did; rather, it is to put it in a historical context.

ONE HUNDRED MEN AND ONE WOMAN

It is crucial to keep in mind that Bill Wilson wrote these steps based on his experience with *one hundred men and one woman* (mostly white business and professional men). As described in *Pass It On*, the inscription on the title page of the first edition of *Alcoholics Anonymous*—"The Story of How More than One Hundred Men Have Recovered from Alcoholism"—was suggested as the book's title before Florence R., who wrote "A Feminine Victory," argued against it.

I envision Florence R. as writing her story for the book and then feeling upset when she saw the proposed title about one hundred men. I can imagine her arguing with them—a brave act for the only woman in the program. She eventually left the program, returned to drinking, and according to *Pass It On*, died of an apparent suicide.

When Bill Wilson wrote the chapter titled "To Wives," his wife, Lois, was mad because she thought she should write it since . . . well, *she* was the wife of an alcoholic. Bill argued that the style should stay consistent, and he prevailed. So *Alcoholics Anonymous* remained consistent—written totally from a white male point of view, with no input from women except through Florence R.'s personal story. Though the second and third editions include stories from women, the chapter "To Wives" remains, locked in the consciousness of the thirties, and discussions about personalities of alcoholics refer to heterosexual men, while discussion about partners of alcoholics are usually directed at heterosexual, married women. That leaves out a lot of people.

> *"We simply wish to be helpful to those who are afflicted."*
> —BILL WILSON'S INTRODUCTION
> TO *ALCOHOLICS ANONYMOUS*

According to the major text of *Alcoholics Anonymous*, the criteria for deciding if you are alcoholic is: "If, when you honestly want to, you find you cannot quit entirely, or if when drinking you have little control over the amount you take, you are probably alcoholic."

AA philosophy maintains that only a spiritual experience will conquer the illness of alcoholism (and other addictive or compulsive behaviors); that without God or faith in a Higher Power, recovery is not possible. It further maintains that once you are an alcoholic, you must never drink again, and you must attend AA support groups on a permanent basis. Maintaining sobriety depends on life-style changes and embracing a daily spiritual program. Only by practicing this program *as a way of life* can one expel the compulsion to drink.

For many people, AA has been a lifeline. For others, it has not. According to James Christopher, author of *How To Stay Sober: Recovery Without Religion*, "Only *five percent* of this nation's ten to fifteen million problem drinkers are helped by AA [emphasis mine]." According to Charles Bufe's review of outcome studies for AA in *Alcoholism, Cult or Cure?* at best only 2.4 percent to 4.8 percent of alcoholics who have investigated AA remain in the group and are sober after one year. Even using AA's figures, only 29 percent of AA members (in comparison with the total number of alcoholics in the United States) are sober after five years. We will explore Christopher's approach to recovery/discovery in greater detail in chapter 7.

Important Contributions of AA

The powerful, revolutionary aspect of the AA model in the later 1930s and early 1940s is that it suggested a nonhierarchical, peer support structure in a hierarchical, patriarchal system that revered experts, the medical model, leaders, status, and rational thinking. The philosophy of men coming together as equals, regardless of status, age, and ethnic background, was fundamental to the success of the program, particularly for men who were not used to a format that allowed vulnerability and stressed service to others.

While I believe it is important to give Bill Wilson due credit, it is also important to remember that, historically, he did not create the idea of peer support. Women have routinely come together to talk at a personal level. Historically there is evidence of women in prepatriarchal times creating many rituals to mark life transitions and connect with the awe and wonder of the universe through rituals intertwined with nature and the cycles of the earth. Native Americans and other indigenous peoples have reinforced community bonds and sought to connect with the spiritual forces through talking circles, vision quests, counsels, discussion, and rituals to mark birth, death, marriage, and life passages as well.

THE TWELVE STEPS

This section is included to introduce those of you who are unfamiliar with the twelve steps to the program. For those of you who know the twelve steps, it also lays the foundation for the coming chapters, where I will talk about the difficulties people have encountered in twelve-step groups.

A fundamental question arises at this point. Is a spiritual path *as suggested in twelve-step programs* necessary for someone who wants to cease their addictions to substances or behavior? The answer is, not necessarily. Atheists, agnostics, and lots of other people stop their addictive use of alcohol and drugs without ever attending twelve-step support groups. Put in its simplest form, sobriety is sobriety and a spiritual journey is a spiritual journey. Many people who become sober decide to embark on a healing journey but it is not necessarily the criterion for sobriety.

From a life-loving spirituality perspective, however, anything that moves toward life is a form of spiritual journey; thus healing from addiction and codependency are by nature spiritual endeavors. That moment of truth when one hits the wall with their addiction and says, I'm out of control, I need help, I've got to stop this, is also a spiritual awakening because it is self-knowledge, and knowledge of God/dess begins with knowledge of self. But self-knowledge is not necessarily linked to Christianity, Judaism, Buddhism, Paganism or any particular religion.

Many people start attending meetings in order to maintain sobriety, but stay for spiritual growth. What I see happening is that people stay in twelve-step groups for years not so much because their sobriety would be threatened if they stopped going but because they value the bonds with others, which for men in particular are not readily accessible elsewhere.

THE TWELVE STEPS OF ALCOHOLICS ANONYMOUS*

1. We admitted we were powerless over alcohol—that our lives had become unmanageable.
2. Came to believe that a Power greater than ourselves could restore us to sanity.

---

*The Twelve Steps are reprinted with permission of Alcoholics Anonymous World Services, Inc. Permission to reprint the Twelve Steps does not mean that AA has reviewed or approved the content of this publication, nor that AA agrees with the views expressed herein. AA is a program of recovery from alcoholism—use of the Twelve Steps in connection with programs and activities which are patterned after AA, but which address other problems, does not imply otherwise.

3. Made a decision to turn our will and our lives over to the care of God, *as we understood Him.*
4. Made a searching and fearless moral inventory of ourselves.
5. Admitted to God, to ourselves, and to another human being the exact nature of our wrongs.
6. Were entirely ready to have God remove all these defects of character.
7. Humbly asked Him to remove our shortcomings.
8. Made a list of all persons we have harmed, and became willing to make amends to them all.
9. Made direct amends to such people wherever possible, except when to do so would injure them or others.
10. Continued to take personal inventory and when we were wrong promptly admitted it.
11. Sought through prayer and meditation to improve our conscious contact with God *as we understood Him*, praying only for knowledge of His will for us and the power to carry that out.
12. Having had a spiritual awakening as the result of these steps, we tried to carry this message to alcoholics, and to practice these principles in all our affairs.

Here is a brief description of the purpose of the Steps. I go into much more detail in chapter 13. In the First Step, by admitting to powerlessness, one cracks the denial about the harm of their addiction. The purpose of the Second and Third Steps is to believe in a power greater than oneself. This again attempts to bring the ego down to size (assuming one has an inflated ego).

The Fourth and Fifth Steps are modeled on the Christian concept of confession and forgiveness, which is intended to heal one's relationship to oneself. By owning up to personal "defects," one is humbled.

Underlying the Sixth and Seventh Steps is the belief that, with the help of a spiritual power, change is possible.

The Eighth and Ninth Steps are intended to repair one's relationships with others by making amends for harmful acts toward them. This helps clear out shame and guilt, which makes a person feel safer bonding to others. The ability to say, "I'm sorry, I made a mistake," is especially humbling for a controlling ego.

Steps Ten, Eleven, and Twelve are sometimes called maintenance steps; they stress the importance of continued self-examination, staying honest in relationships, and service to others.

These Steps are particularly relevant to males who hold power. Envision leaders of countries stressing the need to see all people as equal and coming to believe that honesty, service, and fellowship are key to individual health. Imagine the leaders of the United States and heads of the CIA and the Pentagon and Wall Street getting together to do a moral inventory of all the people they had harmed and to make amends and restitution. That would be wonderful.

But for myself as a woman it is only a tiny piece of the picture. It is important to apologize when I've hurt someone, but as a woman my eyes have been trained to stay focused on my faults and to feel guilty for being successful, assertive, passionate, and alive. The focus of my attention needs to be gaining support to accept my power and wisdom, to take action, to feel alive. Self-blame comes all too easily.

The Twelve Steps as a Religious Program

In a major mixed message, *Alcoholics Anonymous* asserts that the program is not religious, while the language is but one step away from fundamentalist Christianity. AA uses the words *wrongs, defects of character*, and *shortcomings* instead of *sins*. It suggests a fearless moral inventory rather than confession. Instead of proselytizing, *Alcoholics Anonymous* refers to "carrying the message." The chapter in *Alcoholics Anonymous* titled "We Agnostics" affirms the AA belief that *only* a spiritual experience will conquer alcoholism (emphasis mine) and pleads with the reader to adopt absolute faith in God. In Step Three, where people are told to turn their wills and their lives over to the care of God. When I say to people in the program that this sounds religious to me, they respond, "Oh, anything will do for your Higher Power—a doorknob, a tree, your car." That answer seems to trivialize the notion of a Greater or Higher Power.

"How It Works."

This is the title of the chapter in *Alcoholics Anonymous* that is read thousands of times each week in twelve-step meetings around the world. It sets the tone for the program. Here is the opening statement, which I will critique as written and also examine in a historical context.

> Rarely have we seen a person fail who has *thoroughly* followed *our* path. Those who do not recover are people who *cannot* or *will not* completely give themselves to this *simple* program, usually men and women who are *constitutionally incapable* of being honest with themselves (emphasis mine). He goes on to describe people who do not avail themselves of the program as

"unfortunates" who were "born that way," and are "naturally incapable" of "rigorous honesty."

This opening paragraph is a strong admonition to the misprogrammed survival brain; it says that there is a path that brings a new kind of survival. Follow it completely and you'll be okay. This intention is great. Unfortunately, it is again the *one* road, one journey approach as defined by privileged males. If you don't do it our way, or if you don't succeed, you are an *unfortunate* who is *born constitutionally incapable of being honest.* Thus we have a male model that has not worked well for many women and that blames them when they fail. The words used in the above paragraph to describe failure are words often used about women and poor and minority people in this society: *naturally incapable, unfortunates, born incapable of being honest.* Here we see the patriarchal switch in full bloom. Humility is repeatedly stressed, but there is no humility about the viability of the program.

This opening paragraph is incredibly shaming and parallels statements used to draw people into cults. We have the answer; follow us and you'll be saved. If you don't stick with us you are inferior and terrible things will happen to you. When people in desperation hear these kinds of statements, they often absorb them quickly and deeply and become afraid to think for themselves.

While the survival brain does indeed need a strong jolt to get it to switch gears, I find this opening chilling because it echos the Christian righteousness that has been responsible for incredible violence against women and other people who worship their creator in other ways—for example, Native Americans and Africans who are called savages as a result.

Concerning the notion that someone may be born "constitutionally incapable of being honest with themselves": I do not believe there is a gene for honesty. Also, honesty is not the only variable in maintaining sobriety. Some very disagreeable, dishonest people have managed to stay sober (meanwhile abusing and battering children, or taking sexual advantage of vulnerable newcomers at meetings). Conversely, some lovely, kind people have had a terrible time maintaining sobriety, relapsing over and over again due to a wide variety of variables related to the physical ecology of the body, incest pain, or being battered or abused in dependent relationships.

The phrase *"thoroughly* followed our path" reinforces the idea that the survival brain needs to be serious about this new path. For a perfectionist, however, this kind of statement has the effect of keeping them scrambling to do it better and better and better in order to reach the promised perfection. I remember one woman who had done five fourth steps ("a fearless and searching moral inventory") in an attempt to be thorough. She was severely depressed, and the key to feeling better was not confession. It was learning to be assertive, recognizing food allergies, and learning the power the mind can exercise in over-coming depression. She passively followed the dictates of the program because it felt familiar. She was brought up in a fundamentalist, author-itarian family, a "sinner unless saved." So, when several men in her AA group suggested she do another fourth step, she did so without ques-tion. And when it didn't work, she assumed she had not done it right. Her passivity—the core of her depression—was being reinforced in her twelve-step group.

The Danger of Making Promises

The twelve-step programs make promises: "If we are painstaking about this phase of our development we will be amazed before we are halfway through. We are going to know a new freedom and a new happiness. We will not regret the past nor wish to shut the door on it. We will comprehend the word serenity and we will know peace. . . . Fear of people and of economic insecurity will leave us." These promises are beautiful and it is important to instill hope in people. Yet blanket promises such as these can also be seductive for someone who wants magical formulas for perfect cures.

Just below the surface implies a lot of shoulds—you should be happy, you should not regret the past. This is a terrible set-up for people who don't succeed to beat on themselves.

Several years ago, during a two-week period, five women came to me for therapy intakes with virtually identical stories. They were all in AA, had been sexually abused as children, and each had been told in her AA group that if she worked the program thoroughly, she would not need therapy. As one woman said with desperation, "I have fol-lowed the program perfectly for three years and I feel worse than when I started. If I don't feel better soon, I will either go back to drinking or kill myself."

I felt sad at the needless suffering of these women, who had been victimized in the culture and victimized in their twelve-step group. Although treatment programs in the late 1980s and early 1990s are more likely to refer survivors of abuse to therapists, and twelve-step women's groups usually support members having therapy, I still hear many people report that members of twelve-step groups and some treatment programs imply that "if you do the program right you won't need other help." I would also add that some men do support people going for therapy, but usually the admonition to avoid therapy comes from men.

Consider the phrase, "Unfortunates . . . constitutionally incapable of being honest with themselves." We could look at these judgmental words in the context of Bill Wilson's going out on the streets and bringing home down-and-out drunks and trying to save them. While this is purely speculative, he may have been thinking of these men when he wrote those words. Because he was not successful with them, perhaps he concluded they were beyond help. Maybe he forgot his own words: that "we only know a little." Maybe instead of being incapable of honesty, they were in the final stages of alcoholism, their cells so dependent on alcohol they were not able to withstand withdrawal. Maybe some of them were mentally ill or without hope. Maybe some of them were abuse survivors whose underlying pain felt worse than the pain of alcohol abuse. There may have been many reasons why Bill didn't succeed, but he translated his sense of failure into blaming the victim.

I also wonder why honesty came to be the primary variable associated with recovery. While it is very much part of a spiritual path, it is not necessarily the crucial variable in staying sober. Here is one idea. When Bill Wilson started the program, it would have been rare for white, privileged males to speak from the heart and be vulnerable with each other. Usually white males bond through competition, work, status, hunting, and comparing or debating ideas. So, when Bill Wilson, Bob Smith, and the other men who joined AA started talking honestly to each other, the experience must have been deeply felt. Perhaps this honesty kindled a feeling of love, drawing people back to meetings and helping them find hope. Perhaps the healing nature of speaking from the heart got translated into a belief that one must be honest to recover. My sense is that he was talking about human bonds and love.

Let's take the opening statement, give Bill Wilson a feminist and global-consciousness perspective, and say it a different way:

We are thankful to have found a way to stay sober. No professionals were able to help us and we were afraid we would die of alcoholism. We are finding a new strength and joy in our hearts through honest, noncompetitive communication with others, which is new to us as white males, who were taught to be competitive and hide our feelings. Those who have joined our program have done very well, and the ones who have dropped out have often returned to drinking. We don't know why. We need to look for more answers. We've had only one female member, and she did not maintain her sobriety. Thus, our writing is not based on any firsthand knowledge of female experience. We have picked people up off the streets who are alcoholic and attempted to help them stay sober. That method doesn't seem to work and we haven't discovered another way yet.

In chapter 14, I suggest a possible new opening, one that honors different paths and does not shame people who fail.

About an All-Powerful Male God

At the heart of the program is the belief that sobriety depends upon having a High Power, which is usually described as an all-powerful male God. In the chapter "How It Works" in *Alcoholics Anonymous*, Bill Wilson writes, "Remember that we deal with alcohol—cunning, baffling, powerful! Without help it is too much for us. But there is One who has all power—that One is God. May you find Him now!"

Although AA literature is sometimes open-ended about defining one's Higher Power, the "How It Works" introduction to the meeting exhorts people to find God (Him) now, and the twelve steps use God or Him in five of the steps and Higher Power in one step. Again, this presents us with a mixed message.

Bill Wilson was on the right track for people with inflated egos in stressing that there was a power greater than the person's own ego. People who are used to controlling others have great difficulty thinking they can't control alcohol. But Bill Wilson made the leap from needing to tame the inflated ego to surrendering to an external, all-powerful, male God.

I believe that unnecessary leap reflects the fact that Bill was culture-bound by his contacts with predominantly Christian men, the Oxford Group, and his own conversion experience. The only model he knew for deflating the ego came through the Christian model of confession and humility.

And in keeping with his position in hierarchy he took what appeared to have worked for him and assumed it was the only way for all other people. While people need to take the primary step of saying they are out of control with their addiction, and many people find prayer useful, others attribute their sobriety to the use of their rational mind.

Use of the Rational Mind

People who come into the program are often advised to rely only on God or a Higher Power. Self-reliance and rational thinking are strongly discouraged. "Your best thinking got you here" is a commonly used phrase. Again, speaking as a woman, it is crucial to my survival that I use my mind; to think, to observe, and to change my beliefs. Telling people not to use their minds is to shut off the sixth and seventh chakras—perception and knowledge. This locks them into levels two and three of faithing and diminishes the capacity for exploration, creativity, and joy.

In fact, willful, conscious use of the mind is invaluable in helping people access power to maintain sobriety. It is something most people who stay sober do, whether or not they describe it that way. In asking many people what keeps them sober, they say something to the effect of "I never want to feel that way again; it was ruining my life, and I'm much happier now."

Yet *Alcoholics Anonymous* repeatedly warns against using one's mind, and asserts that people have no mental defense against taking that first drink. They must rely absolutely on God. I believe this victimizes people. Thoughts create energy, and with enough repetition they become very powerful. Someone who repeatedly thinks or says, "I must not drink or use drugs, I can't handle it, it's wrecking my life," *is* developing a mental defense against drinking because he or she is reprogramming the new survivor brain to associate good feelings with *not* engaging in their addiction. The first step does work toward this end by having people list and talk about the harmful consequences of their addiction.

It is one thing to admit to powerlessness over one's impulse to use a substance, and quite another to say one cannot take willful action to control their use of drugs. To say one does not have power from within is to lead people to feel dependent and powerless. That is not congruent with healing the whole person or moving to the higher levels of faithing.

God and Higher Power

To return once again to the concept of a Higher Power or all-powerful God, before his conversion experience, Bill Wilson was wary of the God approach. "When they talked of a God personal to me, who was love, superhuman strength, and direction, I became irritated and my mind snapped shut against such a theory. . . . Judging from what I had seen . . . the power of God in human affairs was negligible."

But he was not without a faith that was much broader and sounds similar to what we now call "New Age."

I had always believed in a Power greater than myself. My intellectual heroes, the chemists, the astronomers, even the evolutionists, suggested vast laws and forces at work. I had little doubt that a mighty purpose and rhythm underlay all. But that was as far as I had gone. . . . I could go for such conceptions as Creative Intelligence, Universal Mind, or Spirit of Nature, but I resisted the thought of a Czar of the Heavens, however loving . . .

I resonate to these beautifully articulated thoughts. How did this concept of spirituality, which is broad, mystical, and much closer to life-loving spirituality, end up centered on an all-powerful male God?

I believe it was because of Bill's profound experience of being nearly dead and then crying out to God and having a conversion experience that saved him from drinking. It was highly influenced by his observation of his friend Ebby, who seemed miraculously transformed after he "got religion." (According to *Pass It On*, Ebby later went back to drinking.)

A difficulty with the notion of a "Higher Power" is that it implies a sky-God that makes people lower. It creates duality, the God out there and up there as separate from self. In a life-loving spirituality, God/dess is within us all and permeates all life.

While I believe in miracles and spiritual awakenings, not all people stop drinking because of a spiritual experience. Some are court-ordered into treatment programs as an alternative to a jail sentence. And for some of them, treatment works. I have had clients ask for referrals to treatment because they knew they had a problem. And others have spent several years using on and off before they became committed to their sobriety.

Narcissistic God-Image

The concept of God or Higher Power that many people use in twelve-step programs is a personified male God "up there" who knows all and sees all—as if we're the center of attention of a marionette master who gives full attention to us. This kind of narcissism in relationship to God is common with people in "the program" and I believe it often keeps people from seeing their place in the greater scheme of things or from growing up. People use phrases such as, "Gee, this worked out well, my Higher Power must have been watching out for me," as if there is a benign father pulling the strings and arranging our actions. Every coincidence is attributed to one's Higher Power. Once I met someone who said, "Oh, I was hoping to meet you; this must be my Higher Power at work." When things go wrong, people often say something like, "I guess my Higher Power didn't want me to have this job." When I had dinner with a friend and the waiter said they were out of tortellini, my friend said, "I guess my Higher Power didn't want me to have tortellini tonight."

Developmentally this notion of an all-seeing God reflects the normal self-centered view of a two- or three-year-old child who thinks the parents can see into them and know what they want, think, and feel. Children at that age see themselves as the center of the universe; this view, if continued into adulthood is called narcissism. It's like the magical thinking of children to believe someone is arranging who I bump into or if I get a job. It is grandiose of me to think that God cares if I have tortellini when I go to a restaurant. To think one has a Higher Power who is personally watching everything you do is to remain a trusting child with no sense of inner power or free will.

While it may be comforting to think there is a benign father keeping watch, one could extend this kind of thinking to "My Higher Power must have wanted me to be beaten, raped, impoverished, etc." Do we say to someone who is oppressed, "That's a lesson from your Higher Power"? I think that would be abusive and discount the whole social-political system we live in.

The image of an all-powerful male God up there is an androcentric notion given that plant and animal life on the planet preceded human life by billions of years. Who was their creator if neither man nor woman existed? It is also a reflection of hierarchy and patriarchy and resembles the image of the authoritarian father to be feared, placated, and obeyed without question.

A woman I interviewed who was rethinking her fundamentalist origins said, "I began to note that God was not a him and that it was a childish mentality to think that God was up in the sky waiting for me to come to heaven sometime in the future. I began to re-evaluate, and brought God to an internal experience. And so God is within and God is without; there is no separation and it does not have gender to it." Another woman said, "I changed from thinking that God is Love to Love is God."

Another woman in discussing spirituality said, "Although I've been thinking about this for years, I'm not sure I have a clear concept of spirituality, not really. But I know a lot more about what it isn't. The process has been one of saying it's not this, it's not this, it's not this—it's not a man in a white beard, it's not someone watching over me every minute, it's not somewhere up in the sky. And it's very scary every time you give up one of these ideas. I do think there is something profound however, and it's about energy, but I still pray to a personal God because it is hard to pray to energy. I also believe it is as narcissistic for atheists to hold onto the belief there is nothing there, as it is for people to think it is a white-bearded father who watches our every step."

The Danger of Recovery Narcissism

At a celebration dinner in England for my first book, *Women, Sex, and Addiction*, we got into a lively discussion about the way people in the United States spend so much time on "personal growth." One woman observed that people in the United States seem very self-indulgent. I jokingly threw out the phrase, "Oh, you mean, *recovery narcissism*." Everyone laughed. One woman, Jane, said, "It seems as if Americans are so caught up in themselves they lose sight of the bigger picture." I wanted to defend people who take many years of therapy to overcome the effects of incest and abuse. Still, the term *recovery narcissism* stayed with me.

Because the twelve-step program focuses on faults and gives the impression that one can get rid of all defects of character, it does promote a kind of narcissistic, continual self-examination, preventing people from accepting imperfections and having a sense of humor about the state of being human. I have had numerous clients who were loyal followers of the program continually interrupt themselves, saying, "Oh, am I blaming someone, am I being codependent, am I having a resentment?" In other words, Am I doing it wrong? Talk about constricted flow of energy. It was as if someone—the master marionette man—was watching their every move.

This approach leaves no room for a good laugh at how we can all be jerks, put our feet in our mouths, and make terrible mistakes, and yet are lovable human beings, right now. There needs to be a balance between self-examination and accepting life's imperfections.

OTHER ASPECTS OF THE AA PROGRAM

Approved Literature

In the framework of levels of faithing, where the goal is to create people who have learned to think for themselves, the concept of approved literature is an external authoritarian stance counter to human development. Having approved literature, whether it is wonderful or horrible, is typical of cults or oppressive political systems. It's a form of inculcating certain beliefs while censoring others. When I say this to people in "the program," they usually reply, "But we don't say you can only read approved literature." "Right," I respond. "However, presenting a vulnerable person desperate for sobriety with approved and unapproved literature is like a parent's saying, 'You can have an apple or a candy bar, but I'll love you best if you take the apple.' "

While some groups don't take the notion of approved literature seriously, numerous women reported being in groups where self-appointed leaders strongly advocated reading *only* approved literature. We righteously point our fingers at other countries who control literature, yet having approved literature in AA is overlooked as a repressive measure.

While I have found some of the literature fascinating, particularly the historical accounts, overall, the prescriptions for recovery are full of foreboding and based on fear, which, as we discussed, is inherent to patriarchal control. Repeatedly one sees warnings: If you don't do it right, you'll drink again. For example, in *Alcoholics Anonymous*, Bill Wilson warns that if one is not sorry and continues to harm others, one is "quite sure to drink." This is counter to the idea of reprogramming the misprogrammed survival mind. It's like giving an excuse to drink. "I've been a bad person and harmed others; I will surely drink again." This is in sharp contrast with James Christopher's approach, which gives one clear message to retrain the survival brain: "I don't, drink no matter what." We'll be talking about his approach in the next chapter.

The Need for Balance

Another aspect of twelve-step programs that is common to most support groups is maintaining a daily commitment to sobriety through readings, keeping in touch with other people by phone or in person, and attending as many meetings as needed. I agree that healing is a day-by-day, step-by-step process, and "one day at a time" is important to remember.

On the other hand, the emphasis on going to more and more meetings if you feel scared of using often gets people locked into a treadmill of meetings. This promotes dependency and keeps people from exploring other avenues of help that may be more relevant to their needs. Clients have come for therapy while attending as many as four or five meetings a week. While it is certainly up to the individual to decide, it might be important to have varied means of support, including physical healing of the body, exercise, and simply having fun. It's as if people trip over their own seriousness, and forget that joy, fun, laughter, and relaxation are also part of the healing journey.

The intensity of indoctrination process has been apparent to me because clients I've worked with have repeatedly been scared they would fall apart if they didn't attend so many meetings. When I suggest they could find out for themselves by experimenting, they express both uneasiness and relief. I suggest people have fun, join an interest group, get politically involved—that they do whatever ignites their passion and see how it affects them. I say things like, "Well, try other things and see if you fall apart. You are the expert on your own life." So many people in "the program" seem to lose the perspective that life is now—not some illusory time down the road when you're free of addictions and character defects.

Sponsorship

Having a sponsor can both help a person immeasurably and become a stumbling block preventing individual growth.

Typically, an experienced member of the group takes on the role of supportive mentor and teaches the "fledgling" member how to work the steps and, in a sense, initiates them to the norms of the program. For a person who is afraid of reaching out to others and feels undeserving of care and compassion, having an individual committed to them can be a lifeline. People have described with gratitude the security they found from knowing someone in the world cared for them and was available. For someone who had abusive or neglectful parents, a committed, supportive sponsor is often the first positive role model of a healthy parent figure.

Sponsorship can also block development if the sponsor takes on the role of indoctrinating the new person to uncritically accept the beliefs and practices of the program. The other, more insidious block is when the sponsor feeds their own ego needs by playing the all-wise and knowing expert. This encourages the sponsee to remain a child and seek advice rather than find their own wisdom. It's important that the overall tone communicated by the sponsor be that we are essentially peers here to help each other, and that people not look to others to be gods and that people not play God. The main thing is for the sponsor, like a good parent, to help the sponsee find their own strength and power.

The Twelve Traditions

In an effort to have independent groups while maintaining overall unity, twelve traditions were put together several years after the steps, providing guidelines for membership, handling money, personal and public relationships, management of groups, and other concerns. In essence, the twelve traditions provide rules of operation that have been paramount in maintaining basic consistency and autonomy for groups. I have listed them in short form below.

*THE TWELVE TRADITIONS OF ALCOHOLICS ANONYMOUS**

1. Our common welfare should come first; personal recovery depends upon AA unity.
2. For our group purpose, there is but one ultimate authority—a loving God as He may express Himself in our group conscience. Our leaders are but trusted servants; they do not govern.
3. The only requirement for AA membership is a desire to stop drinking.
4. Each group should be autonomous except in matters affecting other groups or AA as a whole.
5. Each group has but one primary purpose—to carry its message to the alcoholic who still suffers.

---

*The Twelve Traditions are reprinted with permission of Alcoholics Anonymous World Services, Inc. Permission to reprint the Twelve Traditions does not mean that AA has reviewed or approved the content of this publication, nor that AA agrees with the views expressed herein. AA is a program of recovery from alcoholism—use of the Twelve Traditions in connection with programs and activities which are patterned after AA, but which address other problems, does not imply otherwise.

6. An AA group ought never endorse, finance, or lend the AA name to any related facility or outside enterprise, lest problems of money, property, and prestige divert us from our primary purpose.

7. Every AA group ought to be fully self-supporting, declining outside contributions.

8. Alcoholics Anonymous should remain forever nonprofessional, but our service centers may employ special workers.

9. AA, as such, ought never be organized, but we may create service boards or committees directly responsible to those they serve.

10. Alcoholics Anonymous has no opinion on outside issues; hence the AA name ought never be drawn into public controversy.

11. Our public relations policy is based on attraction rather than promotion; we need always maintain personal anonymity at the level of press, radio, and films.

12. Anonymity is the spiritual foundation of all our traditions, ever reminding us to place principles before personalities.

There is great wisdom in many of these traditions that go against aspects of hierarchy and patriarchy. For example, the belief that the common welfare of the group comes before individual personalities is something terribly missing in our culture at the present time, where the privilege of the few increasingly takes precedence over the safety and well-being of the majority.

Yet there is a catch here as well. Because women are so used to sacrificing their individual needs for the needs of men, a woman who is abused in a group may follow her female conditioning, and interpret the tradition to mean she shouldn't complain; the group is more important than she is. So while I agree that overall, in groups and in society, we need to sometimes set aside our personal greed or desires for the common welfare, it is also important for people not to accept being used or abused or violated in any way in any group.

Traditions that prevent the groups from having opinions on outside issues and from endorsing outside enterprises, and that keep the groups nonprofessional, ensure that the focus stays on healing and away from pursuits that tend to inflate the ego. The eleventh tradition, maintaining personal anonymity in the press, radio, and films, has somewhat fallen by the wayside. More and more people are talking about their alcoholism and drug dependency in an open way. This has both positive and negative aspects. On the positive side, when a former

President's wife, Betty Ford, goes public with her chemical dependency problems, it relieves shame in countless people, particularly women who may feel more ready to admit to a problem and seek help. On the negative side, when people write a book immediately after treatment or are in the limelight because they are public figures, they lose some of the comfort of just being a person in a group, no different from anyone else. What is important is that people have a choice and that they think through any decision to be public about their addiction.

Step two is the most problematic in that it reinforces a God/He, and assumes His presence will be expressed in the group conscience. As we will explore in chapter 10, twelve-step groups are not immune to patriarchal values, that is, the exploitation of women by men. And many women have overlooked abuse, saying they believed the group conscience would take care of it.

The second part of the second tradition, "Our leaders are but trusted servants; they do not govern," is part of the positive, nonegocentric belief that we are all working together. No one is the boss; we all serve each other. This implies equality, a step toward empowerment for everyone.

LABELS

In AA and other twelve-step groups, the meeting opens by people saying, for example, I'm Jack and I'm an alcoholic. Everyone responds by saying, Hi, Jack. The positive side of saying "I'm alcoholic" is that it sends a sharp, clear message to reprogram the survival brain: Hey, you're alcoholic—that means you don't get to drink. If the old survival programming is starting to think, "Oh, wouldn't just one drink taste good right now," saying "I'm an alcoholic" can bring a quick reminder that the person cannot handle alcohol. This can be useful in the early stages of recovery/uncovery.

As soon as possible, I like to see people drop the label or use it as only one part of their self-description. "I'm Cathy, a sacred child of the Universe, recovering from addiction to alcohol." I hate to see people reducing themselves to being an addiction. We are so much more than that. If someone has diabetes or cancer, they don't say I'm diabetic, or I'm cancer, they say, I *have* diabetes or cancer. What we say about ourselves has a profound impact on how we view and experience ourselves.

We need to separate from our labels and remember that at our center we are amazing, miraculous miracles of life; we have talents, strengths, humor, love. Remembering this helps tune us in to our connectedness with the earth and all other people. When I realize I'm miraculous simply because I'm alive, I will realize the same is true for all other people.

SUMMARY: CONTRIBUTIONS, CONTRADICTIONS, AND MISSING PIECES

The twelve-step model filled a desperate need in our culture, providing a way for men, and eventually women, to come together and support one another in abstinence from alcohol addiction, and more recently many other forms of addiction. While critics cite the fact that these programs do not help most people who are chemically dependent, we can never discount the fact that millions have been helped. The emphasis on bonding, calling people, and developing community is greatly needed in our transient society. The widespread availability of free twelve-step programs is also very important.

The use of the age-old custom of telling one's story is, in itself, a form of healing, although many people complain that continual recounting of past drinking stories falls into the category of telling back-slapping war stories and never moving on. Contrary to psychoanalysis and many traditional forms of psychotherapy that focus on insight, the attitude in twelve-step groups is one of making concrete changes in one's life. This is all very positive.

On the negative side, the steps are not designed to develop a strong healthy ego, which is often terribly lacking in women. The focus on faults reinforces the Christian sin-and-redemption theme, which is basically a shame-based notion—you're born a sinner and you spend your life making up for it. There are no steps about expressing love to people, having fun, celebrating life, and becoming powerful or healing the physical body. The program creates separateness by taking a righteous stance that separates the loyal followers from those who choose other paths or disagree. There appears to be little understanding of the power of the mind to control addiction or the physical components of substance addiction, and no support for making a decision to leave the program based on one's inner wisdom. The program fosters dependency on the group and an external God. This keeps people from maturing into fully functioning adults at levels four, five, and six of faithing.

Because the program has become sanctified, it fails to open itself to self-examination. This is dangerous because it teaches blind faith and often blocks people from seeing abuse in groups, which we will explore in chapter 10. Sometimes people put too much faith in the program and do not seek help for childhood abuse, battering, or their own violent behavior. In a sense, the ego of AA needs to be deflated so that people realize it is but one part of a very big picture. And because the twelve-step programs have taken on a religious tone, women are often lulled into complacency about acknowledging abuse or practices that are not affirming of them.

Some people complain that there is a phony, "isn't it all wonderful now that we're in the program" attitude that fails to acknowledge that it takes time to connect and become vulnerable to any new group of people. Another weakness is that people forget it is a *suggested* program of recovery and become rigid in their use of the program and shaming toward people who would make changes.

The steps reinforce dualities of good and bad by constantly urging people to get rid of parts of themselves. A more life-loving model of change is one of transformation through acceptance and celebration of life. A typical addictive trait is perfectionism, and the steps reinforce this by suggesting one can become free of character defects rather than learning to accept the fallibility of being human.

The program's promises of "a new freedom and a new happiness" if you simply follow these simple steps may come true for some, but for others sobriety removes the shield protecting a wounded child in need of therapy and healing. To promise that these steps alone will remove fears and insecurities is to seduce the needy child beneath the addict to grab hold to the program with unswerving loyalty. Don't we all want a promise of an easy path to peacefulness? But part of the journey is to give up such utopian dreams. That overcoming addiction is as simple as attending AA is, in itself, addictive thinking: "Just do this and everything will be okay."

AA promotes permanent dependency on a group and does not acknowledge a life beyond recovery that might not include twelve-step groups. It encourages people to stay at levels two and three of faithing. This is not to say that people in the program do not develop beyond levels two and three of faithing. Some do, but often in spite of the program or by getting extra help or secretly rewording the steps, and also through education, psychotherapy, or other spiritual paths.

Finally, twelve-step programs fail to explore a huge piece of knowledge we have about alcohol and drug addiction—namely that there are physical elements of addiction that need physical healing. As we discussed earlier, these physical components have profound effects on one's mental, emotional, and psychological states. Without addressing these issues, many people continue the revolving door syndrome of going through treatment, going to groups, and then falling off the wagon.

AA has helped millions. It has not helped many more millions. It is important to explore some other roads to help us uncover from addiction.

7

Without a Male God:
Other Approaches to Recovery/Discovery

AA and the twelve-step approach dominated the recovery field from 1935 until 1976, when Jean Kirkpatrick started Women For Sobriety (WFS). More recently, in 1985 James Christopher started Secular Organization for Sobriety, or Save Our Selves (SOS). Also in 1985, Rational Recovery (RR), derived from Albert Ellis's rational emotive therapy, entered the picture. It is described in *Rational Recovery from Alcoholism: The Small Book,* by Jack Trimpey, published in 1989. All three of the people who wrote books about these models were pioneering souls who attended AA and left for various reasons, including dislike of the sexism, the powerlessness concept, rigidity, religiosity, the cult-like atmosphere, and the all powerful God approach.

In addition to these three models for recovery, a treatment program based on counter-conditioning (aversion therapy) for alcoholism has been operating steadily since 1935, close to the time Bill Wilson had his spiritual awakening. Originally founded in Seattle, Washington, in Shadel Hospital, the program is currently operating as Schick Shadel in three locations. If it hadn't been for Uncle Ron, whom I mentioned in chapter 1, I would never have heard of this program. He went to Shadel for treatment in 1949 and helped over four hundred people get help through this program. I felt skeptical when I called Shadel hospital. I have a stereotypically negative view of aversion therapy. But in interviewing P. Joseph Frawley, M.D., the chief of staff, and reading their literature, I realized this is a program that could be useful to many people. What is so amazing is that almost no one I've talked with or interviewed knows about this program or this approach. Many people consider aversion therapy a long gone relic of the past. It is an important alternative to understand since it has been extremely helpful to numerous individuals.

It is important to emphasize the one commonality these approaches all share with AA, namely that *people who are physically addicted to alcohol must completely abstain because their body cannot tolerate alcohol in even the slightest amounts.* While *Rational Recovery* is strong in this stance, the Rational Recovery Journal takes a broader view, stating that "The leadership in RR actively promotes a pluralistic (multiple) approach to helping people with chemical health problems. . . . Some RR professional advisors are promoting controlled drinking in some parts of their practices and at the same time using Rational Emotive Therapy/RR abstinence approaches for others. RR views no inconsistency in this regard."

Another commonality is that all three models suggest groups as a means of support, although Trimpey, writing about Rational Recovery, also asserts on the cover of his book, "Just you, that's all it takes."

As we explore these models, it is helpful to keep in mind our survival model of addiction, where the survival brain has been programmed through repeated experience to instantly associate a substance or behavior with relief from pain or distress. Thus in evaluating all approaches it is important to see what techniques they use to help people break the link between the use of a substance and pleasure, or relief from pain.

As we will see, in their different ways, all three of the above self-help programs use the rational mind to create a new type of survivor. They all train the rational mind to discard the idea that addiction means relief and replace it with the belief that addiction equals pain and that a sober life is preferable. They run counter to AA's belief in powerlessness because they believe people can choose to use their rational mind as protection against substance abuse or addictive behavior.

Another common difference from AA is the belief that with time the desire to drink fades away and that one does not need to attend groups forever in order to stay sober. Two programs have specific phrases for this. RR says, "Don't keep coming back," while WFS says, "Upward, outward, and onward." The other common thread in the books written by Kirkpatrick, Christopher, and Trimpey is that while they all express their dislike of AA vigorously, at their core they all support people finding sobriety any way they can because they know from painful experience the devastation caused by alcoholism and addiction.

None of these programs claims to be the only way. Rather, the founders each found a way that worked for them personally, and each has made it available to others, giving people much-needed choices. What will be important in the coming decades is treatment programs' starting to let their clients know about all these models for support and discovery. To help find a program that is right for them would probably save countless people from relapse and pain because they would be free to put their energy into uncovery and discovery rather than adapting to a program that doesn't feel right. And simply presenting people with choices to explore is empowering.

The current dominance of the Minnesota Model—that is, using AA in treatment programs—has led to a virtual censorship of options. When I asked staff of a women's treatment program under the umbrella of a prominent treatment organization if they recommended WFS along with AA, they said they were under strict orders only to talk about AA. If someone just couldn't make that program work, then and only then was it okay to mention WFS. I consider this practice of limiting information on recovery models, which is common in treatment programs, a terrible violation of the rights of clients, who should be allowed to choose for themselves. It is symptomatic of cults.

Even for people who are perfectly happy in AA or a twelve-step group, there is much to be learned from these other approaches that could be useful in helping people avoid a rigid stance toward recovery/discovery models. As we will see, the personal accounts of these people and their philosophies reinforce that there are truly many roads on the path to sobriety from addiction.

WOMEN FOR SOBRIETY

> "We are capable and competent, caring and compassionate, always willing to help one another, bonded together in overcoming our addictions."
>
> —WOMEN FOR SOBRIETY MOTTO

In 1976, in a personal effort to recover from twenty-eight years of alcohol abuse, Jean Kirkpatrick founded a recovery program specifically for women called Women for Sobriety (WFS). She created this model after traveling a long road of life-threatening alcoholism, including hospitalizations, violence, depression, and unsuccessful attempts to get support through AA.

Kirkpatrick had a bright, observant mind and a deeply felt sense of personal spirituality which did not find a welcome home in AA. Unwilling to bend to their rigidity, she left the AA groups and, through trial and error, developed WFS. In her autobiography *Turnabout*, she tells of her decision to leave AA:

> The meetings just did not meet my needs . . . [they] were a big aggravation. The men were set in their ways and ideas, they dominated the meetings, their stories were often lurid and contained an ego element of bragging, their descriptions of women were very often chauvinistic, which they carried with them into sobriety, and their constantly calling me a "gal" began to grate on my nerves. I found that with every meeting I attended, I had a greater desire to go out and get drunk.

She recounts her desire to find physical help to remove her mental obsession and calm the shakes she experienced in withdrawal. On one occasion, thrilled with the results of using vitamins and glutamine as suggested by a doctor, she took her ideas to her AA group. The response was upsetting. "It was to no avail. My suggestion that anyone take vitamins to help with recovery was entirely taboo. I was angry and I felt rejected. It also seemed to be singularly closed minded."

She comments on one of the great paradoxes of AA. "No pills from a physician for high blood pressure? No chemicals? Yet the coffee, not to mention the cigarettes, consumed at each meeting were chemicals."

Kirkpatrick believes women have different reasons for drinking and different needs from men in recovery. As she sees it, women drink because of frustration, loneliness, emotional deprivation, and various kinds of harassment, while men drink for power. She contends that women's being culturally socialized to be passive, to believe someone will take care of them, to have sex on someone else's terms, is not understood in male-dominated treatment programs. Thus her steps are designed to build up women's fragile egos and battered self-esteem through self-discovery, and to release shame and guilt through the sharing of experiences, hopes, and mutual encouragement. She believes that women need separate groups to affirm their autonomy from men and recognize their emerging roles.

Kirkpatrick's program literature takes a more wholistic approach than AA, encouraging women to meditate, eat healthy food, smoke less, and in general treat themselves and their bodies with love and care. This belief is congruent with the policy of not having coffee, sugary food, or smoking during meetings. She encourages women to identify with their power, their health, and with each other. Alcoholism is considered to be "a physical disorder that needs to be treated as a medical/psychosocial problem." In the WFS brochure, Jean lists numerous physical consequences of alcoholism as well as behavioral problems, although none of the thirteen statements for recovery addresses the need for physical healing. To date, this is the only program that stresses the physical aspects of healing.

The WFS "New Life" or "Acceptance" program includes thirteen statements using nonsexist language and refers to spirituality rather than to God or a Higher Power. They are not rigid steps; rather, they are statements people can use as they choose.

The thirteen statements are:

1. I have a drinking problem that once had me.
2. Negative emotions destroy only myself.
3. Happiness is a habit I will develop.
4. Problems bother me only to the degree I permit them to.
5. I am what I think.
6. Life can be ordinary or it can be great.
7. Love can change the course of my world.
8. The fundamental objective of life is emotional and spiritual growth.
9. The past is gone forever.
10. All love given returns.
11. Enthusiasm is my daily exercise.
12. I am a competent woman and have much to give others.
13. I am responsible for myself and my actions. (This was formerly, "I am responsible for myself and my *sisters*.")

In *Turnabout*, Kirkpatrick explains the evolution of these statements, which helped her get past negative, self-deprecating ways of thinking that contributed to her severe depression and continuing to drink even though it was destroying her life.

In Kirkpatrick's words, "The WFS New Life Program is a way of thinking which creates a new way of life. . . . In time, the actions that the use of these Statements provide will soon become automatic and your life will change. We are the architects of our thoughts and these produce actions. We are the mistresses of what we are and what we become.''

In terms of our old survivor, new survivor model, these statements are geared to make life seem more appealing to the new wise survivor than addiction was to the old survivor. The statements encourage the new survivor to be responsible, use the power of the mind, to become excited about life, and to value the power of human love. This is all very important in helping develop a strong new survivor.

For me the first step is not quite adamant enough in warning the old survivor that it had better knock it off with the addiction or there's going to be big trouble. Saying "I had a problem that once had me" might be strong enough for some, but when the old survivor is in tremendous denial about the seriousness of their addiction, it needs sharp, resounding statements such as, "I'm addicted. This addiction is killing me. It is destroying my life," and so on.

I have been familiar with the WFS steps since the early 1980s. At one point, when my use of caffeine was leading to depression and arthritis and I felt upset over my seeming inability to give it up, I attended a WFS meeting for support. I talked to a member before I went because I was afraid my caffeine addiction would not be taken seriously. She assured me I would be listened to. Her assurances notwithstanding, I was very relieved when the women took my problem seriously and nodded in recognition when I said coffee/caffeine was a primary comfort, that my obsession was destroying my ability to concentrate, that I was having numerous physical symptoms, and yet I hadn't been able to stop. I enjoyed the feeling among the women. This was *their* program. It had a different feeling from the AA groups I had attended as part of my training in alcoholism counseling. People seemed open, with differences of opinion. I have since heard this from other women who have attended WFS.

One member summed up the differences commonly cited by women who go to WFS. "First of all, it's by and for women. It's also free of mystique. Jean Kirkpatrick is not a big guru for people to idolize, so it doesn't foster a groupie mentality. There's no religious quality or rigidity compared to AA, with its all-or-nothing thinking. It's also alright to disagree with the statements. Sometimes a woman will say, 'I hate this statement,' and say why. No one gives her a hard time. There's none of this bullshit about whether you are working your program or not. And there's acceptance of people who also attend AA, get therapy, and use other means for recovery. I've found lots of support and wonderful people in WFS. It feels like a mature group where people do things the way they want."

My hat is off to Jean Kirkpatrick for pioneering this program for women at a time when AA was totally dominating the field. Kirkpatrick understands the need for women to have groups of their own that stress choices, the positive power of the mind, imaging, broadening one's perspective, the ability to love, and physical healing. Her approach to self-empowerment through monitoring one's thoughts is well documented in psychological research on cognitive therapy with depression. It makes sense: If you repeatedly say you are worthwhile, lovable, and have the power to take charge of your life, you will feel better and stronger than if you say you are a hopeless, stupid jerk all day.

I like steps seven and ten, "Love can change the course of my world" and "All love given returns," because they feel deeply true to me and are comforting thoughts. (Love is never mentioned in the twelve steps.) They imply a process.

I also resonate with step thirteen, particularly with the old version, "I am responsible for myself and my sisters." It suggests a bondedness and responsibility that reaches beyond addiction to all women. The new statement, "I am responsible for myself and my actions," is good but less appealing to me because it loses the sense of connectedness to others.

Step eight, "The fundamental object of life is emotional and spiritual growth," certainly meshes with my worldview, although it raises the same question I have about AA, namely, Is spiritual growth a necessary criterion for achieving sobriety?

Conflicted Responses to the WFS Thirteen Steps

While I like some of the statements, I have mixed feelings about others, along with their descriptions in the program booklet. Because the statements are not as central to Kirkpatrick's program as the twelve steps are to AA—at least, people don't take them as dogma—it is less important whether someone likes them or not. So my reflections are simply my personal reactions. I believe her excellent intentions, as described in *Turnabout*, don't come across clearly in some statements or the program literature.

As I read through the steps and the program literature, I often feel a defiance welling up in me, as if I'm being told how to be, how to feel, and how to think. In an insidious way, it feels artificial—like saying I should put on a "smiley face," be enthusiastic, and have a great life.

Coming from a middle-class family where everyone faked smiles and happiness, and where unspoken tensions were played out in nervous stomachs, headaches, and depression, I rebel at being told to say "Happiness is a habit I will develop" or "Enthusiasm is my daily exercise." I want full permission to feel upset, down, angry, depressed, lousy, negative, or rebellious.

There is also a paradox in being told to say, "I'm a competent woman and have much to give others." On the one hand, it is meant to build up ego strength, but on the other, it is an external directive, a recipe for what one *should* say. Erica, a woman from a working-class background who was uncovering from drug and alcohol addiction, went to a WFS meeting and had a similar reaction to mine. "It seems so middle class and was mostly focused on alcohol. When all these women went around the room saying 'I am a competent woman,' I simply couldn't relate. Saying I felt competent felt phony and completely turned me off. I felt lousy and needed someone to understand how rotten I felt."

Another step I have difficulty with is, "Negative emotions destroy only myself." I don't understand what Kirkpatrick means by negative emotions, but I know I have worked with survivors of abuse who often want to get rid of "negative emotions" such as anger and grief, when they really need to *feel* these feelings. I spoke with Kirkpatrick about this. She said the intention is to not *think* negatively about oneself and put oneself down. But because her literature talks about negative *emotions*, not negative *thoughts*, her intent is confusing.

Another step, "Problems bother me only to the degree I permit them to," and its description in the program literature is also troublesome: "The value of this statement is in learning that we can control our reactions, that *we needn't react at all*. We permit ourselves to be bothered by people, things, events, action. If we are upset, if we are depressed, if we are sad, if we are lonely, if we are angry, it is because *we permit ourselves* to feel these emotions. And to react to them" (emphasis mine).

I have a strong reaction to this statement, which implies a blame-the-victim stance. I understand the concept of detachment—we try not to allow our self-esteem to be jerked around by outside events. Yet, I constantly work to help women imprisoned by messages that they *should* appear cool and unaffected amid pandemonium, abuse, and betrayal learn that it's healthy and normal to get angry and upset in response to victimization. The implication that a woman is upset because she *permits herself to be* is an invitation to guilt and shame. "I'm angry, and upset, I've failed again by *permitting* this to happen."

If we think of life-loving/creative spirituality and our chakra model, the hope is to open the energy and let it flow, to feel and to be alive. For people who have bottled up their energy and feelings, I encourage expression of *all* emotions, even if they are sometimes "over-reactions" or inappropriate. The first step is simply to feel, to immerse oneself in the truth of the moment rather than creating a duality by implying one should be different.

Other steps that trouble me include, "Life can be ordinary or it can be great," which implies life *should* be great, and if it isn't I haven't done it right. This kind of statement can be overwhelming for poor or depressed women. When I was massively depressed, contemplating divorce, wondering what to do with my life, and wishing the world would crack open and swallow me up, *ordinary* sounded wonderful to me. "Great" was too far off to consider.

As a therapist working with childhood abuse, I also have trouble with the step that says "The past is gone forever." I believe we are a hologram, with our past and present intertwined. Abuse survivors regularly shame themselves for "still having feelings about the past." In the program booklet, Kirkpatrick writes, "Life is centered in the now, in the present moment. We keep the past only if we perpetuate it, keep recalling it, keep reacting to it." She concedes, "Of course, there will be times when we must extract from our past so that we might learn from it. There will be times when we must examine our emotions of anger and guilt *so that they can be dismissed*" (emphasis mine). There is a judgmental implication in saying we should dismiss emotions. It's up to everyone to choose. I have a hard time with any implication that women should totally dismiss their anger. Anger is a survival response to the victimization most women are struggling to feel.

While I understand that these statements are intended to encourage positive self-affirmations, they include a lot of implied "shoulds" that can lead people into the trap of thinking they aren't doing it right, that they need fixing. What's missing are affirmations that say I can love myself this minute, just the way I am—imperfect. I don't have to be enthusiastic, happy, or have the past behind me. For me, transformation starts by accepting our imperfect selves in the present moment.

When I interviewed Jean Kirkpatrick and told her my reactions, she said there was no intent to have people smother their emotions. She said the steps evolved from observing the thoughts that had helped her feel good enough about herself to quit drinking.

I raised my concerns about these statements to women in the WFS program. Some replied, "Well, that's not what is *meant*." "But," I respond, *"that is what is written."* If I am going to show these statements to clients and friends, that is what they will see.

In spite of my differences regarding some of her steps, I have great admiration for Jean Kirkpatrick. She followed her beliefs, pioneered a program that helped her and other women stay sober and, most important, presented a choice. Her books, *Turnabout: New Help for the Woman Alcoholic* and *Goodbye Hangovers, Hello Life,* are inspiring, and I encourage women and men to read them.

SECULAR ORGANIZATION FOR SOBRIETY/ SAVE OUR SELVES (SOS)

> *"Our bond is a human one, natural but not supernatural. . . . We value free thought over mind control and over mindlessness. But most of all, we celebrate and support all alcoholics in achieving and maintaining sobriety, regardless of their belief or nonbelief."*
> —JAMES CHRISTOPHER, HOW TO STAY SOBER:
> RECOVERY WITHOUT RELIGION

I was faced with a pleasant paradox when I interviewed James Christopher and read his books, *How to Stay Sober: Recovery Without Religion* and *Unhooked: Staying Sober and Drug Free.* While secular sobriety is not intended as a spiritual approach, Christopher's flexibility, care, acceptance, and concern for others shines through his writing, imparting a profound sense of love. His approach fits into levels four and five of faithing because people are encouraged to think for themselves, have their own set of values, and to run their groups as they like, using a few simple guidelines.

Drawing from a long history of struggles with alcoholism, recovery programs, therapy, and AA groups where he once was told to "shut up" about his freethinking ideas, Christopher has evolved his own personal approach to recovery/discovery, which he offers but does not impose on others. The origins of the program stem from his article "Sobriety Without Superstition," which appeared in the summer 1985 issue of *Free Inquiry* magazine. There was a strong, positive response, which led to the first SOS meeting in November of 1986. By 1988, there were over a hundred groups, and since the 1989 publication of his first book, the international membership has grown to twenty thousand. Half of the membership is women, which Christopher attributes to the empowerment approach and the focus on building self-esteem. The groups are open to people with all types of addiction and dependency problems as well as their families and friends.

The core of Christopher's approach to abstinence is his "sobriety priority" statement: *"I don't drink, no matter what."* He separates sobriety from all other problems and believes one always has a choice. Thus he takes the stance, "Even if I'm tired, upset, abandoned, or going crazy, I don't drink *no matter what*. If I go crazy, I will go crazy sober."

From Christopher's observations and research into what keeps alcoholics sober, he has reached the following conclusion: "Alcoholics who practice daily and adhere to their individual sobriety priority *no matter what* stay sober for the long term; the others simply do not, whether or not they believe in God." This coincides with my observations over the years. When I ask people what they say to themselves to keep from using again, I hear statements such as, "If I use, it will kill me . . . I don't ever want to go through withdrawal again. It's not worth it." Essentially, these are sobriety priority statements. This is in sharp contrast to AA's suggestion that one will surely drink if they build up resentments, get tired, and so on.

In relation to our old survivor, new survivor approach, Christopher's "I don't drink no matter what" is a sharp, clear, resounding statement that mobilizes the new survivor to take charge. Thus, when the old survivor, the addicted part, starts conning the person to drink, there is an immediate, clear response: "I don't drink no matter what." Christopher sees a cycle, as follows: 1. A person has a chemical need. 2. They develop a learned habit. 3. Recovery involves denial of both need and habit, which is replaced with the cycle of sobriety. 4. The person uses daily acknowledgment of the addiction and affirmation of the sobriety priority.

Christopher concurs with research that shows alcoholism to be a physical disease. He believes emphatically that the 10 percent of us whose body chemistry cannot tolerate alcohol must have complete abstinence, making sobriety the number one priority in their lives. Because it is a physical disease, he sees people with this disease as neither morally superior nor inferior to people without the disease, just as people with diabetes or cancer are not morally inferior or superior. Christopher says that character defects do not cause alcoholism, and therefore are not directly related to recovery. Rather, he believes that people often require medical treatment initially in sobriety, and then must adhere to their sobriety priority, which they can do, character defects and all.

In line with this, Christopher challenges the AA term "quality sobriety." As he says, you can be sober with ugly thoughts in your mind. You can be a sober couch potato. Sobriety means you don't drink or use. He argues that while personal growth is nice, sobriety is sobriety. There is not good quality or bad quality sobriety. There is sobriety, and it is always good, the first priority. You may white knuckle life sometimes, but that is separate from sobriety, which means not using alcohol (or drugs)—no more, no less.

In accordance with his dislike of indoctrination, Christopher does not like the idea of sponsors. He believes that too often older members of the group inculcate the group practices into new members, who may be extremely vulnerable to any teachings when they are so desperate for sobriety. In *How to Stay Sober*, he discusses his experiences with sponsors, and concludes by saying, "In sobriety I think we'd do well to avoid sponsorship, approaching each other as equals, walking side by side."

Christopher has a strong reaction to AA, which he attended at one time. He did not feel accepted in AA because he saw himself as a freethinker and nontheist. Thus he was left to maintain sobriety on his own for many years, which he did with his sobriety priority. While he considers sobriety a lifelong priority, he does not believe sobriety requires AA's "intimidation into mindlessness," nor that one needs to attend meetings forever.

"If one is now sober and staying sober, one need not pay heed to religious or secular priests—the purveyors of a how-we-should feel, what-we-should-think, how-we-should-behave mentality. . . . Being wrapped in the swaddling clothes of cult care can be comforting as long as one doesn't stray from the 'protection' of the AA party line."

Christopher speaks of powerful peer pressure to maintain AA's collective concepts and the rejection faced by those who challenge the groups. He speaks of his early days of sobriety in AA, where he was afraid to voice his concerns because his sobriety was of critical importance, and he believes that many others do the same. Consequently, he believes in support groups when they offer "support without dogma."

Also, in reference to twelve-step philosophy, Christopher encourages people to use their logical, creative minds, learning to depend on themselves and others rather than a Higher Power.

"To accept the concept of utilizing a substitute addiction—reliance upon a mystical power greater than oneself—put forth in the programs of Alcoholics Anonymous . . . is at worst to involve oneself in an oppressive cultist atmosphere. At best, it is to encourage dependence upon something or someone other than oneself for sobriety, rendering sobriety conditional."

Christopher also differs from AA in terms of believing that reaching out and helping others is a requisite for sobriety. He sees it as a choice. He values compassion and care for other alcoholics.

In contrast with AA groups' following twelve exact steps, SOS groups vary. Some use a secularized version of the twelve steps and others do not. Some have blended them with their own ideas. Some groups use these six suggested *guidelines*, as described in *How to Stay Sober*:

1. To break the cycle of denial and achieve sobriety, we first acknowledge that *we are alcoholics*.
2. We *reaffirm* this truth daily and accept without reservation—one day at a time—the fact that as sober alcoholics, we cannot and do not drink, *no matter what*.
3. Since drinking is not an option for us, we take whatever steps are necessary to continue our sobriety priority lifelong.
4. A high quality of life—the good life—can be achieved. However, life is also filled with uncertainties; therefore, we do not drink regardless of feelings, circumstances, or conflicts.
5. We share in confidence with each other our thoughts and feelings as sober alcoholics.
6. Sobriety is our priority and we are each individually responsible for our lives and our sobriety.

Again, relating his approach to our old survivor-new survivor model, Christopher describes his process of weakening his association between alcohol and various situations by eventually learning to go with trusted, sober friends to bars and parties and being able to have a good time staying sober. His description is essentially that of systematic desensitization. Thus his approach is based on a belief that people can change their habits. He believes that the "Pavlovian pull to drink fades with time."

A Secular Sobriety Meeting

In *How to Stay Sober*, Christopher describes a typical AA meeting, and then talks about SOS gatherings. One suggested opening for a meeting:

Hello everyone, and welcome. We are an autonomous, grass roots gathering of sober alcoholics and friends and families of alcoholics. The primary purpose of our group is to support individuals who wish to achieve and maintain sobriety. We define sobriety as abstinence from alcohol and drugs. We also strive to grow as persons, to experience life on a high, human level, free from mind-altering chemicals. . . . We do not base our sobriety upon the intervention of a mystical or supernatural higher power. We reach out to one another in human love, dealing directly with our human problems. We are not anti–AA; some of our members attend AA meetings, some do not. We celebrate every alcoholic's sobriety.

In a conversation with James Christopher, he expressed surprise and delight in finding that people of all faiths have joined SOS.

"In the beginning it was created as a place for secular people. We now have Christians, Buddhists, New Agers, lots of women who often say that AA is a program of learned helplessness. People who are religious have told us things like, 'I already have a religion, I don't need another.' 'I want a separation of church and recovery.' 'God helps those who help themselves.' These meetings are virtually free of judgmentalism. People tend to respect each other, because no one is wagging a finger and saying you should do it my way."

I mentioned my concern that there were few references to drug abuse along with alcoholism. He said that people with all forms of chemical use have been in the program from the outset. I asked him about SOS's attitude toward people having therapy. "We have nothing against therapy—it's a separate issue. We don't offer a quality-of-life program per se—we offer a structure for achieving and maintaining sobriety. You can stay sober if sociopathic. One person called it the AA for grown-ups. You don't use alcohol because your parents didn't love you. You are hooked because you can't process the chemical."

He continued, "We're sort of your free thought forum of recovery. AA is in denial about the fact that they are a religion. Our approach is to keep denial smashed. It's an ongoing thing. Our limbic system has recorded that alcohol equals pleasure. We have the opportunity to put in our conscious mind that alcohol equals pain. We have a journal of recovery where people can log their sobriety priority daily. I see it as freedom from alcohol rather than giving up something. To me it would be like drinking rat poison to use alcohol." Clearly Christopher has a strongly reprogrammed survivor.

I felt a kinship reading Christopher's book and speaking with him in person. His congruence, common sense, clarity, compassion, and humor were refreshing. Though I am not a secularist like Christopher, I favor people's using their minds and thinking for themselves. I don't find spirituality and development of the rational mind to be incompatible. Most of all, I felt I had met a kindred spirit—someone who believes there are many roads on the journey to sobriety.

RATIONAL RECOVERY

A "rational" approach to recovery is explained in the book *Rational Recovery from Alcoholism*, by Jack Trimpey, first published in 1989. He founded Rational Recovery groups in 1986, and by May 1990 there were groups meeting in thirty cities; this grew to 150 cities in 1991. The subtitle, *The Small Book*, sets the tone for Trimpey's rather terse rebuttal to AA's Big Book.

According to Trimpey:

> Rational Recovery (RR) is fast and simple; there are no "higher powers," no moral inventories, and no substitute dependencies or endless meetings to attend. In RR, you will learn that sobriety feels better than addiction right away. And when "the old friend" (the urge to drink) comes around, you'll be ready with a few tricks that will keep you clean and sober.

The model is based on Albert Ellis's rational emotive therapy model, a form of cognitive therapy that has been widely adopted since its introduction in the 1950s. It holds that distorted perceptions are the root of emotional problems; therefore, if you change your thinking, your feelings and behavior will change as a result. Thus if you convince yourself that life is much better without alcohol or drugs, you will be able to stop using.

Trimpey's book is highly critical of AA. In a phone conversation, he said he took this stance because AA thinking is so deeply entrenched in people's minds and he is attempting to jar them loose. Predictably, RR claims that no higher power is necessary for recovery and that there is no need to "admit" that one is "powerless."

In the chapter titled "The Difficulty in Getting Stopped," he writes:

> The philosophy of alcoholism [in AA] holds that alcoholic people cannot control what they put into their mouths, as if their extremities and facial muscles around the mouth are under some strange, alien force that cannot be understood by the common man. It is pure drivel to think that alcoholics are powerless over their addictions. Repeat: drivel, drivel, drivel.
>
> Our so-called powerlessness is learned from other alcoholics, from the media, from professionals who as yet don't know any better, and particularly from Alcoholics Anonymous, the organization which seeks a confession of powerlessness from every American alcoholic. The difficulty in getting stopped stems, in large part, from the extremely popular, irrational,

alcoholic belief that alcoholic people cannot choose to become non-addicted. The truth is that many do it and do it every day.

Trimpey also makes the important connection between AA and the state of our culture/patriarchy/hierarchy. He writes, "As it stands, AA represents America's 'traditional values'—the good, the true, and the beautiful. . . . Taken together [the twelve steps] comprise a philosophy in which one is powerless, submissive to authority, unequipped to function independently, and in endless need of external support and guidance." Along these lines, he also believes AA reinforces guilt because it implies the notion of "variable worth" inherent in patriarchy, that is, that you are morally better if you are not drinking.
He writes:

> If you are still drinking and considering a better life, the time to start feeling good about who you are is now. . . . Better a self-respecting drunk than a guilty one. . . . The idea that you'll have more intrinsic worth sober than drunk is a bigoted, fascist view that holds that members of certain groups are intrinsically less or more deserving than others—a view that has caused more human suffering than any single idea.

From Irrational to Rational Beliefs

Trimpey systematically replaces what he calls irrational AA beliefs with rational beliefs. Some examples:

IRRATIONAL BELIEF: Because I am an alcoholic, I need something or someone stronger or greater than myself upon which to rely.

RATIONAL IDEA: Dependency is my original problem, and it is better to start now to take the risks of thinking and acting independently. I cannot really be an "alcoholic," but just a person who has believed some of the central ideas of alcoholism.

IRRATIONAL BELIEF: Somewhere out there, there is a perfect solution for life's problems, and until I find it, I am doomed to a life of uncertainty and turmoil.

RATIONAL IDEA: Uncertainty is the spice of life, and seeking a perfect solution is silly and a waste of time. I will do better to view life as an enjoyable experiment, seeking my own pleasures and cultivating my own personal growth.

The Beast Within

The concept of a BEAST within that tries to con you into addictive behavior is core to the RR approach. It is used as a device to counteract the urge to drink/use once you have made the decision that alcohol/drugs are bad for you. Here's how it works.

Boozing opportunity: Any time when you consider drinking or taking drugs.

Enemy recognition: Any positive thoughts about using addictive substances—the beast at work!

Accuse the beast of malice: Use any creative means to actively and assertively respond to the beast. For example, "I hear you, Beast, and I know what you're up to. You want me to drink. Suffer, plead, beg all you want, Beast, but you'll not get a drop." Remind yourself the beast does not have your best interest at heart.

Self-control and self-worth reminders: You remind yourself that you stay sober not because it reflects your moral worth— you're worthwhile because you are alive—but because it enables you to feel better, be happier, and live a more fulfilling life.

Treasure your sobriety: Remind yourself that life's pleasures are only available with consistent sobriety.

His BEAST concept is similar to what I have been calling the old survivor—the part of us who discovered pleasure or relief from pain through addictive substances or behavior. His approach is to think of this part as an "ego alien" source which does not have your best interest at heart.

This concept gives people a clear-cut technique to control their impulses, much the same as the statement "I don't drink no matter what" serves as a sharp reminder to stay on the side of sobriety.

I admire his clear, sharp way of setting out ideas for people to use. But while I agree with the concept of recognizing the addicted side at work and having a handy rebuttal, I feel uncomfortable calling part of myself a beast. It feels dualistic—good me/bad me. I prefer the notion of old survivor and the new survivor. The old survivor isn't bad, it's just a misprogrammed way of surviving. So we form a new survivor who talks back to the old survivor: "I know you want drink/food/drugs right now. That's how you survived and comforted yourself for many years. You're not bad for having done that, but it's not working any more. We now survive by *not* using that stuff and trying to have friends and a worthwhile life." This way there is no duality, and eventually the old survivor (the child) merges with the new survivor (the intelligent adult) into an integrated whole.

Slips

Trimpey considers slips nothing more than a loss of vigilance over the inner beast who wants to drink. He believes that one should not get overly upset about a slip, but just get back to reinforcing that one must not drink. In my own experience of working with people having slips, I agree that one should not beat oneself up as a result. I also believe that stressing sobriety is extremely important because once one grants oneself permission to use "just this once," it can take a lot of effort to get the barrier to drinking or using back up. It is like losing trust in oneself, and it takes time to regain it.

What I find missing is consideration of what might be underlying a slip or a sudden impulse to use. Often it is more than the mind losing its vigilance. For some people, that self-destructive voice is tied to feelings emerging about childhood abuse, feelings that need to be addressed. I have repeatedly seen survivors of childhood abuse get close to talking about their memories and then distract themselves by getting obsessed about drinking or using. Often, if they push through their fears and start to talk and get through some of the feelings, the desire to abuse chemicals fades. In other cases, when people have cravings, it can be the body needing physical attention to get into better balance.

Overall, *Rational Recovery* sparkles with "I can do it" thoughts that are empowering for the reader and people in recovery. When I first read it, I had just waded through enormous amounts of approved twelve-step literature that was often ponderous and serious, so it was extremely refreshing to laugh a lot while reading about "recovery."

My reservation about this model is that the approach sometimes seems cut-and-dried. Sometimes, after laughing, I would agree with him and then start thinking, "Yes, but, but. . . ." For example, Trimpey contends that, although withdrawal is uncomfortable, if you say you can *stand* the discomfort, you can get through it. While this might be true for some people, it oversimplifies the fact that physical withdrawal symptoms such as hallucinations, heart palpitations, and delirium tremens are simply overwhelming for most people in the later stages of alcoholism who need a hospital setting in order to have physical attention. Trimpey's response to my statement was, "But that's just your mind telling you it is overwhelming." I felt he was leaving no room for people who feel powerless, and that anything could be solved quickly by the use of the mind.

He writes, " 'I'm powerless?' To whose brain are my arms and legs and facial muscles connected? My neighbor's? Who was it who went to the refrigerator and opened that last beer? Hannibal? Who stocked the refrigerator in the first place? Santa? Could *I* possibly have been the one who chose to wrap my lips around the edge of the beer can and guzzle its contents? Am I really out of control, or is that just what I like to think before drinking some more?"

I appreciate Trimpey's much-needed addition of humor to the sometimes somber addiction field. But while the intention is to reinforce that one can make choices, it also leaves me thinking, "Gee, if I fail it's because I didn't think good enough."

James Milam says about the role of the mind in overcoming addiction that when the cells are starving for alcohol (or drugs), there's little mind left to think with. The cravings feel so overwhelming that even well-intentioned people are unable to stick to rational thinking. I concur with Milam, and believe that, while the rational mind is a major component in sobriety, addressing physical help for physical needs and having support from other people can also be crucial.

Though Rational Recovery says it is not a spiritual program, beneath some of its pungent sarcasm is a concern for the welfare of all people. Trimpey's writing fits with my concept of spirituality, that is, believing one is a worthwhile person by virtue of being alive, living in harmony with one's inner wisdom, and accepting the fallibility of humanness and the unfairness of life.

Finally, Rational Recovery promotes the idea that recovery need not be a heavy, drawn-out, life-consuming experience. "We encourage people to kick the Recovery Habit. Our motto is, 'Don't keep coming back.' " Rational Recovery feels that if anyone is in an RR group for more than a year, it is time to sit down and re-evaluate what is going on.

I have a mixed response to this last statement. While it is good to encourage people to move beyond group dependency, Trimpey is not leaving room for people to make their own choices about leaving. To imply everyone should be ready to leave in a year is too pat. People with hard-core alcohol and drug addictions, lack of bonding, and need to develop trust may need support groups for much longer before they feel ready to go it alone. It is important to have the choice. The part of his idea I like a lot is that if a person is still white knuckling sobriety after a year of attending meetings, it is probably advisable to consider other sources for the pain—the physical effects of alcoholism, childhood abuse, or depression, for example.

Trimpey makes no pretense of being able to solve the problems of the world. He presents an approach meant to reach people who do not relate well to AA, to help train their minds to keep them free from chemicals. To this extent, the Rational Recovery approach is simple, honest, and unpretentious, and provides an alternative program with many valuable concepts. It is also positive in that you learn to stay sober not out of fear, but by remembering the positive pay-offs.

SCHICK SHADEL AND COUNTER-CONDITIONING/AVERSION THERAPY

"There are two ways to stop the craving reflex for alcohol; accidental aversion called 'hitting bottom' which is dangerous and may take many years to occur or safe medically planned aversion pioneered by Shadel" (Dr. O'Hollaren, in the introduction to *Addiction: Who Is in Control?* by P. Joseph Frawley, M.D.).

While this is not a model for a support group, Schick Shadel is a treatment program that has been successfully treating alcoholism and drug abuse since 1935. It is based on synchronizing the use of alcohol or drugs with an immediate unpleasant experience, rather than long delayed consequences. This concept is called counter-conditioning or aversion therapy and is designed to break a person's positive emotional memories with alcohol and drugs, and replace them with aversive feelings, and at the same time reinforce a positive attitude toward life.

This model presents a deep understanding of the physical nature of addiction and programming in the unconscious survivor. Thus it is totally nonshaming, because it views the origins of addiction as a desire for pleasure or as a survival response, just as I have described throughout this book. In his introduction, Patrick J. Frawley, father of P. Joseph Frawley, M.D., writes, "The most baffling problem in personal behavior is the gap between knowing and doing." Aversion therapy addresses this gap in a very direct, simple way.

While aversion therapy is not currently in vogue, Schick Shadel has had an impressive 70 percent success rate with thousands of people. Thus it needs to be recognized as a viable alternative. There are currently three Schick Shadel treatment programs, located in Seattle, Washington; Santa Barbara, California; and Fort Worth, Texas.

I called Dr. Frawley, who is chief of staff at Schick Shadel Hospital of Santa Barbara and he sent me his book *Addiction: Who Is in Control?*, which clearly and simply explains how addiction is programmed into the unconscious memory. It has a positive tone and gives clear steps to follow in the process of stopping the addictive process. "Repetition, precise timing and mild discomfort only when directly in contact with the addictive chemical are the three effective elements of counter-conditioning."

The last page of the book reads, "All addictive drugs suppress a person's natural body chemistry and, by replacement, train the subconscious survival mechanism to feel a need for the drug. Recovery involves regaining confidence in our natural chemistry and reprogramming the subconscious memory with new reactions. The goal of the treatment program is to reprogram the subconscious that *the drug doesn't work but life does*" (emphasis mine).

The book can be ordered through Schick Shadel at 45 East Alamar, Santa Barbara, CA 93105. I would recommend it for people interested in a deeper understanding of the brain's important role in addiction and those who might be interested in this form of treatment to reprogram the memory.

Frawley also sent me a fascinating, easy-to-understand article, "Neuro-Behavioral Model of Addiction," from *The Journal of Drug Issues* (vol. 17, nos. 1 and 2, Winter/Spring 1987), and gave generously of his time to help me understand this form of treatment. While I initially was skeptical about the idea of aversion therapy, it didn't take long for me to realize that the concept closely paralleled the old survivor-new survivor concept, which is actually a form of counter-conditioning on the verbal level.

With aversion therapy, you go beyond words to give a person an immediate, negative emotional experience associated with their drug of choice. It includes smell, taste, and feeling sick. The person is given the drink and told to smell, taste, and drink it, and is then given a medication called emetive which acts on the stomach to cause a person to throw up. This sends an immediate message to the brain which helps to break the memory hold between alcohol and pleasure. Now, instead of "alcohol equals pleasure," the brain gets the message that the smell and taste of alcohol equals being sick. Schick Shadel has also done considerable work to create substances that smell and taste like hard drugs so people can counter-condition themselves against the pull toward these substances.

Through repetition—five treatments over a ten-day period—this negative association with alcohol or drugs creates a barrier to the old, positive associations. Because the other aspect of counter-conditioning is to make a positive association with life, other support groups described in this chapter also work well in conjunction with this model.

I asked Frawley for his views on twelve-step and other support groups. He said in a study at Schick Shadel that support groups did help people maintain sobriety, but they found no differences among types of support, such as AA, church groups, or other support systems. "The main thing," he said, "was that people find the kind of support that feels right for them."

To some, aversion therapy might sound quite awful, but talking to Frawley, with his relaxed, warm style, gave me a different feeling. "You just feel sick a few times," he said casually, "but through the *experience* of counter-conditioning, you are taking away the underlying memory that creates the desire to drink or use drugs."

Patrtick J. Frawley, the father of Joseph Frawley, writing in the introduction to *Addiction: Who Is in Control?*, describes his experience of trying to stop drinking for years. To paraphrase his words: He had heard that people drank excessively because of character defects. But because he was very industrious and tried to be scrupulously fair with everyone, he didn't think he was in any danger of becoming an alcoholic. Yet for many years he couldn't stop drinking, until someone referred him to Shadel in Seattle, where he lost all desire to drink after five counter-conditioning treatments over a ten-day period.

He writes of the incredible relief he felt after his unconscious mind was reprogrammed. "I easily refused drinks with a blessed, instinctive feeling, the same way I refused turnips, which I disliked all my life."

With this method you go beyond white-knuckling sobriety, because the old survivor no longer associates pleasure with alcohol. And it's the old survivor who embodies the cunning and baffling addicted part that can be so overwhelming. According to Frawley, the optimum results come when people finish the treatment program, come for their reinforcement visits, and get support. They also stress the importance of adopting a healthy life-style and being around people who give positive affirmation of worth to help rebuild self-esteem. This helps create a love for life that counter-conditions people against wanting to self-destruct with drugs and alcohol.

CLOSING THOUGHTS

I ponder the paradoxes of these approaches in relationship to spirituality and our levels of faithing. It feels as if it's all turned around. While AA claims to be a spiritual program, it fits with levels two and three of faithing, operating from an external locus of control, often becoming rigid and dogmatic. SOS and Rational Recovery, which claim to be secular, correspond more to levels four and five of faithing, because they teach people to think for themselves, honor differences, and support people's creating the steps that work for them. So, for me, SOS and RR have a spiritual component, while AA is more a religious program based on sin and redemption. AA parallels the patriarchal switch in our culture that values loyalty and obedience and views autonomy and maturity with fear and skepticism.

In the addiction field, you are acceptable if you give rote loyalty to AA and ask no questions. You are a troublemaker or radical if you support people thinking for themselves, being creative in the process, and trusting that they have the power to make choices for themselves. One is also considered a radical for making connections between body, mind, and spirit, because we are supposed to see them as separate entities, understood by experts. My hope is that we make a "patriarchal switch back" and support choice, questioning, creativity, and differences.

8

The Physical Connection

"A physical substance in a physical body has a physical effect."

—JOAN MATTHEWS LARSON,
HEALTH RECOVERY CENTER

This statement sounds simple, but it is a fact largely ignored in the addiction field. Our emotional and mental states are greatly influenced by the substances we put in our bodies, thus uncovery from addiction is often eased and facilitated by bringing the physical body into balance. Our bodies are an amazing ecological system, and when our physical self is malfunctioning it can affect our spiritual and psychological resilience.

There are vast variations in the physiological makeup of different individuals. Thus there is no one diet, one kind of vitamin, or one approach for everyone. Because our culture operates on the second and third levels of faithing, nutrition is taught from an authoritarian stance—you should eat such and such types of food so many times a day. To heal and bring the physical body into balance, people need to move to levels four and five of faithing, where they ultimately rely on their greatest source of wisdom—their own body. I cannot underscore this enough. While we can seek advice and read many helpful books, no doctor, nutrition book, or expert can tell you how your body feels. You are the expert on that subject and ultimately the decision about what you ingest into your body rests with you.

EFFECTS OF PATRIARCHY ON BODY ECOLOGY

We have talked about patriarchy compartmentalizing groups of people, thus creating alienation and separation. This external alienation is reflected in an internal separation that leaves people feeling out of touch with their physical bodies, unaware of the direct effects they experience from ingesting physical substances. Thus people consume sugar, caffeine, nicotine, refined foods, and thousands of unnatural additives and don't realize this can be directly related to lethargy, depression, lack of clear thinking, violent outbursts, feeling weepy, the inability to learn, memory problems, stomach aches, yeast infections, and so on.

The patriarchal tendency to compartmentalize has also led to nutrition being seen as quantitative. People are told to get x amount of nutrients in any form rather than thinking about foods having different effects in combination with each other. For example, beans eaten alone have a different effect than beans eaten with rice, because together they form a perfect protein. We are not taught to be aware of how our digestive system works and how to combine foods to make digestion easier for the body, thus conserving our energy. For example, the digestive system has difficulty digesting starch and protein at the same time. Thus digesting vegetables and pasta takes much less energy than digesting meat and pasta combined, which is why people get tired after a meat-and-potatoes type meal. Getting vitamin A from a carrot is different from getting it from a vitamin pill.

Another reason people have learned to ignore their physical bodies is because we aren't taught a model of health that includes feeling alert, clear, centered, and having abundant energy. We are only taught that health is an absence of pathology or a specific illness. So people drag around, listless and tired, thinking it is "normal." We are taught to relate to our bodies the way patriarchy relates to the earth: we use stimulants to get more work from our bodies than they have to give us naturally; we use chemical fertilizers to get more food from the earth than it would produce naturally, or we feed estrogen hormones to cattle so they will grow faster and produce more milk; at a personal level, we expend more energy than we replenish through rest, relaxation, and healthy food, and culturally we use replaceable resources such as wood faster than they can be regenerated. We also rip from the earth what can never be replaced, such as the rain forests, destroying the natural ecology in the process. We do the same with our bodies when we expect them to digest and assimilate unnatural foods and substances that harm the immune and digestive systems.

Increasingly, our culture colludes in the degeneration of our amazing physical bodies by normalizing feeling tired, having headaches, being stressed out and lacking vitality. The messages we constantly get are: Tired? Drink caffeine; Have a headache? Take an aspirin; Yeast infection? Take a pill; and Overweight? Starve, rather than eat a balanced, natural diet that helps reduce cravings. What we need instead is: Tired? Rest, do deep-breathing exercises, or take a walk; Have a headache? Get someone to massage it, check out if you are angry, or get some exercise; Yeast infection? Stop eating sugar and refined carbohydrates and get checked out for candidiasis.

Another source of people's ignoring the connection between substances and emotional states rests with counselors, psychologists, and medical doctors who frequently assume symptoms like fatigue and inability to concentrate are psychological problems. Paradoxically, while the psychiatric community does recognize that depression and other emotional problems are related to brain chemistry, they often prescribe highly potent substances for them that further throw the body out of balance, instead of exploring all the natural ways to bring body, mind, and spirit into balance. As a therapist I have worked with numerous women suffering from depression who have been able to go off medication through diet, exercise, bonding with others, expressing feelings (anger in particular), and developing a sense of power over their lives.

TIME FOR SOME NEW APPROACHES

As discussed earlier, uncovery rates from alcoholism and drug abuse are dismal. According to James Christopher in How to Stay Sober, only about "five percent of this nation's ten-to-fifteen million problem drinkers are helped by AA." Fewer than half the people who attend treatment programs maintain sobriety, and for drug abuse it is far lower. Stanton Peele, in Diseasing of America, quotes a 1982 study in New York showing that at least 90 percent of heroin addicts return to using soon after treatment.

Thus it seems obvious that it's time to uncover and discover some new paths in this journey toward wholeness. My hope in the coming years is that drug, alcohol, and eating disorder programs will include a strong focus on helping people understand the body as a system and the effects of natural and unnatural foods and substances. I'm not suggesting that all emotional problems are solely about body chemistry imbalance. What I am saying is that there is often a physical component to relapse, depression, mood swings, violent outbursts, fatigue, and other physical symptoms that can be altered with natural healing.

While understanding nutrition and body ecology are not stressed in most approaches to recovery/uncovery (WFS being the only major exception), many people are discovering on their own the importance of physical health. In response to my questionnaire, over three-fourths of the women said that "help with nutrition" was a part of their recovery; about half said it was an important or very important part, and one out of four said that awareness of allergies was important. This suggests that these women were making important links between good health and sobriety. I am hoping there will be more research on the effects of caring for the physical body and maintaining sobriety from all forms of addiction.

ADDICTIVE FOODS: STARTING YOUNG

In this country, heavy, fatty foods, sweets, highly processed grains, caffeine, and nicotine have become a way of life for many (particularly teenagers). Increasingly, we see little children being given cola drinks, sugar, and highly processed foods on a routine basis. With the current concern with children's learning problems, lack of ability to read, and increased hyperactivity I find it amazing that we don't look more at what kids eat. I know if I drink Coke and eat red meat, fries, and hot fudge sundaes, I don't feel well and my mind feels foggy. This is relevant to our discussion of addiction because early addictions to caffeine and sugar affect young people immensely. They have difficulty concentrating, they weaken their immune systems, and they don't feel good. This lowers self-esteem and the ability to succeed, which is part of the set-up for addiction or addictive behavior.

One addiction becoming more prevalent with young children and teenagers is caffeine, a drug that can be highly addictive and damaging. I remember taking a group of teenagers on a weekend trip to a church retreat. When two of them who seemed especially restless pressed me to stop at a gas station, I obliged, thinking they needed to go to the bathroom. They rushed to the soft drink machine, and as soon as they slugged down the first few gulps of cola, they appeared to be more relaxed. I felt like I was watching a couple of junkies. In chemical dependency jargon, gulping down that first drink or bite of food is called "hurried ingestion," and it alleviates acute symptoms of withdrawal.

At the camp, there were no soft drinks available, and the two "addicted" children were listless, restless, had difficulty participating in the weekend activities. They kept asking, "When are we leaving?" On the road home, not surprisingly, the first question was, "When are we stopping for gas?" With the first cola drink they perked up again, and both bought a second to have with them—in other words, like addicted people, they made sure they had a stash. They had missed out on all the weekend activities that could have enriched their lives due to their caffeine addiction. Sadly, I have seen children as young as three or four addicted to caffeine in soft drinks.

PHYSICAL CHEMISTRY AND PSYCHOLOGICAL RESILIENCE

Another important aspect for people to discover is that one's physical state is strongly connected to one's psychological resilience. In other words, how you feel physically affects your moods and your ability to face difficult situations and to get your life in order and face childhood pain. It takes energy and discipline to create a new survivor. It's hard to build a new home when you are exhausted.

An important aspect of psychological resilience that is highly affected by one's physical state is the ability to put past hurts on the shelf. Sometimes, when we are tired or sick, past painful memories rain down on us as if someone opened a Pandora's box and dropped it on our heads. While I support psychotherapy for emotional problems, sometimes people get lost in processing old wounds because they lack psychological resilience. When people balance the physical body, get exercise, start to feel vital and alive, and engage in enjoyable activities, often the sting of past memories seems to fade. It's a matter of balance—of reckoning with the past but not getting lost in it and missing the possibilities of the present.

Depression and suicidal thoughts that sometimes accompany new sobriety or looking at childhood abuse are exacerbated by living in a body that is physically malnourished and unbalanced. This is often related to widely fluctuating blood sugar levels which a person controlled to some extent with alcohol or drugs. When I had a major depression during my marriage, I used to have fantasies of dying so I wouldn't have to wake up to another day of feeling so bad. It wasn't that I wanted to die; I just didn't want to live that way. I am convinced now that while some of my chronic depression in my twenties was due to an unhappy marriage and not having a clear sense of myself, another part was due to lack of any regular exercise, systemic yeast problems from taking antibiotics, caffeine addiction, and eating many foods to which I was allergic or addicted and which kept my blood sugar out of whack, leaving me chronically exhausted and depressed.

CANDIDA ALBICANS, OR SYSTEMIC YEAST IMBALANCE

I include a section on *Candida albicans* because it is such a common syndrome among people uncovering from addiction that is often overlooked. It is more prevalent among women and is often linked to a myriad of emotional and physical problems that go undiagnosed and that can make it difficult to maintain sobriety. After I mentioned *Candida albicans* in an article several years ago, I was amazed at the response. People came to me for therapy because they wanted someone to take seriously their concern about this condition. They had been called hysterical females or hypochondriacs, or were told it was all in their minds, by various medical practitioners. Two references on the subject are William Crook's *The Yeast Connection*, which clearly defines the problem and the kind of diet and supplements that are helpful, and Orion Truss's *The Missing Diagnosis*, which includes histories of many children terribly affected by this syndrome.

I can attest to the misery this syndrome causes because I've had it. I got it the first time after taking antibiotics and didn't discover what it was for twenty-one years. When it was active, I was overwhelmed by the simplest tasks, tired after nine hours of sleep, had an elevated heart rate of 160 from running a couple of blocks (three miles had previously been easy), and got dizzy going for an overhead in tennis. I also had many symptoms of depression: I started feeling sad, was suspicious of people's motives, and started hating myself if someone slighted me or left me out. My self-esteem plummeted. In addition, I had yeast infections, and outrageous cravings for sugar, chocolate, ice cream, and carbohydrates that wouldn't quit. I went to numerous traditional doctors. Nothing helped.

Then a chiropractor who did applied kinesiology, which can access information about the body systems through muscle testing, said I had *Candida albicans*. That means that the natural yeasts that live in the body have become imbalanced and the yeast called *Candida* is colonizing and spreading, creating toxicity in the system and affecting the digestive system. The imbalance is often set in motion by drug and alcohol abuse, birth control pills, stress, sugar, refined carbohydrates, pregnancy, and antibiotics, which have a profound impact on the body ecology. There are many other symptoms listed on a screening test in the appendix. It feels like there is an inner tyrant demanding sugar and carbohydrates. It feels like an addiction because you get relief by eating these foods, but you feel much worse later.

The good news is that with proper diet, exercise, and natural supplements one can usually control this syndrome. Few doctors know about chronic candidiasis, believe it exists, or are interested in treating it with diet and natural substances. Insurance companies often do not recognize the diagnosis. Doctors still tell me I couldn't have had *Candida*, that it is very rare and I probably had something else or was under stress, but I know from reading *The Yeast Connection* that I had all the symptoms they described. I followed the diet and many of the suggestions for natural supplements they suggested, and I felt incredibly better very soon.

Knowledge of *Candida albicans* is especially important for chemically dependent mothers, past or present, because they pass *Candida albicans* on to their unborn children. These infants have endless problems with thrush, ear infections, and rashes, and can be very fussy, unhappy little babies. When they get ear infections, they are routinely given antibiotics—one of the *causes* of yeast infections and body imbalance—which help for a while, but are usually followed by a more severe recurrence of infection. It is a terrible spiral with devastating effects on children's physical, emotional, and mental well-being. Naturopaths and chiropractors with a knowledge of nutrition are most likely to treat this syndrome.

I have worked with numerous recovering chemically dependent mothers and their children. Because the children either had candida or inherited the low blood sugar of their parent, they craved sugar, carbohydrates, and highly processed foods. I could literally see the child going into withdrawal and begging and screaming for candy and cookies. When this happens, often, the parent, frustrated by the whining and begging, gets mad and shames the child: "Stop begging." But then they often capitulate, saying, "Just one piece of candy (or cookie, etc.)." That's like one drink for the alcoholic. The child then wants more, and the parent, often projecting their own self-hatred for their addiction, further shames the child, who then has a tantrum. The child is going through physical withdrawal that is mistakenly reframed as a behavior problem. It is not unusual for four- and five-year-olds to be hooked on sugar and caffeine.

We are constantly teaching children to make paired learning associations between happiness, celebration, pleasing Mom and being good with sugar and soft drinks. Recently, at a grocery store, I saw a tiny little girl having a fit, grabbing for the candy that lined the check-out aisle. The mother was patient and firm, saying, "No, no candy today." Many of us know the feeling of being just fine until we have to stand for five minutes looking at candy bars waiting in a check-out line. There should be some candy-free aisles to relieve parents of having children constantly seduced by sugar.

A WHOLISTIC APPROACH

Our emotional states are directly related to the chemistry of the brain. The chemistry of the brain is profoundly affected by what we eat. Most people have little trouble understanding that if we put 50- or 60-octane gas in a car and only change the oil every twenty thousand miles, the car won't run very well, if at all.

We don't have to have a degree in nutrition to test the theory that what we eat affects how we feel. Try switching from substances that take your body to extremes, such as red meat, dairy products, fruit juices, sugar, caffeine, salt, oils, and highly processed flours and grains. Then try cutting way back on oil and butter and eating brown rice, beans, whole wheat bread, veggies, squash, fruit, and a little fish. You may go through a period of withdrawal as your body adjusts, although daily exercise can usually reduce the symptoms, but after a month or two, see how you feel emotionally as well as physically. The changes can be subtle or striking. You may want guidance from a natural food nutrition counselor or a book on the subject. Eventually, on a natural diet people start to feel grounded and more relaxed. Often the memory improves along with the ability to concentrate, sleep, and be less reactive to difficult situations.

Changing one's diet often needs to be coupled with a shift in thinking from wanting quick fixes to accepting slow change. We are so habituated to using stimulants when we get tired we forget that good foods, exercise, deep breathing, or a momentary rest will often give us the pick-up we want in a natural way, although it takes longer.

A negative eating cycle gets people on a merry-go-round of feeling tired, depleted, irritable, and fragile, and reaching for quick fixes of sugar, highly processed carbohydrates, caffeine, nicotine, or alcohol to feel better. It works in the short term but not in the long term. The cycle gets entrenched and people end up on a physical and emotional teeter-totter.

RELAPSE AND BODY ECOLOGY: WILL THESE CRAVINGS EVER GO AWAY?

My friend Anne has watched her husband relapse four times into alcohol addiction despite his obvious desire and commitment to stay sober. She says she always knows when it is coming.

"First he starts eating candy, then he has more caffeine, then he starts smoking again, getting irritable and picking on me and the kids. Then he starts sleeping in and missing work and feeling bad about himself, and then he's using again. When he goes back to treatment, all they talk about is shame and character defects and higher-power stuff. I'm not saying that's not important, but I think he needs to change his diet." Anne, who is also chemically dependent, had one relapse and then took steps to change her diet based on *Food for Thought: A New Look at Food and Behavior*, by Saul Miller with Jo Anne Miller.

Kim joined one of my therapy groups to uncover from mother-daughter sexual abuse, substance abuse, sexual addiction, depression, general chaos in her life, and an explosive temper that often exploded at her partner, Jay. The tension would build up, and wham! she'd let him have it, no holds barred. If he tried to walk away she would follow him. After blasting off, she would feel relieved and could function again, although she realized it was harmful to the relationship and left her feeling hopeless about ever changing. She said it was like an addiction.

While we spent time in therapy talking about her childhood and her shame, which was a trigger to her rage outbursts, a huge part of Kim's early recovery was to heal her physically imbalanced body that kept her on emotional edge. She had numerous allergies and *Candida albicans*. Over time, with both psychological and physical healing, she started to feel better and was usually able to control her desire to verbally assault Jay and to feel more hopeful about life.

Then, suddenly she came back to the group, saying she was "losing it" again. She was upset all the time and blasting Jay. On a hunch, I asked, "What have you been eating lately?"

"Ohh," she said with a groan of recognition. "My diet has been out of control—lots of sugar, caffeine, and junk food."

"Tell you what," I said. "Clean up your diet for a week or two, and then we will deal with the other behavior . . . if it's still present."

Some members of the group thought I was mean to dismiss such serious problems and make her wait it out for a while. I told them it might be more physical imbalance affecting the brain than any psychological problem. When our brain is chemically depleted, what should be a small annoyance can suddenly feel like a major catastrophe. I wanted to check that out first.

The next week, Kim came back, looking and feeling better. "I started eating right again, and I only yelled at Jay once, and not for so long." Two weeks later she said she was feeling more hopeful and had even apologized to Jay, curbed her desire to blow up, and felt more affectionate as well. Thus much of the solution was in nurturing her body and correcting her brain chemistry rather than delving into psychological causes. Again, the negative cycle is circular. While childhood abuse and stress probably played a part in leading her to get hooked on a lousy diet, the current problem was about an imbalanced brain that was drastically affecting her emotions.

UNDERSTANDING PHYSICAL CRAVINGS, OR YIN AND YANG

Here is a bare-bones explanation about the principles of ecological stability in the body, or, in other words, how to get beyond all those cravings. The information is taken from *Food for Thought* by Saul Miller with Jo Anne Miller, *Food and Healing* by Anne Marie Colbin (a book I highly recommend), and *The Cancer Prevention Diet*, by Michio Kushi. Additional information comes from Shelly McCoy, my experience with clients, and my own personal struggles with substance and food cravings.

According to Anne Marie Colbin, food cravings are generated by three sources—addiction/allergy, discharge, and imbalance of systems.

Addictive Substances

A food or substance addiction begins when a substance initially makes us feel good but eventually leads us to such feelings of imbalance as tiredness, headaches, cravings, restlessness, fatigue, and skin problems. Paradoxically, the symptoms of withdrawal are temporarily relieved by having more of the same food. It often works on a twenty-four hour cycle. Eat chocolate this afternoon and at just about the same time tomorrow, you might start thinking, "Oh, wouldn't some chocolate taste good now?" Caffeine and sugar withdrawal often happen sooner and escalate over time.

Because the addictive food alleviates the withdrawal symptoms, most people think it is what they need. The opposite is true. Generally, when people say they "just love" some kind of food, or that they have to have it every day, or that "I couldn't live without it," their body is physically addicted. It is hard to give up these substances because it requires the discomfort of physical withdrawal. That's when we need to strengthen our new survivor, because when the cravings become intense, the new survivor loses its control and the old survivor often takes over, thinking only of the pleasure the substance will bring. That's why we're often bewildered about what we've done. "I knew better than to eat that. How could I forget?"

With a *food allergy*, one feels symptoms shortly after ingesting the substance. The unpleasant symptoms could include fatigue, skin irritations, headaches, or a number of others. In the case of allergies, it is best not to consume the food and easier to stay off it because even though it may taste good at the moment, it doesn't give that initial lift.

Discharge can also be the source of cravings. As Colbin explains, "According to the holistically oriented natural-healing schools of thought this is what probably happens: Over the years, you have stored toxins in the intercellular spaces of your body. . . . When you change your diet to a healing mode, it seems that the immune system begins to sweep out those toxins. . . . Before they leave the body, these elements or charges get a free ride through the circulatory system. In the brain they pass by the hypothalamus, which acts like a tape recorder picking up information from the bloodstream as if the latter were a magnetic tape running by. The information the hypothalamus picks up from the residue in the blood activates memories of hamburgers and mother's key lime pie, and cravings for the old familiar food appear as if out of nowhere."

Imbalance. Cravings created by imbalance in the body are related to the concepts of yin and yang, relating to expansive and contractive foods and their acid or alkaline nature.

The underlying concept of yin and yang is that the body is always seeking balance; thus when we go to one extreme—sugar and drugs—we tend to swing to the opposite extreme—red meat and fatty foods. Keeping in mind that the nature of the body is to seek balance, take a look at the following chart.

The expansive alkalizing foods to the extreme left—the yin side—create cravings for the foods at the extreme right, and vice versa. That's why McDonald's type foods sell so well. The heavily contractive, acid-forming red meat and oily french fries create a hunger for sugary desserts, milk shakes, and cola drinks or maybe even a beer when you get home. The body is desperately seeking balance, so it yo-yos between one extreme and the other. If you eat a lot of yang food you will

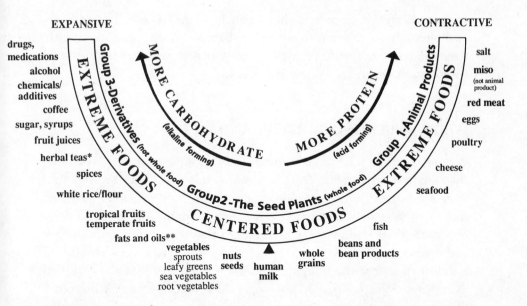

*In general herbal teas vary from yin to yang according to whether they are flower, leaf, seed, or root in that order.
**The effect of oils varies based on whether they are plant or animal derivatives, quality, and method of processing.
Overall, the effect of yin and yang varies based on quality, freshness of food, preparation, cooking time, seasoning, etc.

Adapted from a model by Sol Miller with Jo Anne Miller.   Placement of foods on the scale by Shelley McCoy, certified macrobiotic cook.

Yin-Yang

crave yin food, and, according to Colbin, the cravings are usually so strong as to "demolish all willpower."

If one eats natural foods (Group 2), cravings will eventually abate. It is boring at first because there is no "kick" from those foods. When I started learning macrobiotic cooking and the teacher came to the house to help me cook with a few friends, we called it peaceful food for peaceful bodies. But it's tough when one has used food as a stimulant to fulfill a craving as opposed to a substance that is gently pleasurable and fills a hunger instead of an aching need.

Acid versus alkaline foods. The other part of understanding food's effects on the system is to understand food combining and its effects on the digestive system and energy levels. If you get tired after eating, it is because the digestive system is exhausted by trying to digest alkaline-forming and acid-forming foods at the same time. Essentially, when one eats starch and protein, the digestive system is stressed because they require different digestive juices that tend to neutralize each other. A good resource on this subject is *Fit for Life*, by Harvey and Marilyn

Diamond, and an excellent chapter in *Unlimited Power*, by Anthony Robbins. This is relevant to addiction, because when we are constantly tired we tend to reach for stimulants, which throws the body out of balance and can trigger addictive urges.

WHITE-KNUCKLING SOBRIETY AND DIET

People are often told to go to ninety AA groups in ninety days when they are first sobering up from substance addiction. They are also told they need AA for life. I believe one reason many people need this intense involvement or stay in twelve-step programs for years and years is because their bodies are so unbalanced that their craving for alcohol and drugs is always just around the corner. They are always hanging on for dear life, or white-knuckling sobriety. And many of the so-called "character defects," that is, the anger and resentments AA literature discusses at length, are *augmented* by the effects of chemical imbalances in the brain caused by a poor diet and an imbalanced body.

THE PROTRACTED WITHDRAWAL SYNDROME

In a study entitled Symptomatology in Alcoholics at Various Stages of Abstinency (translation: how recovering alcoholics feel physically and emotionally in the years following sobriety), Clinton B. DeSoto, Ph.D., tracks symptoms of recovering alcoholics over a ten-year period. This study is presented in James Milam's book, *Under the Influence*. DeSoto's scale includes depression, obsessive-compulsive thinking, interpersonal sensitivity, anxiety, psychoticism, paranoid ideation, somatization, phobic anxiety, and hostility. He drew his subjects, both men and women, from AA groups. Results of his study showed that *even after five years of recovery*, people had significantly more difficulty than the general population on numerous dimensions I often see related to self-esteem and the ability to function effectively. The dimensions are:

- Trouble remembering things
- Feeling blocked in getting things done
- Difficulty making decisions
- Mind going blank
- Trouble concentrating

Our emotions can be affected by an incredible number of sub-stances in the brain, including serotonin, zinc, copper, and so on. Many people in recovery, while not pathologically sick, are walking around like someone in extremely depleted shape—kind of like a car with an oil leak, old spark plugs, bald tires, worn-out shock absorbers, and broken door handles. The car may still run some of the time, but it might not get over the mountain, make it through a rain storm, or start on a cold day. That's how many people live. The symptoms of unbalanced brain chemistry are insidious and pervasive, affecting thought, memory, paranoia, aggressiveness, initiative, stamina, energy, optimism, and the ability to be psychologically resilient in difficult situations. People with unbalanced brain chemistry are more likely to flare up, get crabby, be short-tempered, violent and be unable to move through grief or loss.

AUGMENTATION AND PROTRACTED WITHDRAWAL

While we know alcohol has a profound effect on behavior, the pro-tracted withdrawal syndrome is also *related* to violence and abuse because it tends to augment one's feelings. Thus protracted withdrawal is related to abuse, battering, violence, and incest. In many studies with animals—cats, for example—a certain type of stimulation to the brain will elicit purring and friendly behavior while another type will send the cat into an attacking frenzy. This is described in fascinating detail in *The Brain*, a book that accompanied a PBS special series by that name.

Most of us know that when we are under stress we are more likely to lash out at people or be irritable. Protracted withdrawal is like constant stress, weakening the brain's ability to control impulses. Thus something that would be a nuisance, or 10 percent aggravation to a healthy mind and body, becomes a 90 percent blow-up to a chemically unbalanced body. The teenage son takes the car without permission, or the teenage daughter stays out beyond her curfew and comes home with a hickey on her neck. A parent who feels grounded and stable handles the situation in a reasonable way, talking, setting limits, and handing out consequences that are fair and nonshaming. For a parent living on an emotional edge, the event triggers rage that results in screaming, shaming, and beating. Again, I am not saying that brain chemistry is the only part of this; certainly socialization and family training plays a part, but because we see such vast differences in abuse survivors, we need to look for other variables. I talked about this with Dr. Milam.

Milam agreed with my argument that people who blow up are also children of abuse, but he indicated that not all people who were abused scream at, shame, and beat their children. Again, diet and balancing the body isn't the only road, but it is important to be considered along with psychological help. Protracted withdrawal and augmentation are extremely painful. Whether one turns anger outward in the form of violence to others, or turns it inward as self-hate, loathing, and depression, it exacts a terrible human toll. Whatever the percentage of abuse that is attributable to protracted withdrawal syndrome, it is important to address this issue.

A TREATMENT PROGRAM FOR PHYSICAL RECOVERY

Nestled in the midst of Minneapolis, Minnesota (sometimes called the Land of Ten Thousand Treatment Centers, nearly all of which use the AA model), is the Health Recovery Center. It is run by Joan Matthews Larson, a friendly, sparkling, determined woman, who has long believed that alcoholism is a physical disease that requires a physical cure. She has been of invaluable help in my life and I have learned a great deal from her. She is also in the process of publishing a book on the subject titled *Alcoholism: The Biochemical Connection*, to be published in the fall of 1992. According to Larson, protracted withdrawal can be greatly assuaged, and for many people it can be avoided almost completely. Larson believes that a significant stumbling block to staying sober is that people don't look at damage to the brain, nervous system, and immune and endocrine systems. They go around feeling lousy and white-knuckling cravings until they finally give in.

As Larson says, raising her voice in exasperation about all the people who just keep going to AA, "*A physical substance going into a physical body has a physical effect.* When you change the chemistry of the brain, you change emotions and thought processes." When people come into her program, they are given large intravenous doses of vitamin C and other vitamins, and they are encouraged to give up nicotine, caffeine, white flour, and refined sugars. They are tested for food sensitivities and get lots of education on nutrition and the functioning of the brain. While some people do need more psychological counseling than is provided in this program, the physical component is crucial to many.

Larson has had excellent results, especially with the revolving-door people (those who have been in treatment many times), whose glowing letters of thanks are touching to read. Many of them talk about finally feeling physically well and free from cravings. Repeatedly, I have seen friends and clients who spend a couple of years healing their bodies and changing their diet feel less and less need for AA. One woman said, "I'm not 'in recovery,' I'm recovered. I've done a lot of healing on my body and on my childhood. Alcohol is simply something I don't use, and I don't ever think about it."

THE UNDERRATED ADDICTIONS: CAFFEINE, NICOTINE, TV

Caffeine is a highly addictive substance for many people, myself included. As with alcohol, the mind connects the taste of coffee or cola with relief from withdrawal symptoms. Our culture encourages and promotes addiction to caffeine in the form of coffee and cola drinks.

According to Harvey and Marilyn Diamond in *Fit for Life*,

Caffeine is a stimulant of the central nervous system, similar to cocaine, and has been linked to a host of maladies, including increased heart rate, change in blood vessel diameter, irregular coronary circulation, increased blood pressure, birth defects, diabetes, kidney failure, gastric ulcers, cancer of the pancreas, ringing in the ears, trembling of muscles, restlessness, disturbed sleep, and gastrointestinal irritation. It also upsets the blood sugar level, as it forces the pancreas to secrete insulin.

While I am not alcoholic, I have been addicted to speed—most notably caffeine—and at one point used diet pills to "get me in the zone" to write. Caffeine (in coffee) has been the most pernicious substance for me. Quitting cigarettes was not easy, but in comparison to caffeine it was a breeze. While caffeine does not affect all people as dramatically as it did me (although I was in my mid-forties before I was aware of any serious symptoms), I believe we grossly underestimate the addictive nature of caffeine for many people.

I totally agree with Colbin's statement that addictions, allergies, and imbalance can demolish willpower. I can testify to how it feels to be completely controlled by a craving and to persist in using something harmful even when I wanted to stop. If I drink coffee with caffeine, I get arthritis in both hands, making it hard to play the piano, hold a tennis racket, or type; I need up to two more hours of sleep each night;

I get breast lumps; I cannot concentrate through a tennis match; my energy drops and I start getting depressed and anxious. One could argue, but that's not like people who lose their jobs and their homes. True. But from the perspective of a life-loving/creative spirituality, anything that takes us away from the fullness of life is to be taken seriously. I think it is this culture's normalization of stress and lethargy that keeps people from examining the negative effects of caffeine.

My pattern of use paralleled that of an alcoholic. I tried to limit myself to no coffee before 2:00 PM (the typical addict trait of making rules), but little images of coffee in pretty china cups started running through my mind like ticker tape at about 10:00 in the morning, constantly interrupting my thoughts. I would feel restless. And as with any addiction, if I had a cup of coffee, it felt great—for a while—and then a few hours later I would pay the piper. The cravings would return, along with a desire for sugar and chocolate. Toward the end of my caffeine-using days I got to the point where I was falling asleep practically anywhere if I sat down. By evening, I was incredibly exhausted and I had a gritty feeling behind my eyes.

For me, withdrawal from coffee included headaches for three or four days, anxiety, and sleepiness. I took a vacation in order to stop so I could get all the sleep I wanted, take walks, eat right and not have any stress or deadlines. Eventually, when I got through the physical withdrawal, I felt better. Much better. I *feel* better now. As of January 1992, I've been off coffee for three and a half years, in this round two of caffeine abstinence. (I was off for four years before that, with a nine-month slip.)

Giving up one substance is often linked with giving up other foods or substances that stress the body. In my quest to feel better and give up caffeine the first time, I consulted a homeopath who discovered I was allergic to dairy products and wheat, which were making me tired and thus exacerbating the caffeine cravings. Within a week of stopping dairy products, I was able to give up coffee.

It took a couple of years to feel as good without coffee as I did with it (at least during the initial caffeine rush). In my first year off coffee, it was hard to imagine I was actually surviving without it. After about a year, coffee faded from my thoughts. For the most part, I could see it all around me and not drink it and not want it, and I experienced little difficulty even when it was the only substance available at gatherings. While the desire has faded, I'm still careful, however, and always will be now that I fully respect the power of that physical addiction and how it debilitates my life.

My caffeine addiction was not psychological to any great extent, although I had numerous therapy visits and even hypnosis sessions relating it to my mother's love of coffee, my attachment to pretty china cups, and the like. While my old survivor certainly had some pleasurable associations with sitting and drinking coffee with my mother, most of my caffeine addiction related to my mother's love of coffee because I inherited her chemistry. She "loved" coffee for the same reasons I did—it felt so good to relieve withdrawal symptoms. Even when she had a serious heart condition, had been hospitalized, and was told not to use it, she did not quit. She died in her early seventies of a heart attack—still drinking coffee.

Nicotine Addiction

I have a friend who went to every conceivable kind of workshop and clinic and spent months having hypnosis sessions in an effort to quit smoking. She finally started praying, "God help me with this," and two weeks later she was hospitalized with emphysema. She returned home with oxygen tanks. She was carrying them with her when we met at a restaurant for dinner. I ached when I saw her sitting at the table with her oxygen tanks, but she gave me a big grin and said, "I've quit smoking."

Nicotine, for some people, is one of the most tenacious physical addictions. Elizabeth Hoffman, author of *The Smoking Papers: Recovery from Nicotine Addiction*, was hospitalized with a collapsed lung, filled with tubes to keep her alive, and still she smoked every time the doctors or nurses were out of the room. She said she was so steeped in denial that it never occurred to her to quit smoking. After her life nearly fell apart, she finally recognized the source of her problems, and she quit.

Not everyone reacts to nicotine as did Hoffman. Like all addictive, mind-altering substances, people have different tolerance levels and addiction levels for various substances.

According to Hoffman,

Nicotine is a stimulant similar to cocaine and amphetamines. Also present is acetaldehyde, the first metabolic product of alcohol, much stronger than alcohol and having strong sedative properties. . . . Tobacco can be used to wake us up and calm us down at the same time! Nicotine is six to eight times more addictive than alcohol. Nearly 90% of the nicotine addicts still smoking have tried, but failed, to quit, and relapse is higher among smokers than it is among heroin users. Nicotine is a mood-altering drug that meets all criteria for addiction; tolerance (more is required over time to achieve the same effect); withdrawal (symptoms develop when the drug is discontinued); and nicotine-seeking behavior when deprived of a cigarette.

We have many treatment centers for substance abuse, but very few inpatient facilities for people addicted to nicotine. We are missing the boat. Smoking is life-threatening, and many people need a safe place to go to quit smoking and get through the intense withdrawal symptoms and gain the courage to face life without nicotine.

They also need help to bring the body into better physical balance. Because stop-smoking clinics are *not* usually connected to twelve-step programs, they often take a different approach, retraining the rational mind to believe a person can survive withdrawal, and some of them put emphasis on restoring balance to the physical body with the use of diet and nutritional supplements. What is most striking is that many people cease their addiction to nicotine without ever attending a twelve-step group or any other support group for more than a few months.

Why the difference? Some of the answer lies with the use of a rational approach and the *expectation* that people can and will quit and then maintain abstinence. Information to help people stop smoking often focuses on discussing the hazards to health, mind, and body. It also stresses how much better you will feel when you quit. It is a cognitive approach that empowers people to think in a way that helps them *want* to stop smoking because they care about themselves.

The difference between uncovering from alcohol and nicotine addiction demonstrates the degree to which institutions such as twelve-step programs have affected the way people think. Although there are a few twelve-step groups for people wishing to abstain from smoking, most people who quit nicotine have no choice but to use their rational mind to stay abstinent, and many people have been successful at doing so.

Television as Addiction

Television watching is an insidious, damaging addiction that is plaguing our country. It might seem strange that I would include this in a chapter called "The Physical Connection," but bear with me. Early TV watching affects the development and integration of children's brains and for many adults is a compulsion or addiction that thwarts creativity, intimate relationships, exercise, and so on.

Two aspects of TV watching affect children. One is the content; the other is the fact that they are watching images rather than learning to create them. To explain the latter: Throughout history adults have told stories or read to young children. Along with creating a loving bond, it plays an important role in brain integration and development.

We have three parts of the brain that develop and integrate throughout a child's development. The three parts represent various functions. We can call them reptilian, mammalian, and human. The human part of the brain must be developed in order to be creative and imaginative, to understand abstractions, and to learn in an integrated way. When someone reads to a child, the words go in through the reptilian and mammalian parts of the brain and finally reach the human brain, where the child creates images to go with the stories. Because TV provides the images, when children are watching they do not use or develop the human part of the brain; thus they do not develop creativity and imagination.

Joseph Chilton Pearce, author of *Magical Child*, said in a workshop, "TV floods the brain with a counterfeit of what it should create itself, leaving children dependent on a constant flow of images from an outside source. The child's ability to create an image not present to the sensory system is annihilated by TV watching." The negative effects are particularly strong when there is little creative stimulus in the home and the child watches TV for long periods of time.

The other terrible result of not developing creativity and imagination is that it leaves children more prone to depression or violence. When shamed, hurt, or neglected, an imaginative child has an infinite internal world for escape. They can create images, stories, scenes of being loved or rescued. They can express their feelings through play or drawing or take refuge in reading. This gives them a sanctuary that belongs to them, a refuge from the pains of life. Without this escape hatch, children are far more prone to either become depressed or to lash out at others. In his talk on child development, Pearce said that in 1950 there were no known suicides of children under fourteen; now, in 1990, every 78 seconds a child attempts to take his own life. He attributes a great deal of this to TV.

The other damaging aspect of TV watching is the content, which affects developmental patterning and behavior. Children take what they see on TV as a model for human behavior. According to Pearce, "By adolescence, a child has seen 18,000 violent murders, which results in a strange apathy toward violence and toward the meaning of self."

The other concern about content is that when cartoons show someone getting flattened against a wall or blown up, it's supposed to be funny. This pairs violence and humor. Moreover, the person who got flattened then gets up and is okay. Children following this model are confused when they poke, hit, or smash a friend or pet and they don't bounce right back. I thought about this when I read that a teenager was arrested for dropping a huge rock off an overpass onto a car which then crashed, killing the driver. In reading about the teenager I got the impression that he hadn't meant to hurt anyone, but he didn't have the ability to make a connection such as: the rock drops, it breaks a windshield, the driver is hurt or shocked and swerves off the road or hits another car, and someone dies. His statement when asked why he did it—"I just wanted to see what would happen"—rings of the same kind of detachment expressed by children who watch endless hours of TV.

There is a chilling parallel between the rise in murder rates since the widespread use of TV. *News and Notes from All Over*, the newsletter of The Society for the Eradication of Television, refers to Brandon Centerwall in an article titled, "TV's Chilling Link to Murder": "In his research . . . Centerwall analyzes the murder rates in three countries—the United States, Canada, and South Africa. His discovery: Almost like clockwork, 10 to 15 years after television is introduced, a country's murder rate shoots up dramatically. That's just enough time for the first generation of children weaned of television to reach adulthood and move into their most crime-prone years." He continues by saying that South Africa did not have television until 1974, and the murder rate stayed steady until the eighties, a decade after television was introduced, when it soared by 56 percent. The studies measured murder rates among whites only.

The specific physically addictive aspect of TV itself is that the person becomes dependent on fast, external images and stimuli and becomes increasingly unable to relax, self-motivate, and be creative. Thus normal life seems slow and boring and the person has difficulty seeing the beauty of nature or being able to relax. This takes them away from a life-loving spirituality into an artificial world that profoundly affects concentration, learning ability, and the capacity for joy. As a result, people go into withdrawal when they don't have TV as well as computers and computer games, movies and so on. They become restless, agitated, and bored.

The cultural effects of the widespread use of TV cannot be underestimated. It's as if we bring children into the world and then do not give them the natural stimulus they need to develop their brains, which in turn leads to problems in learning, violence, and self-esteem.

TV also creates or exacerbates spin-off addictions such as food. According to Dr. Steven Gortmakes, associate professor at the Harvard School of Public Health, "We are seeing the fattening of Americans." Obesity increases by 2 percent for each additional hour of television a day.

Often, in my practice, when a person has typical addictive symptoms such as being stuck, not following through on tasks, not pushing through emotional problems, and always seeming to keep one foot out the door in relationships, TV addiction has been the hidden culprit. I have often discovered this after checking for other active addictions, feeling bewildered and then remembering to ask about TV. Typically I find out that the person walks in the door and turns on the TV and sits mesmerized feeling unable to turn it off and do something else.

TV has profound effects on many relationships. One "zones out on TV as a way to make distance and avoid intimacy in the relationship. The partner often feels angry and rejected.

One can substitute computers, computer games, and so on for TV throughout this discussion. In my practice I frequently hear complaints such as, "He's always with his computer." One woman said, "He gave up his mistress and married his computer. I still feel left out."

If people are interested in *News and Notes from All Over* and The Society for the Eradication of Television, they can write to Box 10491, Oakland, CA 94610. I am not for eradication of television, as they are, but I find their articles useful.

WHY THE RESISTANCE TO UNDERSTANDING THE BODY?

Why is there such resistance to making links among sobriety, physical and psychological health, well-being, and natural eating? If relapse rates are so high, why don't we explore new roads to help the journey? With so many people feeling poorly physically, why don't treatment programs and addiction literature educate people? I see several general reasons.

If an approach to healing doesn't benefit the patriarchal male system—in this case, M.D.s, pharmaceutical companies, hospital conglomerates, and so on—it won't get widespread support without a struggle. (Some M.D.s are helpful, but, as a whole, they resist this sort of approach.)

The second reason goes back to our levels of faithing. The use of diet and nutrition is at levels four and five of faithing and requires questioning traditional values, trial and error based on internal experience, and autonomous decision-making. AA and most treatment programs are part and parcel of our hierarchical system, which rigidly adheres to levels two and three of faithing, where individuals turn over their wills and their lives to external patriarchal authorities or systems. When it comes to going inside and trusting yourself rather than some "expert," you are unlikely to find support in the dominant male system, because it is based on control rather than on self-empowerment. Thus the practices and beliefs of women, chiropractors, healers, and wholistic practitioners are discounted or looked at askance.

It is particularly difficult for women to realize what an incredible stake the patriarchal system has in maintaining the status quo by controlling health care and attitudes toward self-empowerment and natural healing. Remember, over a period of three hundred years, starting in 1484, it is estimated that nine million persons, mostly women, were put to death for witchcraft.* These women were often midwives, healers, herbalists, and independent thinkers. Patriarchy has gone to extreme lengths to eradicate women's power, which is closely interwoven with harmony, balance, and belief in natural healing. The history of the American Medical Association's taking control of birthing and medical practice is an incredible story in itself, which is described in painful detail in *Of Woman Born*, by Adrienne Rich.

In short, you cannot count on traditional medicine to help you with wholistic healing. When people in the medical establishment do make changes in that direction, they seldom acknowledge that many people—often women—have been saying the same things all along. Now that the American Cancer Society and the American Heart Association are recommending diets similar to those suggested by naturopaths and "health practitioners" for the last twenty years, popular magazines are full of articles on these diets (which are healthy and natural, although they seldom talk about the use of organically grown food). These practices have still not made their ways into hospitals, however. In a hospital stay on a cancer ward in 1991, I was served scrambled eggs, bacon, and heavily buttered toast for breakfast the day after surgery. I remember groaning as I looked at it and saying, "Are you getting me ready for the heart attack ward?"

---

*Historian Matilda Joslyn Gage also states in *Woman, Church, and State* (2nd ed., 1972) that a vast number of women were also sacrificed preceding this time.

SUMMARY

Here is a summary of some reasons why people resist considering diet and natural healing when uncovering from addiction.

1. Twelve-step philosophy does not include self-empowerment through physical healing, and does not address the physical-behavioral links of alcoholism and drug abuse after one achieves sobriety. In fact, they are often discounted.

2. Nutrition and diet coupled with exercise is a simple empowering model, requiring short-term professional guidance. People are encouraged to discover their own diet based on education and personal experience. This is a level four and five faithing process that runs counter to the AA tendency to want external rules.

3. The type of diet that rehabilitates a body is not easily available in traditional grocery stores, which have highly processed foods, produce sprayed with insecticides, and meat containing estrogens, hormones that tamper with the body's natural hormone balance. Organic, natural foods are usually available in co-ops, which are more expensive and often not readily accessible for many. Even so, one can make tremendous changes shopping only at a traditional grocery store by switching to fresh vegetables, brown rice, beans, fruits, and so on, and avoiding stimulants and processed foods.

4. Change in diet is a long-term gradual life-style change that doesn't happen overnight. It is very difficult for people with addictive, quick-fix thinking to accept a long-term process and take the time to learn new ways of food preparation.

5. People with victim programming ("The world is doing it to me and I can't change anything!") have a terrible time believing that something as simple as changing a diet, something they can do themselves, could actually make a difference. Our patriarchal hierarchy constantly tells people they don't know the answer and to leave it up to the experts in charge. As a result of this victim programming, many people prefer to go to "experts" and be told what to do rather than think for themselves. And if we stop being a victim of experts in one area of our lives, it challenges all the ways we are victims, consciously or unconsciously, in other areas of life. In other words, taking our health into our own hands and using natural substances is seen as a rebellious act in patriarchy.

6. The ability to feel pleasure from natural foods, lightly seasoned, has been programmed out of many people. In our patriarchal capitalistic society, foods have increasingly been processed to give a quick high through the processing, which adds artificial flavors and sugars. With time and reprogramming, the ability to find pleasure in natural foods does come back.

7. We have been taught to eat all kinds of foods all year round. We have little notion of a natural diet based on season and location. In other words, pineapples grow in hot climates because they are cooling foods appropriate for people living in that area. They never grow in climates with a severe winter. Grains grow in cooler northern climates because they are warming foods which people need in winter. Thus it is not within some natural diets to eat pineapples in January in Minnesota. Because of our high-tech shipping methods we often eat fruits and vegetables that were picked early, sprayed, and are not natural to our geographic location.

8. Finding one's individual best diet means tuning in to one's own body, requiring a journey of inner awareness that is scary for lots of people. As one woman said, "Before I can go inside and deal with the fine-tuned parts inside of me, I have to deal with the exterior flesh and all the discomfort I have about my body—thick thighs, pot belly, the works. How can I be tuned in to my stomach, adrenal glands, and digestive system when I rarely even notice how I'm standing, breathing, or if my clothes are comfortable? The inner world is mysterious, unknown, and frightening."

Change as a Process

In general, change is a process that involves greater awareness of one's body as well as education. I remember being profoundly affected at a health center by seeing a movie on digestion and realizing how the body works nonstop to assimilate and process food. It makes me think twice about what I eat, how I chew, and, in general, what I ask of my body.

For most people gradual change works best because it gets away from the binge-and-starve mentality of addiction. The old survivor is strongly programmed to be comforted by stimulants and various foods and it takes a while to develop a new survivor who associates pleasure with veggies and brown rice rather than hamburgers and fries. Some people make dramatic changes in diet and exercise following a heart attack or relapse. Some can just give up sugar or caffeine overnight. Others need a slow decrease and help that might include nutritional counseling, supplements and exercise.

The most important thing is *not* to approach change from a viewpoint of deprivation because it will surely backfire. The idea is to program the new wise survivor to love the body and to change because it makes you feel good. My approach is to *add* healthy foods and exercise and to keep noticing how much better I feel. When hit with sudden cravings, the new survivor learns to say things like, "Well, you could have a hot fudge sundae; it's one choice and I know you will feel better for a while. But remember, you will feel tired later and then have cravings for the next couple of days and will start needing more sleep. Let's see; is there something else that will quell this craving that doesn't have such negative side effects? How about cinnamon toast? An apple? A banana? Dried fruit?" And sometimes it is not a physical craving that needs filling, it is a psychological craving for human contact, the need to express feelings, or the need for exercise.

The art of making change is a dance between giving yourself foods you like and developing a new survivor who makes positive associations between healthy foods and feeling good. From our life-loving/ creative spirituality perspective, wellness and vitality are seen as a natural state of a body in harmony with itself and with life.

9

❦

Slogans, Jargon, and Program Literature

Rusty decided to come for therapy with me after hearing a talk I gave on childhood abuse and dependent relationships. He was a very attractive, friendly, considerate man in his thirties. He had been going with a woman who broke dates at the last minute, cut him down in front of his friends, flirted with others in front of him, and then became seductive and charming whenever he tried to leave her. Sometimes she was very friendly, other times extremely hostile. After eight years of sobriety, Rusty was depressed and obsessed with thoughts of drinking. He hated himself for feeling powerless to leave her and risking his sobriety over what he realized was an extremely harmful relationship.

When I asked if he felt angry at her, he said, "I shouldn't have resentments." I noted a knot in his throat and commented that the situation sounded painful. He quickly controlled the threat of tears, saying, "Oh, I shouldn't feel sorry for myself."

Later in the session he described how his mother had him kneel before her with his pants down while she shamed him and beat him. I asked him if he ever felt angry about it. He looked at me incredulously. "Wouldn't that be blaming my mother to be angry at her?"

Every avenue I approached in an attempt to reach his internal world had a traffic sign imprinted with a slogan or piece of jargon from the AA program. He had internalized those slogans as commandments,

212

and he used them without reflection to defend himself against his pain, his rage, and his sorrow—in short, to block himself from being both human and conscious. Rusty had switched from the rigid thinking of his addiction to the rigid use of the AA vernacular of recovery. He was still operating by rote, loyal to external rules rather than his own internal response system.

On another occasion, a woman named Arlene came to see me. She had completed treatment for alcoholism and had maintained nearly three years of sobriety. "I feel terrible coming here," she said, her distress showing. "I feel like a failure for needing therapy. I've done everything they told me to in treatment. I've been to meetings every week, worked the steps, and stayed sober." There was exasperation in her voice. "They said the first year would be hard, but this is the *third* year, and I still feel terrible." Her desperation was obvious. "If this is what sobriety is like I'm either going to kill myself or go back to drinking." Her voice cracked and she burst into tears. A few minutes later she looked up and said, "I want to know if it's possible for me to feel better."

My heart ached for her. Though I didn't like assuming the role of an oracle, it felt right to say, "Of course you can feel better."

Struck by her shame in coming for therapy, I asked why she had hurt so long before she came for help. "In treatment they told me not to have therapy for at least a year," she replied, "and in my AA group, when I've said I'm depressed, people kept saying, just work the program and you won't need any of that stuff—kind of like you're bad to need help and that if I really did it right I would feel better."

"So what's true for you?"

"I feel suicidal."

I paused. "Do you know the phrase, 'Don't take my inventory?' "

"Yes."

"Were the people in your group taking your inventory?"

"I guess so." She smiled. "I never thought to question them."

"So who gets to decide who needs help?"

"I do?" She said it as if she hoped it was the right answer.

"You've got the right answer," I said. "The next step is to believe it for yourself."

A brief investigation into Arlene's childhood revealed a familiar story of incest and abuse. She had been besieged with memories and dreams since she gave up drinking, but she constantly told herself she shouldn't be angry because the program says to give up resentments. The current landscape of her life painted an equally bleak picture. She was feeling hopelessly dependent on a man who was emotionally abusive. She worried about her ability to parent her daughter, who was having difficulties in school, and she was struggling to get by on welfare. A screening survey for chronic candidiasis indicated it could be part of the reason she had little energy and felt depressed. When I asked about the last time she'd had some fun—gone to the movies with friends, had a good belly laugh—she seemed more hopeful.

"So you really think I could feel better?"

"Absolutely, If you want to do some work."

"I'll do anything," she said, her voice becoming stronger.

"My guess is that your depression has many causes that you could change. It seems perfectly natural to me that you feel resentful when you remember your childhood abuse. But you keep blocking your anger. Your energy is being drained by your relationship to a man and by worrying about your daughter. You're not having any fun and you may have a physical problem. There's nothing coming in to sustain you. Of *course* you are depressed." Her face lit up.

"So you really mean I *could* feel better?" she asked again, as if to reassure herself.

"Absolutely," I assured her, leaning forward. Again, she burst into tears, tears of relief.

After her tears subsided I said, "There are some definite steps you can take to be less depressed. One is to talk about your abuse."

"You don't think that would be blaming my parents?" she asked, and then smiled as if she heard herself quoting the AA vocabulary.

"It's not blame to know what's true!" I said. "You need to put the puzzle pieces of your life together and understand your history. The important thing is to feel better . . . right?"

She nodded.

"There are no rules for that. You try things out and decide what works for you. Those treatment phrases weren't handed down from a mountain, and," I laughed, "even if they were, I would still not take them for my truths unless they felt right to me."

Arlene was grinning.

I smiled back, sharing in her relief and at my own intensity. "I get on a soapbox sometimes, but I get so angry when people are fed these lines and then use them to hurt themselves. I'm not blaming you; that's what you were taught to do, and you did it in good faith. Many women have come to me with the same experience. There's nothing wrong with you except that you were taught to listen to others and not yourself."

Arlene's and Rusty's stories echoed those of numerous women and men who have come to me over the years. They had put blind trust in "the program," accepted the slogans without digesting or considering their value and felt like failures because "working the program" had not brought them the promised sense of peace they longed for. Almost always, these people were survivors of childhood abuse. In many cases, there were also numerous physical factors exacerbating their depression.

STRUGGLING TO BOND

Many people who come to twelve-step recovery groups have difficulty with intimacy. They have little sense of how to relate to others without the superficial camaraderie of their using/drinking buddies, their work associates, their sexually addictive roles, or their gambling pals. The great longing to feel better, to belong, and to short-cut the long path of uncovery/discovery makes it extremely inviting to take on group language and group thinking that requires no self-reflection.

A primary technique of indoctrinating people into cults is mindless repetition of slogans or jargon. Not only are people in twelve-step programs encouraged to mouth slogans mindlessly, the slogans themself rail against critical thinking with phrases such as "Utilize don't analyze," "Fake it until you make it," "Act as if" or, "Your best thinking got you here."

While a rote sort of recovery language may serve a function in the initial stages of sobriety, it will not help develop the ego, or heal inner emptiness, because true intimacy is built on sharing inner truths rather than prepackaged statements. People who don the mask of recovery-speak often seem very serious, have difficulty laughing at themselves, and lack a broad perspective. This is reminiscent of levels two and three of faithing—using rote language undigested and unquestioned, and lacking the ability to be introspective and to reflect. You don't realize that your beliefs are just one way of believing as opposed to "the Truth." That's why these people often take them seriously.

A delicate balance exists between accepting the wisdom of slogans and sayings while not applying them like superficial Band-Aids to avoid inner conflict and feelings. One common aspect of an addictive personality is all-or-nothing, right-wrong thinking. Believing one hundred percent in something is a childlike state that quells anxiety and inner turmoil at the cost of personal growth. True discovery involves awareness of inner conflict as one struggles to birth the emerging true self, long overshadowed by addictive behavior.

For many like Arlene and Rusty, there is a great deal of motivation to get well, but they need to learn to operate from an internal frame of reference. In other words, they need encouragement to move to levels four and five of faithing, where they question what they are told, listen to their gut, and make decisions based on internal awareness.

THE USEFULNESS OF SLOGANS

Typically, slogans are simple, uncomplicated statements that embody important truths. They can be called to mind quickly to help one gain perspective on a situation. In terms of the old survivor/new survivor model, the slogan is a quick tool the new survivor can use to keep from slipping into old survivor behavior, almost like a positive hypnotic cue. For example, if someone is obsessively worrying about the future, the thought "One day at a time" can help bring them back to the present. "Easy does it" or "Let go and let God" can have a calming effect if someone is losing their temper over a situation they can't control. Slogans can be helpful when people *choose* to use them.

In the questionnaires, I asked people to tell about ways slogans had been helpful and ways they had been limiting or harmful. Many people were very positive about slogans. "Slogans give me a way to get back on center." "They help me feel better." Others mentioned both positive and negative aspects of slogans, while a few people disliked them intensely. One woman said, "Slogans sour in my mouth. It's hard to treat [them] with any seriousness." Another said "They sound too much like advertising jingles." Kelly, whom you met in chapters 2 and 3, said, "I'm probably not a good person to ask right now because I hate it all. It's insulting. I don't want to hear anything that isn't truly from the heart."

Here are some of the positive responses to the most frequently mentioned slogans.

One Day at a Time.

"Sometimes, when the pain was so great, I'd condense it to getting through the next five minutes."

"If I get looking into the future and become overwhelmed, this can and does snap me back into the reality of the present."

First Things First.

"I use this when I feel overwhelmed by all the different things I need to do. It also is used as self-talk to combat my workaholism."

"I can get overwhelmed. I've had so much responsibility in my life—this helped me prioritize. Now I do it automatically."

Serenity Prayer.

God, grant me the serenity to accept the things I cannot change, the courage to change the things I can, and the wisdom to know the difference.

"I use it as a mantra, especially when I fly or have anxiety."

"I use this when I am obsessing about someone and trying to figure them out—it helps bring me back to myself and to realize I can't control what they do."

Let Go and Let God.

This is often the short version of the third step.

"It means to me not trying to push for a particular outcome, but expecting a sort of Force for Good to prevail over all."

"It pulls me back from my self-centeredness and makes me realize He's running the show—quiets me down, gets me God-centered, restores my faith that everything is going just the way it should and faith that everything happens in God's Good Time—not mine—relieves me of my impatience."

Don't Take My Inventory.

This refers to times when someone is telling you what to do, giving unsolicited advice, or analyzing you.

"I use this in meetings when someone starts giving me advice."

"I've learned that when I get a knot in my gut, it's often because someone is taking my inventory."

"Saying please don't take my inventory has helped me have a polite way to tell people to back off."

"It also reminds me to notice when I am butting into someone else's business—and taking their inventory."

HALT (Don't Get Too Hungry, Angry, Lonely, or Tired).

"I love this statement because it reminds me to take care of myself."

"I never used to notice if I was tired or hungry. This helps me keep from getting on the edge of exhaustion."

NEGATIVE USES OF SLOGANS

Some of the negative reactions to slogans people mentioned in the questionnaires were:

Let Go and Let God.

"I see some people expecting results without doing any work for themselves. Also they use this slogan in a very negative way: 'God doesn't intend for me to be happy—so why try?' "

Get Off the Pity Pot.

"A man said this to me in my AA group when I was grieving a loss. It made me feel ashamed at the time, but I feel angry now. I needed to feel sad for myself and my childhood."

"Sadness and loss are real important aspects of my recovery."

Violating Others with Slogans

Slogans need to be a person's choice. Too often a person throws a slogan at someone else to stop them from expressing strong feelings. Sometimes well-meaning chemical dependency counselors and people in "the program" put on the mask of being all better without doing the internal work required to make healing a reality. They shield themselves from their inner world and automatically impose their fears on others. They often take on the role of benevolent guru or a kindly father/mother figure, handing out advice while staying detached from the aches and pains of their own lives . . . and those of their clients.

Many slogans can be used in an insulting, discounting way. A woman in a drug treatment program was told she had to do her fifth step with the male minister on staff at the hospital before she could graduate. She complained to her therapist about not having a choice. He tried to convince her it was a good idea. She refused to back down and got angry at him. He stayed calm and smiled at her, saying, "Easy does it."

She described her feelings about this. "It was a patronizing pat on the head and I was furious. My right not to confide in a man I didn't trust was being violated and I had a right to be heard. Instead of getting real with me, the therapist hid behind that recovery talk."

Other phrases that people said were flung at them in a negative way were: Don't blame; Don't dredge up the past; One day at a time; Don't make any major changes for a year; Take responsibility; Give up your resentments.

Give Up Resentments.

Lou was told to *give up her resentments* when she started talking about her incestuous father in a treatment group. It was extremely harmful to her. In her words, "Bringing up the incest was the scariest thing I had ever done. My counselor listened in a kindly way as if he was very sympathetic. Then he said, 'You know, this is one of the challenges of recovery, to be able to love those who hurt you and to give up resentments.' I felt so misunderstood and ashamed, I went back to my room that night and cut my arms with a razor. The next day they put me in a lock-up unit and I felt suicidal. I was aching for someone to say, 'Oh, that was really terrible, you must be upset.'"

All too often counselors or people in recovery assume this one-up role and attempt to still a person's stormy rage with canned statements rather than be open to the inner discomfort that might arise. Tragically, this results in numerous stories that parallel Lou's, where a warm, understanding response would have brought healing, but the distancing, pat answer brought more pain and shame.

It's scary to hear other people's feelings, especially when they trigger parts of ourselves we would rather not face. For example, a man hearing a woman's sorrow over sexual abuse might feel his own guilt and shame about his sexual domination fantasies, or sexual feelings he might currently be having toward her, particularly as she relates stories of childhood abuse. It is often easier to hide behind a mask of denial and tell the other person to give up resentments.

It *is* wonderful to give up resentments. But to think one can just turn off a resentment is unrealistic. Not only that, each individual must decide when she or he is ready to give up resentments. It can take years to dig into the past, get down to the core of resentments, feel the impact of childhood experiences on one's life, and then resurface with a new awareness and growth that opens the door to forgiveness and letting go of resentments.

Don't Blame.

"Don't blame" is one of the most misused statements in the recovery field. It needs to be separated from acknowledging the truth and assigning responsibility. Blame puts us in a victim stance when we say things like, "It's not my fault that I was abused so I can never have a good relationship." "It's your fault I drink, you never give me attention."

It is not blaming, however, to express one's rightful rage at having been deprived of rights, violated, battered, or abused. To say, "You wounded me, you hurt me, it was wrong of you to do that, it has affected my life, I'm angry," is not blaming. It is a self-respecting statement that kindles the inner spirit and brings dignity and reality back to a person's life. This acknowledgment of the truth is a healthy step toward uncovery and discovery for many people.

Don't Feel Sorry for Yourself.

Too often people take this statement to mean they shouldn't cry. Walling off the heart is at the core of male patriarchal training and crying is an intrinsic part of opening up the heart and feeling one's pain. While some people get lost in their tears or use them as a shield for anger, for others tears are a welcome opening to their inner world.

Over and over I see survivors of childhood abuse in therapy use this phrase to block expressing their sadness. In therapy, they will start to feel sad and suddenly interrupt themselves by saying, "Oh, I'm feeling sorry for myself." It's as if someone walked in the room and threatened to attack them for the crime of expressing their true feelings. Grieving and mourning are important aspects of moving beyond addiction. "Blessed are they that mourn."

Another common misuse of this phrase is to discount feelings from painful experiences or frustrating events. Often clients will start to complain about a hard day where six things went wrong, and suddenly stop themselves, saying, "Oh, I'm feeling sorry for myself." One time when a woman did this, I said, "That's great you feel sorry for yourself. It's about time someone did; you've had a hard time." Usually if people let themselves be upset for a few minutes and spout off, they can then move on. Putting on a Polyanna front separates people from their authentic selves. There's nothing wrong with feeling sorry for oneself unless it becomes an ongoing chronic state that blocks out positive thoughts.

Don't Dredge Up the Past.

In many recovery groups, looking to the past, except to recount stories of using and recovery, is strongly discouraged. This inculcates a feeling of guilt in people for exploring their family-of-origin patterns. In therapy, people will say things like, "Well, the past is gone, it's time to move on." While I agree with the goal, usually the person has come for therapy because their current difficulties with depression, anxiety, and the inability to be intimate are direct results of childhood experiences. Again, I find myself up against the graffiti wall of twelve-step jargon.

Take Responsibility.

Of course, everyone must eventually take responsibility for staying sober or getting well. No one can do it for us. Yet it is important to be careful about the ways this phrase gets used on people—it is susceptible to the patriarchal switch.

If people have been victimized, abused, or left impoverished, it is important that they *not* take on all the responsibility for their situation. They need to assign responsibility where it belongs—with the abuser and the system. It can be very healing for a woman or minority person or someone who has been abused to be supported in seeing how their stress is due more to societal inequities than any personal shortcomings. It helps relieve self-blame and shame. It doesn't mean a person abdicates responsibility for getting well, it means they stop shaming themselves for being poor or abused.

When a counselor or group member says things like "Take responsibility for your situation" in response to someone's talking about poverty or abuse, they are revictimizing that person. Self-awareness comes from balancing both a personal and political perspective. The first step for someone who has been victimized is to realize they are not to blame. Both Rusty and Arlene needed full permission and encouragement to express knowledge of the betrayal with open expression of feelings. When one feels understood and validated it becomes easier to do the hard work of taking steps to improve one's life.

God Never Gives You More Than You Can Handle.

One often hears this statement in recovery circles and in various versions in "New Age" language. It is another phrase that people use to make distance from people who are in pain. When I'm having a hard time I don't want to be patronized, I want understanding and sympathy.

In 1990, I was deciding to move from Minnesota, I was in the midst of a court battle to protect a dear child from being taken away from a safe home, a third of my retirement money was lost due to mismanaged investing, I was being sued, I was stuck in my writing, and then I found out I had cancer. I felt overwhelmed, exhausted, afraid, and extremely sad.

When I told this to a friend and she said, "I'm sure you can handle it. God never gives you more than you can handle," I wanted to scream at her. I immediately got away from her. I needed someone to give me a shoulder to cry on, to say it was tough, to say they were sorry I got cancer, and hold my hand and be with me.

I don't believe there is a God up there deciding that someone will have a car accident, someone will get cancer, or someone will win the lottery. While there may be a mystical quality to why things happen when they do, and I believe there is a synchronicity that comes when one is following one's path, I believe there is also randomness and unpredictability in life. I believe we have free will, and that God, Goddess, and the Great Spirit are within us all and their work on earth comes through our own efforts. I believe life is sometimes tough, sometimes sweet, and it's how we deal with it that reflects our spirituality and our inner strength.

When statements are handed out like authoritarian commands and not options, they put the receiver in a childlike position, discounting their internal wisdom and power. If there is wisdom in slogans and jargon, it will be learned internally by people as it is translated into helpful experiences.

If you are concerned that you are misusing slogans or jargon or feel patronized by others using it on you, you could ask yourself these questions:

- How did you feel after someone said a slogan or used jargon in response to something you said? Enlightened? Helped? Patronized? Irritated? Cut off? Misunderstood?

- How did you feel after saying slogans to someone else? In your head? Distant? Close? Helpful?

- How did the other person respond to your using a slogan? Did they seem to withdraw? Were they polite but distant?

- Are you saying the slogan to protect yourself from inner feelings? Does expression of feelings make you uncomfortable? Do you like being a teacher (which is a way to block intimacy)?

- Who is taking a position of power over another? (Acting one-up? Superior? Wiser? More experienced?)

- Who is getting treated as if they can't think for themselves? As if they are incapable of learning for themselves?

What these interactions usually lack is understanding and a feeling of intimacy, because someone is taking a one-up stance and peer relationships are based on assumptions of equality. If you feel one-down or patronized by someone who uses jargon a lot, you can get out of this position by saying, "Advice is not helpful to me," or "Don't take my inventory," or "I prefer you just listen to me."

If you are concerned that you are making distance with others by using jargon or slogans, you can ask them, "Do you want my opinion?" In groups it is usually easy to see when someone feels offended or distanced by pat statements—they start talking in their heads, pull away, look away, and make bland remarks. If you are talking with someone and the interaction seems to go dead, you can ask the other person if what you are saying is helpful.

Wanting pat answers for difficult problems is understandable. Being lost in an addiction is like dying, and one wants a rope to grab hold of for support. Bonding with a group of people all struggling to get well can feel like a lifeline. All intimate groups develop a personal language as a shortcut to communication. But adopting recovery-speak and using it instead of heartfelt, honest language creates barriers to egalitarian human connections.

Reaching inward to one's authentic beliefs and feelings takes time, but it is the true journey of discovery that leads to personal empowerment and intimacy.

PROGRAM LITERATURE

So far we have been talking about slogans and jargon. As discussed earlier, there is also literature—approved and otherwise—for addiction and "codependency." In addition, there is a growing body of addiction literature, often by people uncovering from addiction, on a whole range of topics from smoking to gambling to sex addiction.

Daily readings of relevant literature can be extremely helpful for someone gathering strength to stave off the pull of addiction. It's like taking time each day to train the new survivor to stay vigilant about the "cunning, baffling" nature of addiction.

Long before before starting this book, I came to know the twelve steps and traditions through attending three different twelve-step groups, all of which had small pamphlets about their type of group. I had read many (nonapproved) books on addiction and sections of several books on the approved list.

When I started working on this book, I took a trip to my local intergroup store to take a thorough look at the material. I was particularly interested in the history of AA and the twelve steps. The store had two sections—approved and nonapproved literature.

I picked out numerous books from both shelves.

I felt excited as I took my new books to the car in anticipation of the coming exploration. To give me a peaceful place to read, I took my little tent trailer out to a nearby campground. Amid walks, sunsets, and camp fires—one marshmallow for me and one for the fire—I started reading.

The first book was *Bill W.*, by Robert Thomsen. As you might guess from my discussion in the earlier chapters, I was deeply moved by Bill W.'s story, and found in him a kindred spirit—creative, search-ing, always open to change. So I looked forward to more.

After I returned from my camping trip, I immersed myself in the approved literature, including the *Twelve Steps and Twelve Traditions*, and Al-Anon's version of the same thing: *Lois Remembers* (Bill Wilson's wife's story), and much of *Alcoholics Anonymous*, to name a few.

In contrast to the way I felt reading Bill Wilson's autobiography, I started to feel annoyed, heavy, and depressed. Everything seemed so righteous, serious, and heavy-hearted. Something felt plastic, and I had a feeling of being dehumanized from all the "we" statements (as if all addicted persons are the same). I also felt a sense of literary starvation. Where was the line, idea, or image to jolt my thinking, raise my spirits, or give me a sense of inspiration?

Most of the biographies in *Alcoholics Anonymous* seemed to be white and middle-class and could be broken down into three parts. I had things and a life; I lost them due to alcohol; but once I adopted the program everthing was okay again and I got things back. It all seemed too easy, and did not match the hundreds of case histories of people I have interviewed, known and worked with. I can understand how reading about people's recoveries can be helpful and inspiring, but it felt like a formula with no room for doubt. What I objected to the most was the sin-and-redemption tone of many of the statements—as if we're bad, we've done it wrong, we're miserable sinners.

For example: "But whenever we had to choose between character and comfort, the character building was lost in the dust of our chase after what we thought was happiness. . . . We *never thought* of making honesty, tolerance, and true love of man and God the daily basis of living" (emphasis mine).

My comment in the margin was, "Makes negative assumptions—how do they know that I never thought about loving God on a daily basis?"

Continuing on: "For us, the process of gaining a new perspective was unbelievably painful. It was *only by repeated humiliations* that we were forced to learn something about humility. . . . So it is that we first see humility as a necessity . . . to gain a vision of humility as the avenue to true freedom of the human spirit. A *whole lifetime geared to self-*

centeredness cannot be set in reverse all at once. *Rebellion dogs our every step at first"* (emphasis mine).

I felt rebellious reading this. Whose whole lifetime of self-centeredness is he talking about? And what's wrong with rebellion or self-centeredness? I thought of all the women I have known (and not known) whose lives were crippled through being geared to *other people's needs*. These were the women for whom self-centeredness and rebellion were a first breath of their own lives.

The strong focus on humility brought back memories of my childhood in the Episcopal Church. I remember my shock at the age of fourteen when I actually noticed what I had been rotely mouthing for many years: We were miserable sinners and had *"erred and strayed* from Thy ways like *lost sheep.* We have followed too much the *devices* of our own hearts and there is *no health in us, but Thou* O Lord have mercy upon us *miserable sinners."* "Spare Thou those that are penitent" and on and on. Grovel, grovel, grovel. (emphasis mine).

I remember clearly the fire of my own rebellious spirit sparking in me as I stood in silence amid the huge congregation while they mouthed those self-deprecating words while I thought to myself, "I'm not a miserable sinner. It's not true. I'm really trying to do the best I can. I won't say these words." I especially hated the line, "We are not even so worthy as to gather up the crumbs from under Thy table." Over a period of several years, I started editing out the parts of the service I didn't like, and by age seventeen, I left the church with great sadness. It was a long search and many years later before I eventually found the Society of Friends (Quakers), where there was no hierarchy, no dogma, I could believe what I wanted, and I didn't have to call myself a miserable sinner to love God and be considered a spiritual woman.

The constant references to humility in twelve-step literature as having to be knocked down again and again *may* apply to people with a big ego. However, as discussed in chapter 1, I prefer the concept of softening the ego through awareness and an open heart that feels compassion for others. The spiritual task is to accept the role one has been handed and give it one's heart and energy. Groveling is not a part of a life-loving/creative spirituality, which encourages us to celebrate human potential and develop a passion for life.

I am not denying that there is wisdom underlying some of the twelve-step literature. There is. But the righteous tone, the "You're probably going to do it wrong" statements make it hard to assimilate the material from a position of strength and self-love. It is especially problematic for women, minorities, and people of color.

In the course of writing this chapter, I received a powerful letter about *Women, Sex, and Addiction* and the *Ms.* article from a Black, Latina feminist woman named Asale. I called her and we got to talking about her experiences in twelve-step groups. She echoed my difficulties with the stress on humility. She had had a terribly difficult time in an OA (Overeaters Anonymous) group where she felt constant conflict between her needs as a feminist woman of color and the whole philosophy of the twelve steps.

Asale told about her sense of alienation when people read from the brochure titled "To the Newcomer" in her OA group. "It was all couched in 'we,' which irritated me since I was the only woman of color in the group and it was never acknowledged. How could they be speaking for me?" She also pointed out the phrase "seesawing for years between *gluttony* and starvation diets has been steadily destroying our health." "That's so shaming," she said, "like the fundamentalist religion I am trying to get away from." She said it also made her laugh, because by recognizing the implied shame, she had outwitted or seen through the oppressor.

Asale referred to other troublesome phrases: " 'Are you willing to admit *complete defeat?*" From *A Guide to the Twelve Steps for You and Your Sponsor:* "Are you powerless over food, and has your life *become unmanageable?*" "All the things I felt proud of in my life—overcoming a sense of powerlessness, defeat, and unmanageability—and I'm told I need to go back there. I've worked so hard to feel proud of myself as a Black Latina woman." She continued. "It's so hard; I need a group, I want to talk with other people and get over these terrible addictions, but why does recovery have to go against feeling powerful?"

Referring to the program's stress on making amends, she said, "It may be that I need to make amends to someone, but that was not what I needed to hear the first day I walked into a twelve-step group. I need to get to that place for myself. When I walk in and see a lot of white people, I think of all the ways white people need to make amends to people of color. So when those phrases get thrown at me, my defenses go up. "I don't want to deny my history as a Black woman and I shouldn't have to give up my politics to heal from addiction."

To someone who has been oppressed, statements like the following from the *Twelve Steps and Twelve Traditions* too closely echo the patriarchal veiling of the nurturer/violator—one who pretends to care while covertly exploiting you. "When we developed still more, we discovered the best possible source of emotional stability to be God Himself. We found that dependency upon His perfect justice, forgiveness, and love was healthy, and that it would work where nothing else would."

What does this mean in terms of everyday life—when you get up in the morning and the heat's been shut off, when you try to make a decision, when you have a flat tire and are broke? How does his perfect justice work? Is there really a God up there handing out justice? And, if so, how can it be a loving, just God when there is so little justice on this earth?

What's missing for me is an affirmation that through our own actions, which can include the use of our intellect, creativity, and compassion, and through listening inwardly we find that wellspring of inner spirit. The living God/dess is one of daily actions we can take charge of. Faith and spirituality are not passive.

"We"-Language

In my group interviews and in talking with others, there has been a lot of debate about the use of "we" in the literature and in the twelve steps. "*We* admitted *we* were powerless." "If *we* were to live *we* had to be free of anger." "*We* avoid retaliation or argument." On the positive side, people say this gives them a sense of belonging and helps them understand that what they did as an alcoholic (or drug abuser) was a predictable pattern related to the chemical abuse. This helps release shame.

The down side of using "we" is that it makes assumptions that all people who are addicted behave in the same way. They don't. My experience when I read endless pages saying "we" all did this and "we" all did that (usually selfish, reprehensible things) is of being violated and intruded upon. I find myself arguing with the words. "No, I'm not that way. Don't tell me how I am." Let me find it for myself. It echoes the authoritarian righteous father speaking down to the children. It creates a double bind, because the listener is either the complacent receiver of the message or the rebellious one arguing back. When I am in a group I don't want to be in either of those roles because they take the focus off finding my own inner voice.

Using the "we" stereotype of an addicted person also suggests they are a separate breed from other people. Stereotypes are dangerous and limiting. Part of learning about racism, classism, and sexism is to realize that within each group we have tremendous diversity. One African American does not speak for all African Americans, any more than one feminist speaks for all feminists. To lump people together because of color, race, addiction, or any label such as "alcoholic" is demeaning and limiting.

In studying Hakome—nonviolent psychotherapy—I have become

more aware of how interpreting other people's experience is an intrusion unless they ask for it directly. And even then it is better to help people seek their own self-definition and their own truths. It may be slower, messier, and take more time, but it empowers the other person to find their own way.

Women, "Codependency," and the Twelve-Step Literature

I have not discussed traditional Al-Anon literature such as *One Day at a Time* (a book of daily meditations) and the chapter "To Wives" in *Alcoholics Anonymous* in any detail here. I have saved my discussion of this re-covery literature for chapter 11, "Moving Beyond Codependency: The Internalized Oppression Syndrome," because of the profound implications for women and other minority people.

Literature for the Mind, Body, and Spirit

In the midst of reading twelve-step literature and feeling heavy and ponderous, I read a speech given at the United Nations in February 1990, by Vaclav Havel, the leader of Czechoslovakia. I was so inspired that I bought his book, *Living in Truth*. He spoke with a richness of spirit, a lively intellect, and a warm heart. I marveled at his fluid, expressive use of language and I had to stretch my mind to understand sometimes. He spoke of our failings as humans as well as a global need for spirituality and love, but in contrast to twelve-step literature, I felt my spirits being lifted.

In speaking of the changes in Eastern Europe (the fall of the Berlin Wall and the changes in Czechoslovakia), Havel writes, "The mask fell away so rapidly that, in the flood of work, we have literally no time even to be astonished." The sheer beauty of his words were inspiring. He goes on to say,

> We still don't know how to put morality ahead of the human heart, in the human power to reflect, in human meekness and in human responsibility. We are still under the sway of the destructive and vain belief that man is the pinnacle of creation, and not just a part of it, and that, therefore, everything is permitted. We still close our eyes to the growing social, ethnic, and cultural conflicts in the world. . . . The anonymous megamachinery we have created for ourselves no longer serves us, but rather has enslaved us.

In reflecting on twelve-step literature, particularly *Alcoholics Anonymous*, we could say that it "still closes its eyes to the growing social, ethnic, and cultural conflicts in the world." It has become a piece of megamachinery that enslaves some people by defining their experience without knowing or understanding who they are.

In *Living in Truth*, Havel talks about about responses to literary works in a culture lacking self-awareness. Once again, I think of twelve-step literature and the proliferation of twelve-step groups in the United States and abroad that lack self-awareness.

> Whether through censorship or self-censorship . . . it will never stray one inch beyond the taboos of a banal, conventional and, hence, basically fraudulent social consciousness that offers and accepts as genuine experience the mere appearance of experience—a concatenation of smooth, hackneyed, superficial trivia of experience. . . . Despite, or rather, because of this fact, there will always be people who find such a work entertaining, exciting, and interesting, although it sheds no light on anything by any flash of real knowledge revealing what was unknown, expressing what had never been said, or providing new, spontaneous and effective evidence of things hitherto only guessed at. In short, by imitating the real world, such a work, in fact, falsifies the real world.

While the emergence of twelve-step programs and *Alcoholics Anonymous* were highly significant occasions that did at one time shed new light on alcoholism, without substantial updating this institution falls into the category of Havel's words: "It no longer provides new, spontaneous, and effective evidence of things hitherto only guessed at." The twelve-step approach purports to be for all people, but its literature lacks knowledge of most people. By continuing to define people who are alcoholic or partnered with an addicted person in a narrow, stereotypical way, omitting discussion of women, minorities, drug addiction, and cultural influences, it indeed "falsifies the real world."

10

Boundaries and Sexual Exploitation, *or Why Do I Have This Knot in My Gut?*

> *"I used to like my group so much, but I can't get myself to go anymore. I like the people. It's meant a lot to me. But, I just get this knot in my stomach and I don't want to go. I feel so confused."*
>
> —ROSA, TALKING ABOUT AN AA GROUP

For nearly a year, Rosa had attended a mixed male/female AA group. She was concurrently seeing me for therapy and making steady progress. One day, when I asked her if she had talked about a particular problem in AA, she began to move uneasily in her chair. She paused for a long time. Then, like a guilty child, she said, "I haven't been going for a while."

"Oh, really," I said, with a sense of curiosity. "What's up?"

She looked surprised at my relaxed response.

"You're not mad?"

"No."

"I was so afraid you'd be mad."

"No, but I'm curious why you decided not to go . . . and why you are scared to talk to me about it."

"I thought you'd tell me I'd relapse or that I didn't care about myself or that I didn't want to stay sober." She was immersed in guilt for having left her group, and a litany of AA rhetoric was pounding away in her head.

I paused. "*Did* you relapse?" I asked.

"No." She looked surprised.

"How are you feeling?"

"Pretty good."

"So, you haven't been going to AA and you're feeling pretty good."

She paused again and smiled.

"Yeah . . . I stayed sober and I didn't relapse . . . and I'm not worried about relapsing." She sounded surprised by her own conclusion.

While leaving a twelve-step support group might be a sign that someone is sliding into a relapse, it is not always the case, and it wasn't the case with Rosa. As so often happens in twelve-step programs, Rosa had ingested information uncritically and, as a result, felt guilty for making an independent decision based on her own observations and experiences—which was just what she needed to be doing. This reinforced her fear of authority figures, which spilled over into our relationship.

We returned to the question of why Rosa stopped going to the group. She said it was hard to find words, but the group had lost something. On the day the group met she had started getting stomach aches or headaches and wanted to stay home and sleep. "Have there been changes in the group?" I asked.

"Not much . . . well . . ." She seemed detached and vague. "Two people who were lovers in the group broke up . . . but I don't know if that's important."

"Well, let's assume it is, since it came to your mind," I responded.

Rosa went on to say that Hank and Joyce, who had split up, were both still there, but Hank was dating someone else in the group who was a friend of Rosa's.

I asked her how she felt about the situation.

"It's kind of weird." She paused. "I don't much like it."

"Say more."

"I keep worrying about getting in the middle. I like Joyce but when she calls me to tell me how bad she feels about losing Hank I get confused. I always liked Hank, and she tells me things I don't want to know. I'm confused when I see him."

As we explored the dynamics of the group Rosa revealed that Hank had also asked her out "for coffee" and she was afraid to say no. She went with him, feeling terror that Joyce might find out and be mad at her. And on it went, as we unearthed all kinds of past and future relationships that were simmering away under the surface of the group's seemingly peaceful exterior.

"I'm not surprised you had a knot in your gut," I said.

"Really?" she said with relief, looking surprised.

I talked about how unspoken sexual tensions often ripple through groups, leaving people frustrated, uneasy, not knowing what to say or do. Whether or not people are aware of what is going on, most people pick up on the tension either physically or in subtle emotional ways. Typically, as a result, individuals withdraw to avoid stress, or talk more superficially, which lowers the level of intimacy.

"So it's not all me," she said.

"No. It's not all you," I replied.

Rosa was fascinated, trying to take in what I was saying, but she was having difficulty believing she was not bad or crazy—things she had been repeatedly told in her original family.

Watching her grope for understanding triggered the memory of a time when I had that same unexplainable knot in my gut. I asked if she wanted to hear a personal story. She nodded yes.

In the mid-seventies, as part of my doctoral work in counseling, I did a summer internship at a women's therapy collective. The women were pioneers in the field of feminist therapy and seeking to get away from a hierarchical, patriarchal approach to therapy. In a sincere desire to change the power balance between therapist and client, some appropriate professional boundaries were crossed and divisions between client and therapist roles were confused or violated.

Coming from a fairly traditional training program, I felt uneasy, but I rationalized it away, saying to myself, "Well, these are feminists. They are the leaders. They know what they are doing."

My relationship to Arlina, one of the founders, took many forms. I was a guest in her home, her peer at the collective, her supervisee, and, as time went on, I became something of a confidante as well. We socialized together, and often had Friday night dinners with other members of the collective.

Boundaries in the collective were equally confusing. Some of the women had been clients of Arlina's before joining the staff. Numerous women had been in dual relationships, as peer and student, lovers, past partners, therapists and clients. There was a lot of unresolved conflict between many of the women, which I knew little about—except in my gut. At the weekly business meeting we often spent most of the time dealing with personal feelings, separate from policy and organization. I sat there anxiously, watching the clock, wondering when we would get to business, but I was afraid to say anything. On top of this, I was a trainer in one of the programs and a trainee in a different one, which was led by various members of the collective.

Arlina was the principal therapist for a training program held in the big group room on the main floor of the collective. At the first meeting, while Arlina was explaining that various women in the collective would be leading parts of it, I became aware of a knot in my stomach. After the introductions she started us on a relaxation exercise. "Breathe, relax." My stomach churned. She had us get up and move around. When she said, "Put your body in any position or any place that feels totally comfortable," my eyes became fixed on the huge open window that connected with the large front porch. We walked around and women settled into new positions on the floor. My stomach kept turning and my eyes kept returning to the window as I tried to relax.

"Be true to yourself," she said.

"Be true to myself," I thought, as an impish feeling of delight started to dance inside of me. I got up went to the window, bent over, stepped through it and walked away. I relished the warm summer air filling my lungs. I headed for a park, and felt the knot in my gut slip away. I knew with everything in me that I didn't want to be there, but I hadn't known exactly why.

I know now, however, that it was about boundaries.

Rosa was grinning ear to ear when I finished the story.

"You did that!"

"Yes." We both laughed.

It didn't take Rosa long to figure out that being in the role of supervisee, trainee, friend, colleague, and housemate with the same woman was confusing. Also, people who had shared personal information about themselves were training me, but on Friday mornings we met as peers.

Using my experience as a mirror, Rosa started to understand how her group resembled her incestuous family, full of unspoken tensions, secret liaisons, and a lot of rage festering under the surface. When she heard one friend talk negatively about another friend, she was stuck carrying secrets that made her uneasy. When Hank asked her out, her needy self was flattered but she also felt scared and betrayed—which was how she felt with her seductive, flirtatious father, who had abused her.

Rosa's experience is not uncommon. Many people who come from families where secrets, reversed roles, and incestuous relationships were the norm don't easily recognize dual relationships in groups. They just know that somehow they don't want to be there. And when this is countered with strong AA rhetoric, many people, fearing relapse, rejection, or being shamed, continue with the group and deny their internal wisdom. As a result they deepen the wounds inflicted by their family of origin by dissociating even more from their true self.

BOUNDARY DEFINITIONS: PHYSICAL, PSYCHOLOGICAL, AND SPIRITUAL

Boundaries define what belongs to an individual on a physical, psychological, and spiritual level. One of the most important survival tools a person can develop in a hierarchical system is an understanding of boundaries. Dominants in a hierarchical system regularly control those below them with a multitude of boundary intrusions—touching, encroaching on their physical space, interrupting, imposing their ideas. If confronted, they usually deny the intrusion flat out or say they don't understand what all the fuss is about, leaving the other person feeling confused and crazy. We can break boundary intrusions into three types which overlap—physical, psychological, and spiritual.

A *physical boundary* defines your personal space and allows you to control how you are touched and how close people come to you. In the course of personal relationships, no one has the right to touch or hug another person without their consent. Often consent is given nonverbally or permission is given over time. Typically, the one higher on the hierarchy assumes the right to touch someone beneath them—for instance, men assume the right to touch women, and everyone assumes the right to touch children any way they please.

A *psychological boundary* is defining your right *not* to be analyzed, shamed, manipulated, lied to, or brainwashed. It is your right to say no and have that respected without having to give explanations or defend yourself.

A psychological boundary is also crossed when people say one thing and do another. They say "I'm here to help you" when they really want to control you or use you for their ego needs. This happens in twelve-step groups, in families, and in the culture. If children lived in families where their boundaries were routinely crossed, they have difficulty sorting out boundary crossings in adult support groups. Abuse of children is often accompanied with confusing statement: "I'm being sexual with you because I love you." "I'm hitting you for your own good." Children try to cope with the mixed messages by saying to themselves, Something must be wrong with me, or Maybe I made it up, or I do deserve to be hit, or I'd better be good or they'll leave me. Unless a person has some form of consciousness raising or empowerment, he often enters twelve-step groups with the same confusion. If limit-setting and rules were capricious, inappropriate, missing, illogical, and based on the needs of the caregiver, a person may resist any type of limit, because limits are associated with unfairness and control.

Psychological intrusions can involve making assumptions about someone's motivation. For example, when a person says "No, I don't want to," an intrusive response would be, "That means you don't care about me, or you don't like me." It assumes motivation and manipulates through guilt. Another common violation I routinely see is men telling women they are prudes, unloving, or too serious when they express dislike of sexist jokes or refuse to have sex. Conversely, a boundary intrusion is also wanting to live through the power of another person because you lack your own sense of power—being Mrs. Powerful man, or using men as status objects. While it is understandable that minorities or people in one-down positions seek power through associating with people in a higher position, it is still a boundary intrusion and a form of collusion when it is done covertly.

A *spiritual boundary violation* is when one person objectifies another in any way (as cheap labor, a sex object, a wife, or a status object) and blocks them from developing to their fullest potential—including the full range of human emotion, passions, power, creativity, and mental capacity. It is about seeing the body but not the soul. Spiritual boundary violations are perhaps the most insidious and cruel because they harm at such a deep level. Instead of seeing others as other human beings, all sacred, all equal in the eyes of our Creator, one separates people with familiar stereotypes: A woman is a chick, and so on. All objectifying, stereotyping, and defining one group of people as *less than* another group of people is a spiritual violation. It is core racism, sexism, and homophobia, resulting in internalized oppression, which we will explore in the next chapter. If we stop to think about this for a moment, we will see that spiritual violation is core to our hierarchical social system, which assigns unequal worth to people based on gender, color, race, or culture.

BOUNDARY CROSSINGS AND DUAL RELATIONSHIPS

A dual relationship is when a person tries to mix two types of relationships with the same person. It results in a form of boundary violation. They try to be supervisor and peer, parent and friend, sponsor and peer, counselor and friend. The greater the power differences, the more complex dual relationships can be. *But the most important thing to remember is that the person with the most power in a relationship has the greatest responsibility to set limits. The one with the least power is always double-binded when the other person is intrusive or exploitive.*

Dual relationships lead to internal splitting, or dissociating, because the rules for peer relationships are different from those with unequal power levels. Being peers supposes equal time and direct communication—"I like what you did. I didn't like what you said."—without analyzing the other person or making excuses for them. In a twelve-step group being a sponsor and sponsee supposes a different set of rules. The sponsor is ostensibly more experienced and assumes the role of teaching the newcomer about the steps and supporting them in their sobriety. It's very important for both to define the relationship and the expectations. There's a lot of gray area, because some kind of interchange is appropriate. Generally, if the sponsor wants to pour out his or her troubles to the sponsee, particularly when the latter calls for support, the boundaries have been crossed.

If the sponsor becomes seductive, it is incestuous and an abuse of power. It can be difficult for the sponsee—the one with the least power—to say no to any type of intrusion because he or she looks to the sponsor for guidance and modeling, the way a child looks to a parent. There is a tacit (but mistaken) assumption that the one with most power knows what he or she is doing. If people want to shift the nature of a relationship they must discuss it. For example, if sponsee and sponsor decide to end that form of the relationship, it must be mutually discussed. Conversely, you cannot get rid of the problems of a dual relationship by trying to talk them away. To say someone is sponsor and peer at the same time is an illusion, because one cannot be both, no matter how much one tries to talk away the power differences.

In a more covert type of boundary-crossing, I have seen situations where sponsors/teachers/clergy assume a counselor-type role because they have needs for affiliation but are afraid to be peer with others—they need the control and safety of being one-up. They say they are there to help the other person, but covertly they are wanting to be admired and have a friend. In sponsor–sponsee relationships, dual relationships can lead to tension and confusion for the sponsee. *It is a form of boundary intrusion to have a hidden agenda in a relationship—to offer to give something, but actually be filling emotional needs and not saying so.*

* * *

When boundaries are crossed in a relationship or in a group—any group—the first recognition is often a knot in the gut, a headache, mental confusion that feels like fog in the brain, or a strong unexplainable desire to stop going to a meeting. Some people suddenly get a powerful urge to eat compulsively, hurt themselves, or use drugs. The distress may spill over into all aspects of one's life. A person may have no idea that the group tensions and boundary violations, often echoing and awakening feelings from one's original family, are the source of these problems. As a result people often blame themselves or even get sick in order to have an acceptable excuse not to attend groups where boundaries are being violated.

Recognizing when a group is troubled can be difficult because it often happens slowly, over time. A member often picks up conflicts at an unconscious level, feeling them physically. To drown out the nagging suspicions that something is wrong, a person may staunchly defend the group and its value more strongly, speak with disdain about people who leave, or have lots of unexplainable physical symptoms.

BLAMING THE VICTIM INSTEAD OF UNDERSTANDING GROUP DYNAMICS

Because we live in a culture that tends to blame the victim, excuse perpetrators, and not understand group dynamics, people who have negative experiences in groups often get blamed. In my questionnaire for this book, a disturbing number of people responded to questions about individuals' being abused in groups by saying, "They should just leave," or "It's up to everyone to be responsible for themself," or "I trust the group conscience." They didn't seem to understand that groups take on norms which are very powerful, and when a person is vulnerable and seeking support they often don't see the dysfunction until they are lost in it.

Most of us have slipped into negative situations, and only after leaving could we see how bad it was. Looking back, we sometimes think, "How could I have let myself get into such a mess? What was I thinking about?" I think it's naive and lacking empathy to say things like, "If a group is not healthy, then it's the person's responsibility to leave." A person like Rosa, with a violent, incestuous family background, has no criteria to use to tell a healthy group from a dysfunctional one. And frequently there are gradual, almost imperceptible changes in a group as the boundaries slip away.

DEALING/NOT DEALING WITH GROUP TENSIONS IN TWELVE-STEP GROUPS

In our culture we have few nonviolent guidelines for dealing with conflict where everyone comes out a winner. Twelve-step groups suffer from the same problem. It is exacerbated because the twelve-step groups encourage unswerving loyalty, discourage questioning, and see themselves as above reproach, which leads people to set aside a watchful eye or forget to trust their own instincts.

Twelve-step programs give subjective messages for handling tensions that arise. The tradition of "principles before personalities" encourages people to "set aside" personality conflicts for the common good of the group. This can be positive in that it keeps people focused on themselves and their sobriety as opposed to picking on others or making comparisons. On the other hand, this policy doesn't validate people's instincts about group tensions that arise from boundary crossings and people being seductive or abusive. Thus people need to acknowledge the positive value of not focusing on others' personalities, yet trust their own instincts as to the health of a group or behavior of certain individuals.

Another phrase that people sometimes confuse with overlooking abuse is "Don't take anyone's inventory." Essentially, it means don't butt into other people's business or tell them what to do, but it doesn't mean don't protect yourself against abuse. And it doesn't mean don't be concerned for the welfare of the group.

The tradition suggesting a group inventory does give people the opportunity to talk about the health of the group. This assessment of how the group is working is typically done once every twelve weeks. In my interviews, it appears that some groups discuss boundaries and tensions in group inventories, but many do not. They either don't recognize them (although they might feel uneasy), don't know what to say, or are afraid to question the group anyway.

The lack of prescribed ways to voice uneasiness when people are crossing boundaries is intensified because many people in twelve-step programs are afraid to deal with conflict. So they deny the problems, avoid talking about them, and keep the nervous tension in their gut. When a group colludes in denial of a problem, it is tremendously scary for a single individual to say out loud what everyone is denying. There is a fear of getting shamed or being abandoned—often a fear mirroring the childhood fear of naming one's abuse or abuser. Thus, if you are upset with a group, it may be wise to talk with others and see if they are feeling similarly to you, and ask their cooperation in having a group discussion.

Even with therapy, it took a while for Rosa to truly believe that her response—avoidance, physical tension, and fear—was typical of *most people* in her position. I suggested she talk to trusted friends in the group to see how they were feeling. She was amazed at the similar problems many were having. I also validated that it wasn't surprising that Rosa had not talked about her struggle in group with me. First of all, she had a hard time identifying it in concrete terms, and second, she didn't want the devastation of being shamed by someone she had dared to trust.

EXAMPLES OF BOUNDARY INTRUSIONS

In interviews and questionnaires I asked about flirting, dating, and sexual violation, along with other boundary violations in twelve-step groups. Here are some examples of boundary violations:

Giving unsolicited advice. "You should take a fourth step since you're depressed." "You should read the Big Book every day."

Hugging members of the group without permission. One woman wrote, "People seem to think they have a right to hug you just because you come to a twelve-step group. I'm very particular about who I touch." This was one of the most common complaints from women.

Assuming friendship on the part of another member. "Some people assume we're all buddies just because we're in the program. Just because I come to a group it doesn't mean I want to talk personally with everyone."

Not accepting a member's saying "no" to phone calls, socializing, and so on. "When I finally told a friend I didn't want to listen to her talk about her husband any more, she said I wasn't being a supportive friend." "When I didn't want to go out for coffee after the group meeting, people kept pressuring me with statements like, 'Socializing is an important part of recovery' or 'You shouldn't isolate.' "

Trying to get a new member to talk. "I was taking a long time to feel safe and several people kept offering to help me. I felt they were trying to get me to talk so they could feel comfortable. I wanted to say, 'Leave me alone, I'll talk when I'm ready,' but I felt too scared."

Preaching. "I was an atheist and kept hearing, 'You can't get well without a Higher Power'—as if they had the only way."

Flirting with a group member. "There was one man who flirted with every new woman who came to the group—if she was pretty." "There was a woman in our Al-Anon group who was very seductive with every man who ever came to the group. It was disgusting."

Seducing a group member. "This man was warm and fatherly to me, showing me the ropes, then he took me out to dinner, and seduced me. I was afraid to say no."

Telling sexist or racist jokes. "Once a man came into AA and, when asked for a topic, he spoke up. 'I'm really in a bad place—[silence]—ah shit—the bottom line is—I really need some pussy today.' The room roared. I was appalled. I wanted to slap him. I really felt violated, like women are just objects to satisfy his sexual needs, and it was totally out of context. No one said a word to him. I didn't know how to say anything to him."

Bringing sex into the conversation. Lots of seduction goes on in twelve-step groups and one early sign is when people start making sexual jokes or refer to affairs or sexual relationships.

Coming to group with the intent of finding a date rather than a sincere interest in personal growth. Repondents to the questionnaire wrote that it felt disrespectful and abusive to the group when people were obviously more interested in finding a date than seeking recovery/discovery.

Disclosing lots of personal information without taking time to create a friendship or find out if the person wants to listen to you. "This person called me and started telling me the intimate details of her life and I didn't even know her. I didn't want to hear it. It felt intrusive."

These are just a sampling of comments from people I interviewed or who completed questionnaires. Recognizing boundary intrusions involves developing the ability to listen to your body and *trust the response.* Many people said they felt uneasy in some groups or with some individuals, but, like Rosa, they minimized the feelings, saying, "I thought it was just me."

Common responses to boundary intrusions are to shut down, numb out, get giggly, say more than you want to say, get a stomach ache, an uneasy feeling, or a tight throat, and after you leave, to feel spacey, "icky," angry, or want to self-abuse.

SETTING APPROPRIATE BOUNDARIES

People are often afraid to set appropriate boundaries in groups because they have never learned how or were abused for doing so in their families of origin. They come from families where the rules were topsy-turvy and children were the emotional caretakers of the adults, were abused when they said no or expressed opinions, and were seen as emotional extensions of self-centered parents. They end up being open to violation and not protecting themselves. They never learned they had the right to say no.

The other reason people are afraid to set limits is because they have internalized rules from our patriarchal training that teach people not to express anger openly or set limits to people above them in the hierarchy. It is important for people in a one-down position to be kind to themselves if they haven't spoken up. Your fears are not necessarily personal pathology. In hierarchy when you do speak up chances are someone will retaliate and you will be blamed, shamed, lose your job, or something else.

That doesn't mean you should not speak up, it means get support, strategize with other people, and be forewarned of the possible consequences so you won't be surprised. It is important to believe yourself and have the validation that (1) your complaint is legitimate—you *were* violated, and (2) you have the right to set limits and take good care of yourself.

Here are some boundaries that people wished they had set, were afraid to set, didn't realize they had a right to set, needed to set, or did set in twelve-step groups.

It is your right to set these boundaries.

- Saying no to someone asking for or taking a hug.
- Saying no to someone giving unsolicited advice.
- Telling a person you don't want to hear a long, drawn-out story about how they were victimized (for the fifth time).
- Saying you don't want to talk in the group.
- Voicing dissatisfaction with the group.
- Saying no to flirtation.
- Saying no to sponsors or others making sexual advances.
- Saying no to someone being your sponsor.
- Changing your mind about someone's being your sponsor or a friend.
- Changing your mind about being in the group.
- Saying no when you don't have time or you don't want to engage with someone. (I will talk about this in more detail because it came up repeatedly in my interviews and I see it frequently in my practice.)

Because fellowship is so strongly stressed in twelve-step programs and women are so deeply programmed to be available for others at expense to themselves, many women said they exhausted themselves listening to other people's problems. It is one thing to be helpful, and another to be a victim.

Remember, everyone has the right to say, "No, I'm busy, I don't have the energy right now; I'd like to talk another time, but not today," or "I have about five minutes but that's all" in response to someone asking for time or help. Women I interviewed told of listening for hours to other women and men telling them about the abuse they were suffering, how hard their lives were, and on and on. As a result they were drained and felt resentful of the caller.

People need to distinguish between being a sponge for someone else's problems and being supportive for someone taking action to change their life. When people tell "how bad it is" stories, it is not helpful to listen to them more than once or twice. You can be kind about saying no, but don't be surprised when someone is furious at you for not being willing to absorb their problems for them, especially if you have done it for a long time. Some signals of being used emotionally in an interaction are when you feel tired, depressed, or drained after listening to someone. If you want to conserve and protect your energy, stop listening to unending stories of woe.

If someone calls wanting support to take action to improve their life or is genuinely seeking insight, you will probably not feel drained afterwards. Sometimes it is important to stretch ourselves a little in an emergency, but other times we reinforce people creating crises and drama if we jump every time they sound the alarm. Many people are habituated to getting attention through trauma and crises, which isn't helpful to them or you.

Likewise, part of maturity in relationships is to learn to accept other people saying "no" without feeling ashamed or disliked. No matter what childhood traumas we experience, we can't expect friends to always be available, or to listen to us talk forever. We have to grieve our losses and learn the rules for peer communication where everyone has a right to say yes and no without being shamed, argued with, or called a bad person. We also need to learn how to draw on our inner or spiritual strength if we can't find someone for support.

RACISM AND SEXISM IN GROUPS

I have referred to boundary intrusions as core to hierarchy. While some groups, often women's groups, were able to bridge differences, the scars of sexism, racism, and homophobia were frequently described in interviews. It didn't matter if I was talking to women, African Americans, Latinos(as), or Native Americans, the theme was always the same. The people higher in the hierarchy often dominated and were insensitive to the subordinate group.

At a Native American reservation, a man described what happened when white men came into a group that was originally for Native Americans. "The white men talked the most, one of them said we should say the Lord's Prayer, they interrupted when we talked about vision quests as part of our healing, and another tried to be all buddy-buddy right away without taking time to build trust." Another person added, "They didn't understand that we often communicate in subtle ways, we don't always say things right out." The same was true when men came into women's groups, or white people came into Black groups. The minority group would typically clam up and quit talking openly and eventually leave the group.

Minority groups will naturally incorporate languages and attitudes inherent in their background. The dominant group, not trained to be sensitive, will often be blind to subtle cues or will be judgmental because they operate from a limited perspective.

As one African American chemical dependency counselor said, "You always sit there wondering, 'What is that white guy *really* thinking about me? Is he faking it? What does he say behind my back?' Class issues also arise: The rich white man is talking about his pain over losing his boat, and none of the poor men can relate. They never had a boat to lose."

BOUNDARY VIOLATIONS IN TREATMENT PROGRAMS

Institutionalized Abuses

Many people have had positive experiences in treatment programs or rehabilitation centers for all forms of addiction or dependency. On the other hand, for some it has been a nightmare. Over the years I have heard numerous stories of inappropriate or abusive behavior in treatment programs. Some of it was institutionalized into the policies of the program, and in other cases individuals perpetrated the abuses.

One example of institutionalized abuse is the shame-based treatment philosophy that was used for many years and has been a source of profound destruction to many people, particularly people without power in the system such as women and teenagers. I refer to a shame-based as opposed to a guilt-based approach to helping people realize the destruction their addiction is causing them.

Early treatment programs geared their approach to highly resistant men, many of whom had sociopathic personality traits, inflated, rigid egos, or were in tremendous denial about their alcohol or drug use. In a shame-based approach, male values of toughness were typically the standard. Clients were coldly cut down: "You think you're so good. You're being arrogant. You're a big baby. You're nothing." These assaults were sometimes called giving a haircut. People were made to wear shaming signs on their chests, were put in diapers, or had their heads shaved.

As is typical in our hierarchical system, what ostensibly worked to keep these men sober was taken as "the way" and applied—or one might better say inflicted—on women and men and teenagers who had fragile or deficient ego development. For many it was devastating. Teenagers' parents, relieved to finally have them in a treatment program, often turned a deaf ear to honest accounts of abuse. The teenagers then had no place to turn.

One young woman of sixteen, Gerri, a survivor of incest and physical abuse, recounted being forced to wear a sign on her chest reading "Big Boobs" because she had flirted with a counselor. (He had flirted with her.) She begged to take it off when family members came for family week, but counselors wouldn't let her. At one point she was told to stand in the center of a circle while men berated her—"You're just a slut, you get off on power-tripping men, we have to clean up the floors after you're around," and the like. Natural feelings of sadness, fear, or feeling little were routinely shamed. Gerri, for example, had brought a little teddy bear with her to treatment as comfort. The treatment counselors took it away from her when they found it and said "Grow up. Don't be such a baby." At that point she started to contemplate suicide.

Other women and men have described similar forms of abuse in treatment programs dominated by this patriarchal approach. One woman from a Synanon treatment program was totally deflated and then encouraged to stay as a counselor. They kept her there by constantly destroying her self-esteem so she wouldn't have the ego strength to leave—a typical tactic of brainwashing and cults.

If it's hard to believe such abuse could happen in treatment programs or you've never heard of it, it's because most people have been ashamed to talk about it. Like sexual harassment it is widespread and still happens.

In these tragic incidents we can see more clearly the dangers of a sin-and-redemption approach. Addiction is treated like a sin and the redemption comes through breaking the will and humbling people through humiliation. It's based on the fear that unless people are controlled, belittled, and demeaned, they will go out of control. How far this is from a life-loving/creative spirituality that affirms that love, joy, passion and kindness are sacred—a spirituality that believes we are born magical and blessed and that life's pleasures are to be savored and will not go out of control if we live a balanced life.

It is important to recognize differences between shame-based and guilt-based models, as well as an empowerment approach. It is also important to remember that battering people's self-esteem is battering people's self-esteem, sexual harassment is sexual harassment, and abuse is abuse, whether it occurs in office buildings, on the street, or in therapy or treatment programs.

My hope for all people is to trust their instincts. It's one thing to be urged to push through your fears in a rehabilitation or treatment program, or for teenagers to be given clear limits and logical consequences; it's another to be abused or shamed. If you think this might be happening to you or has happened to you, talk to someone, talk to several people, or call a sexual violence center or a hotline about sexual harassment. Remember, it's not your fault. It has happened to many people. It's another form of the abuses that go on in hierarchy under the guise of "what's good for you."

Mercifully, the shame-based approach has slowly given way to a guilt-based approach: Don't drink because it's bad for you, it gets you in trouble. And, even better as mentioned earlier, a few programs operate from an empowerment approach: It's your choice not to use because you choose life. Other evidence of a dramatic shift is that instead of shaming the inner child, people are encouraged to heal the inner child. Carrying teddy bears and the like is now encouraged at some treatment programs.

An institutional form of *neglect* that comes from the culture's medical model of seeing pathology instead of ecology is to treat only the addiction and not take into account the rest of the person. Thus important concerns, such as childhood abuse, racism, dependent or violent relationships, poverty, depression, mental disorders, multiple personality disorder, or post-traumatic stress disorder, have typically been ignored in traditional treatment programs.

Instead of treating the whole person, individuals are often reduced to a diagnosis—chemically dependent, codependent, anorexic—as separate from other concerns. I believe this contributes significantly to the high level of relapse, because addiction is often a symptom of deeper problems. It is not surprising that programs run by and for minorities tend to take a broader view. They are closer to the pulsebeat of the kind of deprivation and violation that often underlies addiction.

Individual Boundary Intrusions

Some abuses that happen in treatment programs on an individual basis are often due to sexism, homophobia, racism, ignorance, lack of education, and poor supervision.

Treatment counselors are sometimes fairly new to recovery and can be certified with roughly two years of post–high school training. They may have more training, but not necessarily. Often they don't have the psychological training to recognize important differences in levels of ego strength, or emotional problems or "mental illness." As a result, people have been suddenly taken off medications, been encouraged to open up their emotions when they needed to gain control over them, or told to focus on their faults (the fourth and fifth steps), which exacerbated their depression.

In some treatment programs based on the twelve steps, staff have related to clients with the fellowship norms of "the program" and ignored power differences between counselor and client. There is often resistance to setting boundaries between staff and clients because equality is stressed in twelve-step programs. Fellowship is fine, but one cannot ignore power differences in institutions without running into problems and, in some cases, abuse.

Here are some types of boundary violations from treatment or rehabilitation programs that often have occurred because people do not understand power differences in institutions.

1. *Supervisor and trainee boundary violations.* A supervisor has more institutional power than a trainee. Thus when the supervisor invites the trainee out for coffee and confides about his or her personal life, the trainee has been violated. One woman I worked with became depressed and extremely confused when her supervisor would first ask about cases and then ask about her personal life or talk about himself. Over time, his disclosures became more and more personal and included information about past sexual relationships. He would invite her out for coffee and she would leave feeling flattered . . . and uneasy. As time went on, he started putting his arm around her and she told me she had fallen in love with him.

Even though she was getting depressed and had a flare-up with her ulcer, she was extremely protective of him—"Oh, it's not him. It's just me. I just need to detach." It took months before she realized that because he was her supervisor he had more power in the relationship than she did. His unloading on her emotionally was a violation. In the meantime, she had spent three months getting more and more depressed and anxious; she lost fifteen pounds and spent lots of money in therapy processing his inappropriate behavior and her inability to see it. Heaven only knows what she learned about being a counselor during that time.

2. *After-care counselor and client boundary violations.* After-care groups are created to give continued support following graduation from a treatment program. Often after-care counselors are volunteers, interns, graduates of the treatment program, or people with little therapeutic training who do not get in-depth supervision for facilitating groups. This is extremely problematic because the problems and concerns that come up after treatment are often more complex than initial treatment issues.

In one situation a volunteer after-care counselor got mad at a member of the group for not returning her invitations to be friends. Typically, after their group meeting the counselor and the clients would all go out for coffee and socialize. When the client said, "But I don't want to be your friend," the counselor told her she was selfish. When I did a session with the two of them it was clear that the counselor had no training in appropriate boundaries and had no concept that it was inappropriate for her to expect friendship from the client.

"But we're all really equals," she said to me. "At a spiritual level that's true," I countered, "but when you are the group leader your role is to be there for the clients' needs." This is not to fault that individual after-care counselor; it is rather to suggest the institution should hire professional counselors, train staff to understand boundaries, and provide sufficient supervision.

In another case, a male after-care counselor frequently gave a female member a ride home and asked her to help plan a recovery conference together. He frequently called her and he offered to take her daughter to the circus in the guise of being a helping friend, or wanting to relieve her stressful life. Other members of the group became jealous of her and rejected her, just like in her family of origin. She spent weeks in therapy sorting out her feelings, writing letters, and gaining strength to confront the treatment program. In the meantime she lost her group, went through incredible stress, and was charged by the treatment program for the time in group, which she later protested.

3. *Mixing clients and trainer roles.* In my own history, I was once asked to present a sexuality workshop to the staff where I was in an intense outpatient treatment program for childhood abuse. I was, of course, flattered to be asked, but later I felt ripped off. I needed to bring my vulnerable side to the program, not my well-defended competent self. When a client is in a program he or she should be free to be a client: It is abusive for staff to be peers or buddies with clients, to single some people out for "special" treatment, or to have them do any form of training or allude to future times when they can be friends or peers or professional associates.

4. *Violations from the old buddy system.* In one treatment program where I consulted, the director had hired lots of his AA buddies as counselors, although many were inexperienced. Female staff were incensed that he bypassed usual hiring procedures. He created an old-boy network in the treatment center, and rarely included women in decisions about treatment, although over half of the counselors and clients were women.

At one point, when the women staff proposed an all-women's group (clients were complaining to them about the inexperienced male staff), one of the male therapists said, "But it's too hard to do groups without women—they open up emotionally and keep things going." The women counselors were incensed at this blatant exploitation of the female clients. The director either couldn't grasp the situation or chose loyalty to his AA buddies over female staff and client needs. Many women staff eventually left the facility after suffering symptoms of stress and burnout.

While there are many programs where people understand appropriate boundaries, at least most of the time, these are not uncommon stories.

Here are my recommendations.

Treatment staff needs to operate from the perspective that clients are clients and are not there for the staff's benefit. The question for staff to ask is, Is this policy, behavior, etc., being done for the education and empowerment of the client, or for the convenience, ego, and money-making needs of the treatment program at the expense of the client?

Sexual harassment, exploitation, and using clients for personal needs should all be defined, discussed, and talked about in staff meetings and in-service training sessions.

Directors should not hire close friends. There should be clear guidelines for hiring new staff that include input from all levels of existing staff. Creating an old-buddy or old-girl system is a set-up for power struggles and tensions that will inevitably filter down to clients.

Staff should learn to understand different personality types and ego strengths, and have direction from trained psychologists. A perpetrator or narcissistic person with a well-defended ego needs a much different approach than a depressed person who has been abused and has little ego development. Social histories and psychological evaluations are important in planning the approach to use with a client.

On-line staff should have input into policy decision-making, particularly about therapy methods. Their styles of counseling should be respected. The people delivering direct services are closest to the pulsebeat of the clients and should be seen as an important source of information about needs of clients. They should also be free to operate in a way that feels true to them, so long as it is within the philosophy of the program. While they may have guidelines to follow, they shouldn't have their creativity strangled by overly rigid rules about how they deliver services to clients. It's important to hire good counselors, pay them well, and then support them and give them good supervision.

Staff members in treatment programs (including all administrative staff) should raise their consciousness about patriarchy, hierarchy, power differences, and group dynamics. This can be done with in-service training and outside consultants.

It is advisable to have organizational consultation by a neutral person outside the organization. The goal is to help create an information system in the organization that has a good communication network going from dominants to subordinates and subordinates to dominants. Because of power differences, people in subordinate positions often remain quiet about problems in the system unless there is a neutral outside person for support. As a result, the dominants often make decisions with very little understanding of the needs of the people who are being served by the organization.

It is advisable to have staff supervision by a neutral person outside the organization. In-house supervision can be useful if done by a skilled outside person who is not part of the power structure. The person should be hired with input from the staff and not just be a friend of the director. One way is to have potential supervisors come in for sessions with the staff and let the staff choose. In my experience, in-house supervision rarely goes as deep as supervision in an outside group, but it is a crucial part of the well-being and cohesiveness of an organization.

It is advisable for counselors to have outside supervision by a professional therapist. In outside groups, people can talk openly about problems they are having with clients or in their organization without fear of getting a bad review from a supervisor. Staff should be given paid time for outside supervision, which would probably be cost-effective because of the increased quality of services they could provide—not to mention that good supervision helps prevent burnout.

Guidelines are important, but they can never make up for having an organization where administrators have a strong commitment, good will, and respect for all employees and clients. The two are inseparable, for if staff are poorly treated, disrespected, or not included in decision-making, it invariably filters down to clients, who pick up the tension.

While many programs are now spending considerable money on marketing, it's important to remember that there is a huge network of therapists and counselors who refer clients to treatment programs based primarily on the word of former clients—the true experts of the quality of any treatment program. My hunch is that money spent on better salaries for well-trained, talented counselors, including women, people of color, out lesbians and gay men, providing good supervision and having in-house trainings on racism, sexism, and homophobia, is the most cost-effective approach to fostering a program that has a safe atmosphere, which will automatically attract clients. I remember at one time in the Twin Cities there was a program with a woman counselor who was openly lesbian. Therapists routinely referred lesbian clients to that program as well as women seeking a feminist atmosphere. After she quit because of the sexism in the program, most of us stopped referring lesbian and heterosexual women there—which meant hundreds of women. This is just one example of how quality of staff affects referrals.

SEXUAL VIOLATION IN TWELVE-STEP GROUPS

"In both straight and gay and lesbian groups the usual kind of bar behavior went on—a lot of cruising, going through multiple partners. This always creates tension. . . . One of the profound insights I gained was that people in AA are like people anywhere."
—WOMAN FROM AN AA GROUP

I have mentioned sexual boundary violations throughout this chapter. This section underscores the immense importance of recognizing seduction and exploitation in groups so people will be alert to either ceasing their exploitation of others or to protecting themselves. My hope is also that more groups will develop guidelines.

While many treatment programs have guidelines or rules against dating and sexual relationships while people are in treatment, most twelve-step groups have no particular policy. In fact, seduction in groups has become so common it is called thirteenth stepping. While one of the traditions talks about putting the group welfare above all else, long-entrenched habits of hierarchy appear to prevail in many groups. About three-fourths of the respondents to my questionnaire said there had been flirting, seduction, and dating in groups, and they described it as uncomfortable, distracting, or extremely frightening. About one fourth had been sexually violated or abused in a twelve-step group. One woman said seeing the flirting triggered sexual-abuse memories, so she left and never came back. Another said she became "emotionally frozen and horrified."

In my questionnaire I asked several question about flirting, seduction, or dating in groups, and the need for rules or possibly a hotline people could call with concerns about a group. It was often painful reading the responses to my questions. I wanted to sleep, eat, take a walk—anything to avoid reading about so much hurt and pain. I felt frustrated at the prevalence of sexual exploitation and abuse, and that so many women seemed resigned to sexual exploitation as a normal part of life or felt hopeless that guidelines or policies about sexual relationships could have an effect. I felt encouraged when women expressed anger, talked about the need for guidelines, and recognized that flirting and seduction were inappropriate in support groups.

There was a wide range of answers to my questions on having guidelines about dating and flirting. They ranged from, "No—mind your own business," to "I'm not sure you could enforce them, people are just that way," to "Yes, recovery groups are for recovery, not dating."

While there is no overall policy for twelve-step groups, Sex Addicts Anonymous (SAA) has very clear limits. No sexual energy, no dating or flirting—and if you fall in love with someone, one person in the couple leaves the group. Also, in the Twin Cities area, most of the SAA groups are either all male or all female. This creates protection for heterosexual members, and the guidelines serve as a reminder for lesbian and gay members. Many people in these groups expressed their relief at having a safe space with clear guidelines. The mixed male-female SAA groups are most often attended by people who have been healing for some time and have learned about appropriate boundaries. At this point, people find that mixed groups can be beneficial.

Flirting and seduction in twelve-step groups has had a profound effect on many people. Some people went to groups, saw the flirting, left and never came back. Other people stayed and were abused. One woman wrote, "A man approached me on a spiritual basis and within a month we had gone to bed together. I came very close to losing my sobriety. I had not hurt so badly since getting sober. The shame and guilt were almost unbearable."

In describing the tension in the group, someone else talked about two women who got into a sexual relationship with each other. "They were very obvious about it and announced their partnership at meetings. Some members felt a power shift take place—they said it felt like there was now a mother/father duo in the group and they felt unsafe. I felt it was inappropriate for them to kiss and hold hands at meetings and whisper and act 'cutesy.' "

And, describing one of the most blatant abuses, one woman wrote:

I met a man in my weekly group who became a trusted part of my life and community. After six months, we dated, then began a sexually, romantically intimate relationship. Six months into the relationship I discovered he had ritually abused and sexually molested my precious three-year-old daughter." She went on to say, "Our OA group was supportive of our romance and friendship. They believed him to be a 'nice guy' too. We all feel very tricked and betrayed by his perpetration."

Many women cited two or three different groups where they had felt the strains of sexual energy being expressed in the group either openly or covertly. A majority of people said that they did not think dating or flirting was appropriate in recovery groups.

Some of the questionnaires showed conflicting information. Some women did not necessarily see a need to set limits or boundaries even though they had been abused in groups. In several cases, women said they trusted that the group conscience would take care of problems, or they saw abuse as an isolated incident. One woman who had been abused "thought it was a relatively safe place to meet people," and she still thinks "dating is okay in groups."

SUGGESTED GUIDELINES FOR GROUPS

If twelve-step groups purport to provide a community for healing, then the community needs to take responsibility for providing a safe place for healing. It simply cannot be left up to individuals. Thus the group conscience needs to consider raising its consciousness about sexism, sexual harassment and exploitation, and the harmful effects they have on people.

Because of the frequency of sexual abuse and exploitation in groups, I believe it is important to have guidelines in groups against flirting and dating. If two people decide to have a sexual relationship, one should leave the group. These rules are not meant as punitive measures, rather to protect vulnerable people and to raise consciousness for everyone. This protects the incest survivor who has not learned to sort out sexuality from friendship.

It is also *not* in the best interest of the person who is doing the seduction to not have guidelines. Seduction is often done as a controlling behavior that masks a deeper vulnerability. The person who is being seductive could be hiding a sexual addiction that has a greater chance of being uncovered if flirtation and seduction are not acceptable in a group.

Exploitive or dependent relationships are common causes of relapse. While no one can prevent this happening, groups could educate people about and model appropriate sexual boundaries and support people in making close friends. It is important to distinguish between two people genuinely meeting and caring about each other and deciding to pursue a relationship and men "hitting on" vulnerable women, or women seducing men, or people seeking sex partners. Because a recovery group becomes the psychological family for many, flirting and seduction of this type feels incestuous and is especially traumatizing to incest survivors.

My impression from SAA and CoSA (Codependents of Sexual Addicts) groups is that guidelines make a positive difference. While people do not always abide by the rules, their very existence makes it easier to confront people who deviate from the norms. Having rules is like having a protective boundary around the group and is consistent with the idea of protecting the welfare of the group. One woman suggested that the group write the rules and then read them at the beginning of their meeting each week.

People cited numerous reasons for wanting group guidelines about dating, flirting, and sexual relationships. One woman wrote, "I feel very vulnerable. I know now that love addiction or codependency is involved in most people coming for help around addiction. I appreciate my SLAA [Sex and Love Addicts Anonymous] sponsor who says 'She'll never date me or be available.' I would like that to be a policy in AA, Al-Anon, OA, and so on."

Another woman wrote, "If clear boundaries are voiced, it may be easier for folks to operate within the group without certain fears. Also—most folks in recovery groups are boundary-less, and any practical experience in learning about boundaries may help."

Some people took a mixed view about having rules.

"I think they [rules] would be pretty tough to enforce. But people should be warned of the dangers of inter-group dating. It slows down— or halts—recovery. . . . There *has* to be a safe place for people who hurt so desperately. How awful to experience that again when you're trying to open up."

There were also the no-rules advocates, who said there was no point in making rules because you couldn't enforce them anyhow. There was a kind of resigned, all-or-nothing thinking—if it can't be perfect, why try. Many people laid all the responsibility at an individual's feet, forgetting that a community by definition needs to have guidelines that foster care and protection for all the members. Without guidelines, it can be difficult to take action with an abusive member.

As one woman wrote, "I don't think you can impose rules on human beings." She later added, "We had a sex addict in denial making new women feel hit on. Five groups told him he was banned. Now he isn't around. We took action ourselves. . . . It took four to five years, though." Five years is a long time to have a group drained of its healing energy, siphoned off by someone who perpetrates.

Apparent contradictions were common in other questionnaires. While women could describe abusive situations, and sometimes acknowledge the personal harm they experienced as a result, many did not take the stance that there should be changes. Their loyalty to the rules and to external control appeared to exceed their loyalty to themselves and their safety and protection. It was as if they couldn't imagine living in a world where safety and respect for them was possible.

Several people cited the fourth tradition as the reason there should be no accountability or hotline for groups. The short form of the fourth tradition reads, "Each group should be autonomous except in matters affecting other groups or AA as a whole." And in the long form, the first statement is, "With respect to its own affairs, each AA group should be responsible to no other authority than its own conscience." One person wrote "I would not be comfortable with twelve-step groups that set these kinds of boundaries, as it violates an important and basic AA tradition re group membership."

The purpose of this tradition was to protect the common welfare of the groups. It certainly was not intended to protect members from confrontation about sexual abuse or exploitation, which has everything to do with the common welfare of the groups. Again, we get in trouble when we adhere to words in the letter rather than the spirit.

And if someone takes the tradition literally, what strikes me as worthy of serious discussion is whether it is more important to protect a tradition or to protect people. I opt for the latter, as I don't believe the fourth tradition, which was written in the early 1940s, took into consideration sexual harassment, incest, and sexual abuse.

The second tradition was also cited as a reason for not having guidelines. "For our group purpose there is but one ultimate author-ity—a loving God as He may express Himself in our group con-science." Using this to avoid making protective guidelines again re-flects a childlike faith that the group conscience is aware of sexism, sexual exploitation, and abuse. Because our cultural conscience accepts sexual exploitation so readily, many people in twelve-step groups do likewise, or don't realize they need to protect themselves. People wrote things like, "I thought that was normal." "I couldn't believe anyone in the program would do a thing like that." Only with education and consciousness-raising will we see changes.

FIFTH STEPS AND BOUNDARY VIOLATIONS

Another important twelve-step institution that has resulted in terrible violations is related to fourth and fifth steps. For the moment, I am not talking about the content of fourth and fifth steps; rather, I mean the ways treatment programs administer them and incidents of boundary intrusions and sexual violation that have happened. We will discuss the many positive aspects of the *content* of fourth and fifth steps in chapter 13, "Moving Beyond the Twelve Steps."

The following boundary intrusions are a reflection of patriarchy being played out in groups because there is so little consciousness of sexism, racism, and power differences. This is exacerbated by the mys-tique built up around twelve-step programs, which lulls people into denial about abuse and exploitation.

The fourth step reads, "Made a searching and fearless moral inven-tory of ourselves." The fifth step reads, "Admitted to God, to our-selves, and to another human being the exact nature of our wrongs."

Many treatment programs require a fifth step before graduating. The fact that it is *required* before graduation is intrusive in that it orders rather than suggests what someone needs to do. While I understand that treatment programs need to set up criteria, a fifth step is an extremely personal, emotional experience. I believe it is against the spirit of the twelve-step program—a *suggested* program—to make this step a "requirement" for graduation.

Taking a fifth step after four weeks of sobriety, whether or not one agrees with the concept, is often too soon for people. One woman minister who worked in a treatment program said that fifth steps taken in treatment programs were rarely a true fifth step. Rather, people simply used that time to take advantage of having a sympathetic ear to listen to their struggles. She commented that many women frequently talked about sexual abuse, saying they had not felt comfortable bringing it up in mixed gender groups. I don't believe that being a victim of incest and abuse should ever be coupled with the concept of taking a moral inventory. Because we live in such a blame-the-victim society, we should take special care not to associate these two concepts. If a woman needs to talk to a caring counselor about incest or abuse, it should not be called a fifth step.

It can also be inappropriate to do a traditional fifth step in treatment programs when someone has little ego development or is depressed, which is common in early sobriety. Typically, a depressed person has tremendous cognitive distortions resulting in persistent negative thinking. They think everything is their fault, and are constantly blaming and berating themselves. To make a list of one's faults is all too easy for a depressed person and the opposite of what he or she needs to be doing, which is to reach for their strengths and start to take charge of their life.

The other intrusive aspect of fifth steps in treatment programs is assigning someone to hear a fifth step. One young woman, Jane, was required to take the fifth step with a male minister appointed by the treatment facility. She had heard him talk and didn't particularly like him, but the counselors pressured her, saying he was very nice and that he did all the fifth steps for their program. One counselor even shamed and threatened her saying she was being controlling which would get in the way of recovery. This kind of pressure was in itself a violation of Jane's own good instincts.

When Jane described a recent rape as part of her "moral inventory" to the minister, he asked her to come sit beside him. She felt terror and a sense of panic but obliged. He starting fondling her hair and stroking her shoulders, saying, "Oh, you poor thing." She recalled feeling sick, horrible, and paralyzed. He asked numerous questions about her sexual behavior, which she later labeled as voyeuristic and intrusive. He held her. It felt like rape. She couldn't find her voice to say no. When it was over she had a relapse with her bulimia.

This is a blatant misuse of power, a form of sexual harassment or abuse. She was told to trust and be honest, to literally bare her soul, and she was abused. Then, when she confronted staff in the program after a year of therapy, the response was the same old story—they didn't believe her. It was a young female "addict's" word against that of the staff minister. A year later, another client from the same treatment program told an almost identical story. She decided to take action, but was also rebuffed and shamed by male and female counselors at every turn. He was a nice man, he couldn't do anything like that, they told her. After considerable effort, both clients finally gave up. For all I know this person is still hearing fifth steps and sexually abusing women.

Other types of intrusion or abuse are when the person hearing the fifth step touches the person without their consent, implies they had a part in creating abuse, minimizes the impact of abuse, tells them to give up their resentments, makes sexual jokes, or keeps the focus on sex or repeatedly asks about it.

Reverend Elaine Marsh, a minister who has heard upwards of five hundred fifth steps, suggested to me that women interview the person who will take the fifth step. I asked her about men hearing women give fifth steps. She said that, for many women, sexuality, sex abuse, and sexual acting out are frequently part of a fifth step. Did she think a man could do a fifth step with a woman?

"Of course, everyone gets to choose for herself," she said, "but I would *never refer* a woman to a man for a fifth step. I have spent twenty years picking up the pieces of women who went to male counselors, male clergy, and male therapists, and while I'm not saying there aren't a few who couldn't do a good job, the risk is simply too great."

I want to underscore the word choice and suggest that treatment programs *never coerce, pressure, or force anyone to take a fifth step against their will or with someone they don't know or like.* It's like asking someone to prostitute themselves. If someone wants to take a fifth step while in treatment, they should get to choose who hears it. If we remember our levels of faithing and the goal of moving to a level where we question what we are told and take charge of our lives from the inside out, then we can easily see that it is counter to the goal of empowering people to force them to do something against their wills.

Suggestions for Taking a Fifth Step

I have put together a brief list of suggestions based on interviews, questionnaires, and my own experience for people taking a fifth step.

1. Do a fifth step when you feel ready and believe it would be helpful to you.

2. Interview the person hearing the step in advance. Let yourself know how you feel talking with that person, and *trust your reaction.* One woman wrote, "Make sure you trust the person, that they listen and hear well and are nurturing and supportive in a respectful way." Ask how long they usually take. Rev.

Marsh said she often spends three or four hours. Where will they hear the fifth step? Is it a comfortable, private place?

3. If a treatment program says you have to take a fifth step to graduate, let them know this is a violation of your right to choose. It is better to be true to yourself than get a graduation certificate. Even if you are a client in a program, it's still your life. The goal is to heal and stay sober.

4. The person hearing the step does not have to be clergy. Several women in SAA did fifth steps with other group members whom they trusted would understand and not shame them. Sometimes they did it with two or three other women. Others did it with their sponsor.

5. If you start a fifth step and it doesn't feel okay—if you start to feel sick to your stomach, if the person encourages you to talk about sexual matters and it feels uncomfortable, or if they touch you in some way that feels bad or inappropriate—leave. Get up and walk out. You don't owe it to anyone to stay. You owe it to yourself to protect yourself.

6. If you are a woman, seriously consider doing your fifth step with a woman.

7. If you don't want to take a fifth step, you don't have to. Many people have stayed sober without one, and there is no evidence showing a correlation between sobriety and the fifth step.

Suggestions for Treatment/Rehabilitation Programs

1. Give clients a choice of whether or not to take a fifth step. Explain it carefully. Let them know they may often think of much more they want to include in a fifth step at a later time.

2. All people should have a choice of who they take the step with and should have the opportunity to interview the person.

3. Women should be *encouraged* to see women, because there is less danger of a woman's listening voyeuristically or reinforcing that rape, battering, or abuse was in some way the woman's fault.

4. Minority people should be encouraged to find people they feel comfortable with in their own community.

5. If the client has little ego strength or is depressed, have them inventory their strengths and ability to take power over their lives as opposed to their shortcomings.

6. The step could be renamed to be a time to talk about anything one feels guilty or ashamed about—which could include ways they have been victimized.

For People Hearing the Fifth Step

It is hard to make guidelines, because being a good listener and knowing when to respond and when to stay quiet is an art that grows out of one's own personal work and awareness. People who do abuse or sexually perpetrate usually do so in secret and deny what they are doing. They are often sexual abuse victims themselves who need considerable help, far beyond the scope of a list of wrongs.

It is a given that the role of the person taking the fifth step is to listen, understand, be supportive, and help alleviate the person's guilt and shame. It is not all right to touch, caress, have sexual fantasies, be voyeuristic with, press the person to talk about sex, or in any way use them emotionally to build up one's ego. Being present for another human being has to come out of a caring heart and a sense of personal vulnerability so that you see the other person as a mirror, not as someone beneath you.

LET'S EXPLORE THE PROBLEM TOGETHER

We live in a culture rampant with sexual exploitation and psychological boundary intrusions. They are the nature of our hierarchical system, where the people holding open power are taught to presume ownership over people below them in the system. Women, no matter what their race, class, or status, are one-down in the system and the most likely to be psychologically abused or victimized by sexual abuse and exploitation in treatment groups or recovery groups.

A huge number of people coming into recovery/discovery groups—both women and men—are survivors of childhood abuse and victimization. They are scared, insecure, they don't understand appropriate relationships, and they have a longing to belong, to be connected and heal. Some people coming into groups have perpetrated violence and sexual abuse, and others are sexually addicted.

As a community promising healing and recovery, it is time for an open, honest moral inventory of seduction, flirtation, and emotional violation in groups. While humans will always be fallible, education and increased awareness about the dangers can help countless people avoid painful experiences. As a community, we all need to take responsibility for creating a safe place for everyone.

PART IV

❧

Discovering New Roads

11

❧

Moving Beyond Codependency:
Understanding Internalized Oppression

"Even though I was addicted to alcohol and drugs for twenty years, the real problem was that I never learned to be a person. . . . The hardest thing for me to give up was the hope that someone would come along and take care of me . . ."
—KELLY

Kelly made that statement after being hospitalized for depression nearly five years into her chemical sobriety. Kelly is the woman you met in chapter 2 who had worked for me and joined one of the first sixteen-step empowerment groups.

Hospitalization or a time of intense emotional upheaval after an initial period of sobriety is not uncommon. Often, as a person moves through the survival period of sobriety and feels more secure, deeper problems begin to surface. Often these problems relate to infancy and early childhood and the lack of a trusting bond or attachment to a parent or caregiver. These buried childhood traumas are then reflected or reenacted in dependent or addictive sexual relationships. Such was the case with Kelly. In addition to the scars from her childhood, Kelly's lack of identity and tendency toward depression was further intensified by being a single mother on welfare without a supportive family or a meaningful vocation.

Even so, her slide into depression caught Kelly by surprise. Life had started to look promising. She'd been doing well in vocational training, feeling good about her empowerment group, and she was making friends who shared her beliefs.

So what happened? Kelly's fragile ego strength dissolved in a sexual relationship with a man named Bob, who was at once charming and fun, and yet emotionally withholding, unreliable, and seldom vulnerable to her.

Her intense longing for someone to take care of her and lack of being trained to believe her instincts left her confused. She was unable to translate the chronic knot in her gut into the knowledge that Bob was controlling and seducing her emotionally by giving her crumbs of attention and then withdrawing his affection. One day he would smile and hug her when he saw her, and then the next day when she reached out to put her arms around him, he was like a corpse. He would allude to future plans for a summer vacation together, but when Kelly asked where he would like to go, he intimated that she was being pushy. He was often late, and whenever she confronted him, he made it look as if Kelly had the problem—she wasn't spontaneous enough, she wanted to control him, she was too dependent.

She became obsessed with him. Like a child trying to prevent a parent's abandonment, she continually tried to find the "right" things to say to please him, and held back her anger and frustration so as not to upset him. She couldn't sleep or concentrate and was exhausted much of the time.

When the relationship problem became intense, Kelly went to Al-Anon. "In the Al-Anon group I kept looking at how it must be my problem—I had abandonment fears, I was too controlling. And nearly everyone kept the focus on what I could do to be more detached and less upset by his mood changes, his breaking dates, and his subtle forms of control. I never really expressed how upset I was. I just kept examining my 'dependent' behavior, and got more and more depressed."

Kelly finally persuaded Bob to go to a therapist with her. On the way home from the first session, he broke off their two-year relationship, leaving Kelly devastated. Her consuming emptiness left her feeling incapacitated. She started driving by Bob's house. Sometimes she followed him. While that gave her temporary relief, in the long run it made her more depressed. Eventually she took stock of her behavior and decided she should stop. After five days of staying away from him, she was more depressed than ever. In her words, "It was like the walls closing in—a feeling of sinking into oblivion."

Kelly was extremely disturbed about herself when she started making plans to follow him again. It was like there were two parts of her battling away inside, but the new survivor part that wanted to stay away from him was not strong enough to control the childlike part craving love and connectedness. At least when she followed him she did not feel so terribly alone and abandoned. Desperate to gain control, she went to a spiritual counselor.

After the counselor heard Kelly describe her overwhelming and frightening compulsion to follow Bob, along with the fact she had lost weight, felt frantic, and couldn't concentrate, she said, "You are depressed and should probably go to a depression unit in a hospital." Kelly was surprised but relieved. In her words, "Someone took me seriously and realized what terrible shape I was in." So, two months after the end of the relationship, Kelly committed herself to the depression unit of a hospital and had her young son placed in a foster home—history repeating itself. She was there for one month.

WHAT'S THE DIAGNOSIS? CODEPENDENCY, DEPRESSION, OR SOMETHING DEEPER?

Given typical definitions of codependency, one could say that Kelly's behavior was "codependent." She was unable to say no to Bob when she needed to, did not express her anger directly, kept hoping he'd change, abandoned her personal needs, neglected her other friends, tried to please him, took all the responsibility for the success of the relationship, and felt powerless to leave even though her life was disintegrating.

But is the solution for Kelly to label herself codependent, have cognitive therapy for depression, explore her family of origin, and go to Al-Anon? While these are certainly important parts of the picture, a fundamental ingredient is missing. Kelly needed help to look beyond individual or family pathology and to see her situation from a cultural perspective. To alleviate her self-blame, she needed to be told that her depression and dependency were *natural* results of her family neglect, her female socialization, and her current situation as a single, overwhelmed mother on welfare with limited resources for education. In other words, she needs some feminist consciousness-raising. She wasn't crazy, but she was feeling crazy as the result of a neglectful social system. She needed support to develop her personal power and take charge of her life and not be seen as sick.

DEFINITIONS OF "CODEPENDENCY"

"Codependency" is about lack of Self or ego development. (I use capital S for Self because I mean the holy, powerful Self.) It almost always involves strong negative programming against expressing anger, wants, and beliefs. It is a childlike state that results in having one's self-worth dependent on external validation. It's about living from the outside in, molding oneself to fit around others' lives instead of directing the course of one's life from internal cues, hopes, dreams, wisdom, and power.

Lacking internal security, a person hands their self-esteem and need for security to someone else. The underlying cry is, "Am I good enough? Do you love me? Take care of me. Please don't leave me." Some typical behaviors include being passive, submissive, dependent on others, pleasing others (sometimes to have them indebted to you), helping others while neglecting oneself, and covert expressions of needs, wants, and feelings. Because a dependent person doesn't believe they have the right to respect and care, they hint at things they want, or act super-nice, hoping the other person will figure it out. Unfortunately, when no one responds they control the internal rage, which further saps their energy and ability to develop a sense of personal power.

The *goal* of codependent behavior is to find externally the security and power that is lacking internally.

The *underlying feeling* is fear—fear of experiencing the terror and emptiness within, fear of being alone, fear of responsibility, and the fear of not being able to take care of oneself.

The *belief system* is that one cannot exist on one's own, and one therefore must do whatever it takes to keep a partner and any other symbols of security, such as a home, children, and financial support. For women in general, being taught to feel inferior to men increases the belief that approval from men is the source of self-esteem. For men, codependency often involves attaching self-worth to status, money, and sexual partners, and hiding a strong dependency on the emotional support of women.

Withdrawal from "codependency" comes when a person starts saying "no" to things they don't want to do, "yes" to things they like, and in general asserts their Self-identity by directly expressing needs, wants, hopes, beliefs, and feelings—particularly anger. The major symptoms of withdrawal are profound guilt and anxiety for going against one's upbringing and the cultural conditioning that says that affirming the Self and speaking up is arrogant, out of place, and will be discounted.

For women, withdrawal is doubly acute, because they are going against both family conditioning and female cultural conditioning that says they are selfish, controlling, pushy, cold, unloving, or mean when they act on their own behalf. Women and minorities face a very real threat of being ostracized and losing jobs and friends when they start speaking up for themselves. Thus it is *natural* that they are often afraid and exhausted from walking a fine line between pleasing the people with power over their lives and trying to be true to themselves.

It is not surprising that the vast majority of people in Al-Anon are women. From birth on, every institution of patriarchy inhibits their earning capacity and rewards them for being submissive, unassertive, and preoccupied with their bodies and looks, and then diagnoses them as having mental disturbances for their resultant depression and anxiety. Finally, they are ostracized when they get angry, become assertive, and take charge of their lives.

Men's codependency is categorically different from women's because society does not categorically punish men for asserting their power. Men often become dependent on their boss's approval and on women who provide the love and nurture they are unable to create for themselves. This varies in degree by class and race, but within all groups men are assigned a dominant role over women. Thus, while men may have strong traits of codependency—fear, passivity, and difficulty expressing anger—they typically have stronger sense of self and ego development.

Codependent behavior is women's basic programming. It is oppressive programming and we need to look at the source. While codependency groups have been very helpful to women, I believe they do not fully empower women because they do not raise consciousness about the politics of patriarchy, which are inseparable from our self-identity, values, and struggles as women.

If we read through traditional codependency literature such as *One Day at a Time in Al-Anon*, or the chapter "To Wives" in *Alcoholics Anonymous*, we see a multitude of blame-the-victim statements in many guises and forms. For example, the August 21 reading from *One Day at a Time* says that hopelessness is seen as "doubting the power of God." What about validating that hopelessness is sometimes about real things that happen in an inequitable system—rape, sexual harassment, poverty or racism? The same reading contends that we are "not at the mercy of a cruel or capricious fate." Yet people who are abused as children, raped, or left impoverished have been at the mercy of a cruel and capricious fate. It is extremely classist, sexist, and racist to deprive people of access to safety, education, and minimum living standards and then tell them their problems reflect a lack of faith in God, or that their situation is not capricious.

One Day at a Time repeatedly stresses that if you are suffering, it is of your making. By suggesting it is solely up to the individual to change their situation, this reading reinforces the idea that an individual is responsible for pain that is generated by an unjust, "cruel and capricious" society. This increases shame and guilt. Of course we have to take action to change our lives, and praying for strength to do so might help, but the changes needed to empower women so they don't feel so dependent must also come through group efforts to effect social change.

The chapter "To Wives" in *Alcoholics Anonymous* is more like a codependency manual (that is, how to be one) than a resource offering any real source of empowerment. Nearly all the advice is about how to act in relationship to the partner . . . uh, husband. Throughout the chapter, the option of leaving a "husband" who is alcoholic is only whispered, while the pervasive message is to stick it out with the patience, kindness, and goodness of Mother Teresa—regardless of violence, neglect, or emotional abuse.

There are constant implications that if the woman does it wrong, the "husband" might not recover. For example, "Family dissensions are very dangerous, *especially* to your husband . . . often you must carry the burden of avoiding them or keeping them under control. . . . The slightest sign of fear or intolerance may lessen your husband's chance of recovery." Why family dissensions are more dangerous to the husband than the wife is never explained.

Double messages to women abound. While women are rightly encouraged not to blame themselves, tell lies, or cover up to protect their husbands' drinking, they are also told, *"The first principle of success is that you should never be angry"* (emphasis mine). There are two oppressive messages in this statement. First is the implication that success equals changing your partner's behavior, and second is the admonition to squelch anger. As we discussed at length in chapter 3 on patriarchy, a primary goal of the dominants in a hierarchal system is to repress the anger/power of subordinates. When you are separated from your anger, your basic survival mechanism is wounded. Anger is a cue to help people know they are being violated, and anger energizes a person to set limits, rebel, or take flight.

The double messages extend to sexual infidelity. "Make him feel absolutely free to come and go as he likes. . . . If he gets the idea you are a nag or a killjoy, your chance of accomplishing anything useful may be zero. *He may seek someone else to console him—not always another man."* Again, his sobriety is her accomplishment, and the "wife" is blamed for his sex addiction. Where is support to express her feelings about him "seeking someone else to console him?"

Not surprisingly, there is not a chapter that tells *a man* to make *his wife* feel absolutely free to come and go as she pleases, and not to be a killjoy or else *she* might have an affair, or that he should take on the burden of controlling family dissension. The chapter "To Wives" sounds like popular women's magazines telling women how to navigate in a man's world, keeping "him" comfortable and maintaining peace at tremendous cost to self.

Nowhere does it say, Be honest, be yourself, be true, find your power, don't be abused, or abuse is not your fault. Reading between the lines, and sometimes just reading the lines, the chapter seems to be more for the "husbands'" comfort than for the well-being of the "wives."

When I have brought up the sexism in "To Wives" to people in treatment programs or recovery groups, many agree that it is outdated, but dismiss my concerns, saying, "But there's good stuff in the book." That response is like telling a woman to tolerate a little abuse, because "he's nice sometimes." And if people know it is outdated, then why isn't it revised and why is it still being handed to thousands of women to read without a warning about the sexism?

Given Bill Wilson's conditioning in the 1930s, it is not surprising that he approaches the chapter with traditional stereotypes of "husbands" and "wives." What disturbs me is that more than fifty years and three editions later, *Alcoholics Anonymous* has not been changed to reflect twenty-seven years of the feminist movement, along with the civil rights and gay and lesbian liberation movements. Judging from the questionnaires and interviews, this lack of attention to women, minorities, race, and class in many ways does reflect the current dominant thinking in AA circles, which is still sexist, resists dealing with diversity, and is threatened by change.

RESERVATIONS ABOUT THE TWELVE-STEP MODEL FOR CODEPENDENCY

The following list of reservations about use of the twelve-step model for women with "codependent" traits comes from interviews, questionnaires, client input, my personal experience, and feminist analysis of codependency literature. The list includes problems women encounter in Al-Anon groups as well as problems with the model itself.

I want to underscore that my reservations are not intended to criticize individuals who attend such groups—I have attended them myself—and, as I said at the outset of this book, all healing and finding one's true Self is sacred. Groups vary enormously. Many women have had wonderful support in codependency twelve-step groups, while others have not. The reservations I list are true for *some* groups *some* of the time.

The questions I'm operating from are: Does this model help women and men become their most powerful, evolved selves? Does it lead to a life-loving/creative spirituality and take us to an integrated level of faith?

Reservations About Twelve-Step Programs for Dependency Traits

1. *The steps stress powerlessness over others, rather than power within and the need for women's collective power in the culture.*

2. *Women get reinforced for staying in relationships where they give much more than they get.* They are not taught to expect love and care equally from a partner. Not taking stock of the emotional costs of a relationship leaves many women exhausted and depressed.

3. *The goal of detachment fails to take into account that living with an abusive or addicted person is often painful, hard, lonely, exhausting and no fun.* People drain their energy by continuously trying to figure out how to function "happily" with a cruel, neglectful, uncaring partner. They repeatedly discuss strategies for being "detached" from the partner. I believe this reinforces delusional thinking. *We* are *affected by the people we live with—there's no getting around it.* People emanate negative energy, just like toxic waste, and we inhale the fumes and get sick when we stay too long. It is important that women learn to value their energy, to use it for their own growth and creativity and not give it away needlessly when there is no return.

A role reversal illustrates the sexism inherent in the concept of detachment. When a white privileged man from the United States is released from being held hostage in a foreign country, front page news stories ooze sympathy and kindness to him for his trials and suffering. Yet when a woman is held hostage in an abusive relationship, threatened by losing her children or her life if she leaves, she is told to be more detached, try this and that technique and blamed when once again he beats her up. She didn't do it right or detach enough. Can you imagine telling a recently released hostage who appears to be disoriented and upset that he should have been more detached while incarcerated?

The concept of detachment fails to let women or men know that their feelings of frustration, hopelessness, rage, anger, and fear are *natural* responses to having an unpredictable, sometimes violent, emotionally abusive partner whose primary relationship is with his or her addiction. People with abusive partners often ask me, "Do you think if I go to Al-Anon I could be happy staying with my partner?" My response is, "If you were strong and happy, would you *want* to stay with a partner who is cold and abusive often?"

4. *Women bond in pain instead of power.* Women in these groups often give lots of energy to women who are suffering but withhold energy from women who are becoming powerful and outspoken. I have repeatedly heard women report that statements about feeling successful or powerful were greeted with a deadly silence or polite affirmation, followed by a subtle withdrawal of support. As women, it is crucial that we cheer for each other's successes and reinforce our strengths. Otherwise we reinforce others staying in pain and creating dramas. I speak from my own experience as well. When I once said in a group that I felt good and happy about my life, one woman told me I was being cocky (an interesting epithet) and that I wasn't being humble. I struggled not to feel ashamed, and then suddenly felt angry because I wanted to bond in power and joy with other women. One is somehow suspect in some codependency groups for feeling good about oneself.

When I asked women in a group to shed some light on this kind of response, one said, "It's scary when a woman shows her power, because I am so afraid of my own. If I get angry or am strong I'm afraid my partner will leave or no one will love me." Another said, "It reminds me that I need to take responsibility for myself, and part of me wants to stay little and be taken care of."

5. *Women's wonderful ability for care and nurture is sometimes pathologized or seen as codependent.* This may seem to contradict the above statement, but my perception is that women often devalue their wonderful capacity for showing love and care for others. I see the ability to love as part of being powerful. Reaching out, thoughtfulness, and kindness are not intrinsically codependent traits; rather, they need to be brought into balance with care and love for oneself. They need to be done honestly and not out of guilt, shame, duty, or as forms of manipulation.

6. *Stress, pain, and suffering are all seen totally as one's personal*

responsibility, not in the context of an abusive, inequitable system. Again, this blames the victim and keeps women (and men) from seeing themselves in the context of patriarchy.

7. *Women set aside their feminist perspective.* Because the mystique around twelve-step programs is so pervasive and the sanctions against questioning so strong, some women set aside their feminism or muffle their inner voice in order to be accepted in a group. Unless women apply a feminist analysis to their lives, they are left to carry the burden of their "codependent" traits as if they were individual pathology. We need to ask questions such as, "What is the value system I learned? Who taught me to believe this way? Is it good for me?" The twelve-step model needs to be subjected to feminist scrutiny just the same as any patriarchical insitution.

8. *There is little direct encouragement in the steps and the literature to be one's authentic self and to speak one's truths.* I rarely see anything in the approved literature that says directly to be passionate, powerful, express feelings openly, speak the truth, and seek the joy of the spirit. Nearly all the approved codependency literature is written in relationship to the partner. Some of the more recent daily readings are more directed at self-empowerment, but the messages are often mixed with those laced with self-blame or they lack social consciousness.

9. *Group interactions stay superficial.* Because the steps do not reinforce developing the authentic self, many people remain immersed in fear. Fear, and a lack of connectedness to one's inner power and wisdom can lead to superficial conversation filled with platitudes. One of the biggest complaints I hear about codependency groups is that people give superficial advice or lack authenticity when they talk.

10. *Staying in sick relationships gets reinforced.* Sometimes codependency groups exert subtle, almost unconscious pressure on a woman to stay in a destructive relationship. As one woman said, "So many of the women are terrified of leaving their partner, so they are threatened when someone else does." Another woman said, "When I was being abused by my husband, women gave me all kinds of support and sympathy but little encouragement to leave. Later, when I did get in a good relationship, they kept questioning and undermining me—was I getting involved too fast? Was I aware of his family history? Did I really want to be with him?" Those were the questions they should have asked about my abusive marriage.

11. *There is not enough focus on forming healthy, strong, nurturing attachments to others.* Women need support for wanting nurturing, intimate, warm attachments. The notion of detachment subtly undermines women's deeply felt desire to have intimate bonds with others.

Instead of struggling to stay in empty or hurtful relationships, women need to support each other believing they deserve and are capable of forming positive, intimate, affirming relationships.

Applying the twelve-step program to dependent women and men is a little like taking a cure for violent men and applying it to depressed women. The basic need of people who feel dependent is a sense of Self. And even when women have addictions to drugs, alcohol, sex, or something else, the underlying problem, as Kelly said at the opening of the chapter, is usually a lack of Self. The steps simply are not designed to create a sense of personal power.

POPULAR DEFINITIONS OF "CODEPENDENCY"

Virginia Satir's theories about family systems influenced people in the addiction field to look at alcoholism as a family disease affecting everyone as opposed to an isolated individual problem. Codependency is a term that came into use in the Twin Cities in the mid-seventies and was adopted nationally in the eighties. The purpose was to describe common traits of the partners or children of addicted people. Before that, partners of addicted people were called enablers, meaning they carried the worry and frustration of the partner, which enabled the addicted person to continue drinking. This is a flawed theory in light of alcoholism's being a physically inherited disease. It is also sexist in that it subtly blames the victim, implying that if the partner—usually the woman—didn't take on all the addict's feelings, he would change. It's not necessarily so.

Timmen Cermak defined codependence from a family context in *Diagnosing and Treating Co-dependence*, published in 1986. "Co-dependence is a recognizable pattern of personality traits, predictably found within most members of chemically dependent families, which are capable of creating sufficient dysfunction to warrant the diagnosis of Mixed Personality Disorder as outlined in DSM III."

If you don't know what a Mixed Personality Disorder is, you're not alone. I can't give you much help. The Diagnostic, Statistical Manual of Mental Disorders (DSM III) lists personality disorders, with no subtype of "mixed." The only relevant listing under "mixed" in the index is, "Disturbance of emotions and conduct, Adjustment disorder with." The diagnostic category that comes closest is listed as an "Adjustment Disorder with Mixed Emotional Features," which includes emotions such as anxiety and depression or other emotions. An example they cite would be "an adolescent after moving away from home and parental supervision, who reacts with *ambivalence, depression, anger and signs of increased dependency*" (emphasis mine).

Two points about this diagnosis. First, it is so general its use is highly influenced by the person making the diagnosis. Second, to use this diagnosis for "codependency" is another way of pathologizing traits of women brought up in a repressive system. The words I have emphasized—ambivalence, depression, anger and signs of increased dependency—are feelings experienced by multitudes of women who have been brought up to be passive, dependent, and look for life's meaning in marriage.

As people recognized typical "codependent" traits in themselves, even when they didn't come from a family with alcoholism, the use of the term codependency was expanded to include anyone from a "dysfunctional" family. Numerous books on codependency and adult children of alcoholics became best sellers because they named a personal experience for many people.

Sharon Wegscheider-Cruse defines codependency as "a specific condition that is characterized by a preoccupation and extreme dependency on a person or object. Eventually, this becomes a pathologic condition that affects the person in all other relationships." She also includes in her definition of a codependent "(1) all persons who are in a love or marriage relationship with an alcoholic, (2) have one or more alcoholic parents or grandparents, or, (3) grew up in an emotionally repressive family," which she claims includes approximately 95 percent of the population. This relational definition of codependency has an eerie parallel to racism and sexism. You are automatically inferior if you are born a woman. In her case, if your partner is alcoholic, you are automatically "codependent." No evidence of your behavior is considered, you are codependent no matter what. While I agree with a systems approach, any responsible type of "diagnosis" needs to include the person being diagnosed. And again, just as when we talked about dysfunctional families, there are a multitude of gradations in functioning within families where one or both caregivers are alcoholic. There are other extremely important variables in outcome which Valliant discusses at length in *The Natural History of Alcoholism*. For example, a child brought up with one alcoholic parent yet who has many positive experiences as a child often does better than a child with no alcoholic parents who is brought up in a bleak environment with no mental or emotional stimulation. People simply cannot be categorized based solely on being in a relationship with someone who is alcoholic.

In *Codependent No More*, Melody Beattie writes, "A codependent person is one who has let another's behavior affect him or her, and who is obsessed with controlling that person's behavior."

What is missing in these definitions is cause and effect. It is descriptive to say that codependent people *let* another's behavior affect him or her or that they are *extremely* dependent, *obsessed* with *controlling* others, and that they behave in *self-defeating* ways. But why do they do so? These definitions do not mention people's motivation and training to be that way or include discussion of cultural socialization and power dynamics. An accurate diagnosis must get to the cause in order to prescribe the cure. If someone has abnormal bleeding, it's not enough just to describe it, you have to find the cause.

Reading between the lines, these three definitions take a subtle blame-the-victim stance. Saying you *let* someone's behavior affect you is shaming, for it implies it's your fault—*you should not have let* someone's behavior affect you.

In an attempt to follow this model, Kelly focused on herself as hard as she could, struggling not to be affected by Bob. It was an inhuman expectation. If we think back to our chakra model, we remember that the goal is to open up our energy system, not shut it down to survive being around abusive people. And, as mentioned earlier, people emanate energy, and when we are around them we pick it up. As social beings, it has been repeatedly documented that we *are* affected—body, mind, and spirit—by brainwashing, poverty, cruelty, rejection, or abuse. It is another example of the patriarchal switch to tell women (or men) that they should not be affected by neglect or abuse.

From the perspective of a patriarchal switch back, we could say that it's hell to live with an addicted person. At best, they keep their distance and are deceptive, preoccupied, and unreliable. At worst, they lie, cheat, steal, blame, shame, become abusive, or lose the family's financial security.

Men seldom put up with that kind of behavior, yet women, under the guise of codependent *recovery*, are often glorified for doing so. The goal so often seems to be martyrdom as opposed to finding joy, companionship, and nurture. To say to someone like Kelly, "Don't let his behavior affect you," is to gloss over the fact that his behavior *has* affected her—and she *is* in pain and *needs* understanding.

When we talked about her experience, Kelly said that some of the women did seem supportive of her taking good care of herself, but, overall, the message was confusing. As we were talking, she picked up *One Day at a Time* and opened it to August 31 and read out loud—"I will make up my mind to be cheerful every waking moment of this day"—and then to August 30—"Let me be *patient* a little longer while I *weigh the alternatives.* Will a radical change really work out better for me, for my children, and yes, for my spouse?" (Emphasis mine.)

Kelly banged the book down on the table. "Cheerful! Patient! I need to learn to be impatient, to stop putting up with so much crap and to take action. Weighing alternatives is a way I con myself into staying in terrible relationships."

THE CODEPENDENCY CONSTRUCT AS OPPRESSIVE

What the addiction field has done in labeling women or minorities who have this syndrome of behaviors "codependent" continues to promote their oppression by pathologizing the very traits they are encouraged to develop.

Kelly told of a codependency speakers' meeting she went to. "The women got up and talked about how detached they had become and how they were perfectly happy living with using alcoholics. They all seemed so plastic and unreal, but everyone looked up to them. I just got frustrated listening to them because it simply didn't match with my experience of being around addicts." The sad thing is that these "plastic and unreal" women were excelling at the teachings so clearly epitomized in *One Day at a Time in Al-Anon,* particularly the constant reinforcement not to be angry.

In the Al-Anon readings, it's as if authentic expressions of anger, fear, resentment, unhappiness, and hopelessness are signs of weakness, and creating an unauthentic cool, detached facade is the goal. This implicitly reinforces sexism, racism, and homophobia because, as mentioned earlier, experiencing anger is often the first step in recognizing one's oppression. When a person is being used, exploited, or blamed, recognition of this intrusion usually comes with a burst of anger. When someone is told to repress anger, it is like removing the power of the individual to recognize abuse and take a stand against it.

Additionally, in *One Day at a Time,* solutions are usually individual and there are no readings where one is encouraged to hold others accountable for their behavior. There is repeatedly a shaming, chiding tone if one takes strong actions. The August 1 reading suggests that thoughts of running away from a situation and starting over "should make us a little doubtful of our maturity" and are "clear proof that many of our troubles are self-created—many of our personal agonies self-inflicted."

Was Kelly *childish* and *immature* to want to get away from Bob? Is it childish to want to run away from an abusive situation? I realize that sometimes people are deluded into thinking a move or a new place will be a magical cure, but telling a woman she is childish to want to run away from an abusive situation is yet another example of the patriarchal switch.

For many women, the moment of truth is a clear, energetic awareness that "this isn't working; I'm dying here and I need to get out." It is these surges of the authentic Self—these expressions of anger or indignation—that need to be fostered and nourished, not shamed and chastised.

Where is the daily reading that says that we need to hold others accountable and stop taking the blame for what they do? Where is the daily reading that says it is human and natural to get upset, be resentful, have blue days, and that the greatest thing you can do is accept yourself this moment—resentments, fears, and all? While approved codependency literature talks about acceptance, it is usually referenced to other people—accept that they drink, accept that they are inconsiderate or injurious to you. And while it is indeed important to realize we can't change other people, it doesn't mean passive acceptance of what they do, particularly if it is injurious to oneself.

The confusing part is that there is a grain of truth in some of the daily readings. We do need to take responsibility for our lives and we can make some choices not to have our self-esteem devastated by others, but that is only part of the picture. We also need to acknowledge our vulnerability, express our feelings, and accept that some situations are exhausting or overwhelming and beyond our capacity to handle.

EXTERNALIZING THE PROBLEM

A turning point came for Kelly when, after leaving the hospital, she read Men Who Can't Love, by Steven Carter and Julia Sokol. Bob's behavior fit Carter's description of a "commitmentphobic"—a man terrified of commitment who at first seems to hunger for love and closeness but then pulls away. The book helped Kelly externalize her problem by seeing that Bob had a problem and that trying to be with him was a no-win situation. According to the book, these men will rarely commit, no matter what you do.

I asked Kelly how the book gave her a different slant from her Al-Anon group. "Al-Anon says to take care of yourself, but the implied message is that if you do it right, you can be happy with (laughter) a jerk. The book led me to see that Bob had a big part of the problem and that it was natural for me to get confused, upset, and hurt around him. *It validated me.* I stopped thinking the problem was all mine or that my reaction was abnormal."

Reading the book helped Kelly get out of the dangerous cycle of examining her own personal behavior as the source of all the problems in the relationship. Thus she externalized some of the problem and stopped carrying the feelings for both of them.

A few weeks after reading the book and feeling better about herself, she took another step that helped her further externalize her problems. She enrolled in a women's studies course in a community college and started to examine women's socialization in the culture. She also continued attending her empowerment group. For years in therapy Kelly had talked about her neglectful childhood. While this was certainly a huge part of her problem, it also kept her blinded to the hidden perpetrator—a system that did not validate her right to be a full-fledged human being. The women's studies course helped her see herself in a broad perspective.

I asked Kelly about the effects of her course. In her words:

"It opened my eyes to *oppression.* Up to that point, I wasn't getting the message. No one had ever used that word in my Al-Anon group. I had spent all my time being 'self-aware' and *'owning my stuff.'* My problems were *my* insecurities, *my* 'codependency.' It was so helpful to see how I had been caught in a system. I finally started getting that it wasn't my fault I abused drugs and alcohol for twenty years and was still cleaning houses at forty and could lose myself so totally in a relationship. I wasn't a *bad* person, I was an *oppressed* person, same as my mother and father. It also made me realize no one would ever come along and take care of me. I would have to take charge of getting what I need in life."

OPPRESSION AS SOURCE OF CODEPENDENT TRAITS

Here is a definition of "codependency" that introduces the notion of oppression. It is by Robert Subby, in *Co-Dependency: An Emerging Issue* (1984): "An emotional, psychological, and behavioral condition that develops as a result of an individual's *prolonged exposure to and practice of a set of oppressive rules,* rules which prevent the open expression of feeling as well as the direct discussion of personal and interpersonal problems." (emphasis mine)

This definition suggests a cause of codependency: *oppressive rules that are learned.* While his reference point is largely with the family's oppressive rules as opposed to the culture's, we finally have a sense of cause and effect.

Ann Wilson Schaef considers codependence "a *disease* that has many forms and expressions . . . that grows out of a disease process that is *inherent in the system in which we live*" (emphasis mine). She calls the disease process the *addictive process* that manifests itself through chemical dependency, mental health problems, unliberated men and women, and family dysfunction.

In *Women, Sex, And Addiction, A Search for Love and Power,* I describe a codependent person as

> someone whose core identity is undeveloped or unknown, and who maintains a false identity built from dependent attachments to external sources—a partner, a spouse, family, appearances, work, or rules. These attachments create both the illusion of a "self" and a form from which to operate. Codependency is a disease of inequality in that any minority person who has to survive in a world defined by others will know more about those in power than about himself or herself.

I would now modify that definition to read: *"Codependency" is a disease of inequality—a predictable set of behavior patterns that people in a subordinate role typically adopt to survive in the dominant culture. Codependency is a euphemism for internalized oppression and includes traits of passivity, compliance, lack of initiative, abandonment of self, and fear of showing power openly.* These traits are taught and reinforced through institutions of family, education, church, traditional medicine, and mental health practices and philosophy in order to maintain patriarchy, capitalism, and hierarchy.

SUBORDINATE BEHAVIOR IN A DOMINANT GROUP

Recognizing symptoms of oppression is not new. Here is Jean Baker Miller's eloquent description of behavior of subordinate members of a dominant-subordinate hierarchical system, from her landmark book *Toward a New Psychology of Women* (1976), which I recommend to all readers interested in understanding the effects of hierarchy on all people.

> It follows that subordinates are described in terms of, and encouraged to develop, personal psychological characteristics that are pleasing to the dominant group. These characteristics

form a certain familiar cluster; submissiveness, passivity, docility, dependency, lack of initiative, inability to act, to decide, to think, and the like. In general, this cluster includes qualities more characteristic of children than adults—immaturity, weakness, and helplessness. If subordinates adopt the characteristics they are considered well-adjusted.

Nothing could more clearly describe what has been routinely called codependency.

In *Pedagogy of the Oppressed*, Paulo Freire writes,

The oppressed suffer from the duality which has established itself in their innermost being. They discover that without freedom they cannot exist authentically. Yet, although they desire authentic existence, they fear it. They are at one and the same time themselves and the oppressor whose consciousness they have internalized. The conflict lies in the choice between being wholly themselves or being divided . . . ; between following prescriptions or having choices; between being spectators or actors; between acting or having the illusion of acting through the action of the oppressors; between speaking out or being silent, castrated in their power to create and re-create, in their power to transform the world.

How well he describes the exhausting inner struggle any subordinate person undergoes in a dominant group. Whether it be a migrant worker, a woman being sexually harassed, a mother being mistreated by welfare workers, someone being exploited in a factory, the constant struggle between speaking out or being silent winds like a thread through the fabric of one's existence affecting relationships, peace of mind, self-esteem, and physical health.

INTERNALIZED OPPRESSION SYNDROME (IOS) VERSUS CODEPENDENCY

Why use the term codependency at all if what we are really talking about is internalized oppression?

My suggestion is that we begin to develop a language to help us incorporate internalized oppression into our understanding of codependency and eventually relinquish the term codependency altogether or use it only when it applies to extreme cases of dependency.

Instead of saying I'm a codependent or I'm a caretaker, people could make powerful statements such as, I am casting out my traits of internalized oppression. I am developing an authentic Self. I was taught to be nice to people in order to be loved.

Reflecting on the old survivor/new survivor model: We need to validate that we survived in the dominant culture by adopting these so-called codependent traits, but that they have become maladaptive in terms of creating a life-loving/creative spirituality or an authentic Self. So we can say thank you to the old survivor for doing whatever it took to survive, and then affirm that we are now learning to survive and be powerful in a new way. To do this we must bond together for mutual protection against the dominants in hierarchy whose teachings are either openly hostile or subtly undermine the empowerment of the subordinates.

We once again need to incorporate the personal with the political. In other words, along with talking about the damaging results of incest, abuse, and battering, we need to also talk about why these atrocities happen and how patriarchy perpetuates this abuse as a form of social control over women.

Following this, we need to talk about what we can do as a collective voice to make changes. This includes moving from speaking in our small groups to speaking out in our communities about rape, sexual harassment, abuse, racism, sexism, homophobia, and so on. For example, instead of having codependency recovery groups, we could have empowerment or discovery groups where people expand their understanding of their problems—where people could explore not only their personal issues but larger social and political factors that affect their lives.

Reasons for Using an Internalized Oppression Concept

If we are ever to truly heal as women and minorities and change the system we live in, we must move beyond the concept of codependency and talk about internalized oppression. Here are some reasons why.

1. The internalized oppression model is a more accurate diagnosis of the problem than the codependency model; thus it suggests more accurate implications for the "cure." Internalized Oppression Syndrome suggests both a personal and social problem needing a personal and social remedy.

2. The internalized oppression model suggests cause and effect, which is more respectful than calling someone (or yourself) codependent (which has a negative connotation). Traits of internalized oppression are understood as forms of survival in both oppressive families and the culture. For example, when someone screamed and yelled at you, you *survived* by numbing out. When you were sexually abused, you survived by drifting off into a fantasy world, or even cutting and abusing yourself to divert your attention from the emotional pain. When your mother was drunk you learned to walk on tiptoe. When you were sexually harassed or discriminated against, you numbed out your emotions, became extremely angry, or medicated yourself in order to relieve the pain. And while these survival behaviors eventually became maladaptive, they were initially adopted for purposes of survival.

Use of the Post Traumatic Stress Syndrome (PTSS) diagnosis for incest or abuse is an example of shifting from shaming diagnoses such as paranoid, histrionic, avoidant personality, to one that suggests a cause and effect. Widespread use of this diagnosis occurred in the seventies, when therapists working with incest and abuse began networking and discovered that many had started using the PTSS diagnosis (frequently associated with war veterans) because it was more respectful and more accurate than pathological labels that did not suggest a cause. The PTSS diagnosis said to a person, "You experienced the trauma of physical or sexual abuse which is related to the difficulties you are having now. You are not intrinsically sick. You were abused."

Changing from the codependency model to an internalized oppression model would be a similar move to correct the patriarchal switch inherent in the concept of codependency. We could even incorporate the concept of post-traumatic stress, and say things like, I'm uncovering from sexist stress syndrome, racist stress syndrome, welfare mothers' stress syndrome, or poverty stress syndrome.

3. Codependency has become a catch-all phrase that leads people to use jargon rather than to accurately describe their experience. For example, saying "I'm feeling codependent around you" is subject to numerous interpretations. It would be more accurate, simpler, and clearer to say, "I'm having difficulty concentrating because I'm worried what you are thinking about me," or "I'm suddenly wondering if you like me." Instead of saying "Don't be so codependent with me," people could say, "Please don't look to me to make you happy, or please tell me directly when you are angry."

It is important to focus on actual thoughts and to make specific requests and not lump them together in an amorphous mass called codependency. Speaking clearly of specific incidents increases inner awareness and results in better communication with others. It is part of becoming responsible and not hiding behind mushy, vague language.

4. Operating from a framework of internalized oppression creates a common language that potentially can help create a bond among diverse groups of oppressed peoples. If minority and underprivileged people got together and told their stories in the context of internalized oppression, the common threads resulting from their subordination could be seen. In listening to each other, they could also come to see and appreciate their differences. This would help people bridge diversity and cut through racial, ethnic, and sexual preference differences and move to levels four and five of faithing, where we can then have empathy and care for all people.

5. Using the internalized oppression model would help people externalize problems they are not responsible for and subsequently help lower guilt and shame. Thus, while experiencing pain about rape, incest, poverty, racism, sexism, and homophobia, people would be encouraged to alleviate self-blame by seeing these things as a form of social control inherent to the system rather than constantly exploring what they did to deserve it or how they could have prevented it.

6. It helps us take responsibility for our collusion in the system. Exploring internalized oppression would include consciousness-raising about the subordinate's collusion with the dominant's system. This includes understanding the ways we as subordinates hold back our power—sometimes our bargaining power—and how that undermines our own efforts and abilities, and how we give our time and energy to those who exploit us and make excuses for their behavior. It would also help people realize that alone, one has limited power over a system, but when we bond together we have tremendous power to take action and effect change.

This approach helps people move toward levels four and five of faithing because it teaches people to explore their belief system and determine for themselves what is self-affirming and what is oppressive.

7. The internalized oppression model could lead to new forms of wholistic healing that combine personal healing of the body, mind, and spirit, cultural awareness studies, bonding with diverse people, and, ultimately, organizing to create change. These things would not be seen as separate but as interlinked.

8. The Internalized Oppression Syndrome approach is a more cost-effective and energy-efficient solution than trying to get well through twelve-step groups that lack a cultural perspective, which is like healing half the person. When we combine education, consciousness-raising, and personal exploration, we are empowering the whole person. Otherwise we see people attending recovery groups and therapy groups for years and years because a part of the cure is omitted. This is not to say that it's bad to have long-term recovery group attendance if a person finds it supportive. I am talking about people who never really heal because of the missing pieces.

Getting a cultural perspective can be done through classes, discussion groups, and support groups, and can be an inexpensive adjunct that often speeds up the healing process. Repeatedly I have seen women and men have an enormous leap in their discovery process when they attend classes and workshops on women's studies, sexism, racism, and classism. And it's definitely cost-effective. A community class in women's studies or a study group is a lot cheaper than endless psychotherapy.

9. The Internalized Oppression Syndrome approach is a positive, wellness approach that encourages healthy *attachments* with caring, supportive people and with community groups. The idea is to have an authentic, separate self and strong nurturing attachments to others. In other words, it goes from the sin-and-redemption/how-to-survive-pain approach of twelve-step codependency groups and moves to a life-affirming/creative spirituality that asks, How do we come to love life and love each other?

FINDING A BALANCE

It is also important that the need for personal healing be a significant part of the picture. In early feminist days in the late sixties and early seventies, we may have put too much emphasis on looking at the inequities of the system and not paid enough attention to the need for personal healing. I remember at the therapy collective I mentioned in chapter 10 that a client came to me in 1977, saying, "I don't want to hear any more about how I'm oppressed in the culture. I want to look at my self-defeating behavior and see what I can do to change." Now, with the codependency movement, the pendulum has swung the other way and the cultural analysis has largely been obscured.

Some people fear that if we consider the effects of oppression, people will blame the system and say they can't change. But people do that already with the codependency label. "I'm codependent; I come from an alcoholic family. That's why I can't have good relationships." Obviously, anyone wanting rationalizations for not taking steps to change can find them, but that's no reason not to work toward a wholistic mode of empowering people.

A RETURN TO FEMINISM, OR, GETTING PAST
THE FEAR OF BEING CALLED A WOMEN'S LIBBER,
MAN-HATER, BITCH, OR DYKE

So why did behavior traits that resulted from oppression that feminists focused on in the sixties and seventies get redefined as the disease of codependency? And why do women so readily don the label codependent and resist the term feminist? It's another symptom of internalized oppression and the patriarchal switch.

Here's my historical view of the subject. As part of the feminist movement, women started Consciousness-Raising (CR) groups in the late sixties and early seventies to share life experiences in the context of growing up in patriarchy. Common topics for discussion were childhood experiences, female programming, pregnancy, birth control, giving birth, sexuality, abuse, violence, attitudes of parents, partners, bosses, neighbors, media, and the beliefs one internalized as a result. Ms. referred to the "click" women experienced as they recognized commonalities in experience, including financial discrimination, harassment, discounting, sexual abuse, and battering. Women discovered they were not alone.

Women gathering together to compare notes and bond together was threatening to some men, some women and to the culture. The media, as a weapon of patriarchy, did an incredible blitz on feminism by reducing feminists to images of unattractive, outspoken, hostile, bra-burning women—who were being vindictive because they couldn't get a man. The media campaign did not bury feminism, but it certainly caused many women to shy away from the label.

Feminism became an alienating word and many women took off the label so they wouldn't be viewed with suspicion or treated with scorn. Thus we heard a lot of watered-down "feminist" talk such as "I think women should get paid equally, but I don't like it when they get so angry and pushy." These comments are symptoms of internalized oppression—you water down the truth to make it palatable to the oppressor.

But women didn't stop getting together. Women have always bonded together one way or another. With the advent of the addiction and codependency recovery movement, which started just as CR groups were fading from the scene, women flocked together in codependency groups. I believe this was a massive example of the patriarchal switch in action. Instead of bonding together as normal women to explore their experiences and self-defeating traits in the light of the culture, they bonded together as "codependents," that is, "sick" people in pain. This wasn't threatening to anyone. Women were back in their place, exploring their symptoms of oppression as personal pathology. Thus patriarchy/hierarchy got let off the hook. No one mentioned feminism or oppression and we were back to business as usual. As Kay Hagan says, "If I attempt to 'recover' from codependency without this [feminist political] analysis, the *oppressor remains invisible, my oppression a misnamed affliction*, and I in a cul-de-sac of self-blame." (author's emphasis).

A Rebirth of Feminism

Women across the country have started questioning the whole concept of codependency and the use of the twelve-step model as a foundation for true discovery. In the last two years, I have read numerous articles on the subject. For example, in *Wildfire*, Sonia Johnson includes a chapter called "Twelve Steps Into the Fog," where she refers to AA as a "depressingly moralistic Christian model." She writes, "I think we must recognize that no male institution is essentially different from any other. I think we are required to hold none of them exempt from our fiercest, most self-loving scrutiny." Later on, referring to the groups, she says, "One must always assert one's illness, one's pain, one's inability to recover. In patriarchal models, health and joy are not posited options." Further, she urges women to stop attending these groups.

While I agree with her analysis of the twelve-step model as male, Christian, and patriarchal, and love her fierce spirit, and share her desire that women shake themselves loose from models with external rules, I get uneasy when she implies so strongly that women stop attending twelve-step groups and attend Women For Sobriety. While it takes time, the goal is to raise awareness so women make wise choices from within following their own pace.

While I long for vast social change away from the mass use of the term codependency, it is important no woman feel shame for where she is on her journey. In reading some of the criticism in the articles, I imagined myself as someone who had been in a codependency group for years, someone who had been helped and supported through a rough time in life. Hearing some of the sharp criticism would have left me feeling ashamed, angry, or misunderstood. It brought back a vivid memory from the seventies when I heard a prominent feminist say that she was against therapy. I remember feeling ashamed and thinking, She wouldn't like or respect me because I'm in therapy. Yet therapy was crucial to me.

A truly feminist way to approach a change away from the codependency construct is for women together to brainstorm alternative language and ways to add a cultural consciousness into their groups if they so choose. Change takes time, and integrating new concepts into an old one that provided a helpful framework for many people needs to be a process.

It is important that women not put their sobriety or healing at stake in order to make a political statement. Sometimes, in the early days of the feminist movement, women got torn between being a good feminist and being themselves. It would be sad to repeat this mistake.

Women's consciousness-raising groups often led to political action. Women sharing their experiences of rape in one CR group led them to organize a speak-out on the subject. Codependency groups, however, focus on healing the individual and do not typically move toward social action. This has sometimes created separation between different races and classes of women. Women of color, lesbians, and poor women are often much quicker than their white middle-class sisters to see the oppressive aspects of viewing their personal traits as codependent. A useful book on the subject is *The Psychopathology of Everyday Racism and Sexism*, by Lenora Fulani. If we all start looking at our oppression it will help build bridges between each other.

IT'S NATURAL TO BE AFRAID

It's scary for women to consider relinquishing "codependent" traits through an awareness of internalized oppression. The process of change involves uncovering the false promises, tricks, deceptions, and negative internalized programming associated with being a woman or a person of color in the United States. And the discovery is likely to result in feelings of anger—the emotion feared by oppressed people, particularly women.

When we women shift the focus from pleasing men and other people to pleasing ourselves and speaking our truths, we will feel our power, but our oppression may increase. I believe the increased incidence of incest, rape, violence against women, feminization of poverty, and laws controlling women's reproductive rights are a reaction to the feminist movement. No oppressed people gain power without a struggle. It is scary to confront a system.

Paulo Freire in *Pedagogy of the Oppressed* vividly describes this inner conflict:

The oppressed, having internalized the image of the oppressor and adopted his guidelines, are fearful of freedom. Freedom would require them to eject this image and replace it without autonomy and responsibility. Moreover, their struggle for freedom threatens not only the oppressor, but also their own oppressed comrades who are fearful of still greater repression.

A CHANGE IN THE WIND

I think we are at the brink of exciting changes. For the past few years, there has been a growing sense that "feminine energy" is rising on the planet. The values of cooperation, bonding, understanding all life as part of a wholistic scheme of things, and nonviolence are being more deeply understood by theologians, ecologists, pacifists, and others who grieve the sad state of our society and our wounded planet.

"Imagine," says Kay Hagan, "thousands of meetings in every city and town of the United States where women gathered . . . to discuss their oppression, what caused it, what it felt like, how they collude with it, what they might do about it. I venture to say this one slight shift in focus could galvanize women into radical united action."

I would also like to see men gather to look at their internalized oppression, for it is also oppressive to be taught that you have to be tough, violent, domineering, in control, and independent. It is a great violation of the soul to be trained from infancy onward to be separate from one's heart and ability to love. Male programming that teaches men they have a right to use and exploit others blocks their ability to feel empathy and compassion, precious human commodities at the foundation of a spirituality that connects us to others.

The positive aspect of the emergence of codependency groups in the seventies and eighties is that millions of women who were afraid of associating with the word "feminist" or being part of consciousness-raising groups joined codependency groups. And when women get together and talk, there will be healing. Many women took steps to get out of abusive relationships and started taking action to improve their own lives. The eighties focused on personal, internal reflection, which has naturally led us back to the political.

As women develop more Self and have basic needs for security met, I believe we naturally will recognize the limitations of the codependency framework and internally feel the need to move forward by including a cultural analysis and taking political action. I suggest we proceed further with our collective growth by adopting and adapting the useful parts of the codependency concept, put it in a political framework, and leave the rest behind.

It is utterly impossible to increase one's personal awareness without eventually realizing that this culture is oppressive to women, people of color, and many others who lack access to privilege. Awareness is awareness, and it permeates everything. Thus it is natural that thousands of women—maybe more—have started questioning the concept of codependency and are ready to move beyond it.

12

❧

Healthy Groups,
Dysfunctional Groups:
How to Know the Difference

Some people have had wonderful experiences in twelve-step groups:
   "The group provided people in my life when I had none. It gave predictability and the support for me to stay sober."
   "AA has helped me see that a spiritual life is what I want and has allowed me . . . to find my own path in what I feel about God and Judaism."
   "SAA gave me gentleness to identify shame and learn boundaries to protect myself."
   "If I'm troubled I usually just feel lighter. It feels safe and I lose the isolated feeling" (from an OA member).
   "I learned that my addictions are rooted in my family's sexual dysfunction—I'm not bad or a freak" (from an ACSA [Adult Children of Sex Addicts] member).
   Some people have had negative experiences:
   "It was so depressing—the people weren't getting better. They were so down. There was a lot of seduction and hitting on women" (from an SLAA member).
   "OA did not challenge sexist attitudes and oppression related to

my compulsive eating. They allowed codependent behavior to replace food addiction. . . . It was easy for me to lead a session with a powerful intellectual flair, and all too easy for me to wear the Recovery Mask while continuing to abuse food."

"A severely co-dependent woman 'ran' it. . . . I felt dumped on, I felt exploited" (from an SA [Sexaholics Anonymous] member).

I have attended a myriad of groups and retreats, including meditation, yoga, and Quaker retreats; personal growth centers; a childhood abuse treatment program; Reiki healing groups; twelve-step groups; consciousness-raising groups; support groups; women's spirituality groups; therapy groups; and Native American sweat lodges, prayer circles, and pipe ceremonies. I have also participated in peace and justice organizations, community action and civil disobedience groups. Some were wonderful, some mediocre, and one became a cult-like situation where non-groupies who questioned the capricious, controlling demands of the leader were "excommunicated" (as we laughingly said), myself included. They have all played an important role in my life.

I love groups. I have led two or three therapy groups a week for fifteen years as well as a six-months' couples growth group. I have seen miracles of healing as the combined wisdom, courage, humor, and determination of the group members helped unlock the healing capacity in us all. The gift to me from these sojourns with so many incredible people is the deepening belief in the capacity of the human spirit to heal if given guidance, support, time, and patience. A group of people together, all pulling for one another, can give us what we can never find alone. It can help us trust a human bond and teach us about acceptance and love.

HOW GROUPS CAN HELP

Groups can be a powerful force for good. They can help assuage loneliness and increase self-acceptance through discovering commonalities with others. They can instill a sense of hope through meeting others who have grown and changed.

Groups operate at many levels. They can teach skills for life, positive ways of thinking, and help people explore their life history. At a deeper level, groups can help people develop trust and the ability to be intimate with others. The very fact that people attend regularly, live through change, express feelings openly and respectfully, and struggle together without harming one another promotes trust that may help heal negative beliefs from earlier betrayals.

Ideally, a group helps to free the highest, wisest part of each individual, resulting in a collective wisdom that is greater than the sum of its parts. It takes everyone beyond where they started. In ongoing therapy groups, I have seen new members make incredible changes because they are pulled toward the high level of the group awareness.

An effective group is a subtle dance between the initially stated goals of the group, the personalities of the members, and the model or approach employed to achieve the goals. There needs to be a balance of structure, receptivity to change, creativity, and room for individual differences. Groups operate at both a conscious level and an unconscious level, where people's buried or repressed needs operate outside their awareness. It is important to realize the power of group norms. People have been lifted to new heights in groups, and they have been abused and led to violate their own values.

It is also important to have a sense of what to expect from a group. Here is a list of positive traits you might use as a basis for assessing a group.

1. *There is flexibility and responsiveness to the needs of the attenders.* People are supported in finding their own belief system, and in using parts of the model/belief system they like and dismissing the rest. "Take what you like and leave the rest behind!"

2. *All members are encouraged (but not pressured) to participate but not to dominate.* If a few members monopolize the time, this is processed within the group, giving responsibility to those who talk the most and those who remain silent. No one is blamed. This sort of discussion is more typical of a therapy group than a recovery/uncovery group, but it sometimes happens in the latter.

3. *The sharing is at a personal level.* It is honest, authentic, and not loaded with platitudes, pat phrases, or advice. People share their personal experiences using "I" statements as opposed to "That's how it is (It should be, You should be, This is the way, etc.)."

4. *People attend regularly and are committed to their healing.* Group cohesiveness depends on a core group of steady attenders committed to themselves and the well-being of the group.

5. *Openness to self-evaluation of the process or how the group is working.* Groups should do a "group inventory" or "group conscience" evaluation process at least every twelve weeks and more often if the group is having difficulty. It is important that group members be able to verbalize and discuss the group norms—in other words, to take a participant observer stance and reflect on the unspoken rules and beliefs that are operating without being acknowledged.

6. *The group has clarity of purpose.* The group is clear about its goals and adopts a process or form that logically works toward fulfilling those goals. It doesn't purport to cure everything or everyone or be the answer to all problems.

7. *Sexual or emotional exploitation is not accepted as part of the norm.* People do not emotionally, sexually, or in any other way exploit each other. The group is not used as a place to find sexual or dating partners. (Remember groups often become one's psychological family and it is incestuous to have sex with one's brothers and sisters.) If two members become involved, one should leave.

8. *Group members coalesce to protect the group from exploitation or abuse of its members within the group.* It is crucial that people work together to maintain healthy norms. People being abused or exploited should not be left alone to defend themselves. It is important for others to rally around and kindly confront people who are being inappropriate, as well as to support vulnerable members in standing up for themselves.

9. *People are regarded as whole individuals*—not just junkies, codependents, addicts, or a mental illness diagnosis. While a group may have a specific purpose, individuals are supported in finding all means that support their growth. Outside means of support are respected and encouraged.

10. *People are not coerced into staying if they desire to leave.* They would be supported in weighing their decision, but told it is always their choice. They are not given dire threats such as, "If you leave, you'll surely drink again," "No one will ever love you like we do."

11. *There is a defined process or norm for dealing with conflict.* Groups must acknowledge that there will be conflict among members and have some form for dealing with it. It can be done inside or outside the group, but when a group pretends there is no conflict, members often repress their feelings, which later smolder away, affecting the group's functioning.

12. *The group has a sense of humor about itself.* If a group can't laugh at itself, watch out! Laughter reflects an ability to stand outside our own dramas and see them from a broad perspective. We need to remember the form we are using is only a form, not a credo. It was created by ordinary mortals with biases and imperfections. In other words, a person can be in the group but not of it.

13. *The group does not stay frozen in form.* The group form expands and changes as people grow and change. Instead of fitting people into a form, the form expands in response to people's needs.

UNHEALTHY GROUPS

On the negative side, groups can descend into meaningless, rote rituals that dull the human spirit, block creativity, squelch spontaneity, limit growth, or abuse and violate individuals. I felt that dullness as a child mouthing the words in a traditional Protestant church. Groups can adhere rigidly to a form or ideology and say words in a perfunctory way rather than constantly re-creating the group and the form through the input of its members.

When people are pushed into or submit to a rigid form, it confines their growth to levels two and three of faithing. They are still controlled by outside forces, be it the Bible, the Koran, Alcoholics Anonymous, churches, twelve-step recovery groups, or whatever. Recovery groups for addiction that operate at this rigid level may result in symptom reduction—in people staying sober—but they do not foster growth and self-awareness.

For people with traits of codependency/internalized oppression, a rigid, nonreflective group is totally counter to the goals of the participants, who need to develop an internal Self as guide rather than looking to outside authority or rigid rules.

Negative/Limiting Characteristics of Groups

This is relevant to twelve-step groups, other models of uncovery/discovery, religious groups, or spiritual communities:

1. *The group discourages or blocks outside involvement.* "You should only stick to people who follow this path." "If you do this right you won't need therapy, or other people." When a group starts to isolate itself from the outside world, it is time to be careful. Isolation gives charismatic leaders the ability to act without interference.

2. *The group limits or discourages access to reading material or other forms of personal growth.* "You should only read approved literature." In my own experience, reading from a wide variety of magazines, books, newspapers, and literature brings constant stimulation to my mind. When I am writing and feel dull, I do things to give my creative Self a charge. I start reading from a variety of sources, go to movies, go hiking, attend workshops, tune in to my surroundings, and visit

friends. Being without this kind of stimulation dulls the mind and leaves a person more susceptible to indoctrination to rigid beliefs. According to James S. Gordon, who was part of a think tank on "Why Spiritual Groups Go Awry," the Rajneesh Community had no library (although Rajneesh himself had a huge personal library) and had only six copies of the *Portland Oregonian* for six thousand people. Oppressive systems are known for limiting reading material because they live in fear of losing control. Literature has historically been a catalyst to help people free their minds from oppressive thinking.

3. *Expression of dissension is punished, squelched, or strongly discouraged.* A way to recognize that group norms are against expressions of dissension is to check your fear level when you want to challenge group dogma or norms. If you have sometimes spoken up in other situations, but tremble with fear at the thought of questioning the group philosophy or leaders, very likely you are picking up the fear of the group, which wants to stay in its dogmatic niche. When groups are open to conflict, people typically experience much less fear about bringing up differences.

4. *The group becomes grandiose in its self-definition—"Ours is the one way, the road to salvation."* "We have the answer to everyone's problems." "If only those poor unfortunates would follow our way, they would be saved." This is an us-against-the-world stance and a form of narcissistic bonding. (One might call this the internalized *oppressor* syndrome, whereby privileged men constantly reinforce the idea that the model that worked for [some of] them is right for women and people from different cultures and backgrounds.)

Narcissism, according to the Diagnostic and Statistical Manual of Mental Disorders, includes traits of a grandiose sense of self-importance and uniqueness; a preoccupation with fantasies of unlimited success; being exhibitionistic; having a lack of empathy toward others; and thinking one is the center of all things. Narcissistic bonding is when the group takes on these characteristics and thinks it is the best, the only one.

A healthy level of group narcissism would be expressed as, "This really is a good group. I think it can help me. It's exciting to be here." But when people extol the group with unlimited praise and say it is fabulous, miraculous, and the best there is, they are often blinding themselves to the natural imperfections of the group. They are often projecting their childlike longing for the perfect parent, group, and world onto the group.

Many approaches to personal or spiritual growth have claimed to have *the* answer to serenity, power, and happiness. This has included different sorts of recovery models, therapy models and spiritual communities, along with forms of body work, meditation, yoga, healing, religion, or nutrition. All these methods or approaches can be helpful, but life is still a matter of getting up every day, meeting oneself, and making minute-to-minute decisions based on one's inner voice. The goal is not to transcend life, rather to become at one with it. Life is not a sickness to be overcome. The idea is to accept joy and sorrow, happiness and sadness, as parts of life to be experienced and put in perspective, not fought with like some devil.

5. People get locked into stereotyped roles. This can be based on gender, class, race, or roles such as leader, follower, placator, peacemaker, lackey, or scapegoat. This limits people rather than helping them expand their self-definition.

6. The group becomes paranoid about outsiders or those who question the norm. The leader(s) of the group, instead of expressing their own inner rage, project it onto outsiders. They tell themselves that the outsiders are dangerous. The followers, whose egos have merged with the leaders, agree. This often becomes justification for repression, abuse, or violence toward the outsiders.

For three years straight, the same woman has interviewed me on my perspective on the twelve steps for a newspaper column written by a famous treatment establishment. While listening to my answers, she would sometimes sigh, and say things like, "Oh, I love what you're saying but I know they won't print that, it's too radical for them; they don't support questioning the twelve steps in any way." Twice she called to tell me the article had not passed the review committee. A happy sign of the changing times is that the third year, they did accept an article that included my views on the first step and the use of the word *powerlessness.*

Women counselors in a treatment program have also told me that male directors instructed them not to tell women clients about Women for Sobriety or other models. They were to recommend twelve-step programs and have people come into treatment to "talk up" the twelve-step model. Only if clients attend AA for a while and could not connect were they to be told about other models.

7. People talk like robots. People spout off rhetoric that seems vacant, vacuous, and prerecorded. They can be very nice and polite, but you feel something is missing when you talk with them. You don't feel connected. They don't pause or reach inward for a response to a question; the answers feel glib, rehearsed, and without struggle.

When I was visiting a spiritual community, nearly all the people used the same intonation and phrasing when rationalizing the leader's strange behavior. It felt like they were spouting a party line. I started to feel very lonely, and eventually I began doubting my own reality: Maybe I'm just resistant to joining groups, my ego is in the way (thank heavens), or some such rationalization. Sometimes when people mouth the leader's/teacher's words as if they have been handed to them off a mountain, I want to say, "Can't you get real or have an opinion of your own?"

8. In-group jargon predominates in conversations. All groups, families, and lovers develop a common language. This is a natural part of developing intimacy. What I mean by jargon in this context is the use of language as a superficial translation of deeper human problems that feels one-dimensional, glib, and detached from human emotions.

9. The group exerts pressure on people to stay. The pressure can come from the ideology such as the twelve-step assertion that people need recovery groups for life to assure sobriety. Pressure can also come from individuals who project their separation and abandonment anxieties onto anyone who wants to leave. Because someone leaving triggers childhood memories of abandonment, they avoid the old discomfort by "guilting" people to stay.

10. People use the group for sexual needs. This happens in cults, spiritual communities, treatment programs, between counselors and clients, and in twelve-step groups. It can range from outright sexual abuse to covert sexual manipulation.

11. The group is unable to reflect on itself, its history, and its values from a broad perspective. Instead of seeing that it is just an ideology, a way, a movement, and that its creators were mere mortals seeing things through their programming, people take a fundamentalist stance. This is *the* way, *the* truth.

ARE TWELVE-STEP GROUPS CULTS?

Many people refer to twelve-step groups as cults. In *Alcoholics Anonymous: Cult or Cure?*, a book I recommend, Charles Bufe explores traits of cults and then discusses which ones apply to AA and which ones don't. His conclusion is that twelve-step groups are cult-like in many ways but lack some traits of cults. For anyone joining any group, it is important to recognize traits of cults so you can make conscious decisions. This section on cults is largely taken from Bufe's book, with some paraphrasing and a few additions of my own.

The traits in AA and twelve-step groups he sees as typical of cults are:

1. Religious orientation;

2. Discouragement of skepticism and rational thinking;

3. Dogmatism—while the steps are given as suggestions, the central organization and many people in groups are dogmatic about keeping them the way they are;

4. Self-absorption—Twelve-step groups believe they have the answers to addiction and dependency and therefore have shown little interest in research, other forms of treatment, or in medical or physiological aspects of drug abuse, alcoholism, or dependency. The pamphlets and books talk about the twelve steps and "the program." If they were truly interested in people healing from addiction and dependency, they would be interested in other approaches and be willing to expand their vision.

The other aspect of self-absorption that is cult-like is that people's aspirations for achievement and success beyond sobriety are seen as contributing to alcoholism. Thus people are often subtly cautioned not to expand their creative intelligence, take on exciting challenges, or make dramatic changes in their lives.

5. Mindless repetition of slogans and dogma that work against people using their capacity for critical thinking. While this isn't in Bufe's book, in a personal conversation he said he would add this to the list, because mindless repetition upholding group norms is common in cults. Some of the phrases in AA that fit into this antiintellectual category, which were mentioned in the chapter on slogans and jargon, are: "Utilize, don't analyze," "Fake it until you make it," "Your best thinking got you here," and "Keep it simple, stupid."

Here are ways twelve-step groups are different from cults according to Bufe.

1. They do not have charismatic leaders although, as Bufe says, they do have dead saints, and sometimes people in groups take on a charismatic role.

2. AA is not based on a hierarchical, authoritarian structure.

3. AA does not go to great lengths to retain members. While members may make phone calls to those who stray or guilt them about leaving, AA does not compare with cults that physically restrain people, use armed guards, or threaten to harm relatives.

4. AA does not employ mind-control techniques. Techniques used in true cults are aimed at keeping people in a state of mental imbalance. This is done with sensory overload, sensory deprivation, keeping people malnourished or exhausted, destruction of personal

privacy, sexual humiliation, sexual abuse, physical abuse, and making people sign false documents, to name a few methods.

5. AA does not create a closed, all-encompassing environment and keep people from contact with "outsiders." While twelve-step groups create something of an in-group feeling, it is different from cults where people live together and are repeatedly told that they are totally separate from other kinds of people and must stay separate.

6. AA does not use consciously deceptive recruitment techniques. While AA members may come into treatment programs and say that AA is the only way a person will stay sober, it does not compare with the ways cults create flagrantly deceptive techniques, use front groups, and seduce new members with friendship, attention, and love (known as "love-bombing") in order to gain control over the members for their own narcissistic gains.

7. Twelve-step organizations do not employ violence against or harassment of critics of the programs. This is against their public belief system.

8. Twelve-step groups do not exploit people for money.

The following are AA traits that are somewhat cult-like, according to Bufe.

1. AA's position is that one must submit the individual will to the will of God. But this is mitigated by the phrase "as we understood Him," and it is offered only as a suggestion, although individuals may get rigid about it.

2. AA is separatist only to the extent that any special interest group is separatist. While people develop a certain kind of jargon, they don't take on new names, use distinctive dress, or make other alterations in personal appearance.

3. Manipulation through guilt: The AA dogma creates guilt in abundance, which keeps people fearful and tied to the group. On the other hand, there is no guru, leader, or organization consciously manipulating people to feel guilty.

4. Twelve-step programs have approved literature, which implies value judgments about what people read. On the other hand, the organization has no stated policy on reading other material.

POWER DYNAMICS IN GROUPS

Groups take on a personality of their own and gradually shift as people come and go. Power dynamics are always at play in a group, as people command different levels of respect, take on different roles and participate with differing levels of commitment, interest, and creativity.

Every member makes a difference. The absence of a steadfast, supportive member is felt as surely as the entrance of a new person. The shifts that occur are sometimes subtle, sometimes blatant. If a dominating or very serious person leaves, the group may suddenly feel lighter, and people will interact more easily with each other.

People may not realize a negative shift is taking place while it is happening. I remember an occasion when a woman who was extremely controlling left a therapy group, the other members at first felt guilty. Then, when someone said, "I'm glad she's gone, I didn't trust her," everyone started laughing and saying, "I'm glad too." They all felt the relief of the heavy energy being gone from the group, but only when someone was honest could they speak their truths.

Because the focus is on staying sober, addiction support groups are not organized to acknowledge the shifts in group personality and help people deal with their feelings about them. The twelve-step model suggests that people keep principles before personalities in order to maintain the focus on recovery. This can be a useful boundary, but sometimes it results in people bottling up their feelings and then holding back in group. It is important for people to internally acknowledge shifts in group character and not pretend that everything is just fine when it doesn't feel that way.

When charismatic people use groups to fulfill narcissistic ego needs their negative power can infiltrate the group personality like a sickness taking over. Sometimes it happens so slowly people don't know what happened, although they may say, "It wasn't always like this; what happened?"

Other times there is a subtle shift in balance. For example, a women's group may have 30 percent lesbian women, who slowly leave due to homophobic remarks that no one addresses. Then suddenly a lesbian woman realizes that she is the only lesbian in a group meeting. It's important to be tuned in to shifts, and to explore why they are happening—not to necessarily stop them, but to operate at a conscious level.

People with ego strength and a sense of internalized values are most likely to recognize dysfunction and leave a sick group, although most people have some blind spots that can make them susceptible to exploitation in some circumstances. The people most likely to stay are those who have not worked through childhood victimization, do not have a healthy ego, or are used to being controlled. Unconsciously they feel guilty or fear reprisal for saying no.

For people in discovery who attend support groups, therapy groups, church groups, spiritual retreats, yoga centers, and the like, it is important to remember *there is no guarantee in any group or with any therapist or spiritual teacher that exploitation and abuse will not occur.* We live in an exploitive culture where various groups of people oppress other groups. The norms and internalized values of our culture do not automatically change when a person becomes a psychologist or a chemical dependency counselor, or enters a twelve-step group. Thus it is important to be aware of danger signs that a group is losing its health or becoming exploitive.

TO STAY OR TO LEAVE?

If you are uneasy about a group you attend, read through the above traits and then ask yourself, What's true for me? Try to sort out whether you are afraid because the group supports your growing and becoming strong, which goes against your socialization, or are you bored, uninterested, and not feeling supported or nurtured in the group. You can always experiment by missing some group meetings and seeing how you feel.

Sometimes a person realizes they are in a harmful group but lacks the strength to leave. Once an individual has turned their will and their life over to an ideology or another person, it is hard to function in one's own behalf. If this is happening to you, to garner strength, find people who share a common view of the dysfunction and talk with one another; validate your reality, and remind yourself you have choices.

People often argue that one should stay in and fight when things get rough. Sometimes that is true, but people can also use this as a rationalization for staying in an addictive relationship with a person or a group. For myself, the better part of valor is recognizing a losing situation, knowing when I'm getting hurt (without always knowing why), knowing what I can't handle (or don't want to put my time into handling), and getting out.

It is addictive to believe there is only one group, one therapist, one spiritual teacher or treatment program and to hang on in the face of abuse or extensive personal suffering. It is also human to admit there are some situations and people one just can't handle.

Many groups are not overtly abusive, they are simply dull, lifeless, superficial, and unhelpful. When you realize that life is precious, time is precious, and a good group can be exciting and positive, you might consider either speaking up in the group to help get the energy moving or, if that doesn't work, finding a more highly evolved group with more energy and models of healthy, alive people.

If you have doubts about a group, talk about them with outside people and try other groups for comparison. Simply obsessing or becoming confused about a group can be a sign that things are awry, even though you might not know why. Sometimes it helps to track back to the source of the shift. When did the feeling of the group start to change? Who came? Who left? Did I change? Did the group move to a new place? Did we change the rules? Am I afraid of someone? Am I speaking out or holding back? Who am I afraid of? What is going on? When you talk to others, don't just complain about the group; think of what *you* could do to help it open up discussion and become more vital.

WHICH PART OF ME SHOULD I LISTEN TO?

It can be difficult to know when one should leave a group. In the initial stages of sobriety, or in any group, part of the struggle is discerning which inner impulses come from the healthy self and which come from the addicted or victimized self. It's like listening to two voices inside and wondering which one really has your best interest at heart.

When a person is first uncovering from addiction, they may have strong impulses to leave a group because their addict side is losing control. In other words, the group is good for their healthy part and works against their addiction, so the addicted side wants to leave.

Symptoms of underlying fear can be boredom, wanting to pick at people or feeling sleepy before group. In my own case, the first time I went to the Ken Keyes Center for a three-week personal growth workshop, I started picking at all kinds of things—the split infinitives in the pathways they use, their method for assigning people to morning work, the lights in the hallways, you name it. After a couple of days I stood back and wondered why I was being so critical of these mundane things and asked myself, what's going on with me? The answer that came to me was, "I can either pick at split infinitives or I can get involved in this program and learn something useful for myself." So I quit picking at little stuff and realized I was afraid of buried feelings that were starting to surface.

I have seen people want to leave a group just as they were settling down, making friends, and about to feel close to people. To an abuse survivor, staying in a good situation often feels scary, while being in an abusive situation feels familiar because the survivor carries an internal message that closeness means abuse and betrayal. In cases like this it is important to separate out present reality from past abuse. Some questions to ask are: What happened specifically in this group that makes me want to leave? Who said what, when? Does this bring up fear of old pain? Is this a familiar pattern?

Remember that when you break new ground or let go of the addicted, old survivor part of self, there is often a feeling of loss, fear, or discomfort. With time, people learn to say things like, "My addict part didn't want to come here tonight," or "My little girl is scared to be here tonight," or "I'm grieving letting go of the past and am afraid to let you see me cry."

People also want to leave groups because they are angry at someone and afraid to tell them. In a twelve-step group I attended for two years, one woman put me down when I was feeling good about myself. For a while I didn't say anything and I built up some resentments. I started feeling resistance to going to group, but knew I didn't want to quit going. It was terrifying to call her (I never figured out why), but, finally, after I asked her not to put me down for feeling good, the knot in my stomach went away.

From Fear to Excitement

There are components of fear and excitement when one joins a group. Initially, people often experience lots of fear and a little excitement. As they have repeated experiences of feeling relief or being accepted after telling secrets or expressing feelings in a group, the fear level drops and the excitement goes up. If someone comes into a group for the first time and they are thrilled and excited, and think it's all just wonderful, I suspect they are in denial. They haven't yet realized that it is a long and rocky road and they are going to have to take charge. People who come in to get through a crisis or expect a magic fix often leave within a short time.

Nothing Stays the Same

There is a natural ebb and flow to groups. They may start, gain momentum, and be wonderful for a while, and then lose energy and fall apart or reconstitute themselves. The form is always changing and our ability to deal with the changes and not hold on to a fixed routine or form is part of our growth.

Whatever type of group you join, remember that it is for you. You are the consumer; it's your life, and it's important to listen to your inner voice.

Groups can be extremely helpful for a while, and then one loses interest. Some thoughts people start having when they are ready to move on from a group are, "I'm starting to get bored here. I don't feel as if I'm growing any more. It's all become too predictable. I want something new." Sometimes people will start skipping support group meetings and find they don't particularly miss them. They will say things like, "It's okay to go, but I don't feel I need it anymore."

There is usually a sense of loss mixed with excitement as one reaches out for more expansive horizons. Like a child leaving home in a healthy way, one feels thankful for what they have learned and a little sad to say goodbye, but they know it's time to go. They don't criticize the group or make people "bad" in order to have an excuse for leaving.

13

Finding Your Own Voice:
Moving Beyond the Twelve Steps

"Any situation in which some men [people] prevent others from engaging in the process of inquiry is one of violence; to alienate humans from their own decision making is to change them into objects."
—PAULO FREIRE, PEDAGOGY OF THE OPPRESSED, 1968

About ten years ago I decided to take voice lessons. Like my mother and sister, I had a voice that seemed somehow stuck in my throat, raspy and unclear. I often got laryngitis. So, I thought I'd just take a few lessons, learn how to use my voice properly, and that would do it. Surprise! It wasn't so easy.

After my singing lessons my throat would get sore. I would practice as I had been told, and it would still be sore. My teacher said I was using my voice properly. I was very frustrated. Then one day, driving home from my voice lesson, I had an image of someone trying to strangle me, saying, "You don't get to sing."

"Yes, I do!" I thought, and I started to cry. After that, I cried during my lessons, after my lessons, and when I practiced. I cried for nameless losses, the loneliness of childhood, and the longing for the love of a mother. I cried for all the blocked-up words and anger I'd choked down. And I cried for the loss of myself.

Finding our voices is like finding ourselves. It releases our feelings and helps restore us to ourselves. It takes time, practice, patience, and sometimes a good teacher.

It may seem risky to find our voices and speak our truths. Our feelings might erupt. We might be the target of hostility from people

305

frightened by change or people who uphold the status quo. But what is the risk, really? That someone won't like us? That's probably true already. That someone will attack us? Women, children, and minorities are attacked economically, physically, and emotionally all the time. A better question might be, "What is the safest way to speak up? How can I do it collectively with others? What do I have to lose by speaking my truths?" Better still, "What do I have to gain?"

When people are fearful of or outraged by free inquiry, they reflect uncertainty about their own values. Conformity and deference to authority are highly regarded values in patriarchy/hierarchy. That's why those who question authority or name oppressive practices often become the targets of attack. Some people have implied or said outright that I'm arrogant to have rewritten the twelve steps. Hearing that, one woman laughed and said, "It's pretty arrogant of them to tell *you* you can't think for yourself."

GROUPS AS RITUAL

I believe that much of the attraction of twelve-step groups comes from a need for meaningful ritual in our lives. It is important to differentiate between conscious ritual where people reach for their inner truths, and unconscious, rote rituals where people mouth a script. The greater the creative freedom, spontaneity, and level of honesty, the greater the potential for transformation in a group ritual.

Peace activist, writer, and ecofeminist Starhawk writes, "Any ritual is an opportunity for transformation. To do ritual, you must be *willing* to be transformed in some way. That inner willingness is what makes the ritual come alive and have power . . . *ritual that is alive doesn't become frozen in form*" (emphasis mine).

In an article, "Women's Rites," reprinted in the *Utne Reader*, Francine du Plessix Gray writes, "On a . . . secular level, significant rituals are . . . those that fulfill our sacred need to reinfuse a family or a community with greater harmony and love."

Before patriarchy came to dominate, many rituals centered on the cycles of the earth, the moon, and the seasons. Later when Europeans invaded the United States, Native American rituals that were centered in interconnectedness with earth and its cycles were then called primitive, godless, and even savage.

Thus we lost our meaningful rituals, which tied us to the earth and to nature, and replaced them with somber, rote, religious rituals of the church and eventually secular rituals of watching football, baseball,

TV, or *The Rocky Horror Picture Show*. And on the negative end of ritual, we have cults and satanic groups whose rituals are rooted in violence, sadism, and destruction.

In the United States, so spiritually bereft and lacking in meaningful ritual, it is not surprising that people find comfort in twelve-step meetings. They provide a predictable format where people attempt to be honest and open. This may explain in part why so many people stay in groups for so long. There are few other places for them to find genuine interaction and support. They are a form of ritual.

Du Plessix Gray continues: "Ritual brings us a heightened sense of our own *identity* and meaningfulness." When I started experimenting with rewording the steps in my twelve-step group, other women occasionally did likewise. I found myself listening intently to their words. Our ritual had opened itself to our creative voices, heightening our sense of identity. Because our words came from our inner voices, they were personal, changing, and authentic.

I suggest rewording the twelve steps not because I believe this model is the only way to recovery/discovery, but because it is a program with underlying wisdom that has been supportive to many people. By taking the best parts and transforming the rest, I believe more people will find their inner voice and thus be empowered.

If the traditional twelve steps work for you, that's wonderful. This chapter is directed to people who don't feel comfortable with the steps as written, and who want to open the door to more authentic Self-expression. Uncovering from addiction and dependency should never mean you have to insult your soul.

While many women and men have reworded the steps privately, it is extremely important that we do it openly. To remain clandestine in this activity further reinforces the cultural norm of pretending to accept a rigid, male model when it is not working for us—whoever we are. To break through fear, we need to speak out, to find our voices. Because when we do, we find each other and our collective power.

It is essential to remember that twelve-step programs were created to help people with sobriety. The only thing that is sacred is healing and becoming whole. The rest is form, a shell, a mechanism—nothing more.

A JOURNEY THROUGH THE STEPS

I will outline the twelve steps, discussing their strengths and limitations particularly in the context of being socialized as a woman. Then, taking the spirit of each step, I write one of my own translations and offer several by other people. I present this as an invitation to the reader to listen to other voices and then search for your own until you find words that feel absolutely right for you. The very process of reaching for your own voice is a form of self-empowerment, because it leads to the authentic, creative Self. It was through this process that I eventually made a list of sixteen steps that I call a model for discovery and empowerment. I will present this model in chapter 14.

Step 1: *We admitted we were powerless over [addiction], that our lives had become unmanageable.*

Clearly, to uncover from addiction, we need to acknowledge or admit we have a problem. The purpose of admitting powerlessness is to send shock waves to our ego or old survivor. "I've got a problem. Get it? The old ways aren't working any more—they could kill us." It's like saying that what seemed like survival is now life-threatening and you've got to stop. When a person's life has been under siege from an addiction, they need a sharp, clear, stinging reminder that they have lost control and that their addiction is messing up their life.

I prefer to say,—"I *feel* powerless," or "I *experience myself* as powerless," instead of "I *am* powerless"—because the overall truth is that we are not powerless. We have the power to make choices. Other possible ways to get the message across to the old survivor: "My use of alcohol/drugs/chemicals/food/cigarettes is out of control; my use of chemicals is destroying my life." The first step in Women for Sobriety is, "I have a problem that once had me." Some people prefer to say, "I am powerless over my *impulses* to use chemicals, foods, and so on." In other words, I can't stop the *cravings*, but I sure as heck can control what I pick up and put in my mouth.

The concept of powerlessness can also be helpful when one feels immobilized. Difficulty finishing tasks and keeping life organized is a common symptom for many addicted people. If I get stuck with something—paying bills, writing, returning phone calls—and feel like I'm in a slow-motion dream, saying I'm experiencing powerlessness is often helpful. Note that I don't say I *am* powerless. I just say I'm *feeling* powerless. This separates me from my mired-down state and relieves shame. "I'm not bad, I'm just stuck." This often clicks me out of my trance and helps me reconnect with my will, with the power to take action.

On the other side of the coin, many people don't like the term *powerless* in any form. When I first encountered the twelve steps, I was waking up to feminism and coming out of a depression. The word powerless in any context made me wilt inside. I wouldn't say it. My greatest need at the time was to find a sense of power—power to get up, to get going, to work, to take care of myself, to push through fear.

I am uneasy hearing victimized or dependent women and minority people say over and over again that they are powerless without also talking about the power they do have. It's as if all the focus gets put on their powerlessness and none of it on their intrinsic power. This sounds like the patriarchal switch in action. While it is important to say I can't change another person, it is also important to shift the focus to Self, and to affirm, "I have the power to love myself, grow strong, and take charge of my life." Language generates energy. Try saying to yourself, over and over, "I am powerless" and feel what happens inside. Then try saying, "I have the power to take charge, I have choices," and see how you feel.

Paradoxically, when I have felt more centered in my power, it has felt okay to say I was powerless over my impulses to do something. But it felt totally wrong when I was depressed.

Some people contend that you *must* admit powerlessness in order to recover. That's not true for everyone. I interviewed staff at a women's treatment program that works with all forms of chemical dependency. They have stopped using the twelve steps altogether.

In the words of one counselor, "We rarely use the word powerless. Our model is about empowerment—the bottom line. What we stress are choices so you feel the empowerment. We give people resources of outside support systems, therapists, and other treatment in terms of child abuse, rape, and sexual assault. We see each woman as having individual needs. We also provide an education component to help women understand how the culture limits options and choices, and how that continuously beats up on us. We ask women, 'What can we do to take back our power? What *are* the choices beyond alcohol and drugs? What would help you want to live without them?' We stress that it is a *choice* not to drink or abuse chemicals."

"*My life has become unmanageable.*" The purpose of saying one's life has become unmanageable is to make people aware of the harmful consequences of their addiction. People don't always realize that the lost jobs, house, health, friends, and family stem from their addiction.

On the other hand, sometimes a person's life is unmanageable due to violence, abuse, or poverty, and addiction feels like survival. It isn't that life was once manageable and became unmanageable because of the addiction, although addiction may have intensified the unmanageability. The addiction is an *extension* of the unmanageability.

Thus for some people a more apt statement would be: "My life was unmanageable, addiction has made it more unmanageable, and the only way out is to stop using *and* face the situation of my life. It is important to realize that when many people give up their addiction, their struggles and all the accompanying pain will be deeply felt. This makes it hard to sell sobriety as a *wonderful* idea, but it's important to be realistic and not promise that life is a rose garden if one sobers up.

In a personal interview, a male counselor in an African-American chemical dependency clinic put it this way: "Our program is a holistic approach for our clients, using culturally specific language, information, and history. We talk about how, for Black people, drugs have been part of their lives ever since slavery. We talk about what that piece means for them, and that *life is not going to be great and wonderful just because they are recovering.*"

The statement of unmanageability doesn't hold true for all people who are harming their lives with addiction. For some people, life doesn't appear unmanageable. In fact, they use this as a rationalization to say they don't have an addiction. "I still go to work every day. I jog three miles a day. Hey, I'm fine." Alcoholism or drug abuse can manifest itself in a chronic, controlled form that slowly erodes the ability to be close and intimate, to deal with childhood pain, to express feelings and feel peaceful—but life on the outside may appear to be okay.

Here are some alternatives to Step 1:

- —We admit we are out of control with/powerless over _____, but have the power to take charge of our lives and stop being dependent on substances or other people for our self-esteem and security.
- I acknowledge the pain and suffering I experience because of my addictive use of _____ and commit myself to recovery.
- We admit we are appropriately powerless over people, places, things, and events, but powerful over the daily living of our own lives. Our lives have become unmanageable by trying to live them any other way.
- I am powerless over everything but my own choices and actions.

• In remembering my potential for wholeness, I realize that chemicals have taken me from my true self.

Step 2: *Came to believe that a Power greater than ourselves could restore us to sanity.*

The element in this step is hope—hope that recovery is possible. When we're about to give up an addiction, it sometimes feels like we're sitting at the edge of a cliff, being urged to jump. It seems impossible to imagine how we could live without the addiction. Yet the only way to take the leap is with hope and faith that there's something better, another way. The underlying message is to set aside the addiction, the protective shield that feels like a best friend, and return to life.

I agree there is a power, a mystery, a vast force beyond human comprehension, but I don't see that power as outside us or as a male figure. My image is a cooperative union between the power of the Universe and my own will. I ask the Universe to energize my will. Instead of praying for God to take care of me, I ask for the strength to take action. And I believe we can find that power through prayer, meditation, affirmations, exercise, being with people, going to talks and workshops, and simply opening our senses to all that is around us because God/the Goddess, or the power of the Universe, is every-where, in all living things. It's not "out there." Likewise there is a mystery involved in this process, because while we can take action, ultimately we can't tell a gift how to come. The form of the outcome is still out of our hands to some degree, but we can help guide the course.

In reference to being "restored" to sanity, I don't like the duality suggested by this concept of sanity—that one becomes insane from an addiction and sane after the addiction. While it is true for some, it is not true for all. Some people indeed seem pretty insane (meaning "foolish or absurd," according to the *American Heritage Dictionary*) when they are in the midst of their addiction. They've lost their health and their peace of mind and they're still saying, "Hey, no problem." But not everyone *appears* to be insane. Some people who are addicted appear to be functioning adequately on a job, and haven't lost every-thing. The goal is to interrupt the addictive cycle earlier, before chaos has taken over someone's life.

The phrase "restore us to sanity" assumes sanity prevailed before the addiction took over. That's not true for all people. For some, there are mental or emotional problems that will continue to exist after sobriety.

I prefer the image of being restored to ourselves. Addiction is a journey away from the authentic Self into the protected or defended self, or, as Aaron's (the Native American I spoke of at the beginning of this book) teachings said, from the authentic child to the adapted child. Giving up the addiction, no matter how painful that may be, launches the journey home.

Here are some alternatives to Step 2:

- We *came to believe* that the Universe (Great Spirit, Higher Power, Life Force Energy) will awaken the healing wisdom within us if we open ourself to that power.
- We came to believe that a power greater than ourselves can restore us to health.
- We came to believe that a power greater than ourselves and deep within us can restore our balance and give us wholeness.
- We came to believe that alignment with a higher good can restore us to sanity.
- I came to understand that the collective power of people could restore me to wholeness.
- I came to believe there is hope for recovery."

Step 3: *Made a decision to turn our will and our lives over to the care of God as we understood Him.*

The wording of this step presents a double message: you are to find the God of *your* understanding, but God is defined as "Him." That limits the choice. Others may have a completely different concept of God that is female, genderless, or about a life force energy or spirit.

This step is often referred to as the "let go and let god" step. The message I take from this step is to stop controlling what you can't control, do the best you can, speak your truths, and beyond that let the chips fall where they may.

Letting go is an age-old concept. *What will be will be; what is, is;* and *turn it over* are familiar, related phrases. The Buddhists refer to attachment as the cause of suffering. When we demand that things be a certain way to be happy we are bound to get upset. And, ultimately, giving up attachments helps us deal with death, the ultimate letting-go process.

To surrender, to let go and stop controlling what we can't control, requires faith—faith that we'll survive the outcome and, we hope, emerge with a sense of perspective. But the question remains. Do we find faith by turning our wills and our lives over to a male God?

To me, that image conjures up scenes of women passively, mind-lessly turning their wills and lives over to the care of male doctors, husbands, clergy, teachers, politicians, the military, authority figures, and so on, often with disastrous results. It reinforces the concept of obedience to male authorities as well as teachings that have brain-washed women to trust that men will take care of them when in fact they so often exploit or control them. The last thing women and minorities need to do is hand their wills over to others to control. To do so is at the heart of oppression. Our will is the source of our power for good. So if God is within us, then a strong will for good symbolizes a strong contact with God.

Instead of the image of turning my will and my life over to some-one, I think of inhaling life energy into my being, filling myself up with a sense of spirit, energy, and goodness. It is an image of joy and strength rather than one of giving myself away.

Some alternatives to Step 3:

- We declare ourselves willing to hear the Universe speak its truths into our spirit, and to listen and to act based upon those truths.
- We constantly reaffirm our decision to center our lives on seeking alignment with a larger good.
- We made a decision to ask for help from the Goddess and others who understood.
- I allow the interest and care of others to carry me when I need help.
- We choose to step beyond our daily concerns and listen for the guidance of the goodness within.

Step 4: *Made a searching and fearless moral inventory of ourselves.*

I take this as a cleansing step. The idea comes from the belief that confession is good for the soul. Buried secrets create shame that, like toxic waste, takes on a life of its own. By clearing out our secrets, we deflate the power of the shame and guilt. This frees us to love our-selves. I believe in a clearing-out process, but I don't agree with calling it a *fearless moral inventory*.

For starters, the word *fearless* sounds too bravura. Fearlessness is a masculine goal that causes people to deny their feelings. It is one of those absolute terms that set people up to feel they aren't doing it right. What's wrong with feeling fear? Most of the difficult things we do are accompanied by at least an edge of fear.

It is valid to make a list whether or not you are afraid. I translate fearless to mean reach deep, reach for it all, no matter how bad it is. Write it down, say it, get it out of you. Even this idea has its problems, because for some people it is much better to go slowly, releasing the inner shame bit by bit and not in one fell swoop.

My problem with the moral inventory idea is its obviously judgmental, shaming tone. It may be applicable for some but not for others. The moral inventory concept does apply to those who perpetrate or assault or exploit others, or those with a grandiose ego. It is extremely important that such people own up to the harm they have perpetrated on others.

A moral inventory was a core element of the moral rearmament movement (from the Oxford Groups, which predated AA), which proposed that leaders and businessmen and those who held open power in government assess the harm their need for money, status, control, and violence has done to other people. I think that's a terrific idea. I would love to see corporate presidents, the U.S. Presidents, and Pentagon officials have weekly meetings to take a moral inventory of what our militaristic society and its exploitation of women and people of color has cost in terms of individual human suffering and devastation to the earth.

On the other hand, it may be counterproductive for oppressed, depressed, or ordinary people to immediately look at their faults before they have affirmed their intrinsic goodness, strengths, and power. Most people, particularly the oppressed, tend to blame themselves for their abuse—"How could I have let them do that to me!"—and this step often reinforces self-blame. We are obsessed with guilt and shame in this culture, and spend very little time affirming the magic, wonder, and beauty within us and around us. Thus this step is very unbalanced.

It creates a duality, too, to take a moral tone about ordinary human weaknesses. It is possible to say, "I made a mistake; I hurt someone and I'm sorry" without saying one was immoral, which is implied in this step. Most people I know or work with need to accept the imperfections of their humanness and stop trying to be so pure.

I urge depressed persons to skip this step and read David Burns's book *Feeling Good*. An insidious symptom of depression is distortion of one's culpability for all the negative things that have happened. So this step could serve to reinforce the depression. The important thing for a person with depression is to focus on what they can do to start taking control of their life. So instead of a "moral inventory" they could list their abilities, talents, and strengths. Actually, this could be good for anyone—depressed or not.

Some possible versions of Step 4 are:

- We repeatedly examined our lives, remembering all the things we have done for which we felt guilty, ashamed, or wrong. We also affirm our strengths, accomplishments, positive choices, and things we like about ourselves.
- We made a thorough and balanced moral inventory of ourselves.
- I made a searching and fearless personal inventory of myself.
- I made an assessment of how my life was.
- I searched my conscience and was honest with myself about how my choices, actions, and attitudes affect myself and other people.
- I made a list of every secret and every thought I have inside that makes me ashamed.

Step 5: *Admitted to God, to ourselves, and to another human being the exact nature of our wrongs.*

(With regard to Step 5, I refer the reader to chapter 10, where I discussed certain aspects of fifth steps, including cautions, suggestions for taking them, and selecting someone to hear them.)

This is the extension of step four—a cleansing step. We take our list and, using it as a guide, tell another person all that we have kept locked up inside. It can be a wonderful relief, especially when the person hearing the step is sensitive and caring, and doesn't keel over with disgust or say, "That's too terrible. Get out of here!" It brings new perspective to our secret shame. Maybe those terrible things we did don't mean we should be thrown off the planet. Maybe we're not such bad and shameful people after all. Because secrets shared become sacred truths, this step helps us love and accept ourselves.

What I *dislike* is the religious tone of this step, reflected in the language. The word *admit* conjures up a negative image and a moralistic tone. It reinforces that you've done something bad and you should confess. I reframe this step to mean we *choose* to reveal our *secrets* in order to cleanse ourselves and feel at one with the spirit. In terms of the word *wrongs*, while it applies sometimes, wrong is subjective— some women think they are wrong for refusing sex they don't want. I prefer to stay with the image of a cleansing step without assigning blame.

For guilt-ridden people, a fifth step can help put their perceived crimes in perspective. I remember telling a therapist about the profound guilt I felt as a child after hearing my father storm around yelling,

"Where's my comb?" and seeing that the comb was on my dresser. I quickly hid it in a drawer and played innocent when he came to my room and asked if I knew where it was. The therapist's good-natured laugh was reassuring. "Do you hear what you are saying?" he said. "You accidentally took a ten-cent comb to your room, and when you heard your father storming around, like most kids, you hid it in the drawer and acted innocent to prevent being yelled at. What a crime!" We both laughed.

On the other hand, a person with a narcissistic or perpetrator personality, who doesn't feel much guilt about exploiting others, may need the person hearing the step to guide them in a different way. It is crucial to let the person sit with their pain and take full responsibility for harming others. They need to feel guilt.

Unfortunately, what happens because of our internalized acceptance of society's values is that people who admit to being victimized are sometimes revictimized during fifth steps by a listener who implies they caused the abuse. And people who have perpetrated are sometimes let off the hook by listeners who minimize their behavior.

I suggest the idea of a group fifth step where all people share with each other. At Ken Keyes College, we called it a cop session—copping to your stuff. I have had groups do it around sexuality or anything else that comes to mind. This changes the power imbalance of having a confessor and confessee, and gets rid of the moral tone. We put a pillow in the center of the room, light candles and, in no particular order, everyone says things that come to mind that feel like shameful secrets about things they have done. We do this as equal human beings, in the spirit of the knowledge that we all make mistakes.

Here are some possible versions of Step 5:

- We share with others all things for which we feel ashamed or guilty, not blaming ourselves for what was not our responsibility. We also shared our strengths, accomplishments, positive choices, and ways we like ourselves.
- We admitted both privately and publicly, to the full and appropriate extent that we could, the exact nature of our challenges— our strengths as well as our weaknesses.
- We admitted to a Higher Power, to ourselves, and to another human being the exact nature of our wrongs.
- I admitted to God, to myself, and to another human being the exact nature of my difficulties and problems.
- We told the truth about ourselves without adding or hiding anything.

Step 6: *Were entirely ready to have God remove all these defects of character.*

In spirit, I think of this as a willingness step: I am willing to change, I am willing to be healed. It recapitulates the second step by implying there is hope.

The wording and the imagery in this stage do not work for me. The reference to removing all *these* defects of character implies that what we confessed in the fifth step are all defects of character. If we use a fifth step as a cleansing step, it's not about defects of character, it's about releasing human shame.

The term *defects of character* might be apt for perpetrators, narcissists, and other exploitive people, but it doesn't fit for shame-based or guilt-ridden people who all too easily stay focused on their failings and weaknesses. "Defects of character" is a culture-bound, Christian concept stemming from the idea we are born sinners and must redeem ourselves through a life of confession and atonement. It creates duality—good and bad. And who defines a defect of character? In patriarchy, obedience is usually considered a good trait. Does that mean independence and autonomy are defective? It's a matter of viewpoint.

For example, in my interviews with people at the Blue Bay Healing Center, one man said, "We don't think like white people in terms of right, wrong, good, bad, yes, no. So phrases like 'remove defects of character' do not fit for us." It also doesn't fit in terms of female or Goddess spirituality, where everything is seen as part of the whole.

For me, a God who removes defects of character conjures up the image of a surgeon standing over an anesthetized (passive) woman, knife in hand, cutting out a tumor, a cancer, a defect—or a powerful God out there swooping down and taking away our imperfections. What a grandiose idea. It seems like addictive, all-or-nothing thinking—a miraculous conversion experience. I don't believe God is a person with hands who can "remove defects." I believe we choose to be transformed. We light the fire of love and self-acceptance, which opens the path toward releasing traits we might not like. This is the beginning of change.

I also react to saying "entirely ready." I'm usually entirely ready to go on vacation or to play tennis, but I'm not always *entirely* ready to change everything. What a tall order. What's wrong with being *tentatively* willing to explore one small change at a time? Like putting your toe in the chilly lake before you dive in? Most of us vacillate between wanting to change and wanting to hang on to familiar patterns. While there is a wonderful feeling when one flashes on the knowledge that it's worth doing anything to be well, most people find themselves open to change one minute and strongly resistant the next. Also, a person can be ready to change one behavior and not others. It is a process that takes time. Every step requires a new willingness to let go, to change in one more way, and to face the fear of the unknown.

This step is stated so seriously. We've got to get rid of all these defects. My thought is, lighten up! We *all* have defects, foibles, and blind spots, and they can be amusing, irritating, or a royal pain. We need to realize our programming is separate from our spirits, which are always sacred. We can do lots of wonderful, creative things as fallible, sometimes nutty people. This image of getting rid of defects of character pathologizes life. As one woman said, "I resent the implication that we're never okay right now. We're in constant need of fixing. When is it ever okay to be the way I *am!* I may have all kinds of things I'd like to change, but I need to hear I'm worthy of love right now."

This step feeds into a perfectionistic trap. Part of our humanness is that we are a mixture of behaviors, some that work and some that don't, and many of our attributes are a mixed bag. Being compulsively neat is great if you're cleaning houses, but not so good if you're bringing up children and want to provide a relaxed atmosphere. Suggesting or implying that we can remove all "shortcomings" and "defects of character" leads to constant nonacceptance of ourselves. It also leads to recovery narcissism—a prolonged overconcern with self and an impossibly idealized notion of what it is to be human. We are perfectly imperfect right this moment.

Here are some other versions of Step 6:

- We became willing to let go of our shame, guilt, and any behavior that prevents us from taking control of our lives and loving ourselves and others.
- I declare myself willing to follow divine guidance in order to give up and transform all behaviors that are not self-affirming or self-loving.
- I was ready to trust that I, with the help of God as I understood God, could work to make my life whole.
- We were entirely ready to have a Higher Power guide us to accept ourselves as we are, and grow toward becoming our highest selves.
- We were entirely ready to build our strengths and to transform our weaknesses into strengths.
- We quit fighting ourselves and accept all parts of ourselves as

they are right now. In our acceptance, our shortcomings begin to disappear.

Step 7: *Humbly asked Him to remove our shortcomings.*

The wisdom behind these words is the belief that transformation is possible. Change is, to some degree, a mystical experience, but it also comes from willful acts—like saying affirmations, doing daily readings, meditating, taking classes, exercising and so on. It's a balance of the two. We can take action to change, yet the timing and way it happens remains to some degree a mystery.

Like step six, this step sometimes gets people into a perfectionist trap. "I've got to get rid of all my shortcomings. I've got to do recovery right." Serious sin-and-redemption stuff again! Where is the ability to laugh at ourselves? In our guilt-ridden, shame-based society, I would like to see much more focus on goodness, strengths, celebration, and joy. We need to develop the concept that we can learn and grow through love and happiness, not just suffering.

Beyond that, much of what I have said about steps four, five, and six applies here. The external male God, the implication of instant change, the stance of being one-down from God, do not affirm an image of people celebrating life and accepting our shortcomings as humans. And, yes, some people need to focus on their shortcomings, but I believe it should be balanced with focusing on strengths.

About the concept of humility: Humility in our culture has come to be associated with humiliation. This mistaken belief was the source of the incredible abuses in treatment programs I discussed in chapter 10.

Humility is not about humiliation. It is not about groveling, self-abasement, or being down on one's knees—all the patriarchal images associated with humility. Because so many women have internalized the patriarchal images of female humility as being a vapid martyr, groveling, or being somehow broken, I prefer to use this term with utmost caution.

It is good to celebrate a job well done, a courageous act, or a self-loving action. We need to cheer for each other's strengths. Women are already overly experienced at bonding in humility or pain.

Humility cannot be imposed on a person; rather, it comes from a deep understanding that our path is interwoven into a larger picture. We accept our talents and strengths as gifts from our Creator, and use them, enjoying them fully, without becoming self-effacing or egocentric. Humility is not incompatible with celebration and self-satisfaction. If God gave us our talents and strengths, then to enjoy and use them is to celebrate God.

I'd like to pause here for a personal note. After writing about these steps for several days, I found myself feeling heavy. All this focus on faults, wrongs, moral inventories and defects of character seemed so negative and shaming. I took a break to call a good friend in Al-Anon who has consulted with me on this book and bemoan my heaviness. "I'm exhausted," I told her. "All this focus on badness. Where is the love and goodness?"

She laughed and said, "You'd think you're supposed to lie face down, prostrate on the floor, and then live life from that position. You've already been beaten down, but let's beat you down a little further, somewhere beyond humble. I sometimes wonder where is the bottom line in all this. When is someone humble enough?"

We laughed together and continued our discussion. The idea of getting rid of shortcomings or defects precludes introspection, awareness, and gentleness. It's a dualistic approach to say, "This is bad—get rid of it!" It doesn't promote learning. In a nondualistic approach, we learn from our mistakes by standing back and kindly observing our dance, our soap opera and saying: "Hmm. Why am I doing that? What's that about?"

We also learn to rechannel energy that was destructive. In other words, the cleverness of the addicted person in finding drugs can be rechanneled into cleverness for finding a job or strategies for staying sober. Thus we redirect energy from the old survivor and take the focus off the symptom.

Some versions of Step 7 are:

- We asked the Universe for courage and wisdom to transform our destructive behavior into positive behavior.
- I asked for forgiveness and guidance.
- We learned to ask for help with our self-improvements without embarrassment or shame.
- Without pretense, asked to become all that I am meant to be.

Step 8: *Made a list of all persons we had harmed and became willing to make amends to them all.*

Steps eight and nine help people repair their relationships to others and in doing so opens their hearts. To look inside and think of the ways we have hurt others leads us to feel sorrow for our behavior and the pain it has caused someone. Hopefully, in time the awareness of harm we have done to others will generalize to an awareness of the massive separateness in our culture which leads to so much human suffering. When we tune in and connect with the suffering in the world, we develop a sense of oneness which is often a catalyst for taking action.

For people who operate by blaming everyone, stopping to think how they have hurt others can slowly influence them to realize the implications of their actions. Many people are unconscious of the ways their behavior impacts others. It is difficult for them to realize that blaming actually comes from a deep sense of powerlessness. I can't control what I do, think, feel, or drink, so I blame others. To stop blaming is to take back one's power (except, of course, when one needs to assign responsibility for having been abused).

The focus of step eight is to make the list of persons we have harmed and become *willing* to make amends. Many people find it important to start the list by making amends to themselves. A way to alleviate the shame around our destructive or hurtful behavior is to recognize that there is usually a positive intention of seeking love and personal power underlying every negative act.

Many of our destructive habits started in childhood as mechanisms to survive in a hurtful family or in a negative community environment. It can be very helpful to look for the childhood metaphor in our adult behavior. Most of all, we can remember that a spiritually aware person would not harm themselves or others. It is important that people not make amends because their sponsor told them to or they feel pressured to do so. However, though willingness must come from the heart, with highly defended people a little nudging might help. This process often involves looking inside and bumping into tons of fear. "If I make amends, they will tell me I'm a rotten person, slam the phone down, or tell me I'm a jerk."

Becoming willing is an intrinsic part of the spiritual journey. It means we are willing to do something that could be uncomfortable in order to grow. Remembering ways we have harmed others often brings up shame. "How could I have done that?" I remember a mother who, when confronted by her adult daughter, whom she had sexually and physically abused, said, "I would give anything if it weren't true, but it is."

Examining ourselves to see how we've harmed others often opens the road to childhood abuse memories that may have been buried. Sometimes the harm we have done to others reflects the abuse perpetrated on us. Thus making amends can lead us to feel the full impact of our own abuse, so we can heal and stop the cycle of abuse.

We encounter a cultural double bind with step 8. The people who most need to say they are sorry—those highest in the hierarchy—are seldom aware of it, and the ones who don't need to continuously apologize are all too willing to take the rap for everything. Women routinely apologize for being abandoned, raped, beaten, or poor, because they've internalized society's "blame the victim" stance. There needs to be a balance between taking responsibility for the *harmful* things you have done to others and absolutely *not* taking responsibility for others who have harmed you.

The important step toward healing is to clear out negative energy between yourself and others no matter who generated the harmful behavior.

Here are some possible rewordings of Step 8:

- Became willing to clear out all negative energy between myself and other people, remembering we are all sacred children of the Universe.
- Made a list of all persons I had harmed, particularly myself, and became willing to make amends to them all.
- We made a list of all the persons we had harmed and became willing to make amends to them all; we made a list of all people we had helped and became willing to accept their gratitude with dignity.
- I am willing to apologize to all I have wronged and let them know about the changes I am going through.
- I am willing to be responsible for my mistakes and do my best to clear the air with people I have hurt.

Step 9: *Made direct amends to such people whenever possible except when to do so would injure them or others.*

This step is useful to some degree, but it is again unbalanced. It keeps the focus on one's negative behavior toward others but does not support a person's recognizing when they have been harmed by others, which is a necessary step for empowerment, particularly for women and other subordinated people. This step also maintains the overall sin-and-redemption tone, and does not support people saying what they appreciate and love about each other (which I include in the sixteen steps to follow).

Making amends helps heal relationships. It clears the air, restores self-respect, and cracks through our isolation. Because addiction thrives in isolation, creating genuine human bonds is important. When we learn to make amends, we build a bridge that takes us out of our shame and reconnects us to to others. While some people may not accept our amends, most of the time people are grateful.

I would like to underscore that it is *never* too late. At my twenty-fifth high school reunion, I made amends for something that had rumbled around in me for thirty years. When I was fourteen, a very dear young man dated me. At some point, I froze up and could no longer comfortably talk to him. I just disappeared from his life. I saw him on a bus some months later and went to talk to him, but he turned away from me with a pained look on his face. I never forgot it. Years later, after therapy and introspection, I realized I had frozen up and left him because he was kind and good to me, and I didn't believe I deserved love.

When I saw him at the reunion with his wife of twenty-two years, he was nice to me, but there was some uneasiness. When we had a moment, I apologized for being so cold to him way back when, telling him, "It wasn't your fault. It was because you were loving, and I didn't know how to be loved." The smile on his face and the look in his eyes were priceless. He said, "I always wondered what happened. Thanks for telling me." And we danced together just as we had as adolescents. Thus making amends can help heal the object of our damaging/ignorant behavior as well.

Making amends is a long process. The time and setting need to be right. If we make amends without being sincere, it will not heal the other person. In fact, we will be using them again. And just making amends is not enough if there is a long-term betrayal. A person may have to earn back the trust of the other person through being responsible and respectful.

Some possible wordings for Step 9:

- We cleared out negative energy between us and other people, both owning our part, and sharing our grievances in a respectful way.
- We made direct amends to such people, including ourselves, except when to do so would injure them or others.
- I corrected my mistakes in a responsible manner.
- We made direct amends to such people whenever possible, except when to do so would injure others or myself.

- We acted responsibly on these intentions wherever possible, injuring none—including ourselves.

Step 10: *Continued to take personal inventory and when we were wrong, promptly admitted it.*

Steps ten, eleven, and twelve are often called maintenance steps. Earlier steps help heal the past, and these steps are geared toward staying conscious in the present and keeping our relationships honest. If we make a mistake or hurt someone, we say so. We don't cover it up, rationalize it away, or blame the other person, for that will kindle the inner shame and guilt again.

Once again, this step is unbalanced, breaking down the ego by focusing our eyes on our faults without affirming our strengths as well. It also could be a trap for people who self-blame to feel responsible for being victimized.

It is important to make amends when we have been hurtful and it is important *not* to take responsibility for what other people do to us. For subordinated people to be free from internalized oppression—those voices within that cast self-doubt on one's worthiness and abilities—they must externalize the oppressor who lives within.

Some alternative wordings for Step 10 are:

- I continue to gain awareness of how I hurt myself and others, and when I do, forgive myself and make amends.
- We continue to take personal inventory. When we are wrong, we promptly admit it. When we are right, we assert it nonjudgmentally.
- I continue to assess my problems and to solve them promptly.
- We continued to tell the truth about ourselves moment to moment.

Step 11: *Sought through prayer and meditation to improve our conscious contact with God as we understood Him, praying only for knowledge of His will for us and the power to carry that out.*

As a Quaker, the *spirit* of this step speaks clearly to me. It is about listening to that still, small voice within, hearing my calling and my purpose, and following it with faith. To do this takes discipline and courage and often a significant leap of faith. When we hear our inner calling, it rings with rightness and clarity. While the leadings may not be what we hoped for, to fight what we know is right for us only creates inner chaos. We can only do what feels right and accept the outcome. It may not be what is easy or convenient. It simply *is*.

Again, I do not ascribe to the notion of an external God and grimace at the image of women asking for *His* will, which is the core of our oppression in patriarchy. We need to find our inner Will, which is a woman's voice or the voice of the spirit.

I like the part of this step that suggests finding guidance through prayer and meditation, and I certainly believe we need help in finding the courage to live out our calling. Finding our inner voice and gaining courage also comes through supportive contact with other people. Thus along with seeing ourselves as finding the courage individually, I see us as finding it together as well.

Done communally, this step has potential for unifying large groups of people who, when they tell the truth, will recognize they are being exploited, abused, or ignored. This can spark collective anger, which leads to social action, because for all of us the truth is that we were given a life to lead that has its own special meaning, and we have a right to find our purpose.

Living by the truth is not just about big moves or major decisions. It is about minute-to-minute awareness and honesty—asking myself what do I want to wear today or eat for breakfast; who do I want to talk to, what do I want to read.

Sometimes finding our inner purpose takes a long time. On other occasions one has an epiphany—a leading—that seemingly comes out of the blue. I remember vividly the beautiful fall day when, as a piano instructor at Ohio University, I heard a voice in my head say, "This is not what you will do forever. You're meant to do something else." My reaction was, "Oh, no! I wished I hadn't heard the voice." I could hardly believe it. Until that moment, leaving my teaching career had been the farthest thing from my mind. But, somehow, I absolutely knew that my days as a piano instructor were numbered.

Here are some different peoples' wording of Step 11:

- Sought through prayer, meditation, and increased awareness in all my involvements to listen to my inward calling and gain the will and wisdom to follow it.
- I make a conscious effort to keep my spirituality close and personal, and to use my spiritual awareness to guide and motivate my actions.
- Through inward and outward seeking, I quieted my soul, listening to the spirit within and directing my life accordingly.

Step 12: *Having had a spiritual awakening as a result of these steps, we tried to carry this message to others and to practice these principles in all our affairs.*

Part of the spiritual journey is giving back to others what we have been given. It is a natural process that evolves as we feel abundance in our lives. The danger is that carrying the message can turn into prosely-tizing, or that people feel duty-bound to "carry the message" in order to be good "program people."

We carry the message as we live it. By being loving, open, authentic human beings we naturally have a positive effect on people around us. "Attraction, not promotion" is an apt phrase from AA circles that needs to be remembered. One woman wrote, "I hated all those Big Book thumpers in our group."

Fellowship and caring for others was a huge part of the early AA groups. And to someone in need, it is wonderful to know people are available. While one of the greatest joys of spiritual recovery is in loving and serving others, it doesn't mean one is required to give. Giving is a choice, and best not done from an empty vessel. Again, we need balance between taking in love and kindness and giving it out. Many people are conditioned to give out of fear and guilt, or only to give and not to receive. This can work to defend us against acknowledg-ing needs and becoming vulnerable.

Sometimes people who live in chronic crisis abuse this step by feeling people should always be available to them. It is important to be wise in our giving, not to throw our energy down the drain or enable people by listening to repeated stories told from a victim stance. The only way some people know how to get attention is by creating a drama or telling how they've been victimized, or by acting little and needy.

This step is unbalanced because in following the sin-and-redemp-tion focus on troubles and suffering, it directs us to reach out to people in need, but not reach out in joy, love, or success. As I said earlier, oppressed peoples need to learn to bond in power and joy, not just in pain.

In a life-loving/creative spirituality we grow through celebration, ritual, love, being at one with nature, and taking action for social justice. If we have hard times, they are not glorified as more holy than good times, they are simply seen as the ebb and flow of life.

My favorite phrase when sorting out whether it is genuine to give or not is the phrase, "Don't give presents you can't afford to give." If I will be resentful or feel someone owes me something, then I wouldn't be giving, I'd be faking it. If I want something in return, I need to say so out front, so the contract is clear. I'll do this for you if you'll do (whatever) for me. Being honest is a far more precious gift to a relationship than faking it. Saying an honest "no" or "yes" can be a gift to another person who needs permission to do the same thing. Honesty thus becomes a form of giving.

Here are some versions people have written of Step 12:

- As my consciousness and spirituality grew, I carried my awareness, knowledge, and hope to others, and continued to follow a path toward living a more spiritually centered life.
- Having experienced both emotional healing and spiritual awakening as a result of these steps, we carry this message to others by practicing these principles in all our affairs.
- It is important to share my process and to be responsible to myself and others in all my affairs.
- By practicing these principles, I awaken to my wholi-ness, making it possible for others to awaken to theirs.

Now I will include three complete rewordings of the steps by people with varied backgrounds and different addictions or concerns. The first list is by a Lakota Native American man, the second is by a feminist Witch, and the third is by a survivor of childhood abuse. All three wrote the steps as part of their own healing journey and shared them with others. They consented to include their steps on the condition that the copyright extend only to reprints in publications so that readers would be free to copy them for their personal use.

So with many thanks to these creative people, here are their versions of the twelve steps.

JERRY'S TWELVE STEPS IN THE NATIVE AMERICAN TRADITION

Sobriety Through the Sacred Pipe—Caŋnupa Wakáŋ

1. Admitted we are powerless over alcohol, and that our Indian way of life had become unmanageable.
2. Come to believe that the power of the Sacred Pipe—Caŋnupa Wakáŋ is greater than ourselves, and can restore us to our culture and heritage.
3. Make a decision to turn our will and our lives over to the care of Tȟúŋkašila—Ate through our Sacred Pipe—Caŋnupa Wakáŋ.
4. Make a searching and fearless moral inventory of who we are, and understand the symbolic meaning of each of the four directions.

5. Acknowledge to the Great Mystery—Tůŋkašila—Ate, to ourselves, and our Indian spiritual advisor, the exact nature of our struggles, wrongs, against the tide and its manifest destiny.

6. Be entirely ready to have the Great Mystery—Tůŋkašila—Ate, remove all these defects of an alien culture.

7. Humbly ask the Great Mystery—Tůŋkašila—Ate, to remove our shortcomings through Lakól wicoȟ'aŋ, our tribal ceremonial teachings and spiritual growth.

8. Make a list of all the harms that I created to myself, to our people from alcohol, and became willing to make amends to them all.

9. Make direct amends to our people about our struggle against the alcoholic disease wherever possible, except when to do so would injure them or others.

10. Continue to take a personal, searching and fearless moral inventory of who we are, and when we are wrong promptly accepted, and admitted it.

11. Seek through prayer and meditation to improve our conscious contact with the equality, brotherhood/[sisterhood] of all the Mother Earth's creatures attaining that spiritual balance of the great harmony of the total universe.

12. Having the universal understanding, wisdom of the hearts, minds, spirits, of all people, we carry this message to Indian alcoholics, and we practice these principles in all Indian affairs.

ANTIGA'S THIRTEEN CIRCLES

1. We believe that we are not responsible for creating the oppression that permeates our society.

2. We believe that a Power outside ourselves and deep within us can restore our balance and give us wholeness.

3. We make a decision to ask for help from the Goddess and others who understand.

4. We acknowledge our beauty, strengths, and weaknesses and look at the ways we have been taught to hate ourselves.

5. We acknowledge to the Goddess, to ourselves, and to another person our successes and shortcomings.

6. We make a list of the ways we have acquiesced to oppression.

7. We become ready to say no to oppression.

8. We ask for the courage to resist oppressive situations.

9. We mend our lives with respect for all.

10. We continue to be conscious of our actions and thoughts,

promptly acknowledging our mistakes and enjoying our successes.

11. We seek to improve our conscious contact with the Goddess.

12. We believe that at every moment we are doing the best we can, and that is enough.

13. We accept ourselves exactly as we are, trusting our experience and affirming that health, joy, and freedom are our Goddess-given rights.

(These steps may be copied for personal use so long as credit is given to Antiga.)

SARA'S STEPS

I put together the following version of the twelve steps in my process of recovering from incest. When I wrote these steps I never expected anyone but me to see them. What I wanted was a personalized set of the steps, one that brought together ideas and words that were particularly meaningful to me. My approach was simply to ask, What do I need to hear? What do I need to admit? What do I need to come to believe? I first shared these steps with a member of ARIA (Adults Recovering from Incest Anonymous) and discovered they struck a chord with many others in the group. Since then they have been passed from one person to another and assumed a life of their own, much to my surprise and delight. These steps are based on the words of the SIA (Survivors of Incest Anonymous) Twelve Steps, the Feminist Steps, and the many people who have helped me to recover. Take what you need and rewrite the rest.

1. Admitted that we had been sexually abused, were powerless over the abuse at the time, and that its consequences had deeply affected our lives.

2. Came to believe that a power greater than ourselves and deep within us could restore our hope and bring healing.

3. Made a decision to seek help from our higher power and others who understood.

4. Searched deep within to honestly appraise our strengths and weaknesses, and how they affect our lives and others around us.

5. Admitted to our higher power, ourselves, and another person the exact nature of these concerns.

6. Became ready, with the help of our higher power and others sent to aid us, to discard behavior and thinking that was no longer useful or healthy.

7. Honestly desired to abandon these behaviors and pursue instead those that bring strength and renewal.

8. Made a list of the people we had harmed, including ourselves, and became willing to make amends when possible, change our behavior, and forgive ourselves.

9. Made amends with respect for all concerned.

10. Continued to take personal inventory and, when falling back into harmful behavior, promptly acknowledged it and started again, remembering to appreciate how far we've come.

11. Sought through prayer and meditation to improve our contact with our higher power and inner spirit, seeking to realize our potential for a generous and meaningful life. Came to believe that every time we accept our past and respect where we are in the present, we are giving ourselves a future.

12. Having had a spiritual awakening as a result of these steps, we sought to spread this message to others and practice these principles in all our affairs.

•   •   •

We have journeyed through the twelve steps and explored them from a life-loving/creative spirituality that seeks to create balance and present choices.

Though I have attempted to bring balance to the existing steps—the yin and the yang, the negative and the positive—there are still crucial steps missing that support celebrating strengths, having choices, standing up for ourselves, healing the physical body, expressing our love for each other, and seeing ourselves as part of the planetary community, not just a recovery community. That comes next in my discovery empowerment model.

Rewording the steps has far-reaching implications because it breaks with the patriarchal obedience code that is so deeply internalized in subordinates in patriarchy, especially women. That's one reason rewording or expanding one's interpretation might seem scary. It goes against our internal programming and it is a political act because it affirms the Self. But remember, while it may bring hostility from some, in my experience in talking about this at workshops around the country, there are many people who are eager for changes or already making them.

If the thought of making changes creates a lot of fear within, don't fight the fear, listen to it. What are the injunctions you were taught against thinking for yourself or making changes? Remember, it is internalized oppression to believe we have to take the words of others and use them obediently.

To quote Paulo Friere again:

> In order for the oppressed to unite, they must first cut the umbilical cord of magic and myth which binds them to the world of oppression; the unity which links them to each other must be of a different nature. . . . Only forms of [cultural] action which avoid mere speech-making and ineffective "blah" on the one hand, and mechanistic activism on the other, can also oppose the divisive action of the dominant elites and move towards the unity of the oppressed.

14

Sixteen Steps for Discovery and Empowerment

The principles I have talked about in this book are now integrated and translated into sixteen steps for discovery and empowerment, along with an introductory reading for groups. The goal is a model that helps people move through fear, open up all the energy centers in the body (described earlier as chakras), develop a sense of inner strength, and integrate a cultural framework into their understanding of addiction and dependency.

All of this is embodied in a life-loving/creative spirituality, which affirms passion, expressiveness, creativity, diversity, awareness, and joy. In a life-loving spirituality, people are considered to be born blessed and holy. The goal of life is to grow, expand, and be connected to all life, in contrast with the idea of being born a sinner in need of redemption. In a life-loving spirituality, faults are seen as human and change as a process of transformation, while sin is reframed as lack of compassion and being oppressive to others. It is hoped that the use of this model will spill over to our political system. If our culture operated from a life-loving spirituality the leaders and people with power would be committed to nonviolence, care and compassion for all people, preservation of the earth, and the ability to value and bridge differences.

I present this model as a framework or process, not a rigid model. I hope people will use it as a springboard to find their own inner voice, which is the only way to empowerment.

To underscore that power of language, I return to a quote from Paulo Freire in *Pedagogy of the Oppressed*: "We were blind, now our eyes have been opened. Before this, words meant nothing to me; now they speak to me and I can make them speak. I work, and working I transform the world."

There is a saying that if one woman told the truth, the world would crack open. What this really means is that if women collectively speak their truths, we will be transformed and effect enormous social change. It boggles my mind that a two-page article I wrote for *Ms.* rewording the twelve steps elicited nearly four hundred letters to me, and many others to *Ms.* All but four or five of the ones I received were from women. As women, we are hungry for words that speak to us and name our experience.

Rephrasing Freire: Words speak to *us* and *we* can make them speak. The process creates a circle. We can be healed by words that speak to our hearts because language changes the ways we think, perceive, and know, and in turn, helps us become more able to speak from our authentic Selves. This weaves us together, breaking down the isolation that perpetuates domination and subordination. Unifying our voices gives us power.

Many people wrote that they made copies of the reworded steps and took them to their groups or that someone showed up in their group with copies and initiated discussion.

My friend Kitty talked about taking these new steps to her Al-Anon group when she presented the first step. She said,

> I was reading the AA and ACOA versions of the first step and there was this wall of impassive faces all around me. Then I read the empowerment step: "I have the power to change my life and to stop being dependent on others for my self-esteem and security." I looked up and I suddenly saw lively, interested eyes. But no one said a word. Finally, one woman found the courage to speak. "I really like that. Do you suppose sometime we might spend a whole session looking at rewriting the steps?"
>
> Her words melted many of the icy faces. There were animated smiles, and heads nodded all around. Someone else

said, "It feels scary to mess around with the steps, but I have to tell you what a relief it is to finally be able to say they're not right for me." The nodding continued and I knew something monumental just had happened that bordered on heresy and on . . . something new for all of us.

Responses to the sixteen-step empowerment model echoed similar themes. One woman wrote, "Your article helped restore my sanity. It answered (or put into words) that kernel of 'What the hell is wrong with this picture?' feeling I have always suffered from in the traditional ACA, CODA ideals, meetings, and educational classes. . . . Your ideas have taken away the aloneness I always feel from never being with like-minded people."

My hope is that people who are discontented with their twelve-step meetings will talk about their feelings. There are many groups like Kitty's, where the dissatisfaction simmers under the surface, waiting to find a voice. It just takes one statement: "I want to talk about these steps. I want to change the steps. I want to take out the shaming language. I want to incorporate a feminist analysis of my addiction and dependency." The potential for change is like the Hundredth Monkey concept Ken Keyes describes in a book by that title. He suggests that when the time is ripe for a new idea, people all over make similar changes, and a widespread consciousness change results.

So if you want to speak up, remember, you are not alone. There are many who feel as you do. My experience of starting to change the steps in a small meeting in a grubby church basement here in South Minneapolis was a seemingly small, personal act. But as I started to speak up and learn from others who were doing the same, our small personal acts gained momentum. We brought support to each other.

When I was tired writing or feeling grief over having cancer this past year, I would pull out letters that became like wind beneath my wings to keep me going. "Your words helped me, thanks for speaking out." One particular letter from a Black Latina woman gave me a huge surge of energy. She said both *Women, Sex, and Addiction* and the *Ms.* article were *bold* and *fierce*. How I thrilled to hear those words. It created a circle of energy; I gave, I received, and I could give some more.

Transformation comes through the collective creation of new rituals and myths that affirm a new way of thinking. Here is a quote from Riane Eisler, author of *The Chalice and the Blade*:

Often unconsciously, the process of unraveling and reweaving the fabric of our mythical tapestry into more gylanic* patterns . . . is in fact already well under way. What is still lacking is the "critical mass" of new images and myths that is required for their actualization by a sufficient number of people.

Many women who wrote to me indicated they had experienced that unconscious process she speaks of:

"Thank you so much for validating what I have felt for some time."

"The twelve steps never seemed to fit for me and now I understand why."

The importance of speaking out and not quietly dancing around a patriarchal ritual is to create that "critical mass of people" who will effect change. The isolation created by adapting to a model that doesn't fit was expressed by a woman who directs a sexual assault center. "What I was unable to articulate for myself or anyone else is that I adapted them [the twelve steps] so they would work. At a recent conference on women and chemical dependency, someone pointed out that women are very used to having to rework things that were developed for men in order to get what we need—something I'd been doing without even being conscious of it."

Making constant inner translations is exhausting. When we politely and quietly dance around a male model, it perpetuates our internalized oppression and keeps us from affirming ourSelves. It prevents us from developing a language that will help newcomers focus on healing, and not on translating from male experience.

I know from personal experience how disorienting it can be to try and assimilate knowledge presented from a male perspective. As a child, I had a terrible time concentrating in school. School books were boring, and I had tremendous difficulty memorizing historical dates. Later, going through sociology texts in college, I would stumble and get mired down in the complex words and ideas. I used to think I was stupid.

---

*Eisler uses the term *gylanic* as a combination of feminine and masculine linked together equally in a partnership society. "Gy derived from the Greek root word *gyne*, or 'woman.' *An* derives from *andros*, or 'man.' The letter *l* between the two has a double meaning. In English it stands for the *linking* of both halves of humanity, rather than, as in androcracy, their ranking. In Greek it derives from the verb *lyein* or *lyo*, which in turn has a double meaning: to solve or resolve (as in ana*lysis*) and to dissolve or set free (as in cata*lysis*). In this sense, the letter *l* stands for the resolution of our problems through the freeing of both halves of humanity."

But when I read *The Feminine Mystique* in 1963, followed by other feminist books, I came alive. I gobbled up every page. Someone was speaking to me in a language I could understand. I think much of my former exhaustion and disinterest in reading (along with being mildly dyslexic) was because the books were about some foreign tribe that had nothing to do with my experience as a female, and they were presented in a male style. But because I didn't know that, I thought the problem was mine—the patriarchal switch again.

My rewording of the steps is not intended to set women apart from men. On the contrary, it is intended to help us move closer to an integrated, nonviolent balance between men and women which will benefit all of us. It is our system I oppose, not individuals.

AN INTRODUCTION TO A DISCOVERY/EMPOWERMENT MEETING

I have written an introductory reading for support groups that seeks to affirm diversity and create acceptance of others. It could be read at the opening of meetings.

To review the use of the term *dis-covery* rather than *re-covery*: Discovering suggests opening, expanding, and growing. Re-covery suggests covering up something. Re-covery is defined in the *American Heritage Dictionary* as "to restore to a *normal* state . . . to regain a normal or usual condition." As a woman who has spent close to thirty years deprogramming my mind from what was called *normal* for women and uncovering my inner voice and values, I don't want an image of re-covering. I want to uncover, discover, expand, and move beyond the limits imposed on me by our patriarchal system.

• MANY ROADS, ONE JOURNEY: • WE GATHER TOGETHER

Our purpose in coming together is to support and encourage each other in our healing from addiction, dependency, or internalized oppression. The only requirement for membership is a desire to maintain sobriety as we each define it.

We come together from many backgrounds and we can learn from each other's ways and experiences. None of us has the answers for another person. We describe our journeys of healing, but it is up to each of us to find our own path. We do not impose our beliefs on others or expect others to tell us the way. We have faith that through determination, sharing our histories of discovery and healing, supporting each other, and understanding the impact of our social system on us, we can each discover our personal path toward sobriety, healing, and inner strength.

Healing is a balance between gentle self-acceptance and a firm commitment to sobriety. We overcome addiction and internalized oppression because we want to honor and enjoy the life we have been given. Healing from addiction and dependency is not about moral worth. We are all sacred children of Creation this moment.

These steps for discovery and empowerment are designed to create a healthy, aware Self which, over time, will help crowd out compulsive, addictive, or dependent behavior. We believe that through bonding with others, speaking genuinely from our hearts, forgiving ourselves and others, finding purpose, helping create social change, and accepting the imperfections of life, we will find a sense of fulfillment that we have sought to fill through our addictive and dependent behavior.

The journey is sometimes difficult, sometimes smooth. This is natural. As we let go of our addictions and empower ourselves, some of us may use other resources to help us grow. We may also be faced with difficult circumstances in our lives that need advocacy and assistance. We support each other as we explore all avenues of personal empowerment and growth.

Several things you may want to remember as you use these steps are:

- Many people have healed from addiction and internalized oppression.
- There is no perfect path, only the path you choose one day at a time.
- While we are aware of the powerful nature of addiction, we have seen that our collective will and commitment to healing and growing is even more powerful.
- Change takes time and is made of many small steps.
- The steps are only suggestions; change them in any way you like so they feel true to your heart.

Drawing from the reworded steps of the last chapter, combining some and adding new ones, I have put together sixteen steps for discovery and empowerment. As you read through them you may have an emotional response. My suggestion is simply to be with the feelings for a while. Do you feel scared? Do they energize you? Do you feel sad? Excited? Relieved? Irritated? Scared?

I put the sixteen steps in the present tense, in contrast with the way the twelve steps are presented in *Alcoholics Anonymous* ("Here are the steps we took"). Using the past tense divides the steps between those who have taken them and those about to take them, as if there are recovered people and unrecovered people, another duality. I think we grow and heal in gradations, constantly bringing new awareness to old situations. It is a circle or a spiral without end and we are all on it together.

SIXTEEN STEPS FOR DISCOVERY AND EMPOWERMENT

1. We affirm we have the power to take charge of our lives and stop being dependent on substances or other people for our self-esteem and security.

    Alternative: We admit we were out of control with/power-less over _____, but have the power to take charge of our lives and stop being dependent on substances or other people for our self-esteem and security.

2. We come to believe that God/the Goddess/Universe/Great Spirit/Higher Power awakens the healing wisdom within us when we open ourselves to that power.

3. We make a decision to become our authentic Selves and trust in the healing power of the truth.

4. We examine our beliefs, addictions, and dependent behavior in the context of living in a hierarchal, patriarchal culture.

5. We share with another person and the Universe all those things inside of us for which we feel shame and guilt.

6. We affirm and enjoy our strengths, talents, and creativity, striving not to hide these qualities to protect others' egos.

7. We become willing to let go of shame, guilt, and any behavior that keeps us from loving ourSelves and others.

8. We make a list of people we have harmed and people who have harmed us, and take steps to clear out negative energy by making amends and sharing our grievances in a respectful way.

9. We express love and gratitude to others, and increasingly appreciate the wonder of life and the blessings we *do* have.

10. We continue to trust our reality and daily affirm that we see what we see, we know what we know, and we feel what we feel.

11. We promptly acknowledge our mistakes and make amends when appropriate, but we do not say we are sorry for things we have not done and we do not cover up, analyze, or take responsibility for the shortcomings of others.

12. We seek out situations, jobs, and people that affirm our intelli-

gence, perceptions, and self-worth and avoid situations or people who are hurtful, harmful, or demeaning to us.

13. We take steps to heal our physical bodies, organize our lives, reduce stress, and have fun.

14. We seek to find our inward calling, and develop the will and wisdom to follow it.

15. We accept the ups and downs of life as natural events that can be used as lessons for our growth.

16. We grow in awareness that we are interrelated with all living things, and we contribute to restoring peace and balance on the planet.

Now I will go through the steps, commenting briefly on the ones discussed in chapter 13 and elaborating on the new ones.

1. *We affirm we have the power to take charge of our lives and stop being dependent on substances or other people for our self-esteem and security.*

The word *affirm* is defined in *The American Heritage Dictionary* as "to declare positively or firmly; maintain to be true; to ratify or confirm. . . ." For women and oppressed peoples, to affirm our power is to confront one of the deepest parts of our internalized oppression—namely, that we are inferior to and dependent on men or authority figures. To *declare positively* that we have power to run our lives confronts all the stereotypes of what it is to be an acceptable woman or minority person.

Because oppression is tied to economic discrimination, part of this step is to take action to be able to earn a living so we are not economically tied to destructive, exhausting, or battering relationships. Whether we wait tables, learn a trade, teach, or something else, we need to support each other in believing it is better to live simply and with dignity than to be spiritually dead living with or working for an abusive person.

Earning a living is not easy for women and poor people in the United States because of wage discrimination and the cultural blocks to education for women and minorities. Once we externalize that it is not our fault that these inequities exist, we move to a stance of asking, "What choices do I have? How can I become more powerful? How can I take charge of my life? How can I feel happier? How can we work together and improve our situation?"

I remember joking with a client who always hid behind the thought, "It's too scary to speak up or be on my own." I suggested she write her obituary based on her current behavior. Would her gravestone say, "I lived a walking death because I was afraid?" Do you want to die never having lived?

In this step we don't talk about being powerless over another person as a starting point, because that keeps us talking about other people. We put the focus directly on ourselves, looking at what we *can* do to give up the economic, psychological, and psychic dependency on others or things for our self-esteem and security.

An even deeper level of this step is to give up needing external approval for our self-esteem. While it's important to be around people who affirm us and cheer for us finding our power, it is different to have our self-esteem *dependent* on the approval of others. When we think, I'm worthwhile because I wrote an A paper, cooked a good meal, or was told I look pretty, we are placing our self-esteem in the hands of others. It keeps us in a one-down, dependent position. We need to take our self-esteem, draw it into ourselves, connect it to our own lives, and ask ourselves, "What am I doing that brings pleasure, meaning, and a sense of well-being into my life?"

1. Alternative: *We admit we were out of control with/powerless over _____, but have the power to take charge of our lives and stop being dependent on substances or other people for our self-esteem and security.*

Many people said that admitting/acknowledging powerlessness was important. They had to continually say, "I am powerless over (drugs, cigarettes, alcohol, sexual impulses)" to realize the devastation it was causing in their lives. Although this step starts by acknowledging powerlessness over a substance or person, it goes on to affirm that we can take charge of our lives.

The crucial part of recovery from dependency on people or substances is to admit we have an addiction, and then put the focus back on ourselves. How do we maintain sobriety and then fill the emptiness beneath the addiction?

2. *We come to believe that God/the Goddess/Universe/Great Spirit/ Higher Power awakens the healing wisdom within us when we open ourselves to that power.*

From the perspective of a life-loving spirituality and many indigenous teachings, I believe that a sacred spirit or life-force energy is within us and around us. It is our willingness to tap that power, to draw it into ourselves as an energy source to bring insight and awareness that brings strength for the journey. It is an active union between a person and the power of the Universe. And it's a process—we *come* to believe, we don't *instantly* believe.

Simply saying, "I'm willing to do whatever it takes to heal/be whole" helps open the door. Often people feel a rush of fear when they make such a statement, because the old survivor is terror-stricken at the idea. It's crucial to believe we have within us the power to heal and we can find the power to ignite our will. We may listen to others and take in their words, but ultimately we put them in our holy middle and find our own answers.

3. *We make a decision to become our authentic Selves and trust in the healing power of the truth.*

Knowledge of God/Goddess/Spirit begins with knowledge of Self. If we are to be one with the spirit, we must know ourselves. This means allowing ourselves to meet our inner world of thoughts, feelings, and sometimes buried memories. It means we stop taking directions from others, stop faking the smiles, the bravura, the innocence, the power, the charm, the docility, the orgasm, and that we continue to reach deep inside, asking ourselves, "What is my truth?"

It might help to remember the teachings that Joseph, a Native American, gave me for this book about the natural child and the adopted child. Our work is returning to the natural child, who takes pleasure in exploration, touch, feel, and discovery. The whole movement to heal the inner child is about finding the natural child who has the keys to joy, spontaneity, awe, and love.

Finding our truths often means sorting out our addictive impulses from our wisest self. People often develop phrases to help them reach for the truth. They ask, "What does my wise woman say? What does my highest Self say? What do I *really* believe? Which choice is truly in my best interest? Which way would be loving of myself?"

Sometimes we listen and hear nothing. Sometimes the voices collide inside, and we feel stuck in confusion. One moment we feel sure we have the best solution and a few minutes later we're not so sure. Just as we are about to take a positive step for ourself, the old survivor mounts a counterattack. We may feel a sudden sense of foreboding as if something terrible will happen. Or some part of us might say, "You don't deserve that." Confusion is a natural part of the process. We need to get away from the notion that we must get things fixed . . . now! If no one ever asked you what you think and feel, or gently cared for you, it will take time to trust the voices within. Hopefully, they will eventually say you get to have sobriety, love, success, fun, and friends.

When we are clear about which voices belong to the old survivor, we can affirm them like a parent consoling an upset child: "You did the best you could to get me through, I know you were trying to protect yourself. I'm grateful to you, but now we are learning new ways that work better."

The second part of this step is to take some risks and say your truths to others. "I feel good about that job I did. I disagree with your opinion. I'd like to be sexual with you." You start saying words that have been stuck in your throat. You can keep taking reality checks: Did the world collapse when you spoke up? Probably not.

You may lose some friends or partners because they liked you better when you acted like a victim and spoke out of your "shoulds," but that's part of the process. One woman who left a nine-year relationship said, "It died when I started being real."

Ultimately, we come to trust that if we live by our truths, it is the best we can do in life. It's really the only thing we can do once we commit ourselves to a spiritual path.

4. *We examine our beliefs, addictions, and dependent behavior in the context of living in a hierarchal, patriarchal culture.*

The purpose of this step is to understand all the ways we carry the pain, confusion, and anger of our system in our bodies, minds, and spirits. Many times we receive confusing messages from the system and then think we are the source of the confusion. Have you ever stopped to inventory how much stress you have in your life due to inequities in the system or walking the line between surviving in patriarchy while trying to be true to yourself? This step is crucial in terms of moving to a mature level of faith, developing a healthy, aware ego, and our ability to perceive what's really going on around us.

Another goal of this step is to become wary and wise. We have to give up being naive and innocent in order to see danger and to protect ourselves. We need to know a con when we see it and to recognize when we are being manipulated. This leads us to get angry instead of slithering into shame or feeling stupid when we are being oppressed.

In this step we attune ourselves to the patriarchal switch in all its many forms. One key to recognizing the patriarchal switch is to see who gets protection and who gets blamed in our system. Typically, perpetrators get protection and people who are victimized get blamed. The perpetrator of rape or sexual abuse gets probation, a treatment program, and lots of support, while the one victimized gets shamed and ignored and is offered no provision for treatment or help. Children who have been flagrantly abused are forced by social service organizations to spend time with abusing parents because policy says, "Every parent has the right to fail." The CEO earns five million a year and workers are told they are lucky to earn twenty-four thousand. The boss is late giving the secretary something to finish, then puts her down for not having it done on time. Women are taught to dress attractively at the office and then told it's their fault they are sexually harassed. Men are told it's brave and patriotic to go to war, and then their wounds and pain are ignored when they return. A rich person looks down on someone who is poor and calls them lazy. Men are taught to be macho, and then end up feeling empty and alone.

This step can take a long time. One woman wrote that the empowerment group she started spent five weeks on this step and they were still not ready to move on.

5. *We share with another person and the Universe all the things inside of us for which we feel shame and guilt.*

No matter what the source of our shame and guilt, it is important to talk about it in order to clear out dense energy in the body. Whatever we deny is like toxic energy poisoning our system. It is important that we talk about sexual abuse, loneliness, stupid or mean things we've done—anything that blocks our ability to love ourselves. When we release shame, we are free to connect with the wonder of being alive, of having a life.

This is a cleansing step that is often a long-term process, particularly if we are survivors of incest, battering, or abuse. When we talk about shameful things done to us, particularly sexual abuse, we often feel shame; thus we need to go slowly to prevent being overwhelmed.

If we are talking about harm we've done to others, while we need to hold ourselves accountable for abuse to others, we don't need to flagellate ourselves. We can remember we are sacred children of our Creator and that our actions come out of our programming.

Some people use guilt and shame as an excuse to block intimacy or take responsibility. "Oh, I'm so bad; I'm an addict, I've ruined my children, I've been so selfish, I've blown my career, nothing will ever go right for me—bad, bad, bad." We all have done some tacky, thoughtless, maybe despicable things. We can weep that we were so separated from ourselves and from love, and then take steps to make changes.

6. *We affirm and enjoy our strengths, talents, and creativity, striving not to hide these qualities to protect others' egos.*

This step is for pure celebration and unmitigated self-congratulation. For some, this will be comfortable; for others it will be more difficult. Women's programming is to be self-effacing and to hide our light under a bushel (to use the old expression). In women's therapy groups, when we set aside time to affirm our strengths and accomplishments, there is sometimes enormous resistance compared to how readily we repeat the litany of ways we have messed up and done things wrong.

If words like *arrogant, bragging, boasting, big ego* or *lack of humility* come to mind when you think of talking about your strengths, remember: If our talents come from our Creator, then to celebrate them is to celebrate creation. It doesn't mean we are better than someone, it simply means we celebrate our lives.

It's fine to say, "I'm proud of myself for staying sober. I played a good game of soccer today. I baked a really great cake today. I did a creative job of organizing the office today. I like this brick-laying job I did. I enjoy having musical ability."

This step runs counter to the patriarchal notion of humility, which confuses self-appreciation with arrogance or ungodliness, especially if you are a woman—the patriarchal switch again. Affirming our strength is an important first step toward amassing our collective power so we can energize each other to reach beyond our perceived limitations.

One way to activate knowledge of your strengths is to write down all the wonderful, thoughtful, caring, intelligent, creative things you have done. Then read your list to a group and put it in a place where you will see it daily. You could have a "popcorn group" where you set aside time to sit in a circle and spontaneously say things you are proud of in no particular order.

The second part of the step is particularly directed at women and has to do with not sacrificing ourSelves to protect men's egos. We are deeply conditioned to squelch our intelligence, creativity, and spirit around men, lest their sense of superiority be threatened. Thus many otherwise intelligent and competent women suddenly act seductive, giggly, lamebrained, cutesy, or seriously impressed around men.

Sometimes when a group of women is meeting and a man enters the scene, many women break their connection to the other women by shifting their attention to the man as though an oracle had just walked into the room. Men don't stop their important business when women appear. Changing this behavior is part of casting out our internalized oppression.

You can start doing this step by noticing how you change your behavior around different people. Do you hide your power by getting giggly, scared, turning to mush, or otherwise losing your voice and your convictions with men, bosses, authority figures, women—anyone?

Simply observe your behavior (or collapse) with fascination and interest and listen to the messages in your brain. Make note of what you say to yourself. "He won't like me if I say anything. I'm acting super-sweet because I'm really mad and I don't want it to show. She'll think I'm a lesbian. I'll lose my job. They'll leave me."

After you've observed yourself, start challenging these internalized responses, exposing them to current reality. My mother might have hit me if I spoke up, but will this person do that? What will happen if I tell my friend I'm upset? What will happen if I stop laughing at sexist jokes? Usually the child within fears great disaster, but the monsters we fear are often paper dragons left over from childhood.

7. *We become willing to let go of guilt, shame, and any behavior that keeps us from loving ourselves and others.*

This is where we learn to recognize the voice of our internalized oppressor, be it mother, father, caregivers, clergy, teachers, media, or others. How do their teachings live in our heads and guide our behavior? What can I do to cast out these harmful beliefs and take steps to improve my life? In step four we examined the external sources of our beliefs; now we look inside and release the negative beliefs that keep us mired down.

One way to approach this step is to make three columns on a page. Title them, "Internalized oppressive beliefs," "How I lived out the oppressive belief," and "What I can do differently?" An example of an oppressive belief is: "I'm worth more if I am with a partner." Examples of "How I lived it out" are staying in an abusive relationship, not going back to school, not saying I was angry, being depressed, abusing medication, getting sick, giving lots of attention to my image, and so on. Examples of "What I can do differently" are, I will join a support group; I'll take an assertiveness class; I'll affirm that my body is lovable just the way it is.

Another way to approach this is to look at our internalized racism, sexism, and homophobia and ask how we turn it against ourselves. Did we live it out by self-abuse, such as drinking, quitting school, or feeling hopeless? New beliefs could be, "I am worthwhile, I am as God/dess created me, I can learn, I can stay sober, I can find ways to change my life."

To make these lists is to take responsibility, but also to stop the self-blame, and to realize that many of our beliefs and behaviors stem from internalized oppression. If you get upset when you realize how much you have been influenced by oppressive teachings, remember, it's a given that we collude with our oppressor on occasion. Sometimes it's a toss-up between losing a job or losing self-esteem—a rotten, stressful choice. Being put in such a double bind is part of our oppression. Blaming yourself for the stress is also part of internalized oppression.

We can take our list of statements under "What I can do differently" and use them as affirmations—a great way to reprogram our brains. "I *can* change my life." The more we say it, the likelier we are to believe it. Said enough times, affirmations progress from being vague thoughts, to beliefs, to reality.

The next step is taking action. Unfair as life is, we need to eventually shift our focus from blaming to making our lives better. This can be uncomfortable if we are afraid to take control, but it takes us from feeling victimized to being a survivor. The important words here are *choice* and *consciousness*.

We may *choose* to stay in an oppressive job because we need the money. But we acknowledge that it is an abusive job and cease making excuses for the boss or the organization. Thus, instead of complaining about the job we strategize about ways to protect and care for ourselves on the job and not give our energy away.

When we operate from a victim posture, it is difficult to bond intimately with others because we are always wanting others to take care of us instead of being true peers. The same is true when people operate from a one-up or domineering stance. Either way, relationships are unequal and lack intimacy. So this step involves giving up arrogance as well as giving up operating from a victim stance.

8. *We make a list of people we have harmed and people who have harmed us, and take steps to clear out negative energy by making amends and sharing our grievances in a respectful way.*

This step helps us repair relationships and become free of negative connections to people. When we feel ashamed of how we treated someone, or have resentments toward someone who abused us, we are still connected to them in a negative way. The only way to move toward a positive connection is to clear the air and redefine the relationship. Sometimes we find out it is not possible to clear the air, or we don't want a connection. It's important to find this out, disconnect, grieve the loss, and move on.

Working this step can be a long-term process. It is important that we take responsibility for what we have done, and assign responsibility to others for what they have done to us.

My healing process involved owning that I had lied to some people to keep them from leaving me. It also included calling a man who had raped me and telling him (twenty years later) how he had harmed me. Both actions helped relieve my shame.

Much of the therapy I do with people is clearing out old relationships—particularly those with parents. One rite of passage into adulthood is to talk honestly with one's parents, demystify them as gods, and stop faking it around them. This can be extremely scary, like daring to steal fire from the gods or like David using his slingshot on Goliath, but it is crucial to healthy development. This doesn't mean being brutal or disrespectful; it means to stop being like a child needing one's parent's approval to feel okay. Often, after the anger and hurt is expressed, people find at least some positive ways to be connected. I've witnessed amazing changes in parent–adult child relationships over the years.

9. *We express love and gratitude to others, and increasingly appreciate the wonder of life and the blessings we do have.*

To look someone in the eye and say genuinely, "You are special to me; you helped me; thanks," awakens our loving side and bonds us to other people. If love is God, then showing our love makes the presence of the spirit come alive around us. Thus expressing gratitude to people is a form of prayer that blesses both the giver and receiver. The thanks can be for anything that genuinely touches you—being helpful, patient, tough, a good teacher, a good friend or lover.

Expressions of love and care can be built into simple rituals to mark changes in our lives. Two dear women friends from my tennis team took me out to dinner to celebrate the end of my radiation treatments. We were seated near a window wall where we could see the full moon. We intentionally took turns saying what we appreciated, admired, and liked about each other. It brought tears to all our eyes and it felt like a perfect moment in time. I remember a sense of being filled up. I believe we can grow through love.

Giving and receiving links us together. Remembering back to childhood, I think of Helen Haig, a friend of my mother's, who let me play with a little white china tea set from *her* childhood. To me it was magical. Then, one day when I was six, she took it off the shelf and gave it to me. Tears come to my eyes even now as I remember how special she made me feel. It was unbelievable to me. When I was forty-one, I wrote her a letter saying that I wanted her to know the magic those little white dishes had brought into my life and that over the years seeing them on my china shelf repeatedly kindled warm feelings. I acknowledged it was a rather late thank-you note. She wrote back that my letter had come at a hard time for her and did a lot to ease her pain.

The more love we generate, the more we change the atmosphere. Some people are wonderful about doing thoughtful things for others. Some of us *think* of giving to others and don't follow through. Some of us feel entitled to have people wait on us and do things for us without giving back. Whatever balance you need to strike, the goal is to tune your senses in to the goodness that comes your way and genuinely show appreciation to others.

The second part of this step is to acknowledge the mystery and wonder of life along with the blessings we *do* have. One woman wrote, "Be sure to say this is not about the 'be good or God will getcha' approach" used in Sunday school, or about forcing kids to smile for relatives, or any other Polyanna garbage. I'm not talking about denying pain or putting on a false smile. I'm talking about remembering the richness of our lives. A dear friend wrote into her wedding vows, "I promise to stop looking for what I don't have and realize how much I *do* have with you."

Sometimes we get lost in negative thoughts and forget to remember our blessings. You may think you don't have any, that life has been absolutely rotten, but it's all relative. I recently talked with a Native American friend who has six children and lives on a small income, is finishing a college degree, is already certified as a chemical dependency counselor, and leads healing ceremonies. On the day she called, her car had broken down, the phone company was threatening to disconnect the phone, and she was short on money for groceries. "Well, I've got to keep a good attitude around these kids so they don't feel like victims," she said. "I've got to remember my blessings—I have these children and some people can't have any." And it was genuine, not a bunch of phony baloney. Being around her is always uplifting, because no matter what is going on we can laugh and cry together and there's always a sense of perspective. It's not that she doesn't get upset or cry, but her foundation for life rests on feeling grateful.

Another way to tap into the wonder of life is to take an inward journey into our bodies. We can image billions of cells at work in our body, regenerating themselves. We can stop and listen to our heart beating away as it has all of our lives. Simply breathing air fills us with energy. We wiggle our fingers, our toes, breathe deep inside. We remember that we have a warm bed to sleep in, enough food, and people who care. This is not to minimize our problems; rather, it is to lift the heaviness and restore balance to our perspective.

One woman talked about momentary meditations that helped changed her perspective on life: "Simply to remember to notice the leaves and trees, to hear a bird sing, or to look at cloud formations."

Eventually, counting our blessings helps us bring a sense of gratitude into the moment and become at one with it. We are touched when we see people being kind, we feel joy when we hear the birds singing. This helps us focus on the positive aspects of ourselves and take the focus off our mistakes. It is a process of sensitizing ourselves to the positive so we experience it more deeply, feel more filled up, and become gentler with ourselves.

Many people who are used to a fast pace and constant external stimulation find it extremely difficult to slow down and take pleasure in looking at a flower, enjoying a walk or feeling wonder in simple things. One woman said sadly, "I was with a friend who said with excitement, 'Oh come look at these flowers.' I looked at the flowers, and I felt nothing." Another person described it as looking at everything through a plastic wall—there was no way to connect with the beauty. To develop a capacity to be sustained by natural things often means we turn off the TV, slow down the pace, breathe, spend lots of time with nature, and be patient. Development of this ability may take a long time.

10. *We continue to trust our reality and daily affirm that we see what we see, we know what we know, and we feel what we feel.*

I originally had a second part for this step: *When we are right we promptly admit it and refuse to back down.* However, some people took this part literally and stuck up for themselves and got into big fights and got hurt. So take this second part in spirit and use it with wisdom. Let yourself know when you feel clear and right inside and speak up when it feels wise to do so, but don't get yourself harmed, or at least be aware of the risks you are taking. The purpose of this step is to develop trust in Self.

Step ten is dedicated to women and all subordinate people in hierarchy. I got the idea in a twelve-step meeting when a woman read the tenth step and exclaimed, "Say I'm sorry—I need to say I'm right for a change! I say I'm sorry for breathing air!"

To see what we see, feel what we feel, and know what we know is the antidote to internalized oppression syndrome, where we are trained to see ourselves through the eyes of those who confine us to our limited roles. In this step we grasp hold of our reality and learn to hang onto it. Yes, we listen to others, but we also listen to ourselves. We learn to notice manipulative behavior and not be conned by smooth words. If my gut tells me I'm being harmed, I pay attention to my gut. I don't have to know why, but I start by believing the signals my body is giving me.

With this step, we build a healthy aware ego and self-trust. In therapy, I repeatedly ask clients, "What do you think? What feels right to you?"

With a support group, we can start getting validation for our perceptions. One woman says, "My boss started talking about his sex life to me and it felt icky." Another responds, "Yeah, that's not appropriate. You're right, that's icky." As a result, her self-trust grows. A Native American says, "I didn't trust that businessman telling us they want to use our land for businesses to create jobs for us." Others say, "Yes, look at the history. He's trying to con us."

We need the collective strength of one another to help us learn to trust our perceptions. Ultimately we may be able to speak up even when no one agrees with us, but most of us need support "at home."

11. *We promptly acknowledge our mistakes and make amends when appropriate, but we do not say we are sorry for things we have not done and we do not cover up, analyze, or take responsibility for the shortcomings of others.*

Staying current in our relationships by owning up to ways we are insensitive or hurtful restores our bonds with other people. Truly saying "I'm sorry" means acknowledging the harm we have caused and listening quietly when someone says how our insensitive behavior hurt them. And, as mentioned in other steps, it is important to acknowledge our shortcomings gracefully and not grovel or hang onto guilt.

On the other hand, people in dependent relationships often spend hours a day analyzing or covering up for their partners. They rationalize abuse—"Oh John had such a hard childhood," or, "His boss is so mean"—when the time would be better spent figuring themselves out. This is often a defense against seeing the reality of the situation and having feelings, especially anger.

Making excuses for others also keeps distance. When Mary tells Jane, "I'm so mad at Dick for not calling me," and Jane responds, "Well, maybe he's having a bad day," she breaks the feeling connection with Mary and covers up for Dick. Such cover-up responses, which stop conversation, are typical of people who are afraid of emotions—usually their own.

One woman spoke of how bad she felt for repeatedly making excuses for her husband's abusive behavior toward her children. She would say, "He's had a hard life; he works hard," never acknowledging the pain caused to the children. (This is the patriarchal switch of protecting the perpetrator and asking the victim to suffer in silence we talked about in Step 4). I've heard the same scenario in reverse, with the father protecting an abusive mother but it's far more common with women protecting men.

Covering up for others can perpetuate our oppression. A woman complains about sexual harassment and her friend says, "Oh, he's just teasing you, he's that way with everyone." The second woman is protecting the man . . . as she was taught to do.

A way to stop the cycle of analyzing others is to stop and say, *"The truth is,* I feel _____ about this person." Thus endlessly wondering *why* Mic is being mean and unreliable changes to, "I'm angry at Mic for being mean and unreliable." It shortens the inner conversation considerably.

12. *We seek out situations, jobs, and people that affirm our intelligence, perceptions, and self-worth and avoid situations or people who are hurtful, harmful, or demeaning to us.*

When we connect with people who affirm our intelligence and perceptions, it strengthens our belief in ourselves. Light energy creates more light energy. Ideally, we put ourselves in the most nurturing situations possible.

Unfortunately, in our system, many people are swamped in negative energy—the welfare system, poor housing, dreary jobs. But we all have some choices about friends, what we watch on TV, what we read, and how we think. Every choice we make matters.

We will always have to deal with people and situations that are difficult for us, but we perpetuate our problems when we stay around people who are harmful or drain our energy. In *Women, Sex, and Addiction,* I included a section on taking a lightness reading after you are in situations. Do you feel light, happy, and invigorated, or do you feel drained, dense, and heavy?

There are certainly times to stay in and push through difficult situations, but sometimes the solution is to get away as soon as possible. The sin and redemption belief system perpetuates people's thinking they have to fix others and accept suffering. This is merely an extension of thinking we have to fix our sinful selves to be lovable rather than affirming life is sacred, and joy, self-love, and finding a purpose are holy.

This step is also offered as an antidote to depression, which worldwide is far more common in women than in men. I believe the prevalence of depression in women is, in part, linked to the fact women are not taught to preserve and savor their energy. Rather they are glorified for giving it away, and asking nothing in return. It's like taking the engine out of a car and wondering why it doesn't run.

Healing from addiction, feeling hope, and having the ability to make clear decisions is very difficult when a person is depressed because the mind creates the world as bleak and cannot see choices. Thus I cannot overstate the need for people to treat themselves with care and respect, saying "no" to things that are draining and unfulfilling, and saying "yes" to gatherings and situations that are invigorating, interesting, and fun.

It is important not to underestimate the cost of being in a hostile workplace for eight hours a day, or spending time with people who are emotionally absent, cut you down, or throw cold water on your dreams. In observing clients over the years I have seen people get stomachaches, headaches, feel anxious, start having violent dreams, and a speeding mind when they try to stay in a job they hate. Conversely, I have seen depressed people who hated their job and their partners become less depressed and then view those things quite differently.

13. *We take steps to heal our physical bodies, organize our lives, reduce stress, and have fun.*

A life-loving/creative spirituality seeks to create harmony and balance between body, mind, and spirit. As we talked about in chapter 8, "The Physical Connection," restoring the body to a healthy balance is one important way to bring balance to a person at all levels. This gives us more energy to take affirmative steps on our own behalf.

Getting one's life organized saves energy. The idea is to reach for something and have it there. In one of my favorite books, *Clutter's Last Stand*, Don Aslett writes: "There is a wisdom in letting go of things that clutter and choke your life. . . . Most of us never taste the new, the fresh, the zestful because we have our heads and hearts gripped clear to the quick in clutter. . . . *Hanging on will hang you.*"

I can testify to the difference it makes to clear out clutter. I've learned a lot from my efficient office manager, Linda, who has dejunked and organized the files, my chapters, and my notes. I'm still working on my garage, my yard, and my closet. It's not great yet, but even when I make simple improvements, I feel lighter and breathe easier. It is amazing how much energy is wasted shuffling through excess stuff.

Having fun and celebration are also central to a life-loving/creative spirituality. Laughter and joy spark our energy. Just because someone is in uncovery doesn't mean they can't tell jokes, be spontaneous, or go out and have a good time. It can be wonderful to take up something you've always wanted to do—music lessons, dance, calligraphy, volunteer work, writing—whatever feels good. On the other hand, sometimes we need to be a couch potato. It's important to let the earth lie fallow between planting crops. We renew our creative energy by having a wide array of experiences and stimulation balanced with quiet and solitude.

Living in Minnesota, which is largely inhabited by people of Scandinavian and German descent who are extremely industrious, I have many clients who have been taught that if you aren't doing something *productive*, you're bad. So they never truly rest, and feel guilty at the

mere thought of having a mindless, happy, task-free day, doing whatever comes to mind.

Relaxation and fun are nurturing and healing, but people sometimes carry this exaggerated notion of industriousness into addiction
"recovery" and *work hard* to do it right; they get addicted to being
nonaddicted and forget to laugh at themselves. *My thought is, lighten
up—uncovery and discovery are important, but the moon will still wax and
wane and the stars will still shine, no matter what you do today.*

Reducing stress also comes from learning to change the ways we
think. We change from "It's a catastrophe" to "It's a nuisance"; from
"I can't live without her" to "I don't want to live without her/him, but
I've done it before and could probably do it again. Rats." Again, I refer
you to *Feeling Good,* by David Burns or books on rational emotive
therapy by Albert Ellis. It also comes from not taking responsibility for
problems that don't belong to you.

Meditation, yoga, and deep breathing exercises also renew our
energy so long as we don't become compulsive about them.

Reducing stress also comes from taking enough time for our daily
activities, and returning to a sense of ritual. On a recent trip to Europe,
I realized that Americans don't allow for breaks the way many Europeans do. They don't try to cram as much into one day. It was nice
when people made rituals out of afternoon tea, eating, or visiting a bit
in the morning before leaving for work. Even on business occasions,
people would take a few minutes to chat before "getting down to
work."

Quakers have a saying: "Live simply that others may simply live."
It is a natural part of the spiritual journey to simplify and declutter our
lives so we have more time to know ourselves and to do the things that
bring pleasure.

I recently visited a friend who had sodded over her garden. "I used
to love gardening, but this year I resented it and thought, 'I could be
reading a book, or out riding my bike,' so I sodded it in." The key is
to operate with fewer "shoulds" and more from the heart, accepting
that interests and passions change.

14. *We seek to find our inward calling, and develop the will and wisdom
to follow it.*

In this step we go from *willingness* to *action* based on our own
truths. Quakers call it following one's inner calling.

The toughest part of the spiritual journey is living our beliefs.
Many preach, write, and talk a good line. But fewer people live close
to their beliefs and those who do so are often quiet or modest about
it. This is the fifth and sixth levels of faithing.

It's important not to get pious or sanctimonious about this step and reach for some mythical ideal of purity. The idea is to find our dreams, to sort through our values and journey toward them with a lightness of spirit.

The path is usually a series of small steps that may include taking a walk, attending a workshop, dropping in on a neighbor, finding a career, working less, working more, giving up a fancy, high-paying job, going for a better job, giving up drug dealing, going back to school, getting sexually involved, leaving a sexual relationship, taking a vacation, or resting for a few days at home. It can include moving, writing, or simply deciding that you will risk sobriety, one day at a time.

Following your heart can be scary because it often goes counter to hierarchical conditioning. Yet our souls become liberated when we dare to dream, and the happiest, most content and interesting people I know are those who follow their calling.

Moving toward our values often stirs up resistance. "I want to work less, but . . ." All those rationalizations begin to dance in our mind. That's just our ego expressing its fear, which is why we have support groups or learn to call friends. If we sit in a room with ten other people who all say, "Go for it, I'll support you," their collective energy may spur us on.

15. *We accept the ups and downs of life as natural events that can be used as lessons for our growth.*

It's important that we not see symptoms of life as symptoms of addiction to be cut out, overcome, and cured. All people on the planet go through gradations of being up and down. When people get narcissistic about recovery, they vigilantly assess how they are doing and often try to get over any symptom of depression, sadness, anger, or frustration, as if it were bad. They stay perpetually engrossed in themselves, missing out on fun.

Part of development into maturity is to realize that we all have our personal soap operas. Our ups and downs matter, but in the cosmic scheme of things, they're not serious; they come and go.

When we accept life on its terms, it is easier to relax and just *be*. I remember that when I turned fifty, I said to myself, No more trying to change my personality, and no more seeking out growth experiences or attending intensive workshops. I am the way I am. I am not in need of fixing. I just want to be. I'll follow my heart, and if something hits me in the face, I'll deal with it. If I want to do yoga or go to a workshop, I will. If I don't, I won't. It was incredibly freeing. I'm probably no more or less fun, obnoxious, or opinionated than I was before, but I'm more relaxed about it. And after a period of not meditating or doing yoga, I felt a desire from within to return to my practice, but it came from my heart, not as a "should."

The ups of life can teach us about love. In the sin-and-redemption approach, people learn that they have to pay for the ups with a lot of downs, as if happiness is somehow a sin to be punished. I disagree. As I have talked about throughout this book, I don't believe that suffering and trouble is the only way to grow, although Christian teachings center on this idea.

I remember in Sunday school, when I was eleven, a chaplain came into our sixth grade class and, with arms flailing, shouted dramatically, "It's when I fall off the ladder, when I have nothing, when I'm on the ground that I find God." I remember thinking, "What a stupid idea. If you fall off a ladder, you skin your knees and it hurts."

When I went through cancer surgery and radiation treatments, people would say things like, "It must feel good to know you were strong and survived." Having cancer didn't teach me I was strong. I already knew that. And I survived mainly because I had a routine mammogram and the cancer was caught before it spread. I learned that I didn't like having cancer. But I already knew that too. I don't deny that something changed in me—my desire to live, love, and enjoy everyday has deepened. For some people, tragedy does bring us closer to our friends, but that's largely because people live so trapped in fear of intimacy that only under extreme circumstances does the veil of our separateness temporarily fall.

Patriarchal Christianity has glorified suffering—pretty clever, since this system creates so much suffering. In a life-loving spirituality we don't have to wait for tragedy to tell someone we love them. Closeness, love, and connectedness are the goal. Yes, we have to survive falling off a ladder, but if love is God, then it was Helen Haig, who gave me her white china tea set, who brought me closer to God, because she nourished my heart.

16. *We grow in awareness that we are interrelated with all living things, and we contribute to restoring peace and balance on the planet.*

In speaking of creation theology, which is similar to a life-loving/creative spirituality, Matthew Fox says, "It's not enough to awaken the heart and right brain if you don't also put that energy to work relieving the suffering of the world."

What happens to us individually is a reflection of our culture. The massive addiction problems people suffer reflect a culture in denial and in pain. It's all interrelated. A natural step in the healing process is to want to reach out to others to share what you have learned. In the traditional twelfth step, people were encouraged to reach out to other alcoholics. Now we extend the step and reach out wherever there is need. Thus we move beyond our identity with an addiction group and reconnect with the broader community.

THERE IS NO ONE WAY:
EXPAND, DISCOVER, CREATE

I have presented a model. There is nothing sacrosanct about what I have written. These steps feel blessed to me because they have come through the voices of so many people. I believe they reflect a huge change in consciousness that is underway. Take them, use them, change them, make them your own. Your words are also blessed, simply because they are yours. "Words speak to us and we can make them speak."

If you use these steps in a group, or if you simply use the steps in your everyday life, I would like to hear from you so we can create a central list and build a bridge among more people. It has been exciting to hear how people have integrated and incorporated these steps into treatment programs and support groups, which I will talk about in the next chapter.

I would like to know how you used the steps, what they meant to you, which ones you like, and ways you reword them. If you adapted them in any way to use in a program or in a group, please send a copy. A list of questions and an address is printed in the back of the book.

Finally, I ask that no one pressure another person to adopt this model, for that is completely contrary to the spirit of this book, which is to support people in thinking for themselves and finding their own path.

15

✻

We Gather Together:
Finding or Forming a Group That Fits

In an article on "Why Spiritual Groups Go Awry" in the May/June 1990 issue of *Common Boundary* magazine, Ram Dass says, "For a method to work, you must become entrapped. For the method to complete its work, it must self-destruct. That includes teachers, techniques, and all of it. Otherwise one gets left with being a good meditator, or a good devotee. The process is complete when you've gone beyond the method itself."

Many people start out seeking sobriety and end up on a spiritual journey toward wholeness. While there are many roads on this journey, there are also some common threads binding the process together. Finding support for the journey often means finding like-minded peers who provide shelter and inspiration for the journey. If we accept that people move to different phases of maturity and spirituality, then it makes sense that people need different types of groups to fit their needs.

We could conceptualize healing and uncovering from addiction on a continuum.

The problem with linear models is they don't make room for

Path of Discovery

individual differences. A person doesn't pass from one phase to another on a given day, and often there are areas of life in different phases. These phases can be seen as general categories that overlap, or perhaps as a spiral where we come again and again to a similar situation but bring to it a new perspective or heightened awareness. People might want to be in different phase groups simultaneously.

MANDALA IMAGE

Another way to see this process is with a mandala, where we become whole by incorporating different aspects of growth in our own special way. It's kind of like putting notes and words together, experimenting, trying things out, and eventually creating a song. We may do therapy, improve our diet, do assertiveness training, and take more time for rest, and eventually these seemingly separate acts merge together, creating an integrated whole. Slowly, over time, each part becomes stronger. We don't complete one part and start another; we gravitate from section to section, returning with new insight and strength. In Appendix II you will also find a blank copy of the mandala so you can fill it in any way you like.

DIFFERENT NEEDS, DIFFERENT GROUPS

Through my interviews and questionnaires it became apparent that support groups for addiction and dependency operate in different ways. Some focus primarily on sobriety. In other groups where people's sobriety feels secure, the orientation shifts toward personal

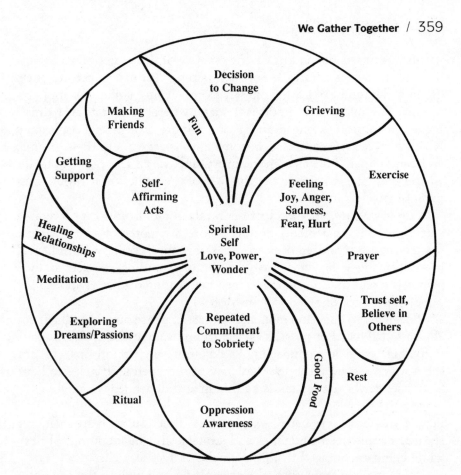

Discovery as Seen in a Mandala

growth. One possibility is to designate different types of groups: Phase one—abstinence/discovery groups, and phase two—empowerment and growth groups. Phase three is where the form fits the people's goals and changes accordingly.

Phase One: Abstinence/Discovery Groups

In phase one, the goal is to dam up the flood of the addiction and convince oneself thoroughly that sobriety, although difficult, is better than addiction. Sobriety is better whether you are poor, rich, white, lesbian, African American, Native American, Asian, battered—no matter what, sobriety is better.

When people "bottom out" and join addiction support groups, they take the lid off their denial and *uncover* the harmful, devastating effects of the addiction, as well as buried feelings and emotions.

In this phase, depending on the severity of the addiction and one's life circumstances, strategies for maintaining abstinence, getting one's life in order, and extricating oneself from harmful situations are paramount. For many it is a survival stage, where "one day at a time" sometimes becomes one hour or one minute at a time. People may latch on to recovery phrases, become enthusiastic about their groups, and center their life on their recovery/uncovery. The point is to do whatever it takes to escape the clutches of the addiction without compromising one's integrity.

Along with maintaining abstinence, the focus is often on survival— staying in one apartment, finding a job, straightening out financial matters, getting children back from foster homes, coping with upheaval in relationships, leaving abusive situations, finding a place to live, paying the rent on time, going to meetings, eating regularly, and calling people on the phone . . . to name a few!

For many women and men, a huge part of phase one is healing from childhood abuse. For most, it is best to find a good therapist and have individual or group counseling. Addiction support groups are not therapy groups, even though they may be therapeutic. It helps to have a counselor who understands addiction and dependency.

People in phase one usually want clear direction to help them get started. People need guidelines and strategies for maintaining sobriety while being encouraged to think for themselves as well.

Many people argue that when people first come into the program, you have to tell them, "Just shut up and do it." I disagree, particularly as this relates to most women. This stance encourages people to blindly adopt dogma, making them victims of "the program." While they may need to immerse themselves in the program and make it the focus of their lives for a time, this does not preclude using their minds and creativity. People don't have to fit themselves into a box to stay sober or to change.

When people present themselves as victims by constantly asking for advice, it is especially important to say, "What do you think is best? What possibilities have you explored?" You can support and help by brainstorming with them, citing how different people solved the problem, but it is a violation to tell people what to do. They need to be supported in their struggle to develop a sense of self.

In phase one, as one addiction gets under control, others often surface—very often around sexuality, dependency, and relationships. It's not uncommon for people to attend three or four different support groups for different addiction or dependency problems. Relationships may fall apart or require counseling to make them come alive again. The camaraderie of one's addiction buddies is lost. A new support system is needed.

Many people spend years in this phase, slowly shifting to a new level as sobriety feels more secure. A common progression is sobriety, therapy, education or vocational training, a better job, leaving old friends, developing support, and finding new relationships—and, of course, a growing sense of self. Many people start incorporating rituals into their lives or exploring their cultural heritages, or looking for churches or spiritual groups that feel supportive.

Many Native American people have used pipe ceremonies, sweat lodges, and vision quests, and kindly include white people who are drawn to such spiritual rituals. African Americans start exploring their literature and history. Women form spirituality groups and learn about the Goddess and their internalized oppression. Men of privilege in hierarchy are also bonding together to look beneath the facade of their stereotypical roles.

Phase Two: Discovery/Growth Groups

In the second phase, we shift the focus from survival to growth. This does not preclude difficulties along the way, but life is no longer quite so difficult, dramatic, or on the edge. Carrying forth all that feels supportive and helpful in phase one, this phase takes people to a new level of consciousness. Expansion, exploration, creativity, affiliation, and purpose are key concepts. People integrate physical, emotional, and spiritual well-being, realizing the need to be balanced in all these domains. People also deepen knowledge of their cultural heritage and their internalized oppression, taking steps to empower themselves to feel whole.

Quality of life and relationships to friends, family, partners, work associates and community come to the forefront. This is balanced with taking charge of one's life and taking steps to reach one's personal goals. People go back to school, continue psychotherapy, get better jobs, develop a support system, and start pursuing interests and hobbies. At this stage, if they haven't done so already, people start shedding their identity as addicts or codependents and see themselves as normal human beings who have had some addiction and dependency problems.

The sixteen steps could continue to be a springboard, or people could revise or create their own steps or work from other models. They could also incorporate into the steps discussion of relevant social issues and literature.

At this level people become interested in diverse groups of people, although they may need to return to the sanctuary of their own gender or ethnic or racial group some of the time. If a group uses closing prayers, each person could bring one that has meaning for them. They could also make a conscious effort to include readings from other spiritual or cultural traditions, for part of this phase of growth is developing a worldview and discovering the universality of wisdom in many teachings throughout the world.

Another aspect of this stage is that we watch the dance of life from the perspective of a nonjudgmental witness. "Oh, there I go doing my crazy stuff. Wonder what's going on inside." Shame becomes less common, since we are more truly convinced that we are sacred because we are alive, which helps us separate actions from worth.

Finally, people at this level increasingly realize the deep interconnections among all life—that we as humans are not separate from or superior to the earth and that how we relate to the earth often mirrors the ways we relate to each other.

The Use of Rituals

In chapter 13, I spoke of rituals as a way to heal and grow and keep us grounded in life's ups and downs. Creating life-affirming rituals become part of people's lives at all levels of uncovery and discovery. Rituals can help people pass through life transitions thus normalize life events by observing, feeling, and talking about them with one's community of friends. In our culture, many products are sold based on the premise that uncomfortable feelings and struggle are something to medicate, get over, and avoid. When we fall into this trap instead of merging with life we avoid it. This is a primary source of addictive behavior.

We can make rituals for transitions—birth, death, success, loss, marriage, partnering, sickness, promotions, moving, healing—that help us move through these times and let go. Rituals do not need to be formal or complex. Several people getting together when someone is going through a hard time and letting them talk about their experience can be a ritual. I think of my friends' taking me out to dinner to mark the end of my radiation treatments and our affirming each other as a form of ritual that acknowledged my illness, bonded our friendship, and helped me to move on.

The AIDS Quilt, which has traveled around the country to commemorate those who have died, is a remarkable ritual that has touched thousands of people. The ritual includes both the people making the quilts and the people looking at the quilts. This is a mass ritual that brings us home to ourselves and the realities of life . . . and death.

Ritual gives us a way to be immersed, creative, and connected in times of grief. When my mother died, my sister Lenore brought a large, fringed square of heavy white silk and embroidery thread to our mother's house. We sat together on Mom's favorite love seat—the one she finally allowed herself to have—holding the lovely material, embroidering flower designs she would have liked.

It flooded my being with memories of happy times when my sister and I were little children—embroidering dish towels, or sitting around together making doll clothes. My mother was a wonderful teacher. She radiated joy in sewing together with my sister and me. She let us try out any wild idea we had, and she never criticized our mistakes or what we made. We didn't have to finish, do it right, follow a pattern, or make it match, and safety pins were an okay substitute for buttons.

So there I sat with my sister, late into the night, sometimes discussing if Mom would prefer green thread next to the coral flowers we embroidered, sometimes crying, and sometimes bathed in wonderful memories. I felt linked through time and space to all daughters mourning the loss of their mothers, and to all sisters feeling a special bond between them. The next day, we wrapped the scarf around my mother in her casket, and she was cremated wearing it. Letting go of the scarf helped me accept death—to put all my love into something, give it away, and let it go. The memories remain secure in my heart.

Rituals for celebrating success are also important. Medallions for having completed a month or a year or more of sobriety are a ritual in twelve-step groups. Often a woman brings a new medallion to therapy groups, talks about her healing, and passes it around for us all to hold and to send good wishes to her.

In my therapy groups I find that people have seldom had celebrations for life events, including birthdays, new jobs, or a personal achievement. So we create the rituals people want—bringing flowers, singing, reading them poems. When people leave groups we also create a ritual. We've had everything from Caesar salad and candlelight, to making collages, to everyone bringing a rock, to singing, to having me play the accordion while everyone danced. Rituals bring us into the present and heighten our sense of awareness. They are both personal and creative.

When we take a personal experience that has intensity and meaning and describe it to others, we are partaking in the age-old ritual of storytelling. At a recent gathering of Minnesota Women Psychologists, a woman storyteller invited participants to tell a story from their lives. They were fascinating. In our Quaker meeting before our gathered worship, we have a time where one individual tells of their spiritual journey. I often learn more about a person in that hour than I have in years of going to meeting with them.

Quakers also have clearness committees that can be a model for community ritual. When you are stuck or in need of help, you can call for a clearness committee to sit down with you and help you sort through your problems. I have done this on several occasions. What I like is the sense of it being a communal, peer form of ministry to one another.

Over time, rituals come to augment and sometimes replace therapy for dealing with life events. A core to changing our understanding of healing or uncovering from addiction is to realize that life is not a sickness, feelings are natural, and there are ups and downs for everyone.

Stage Three

Recalling the quote by Ram Dass, this is where we move beyond the method. Instead of being a good "program person," one is simply an integrated person; instead of being good at prayer or seeing oneself as spiritual, life and spirituality merge, as we bring consciousness to daily activities. As one woman said, "Often when I'm meeting people at work, talking to an old friend, looking out the window at the trees, or peeling a carrot, I feel this sense of thanksgiving move through me." We're no longer going somewhere so much as tuning in more deeply to where we are.

In this stage, group structure evolves by consensus as groups form for varying reasons. The form serves the purpose of the group, and lasts only as long as it is needed. Groups could be for personal sharing, spiritual growth, reaching beyond our social circles, bridging diversity, and social action.

In this phase, one may still join a support group, but addiction and dependency are seldom the focus. While one may never transcend a physical addiction, it ceases to occupy psychic or emotional time. It is like an old story, read long ago and placed on the shelf. It doesn't mean life is without stubbed toes, or addictive thoughts crossing one's mind, but the emotions connected with the trials and pleasures of life are felt openly, allowing a person to move on rather than escape with addiction.

As we become strengthened in our hearts and wills, we speak more simply from our inner voices. The thoughts, "What's the *right* thing to say?" or "They might leave me if I don't do it *right*," have dissolved into "Hmm . . . what's the *truth* about this for me?" "What am I meant to do?" We develop bonds with others that are woven together through common beliefs and goals. We also learn to accept the solitude required in pursuit of our calling.

Diversity Groups

I would like to see people create groups for the purpose of bridging diversity. In the past years, I have found workshops dealing with racism and classism have helped me grow at a deeper level than workshops on psychotherapy. In interviewing a diverse group of people for this book, I learned again and again that my experience and perspectives, the values I hold dear, are very much a product of my conditioning and experience as middle class, white, female, single mother, bisexual woman from Missoula, Montana, who has lived in seven different cities or towns.

When the *Minneapolis Star and Tribune* did a lengthy series on racism, core people in the project kept diaries for several weeks in order to record their encounters with people of other races (and their own). Individual's journals were printed daily in the paper. They were always the first thing I read, for personal accounts of people's experience give us the pulse beat of where we are in developing our awareness. It's through tuning in daily to our own racism that we start understanding the magnitude of the problem in our culture.

The first step of a diversity group is to sit and listen to other people's histories without questioning, arguing, or trying to change their perspective. Rather, to imagine how it would feel to be that person. It is fascinating and often painful to hear others' stories, especially when one's privilege or ignorance has hurt others. What was it like growing up? What did it feel like to be Black? white? poor? gay? have alcoholic parents? Where did you live? What games did you like? What were your sources of strength? What kind of discipline did your caretakers use? Did you have friends? Were you lonely? What were your joys and talents? What were the racist/sexist/homophobic experiences you had? How did your privilege/poverty affect you? It is important that people talk from a personal level in telling their experiences.

Another part of participating in a diversity group could be for people to keep journals as they become more conscious of racism and sexism and report back to others what they are learning.

People could ask other members to read books that promote understanding of their minority groups. The *Star and Tribune* series on racism is a fascinating starting point, and is available by writing to the *Star and Tribune*, 425 Portland, Minneapolis, MN.

Diversity groups could pool knowledge. When we discussed racial issues at the Blue Bay Native American healing I mentioned earlier, I noticed that several white speakers were on their invited list. The woman at the center smiled at me, and said simply, "We're interested in learning whatever we can to help our people." I was repeatedly impressed with the ability of many Native Americans to draw from many sources of wisdom and integrate and adapt them to fit the need at hand.

Diversity group could be formed as part of taking social action. The possibilities are endless, but it needs to start with understanding each other's situation.

Diversity groups can also operate in organizations. It can be people in different echelons of power coming together, like our mandala image. In consulting for troubled organizations, the first step is for everyone to sit in a circle and describe from a feeling level what they are experiencing in their work. What in the system is helpful, what grates on their nerves or has gotten in the way?

In leading a weekend retreat for an agency, I was amazed at how unaware people were of the problems and concerns of people in other sections of the organization. It was like the multiple-personality syndrome I described earlier. It was easy to see why the system didn't work very well. There needed to be understanding and compassion between different segments, and a communication network reaching out in all directions, not just from the top down.

Oneness/Acceptance

In this phase of maturity we realize that falling off the path is *part* of the path. Nothing is separate. We fall, we get up, sometimes alone, sometimes with the help of a friend. It's not good, it's not bad, it's just what is in the moment. So we accept the falling off and know we will get back up.

Physical well-being, illness, happiness, sadness are also accepted as natural parts of life. It isn't that we will be happy all the time, it's that we will feel secure in the knowledge that we can rely on a strong center within to support us in difficult times. I image it as a willow tree in the body—strong, bending, fluid, flexible, swaying with the wind yet still rooted firmly in the earth. At this level, the desire to stay on our path and seek our purpose and the willingness to accept the unknown become secure within us like a deepening reservoir.

According to Fritjof Capra, author of *The Turning Point*, in Chinese medicine "illness is not thought of as an intruding agent but as due to a pattern of causes leading to disharmony and imbalance. . . . Going in and out of balance is seen as a natural process [and] no sharp division is made between health and illness. The individual organism changes continually in relationship to the changing environment."

Likewise, we do not see ourselves as separate from other people and other forms of life. Thus nonviolence is an intrinsic part of this stage, because to harm another would feel like harming ourselves. Love is not seen so much as something we get, but as a way we live and feel on the inside.

Groups could use various types of steps, discuss books, and continue to cast out their internalized oppression. In essence, they would broaden the definition of the traditional twelfth step and bring the focus into the present with creative rituals, reaching out to people in need and participating in social action.

Imagine all the good that could happen if all the people attending twelve-step recovery groups because it has become their primary identity and social network rechanneled some of their energy into serving community needs. I have an image of a lot of AA old-timers who may be bonding together in groups, more because of the fraternity they offer, than because of any real threat to sobriety. In my image, they get together to renovate boarded-up low-income houses, or build playground equipment, or do other community actions that improve our community's well-being. They could have their group for themselves one week, alternating with a community support group the next. The possibilities are infinite.

SUGGESTIONS FOR STARTING A SIXTEEN-STEP GROUP

If you are in a traditional "recovery" group and want to switch to or start a sixteen-step group, here is what others have done.

1. An existing twelve-step group, after discussion and processing, switched to the sixteen steps. A few members left.

2. Someone brought the sixteen steps to their group. Some people wanted to use them and others didn't. The sixteen-step advocates broke off and formed their own group.

3. A woman placed an ad in a local "recovery" newsletter saying she wanted to have a woman's empowerment group for recovery. Several people came.

4. The steps were written up in a women's psychology newsletter with times and dates of sixteen-step groups so psychologists could refer to those groups.

5. A man in an incest survivor's group suggested they use these steps. Some people wanted to, but others didn't, so he broke off and formed his own group.

6. One group had a retreat to talk about changing to different steps and supported everyone in expressing all their feelings.

7. Women used examples from the sixteen steps when presenting a step in a traditional group. Other members were intrigued and started combining the sixteen steps with the twelve steps.

8. One group decided to use the twelve steps one week and the sixteen steps on alternate weeks. Another group read both the twelve steps and the sixteen steps every week.

9. An existing group used the sixteen steps as a base and made a few revisions. They use the new version for a designated time to give the group stability.

10. A group of women friends at a conference talked about the sixteen steps at lunch and decided to start a general support group using them.

11. One woman formed an all-purpose discovery and empowerment group for people in phase two with any and all addiction and dependency concerns included. She advertised in a local "recovery" newsletter and asked me to mention it in a talk I gave.

12. In one group, a woman stood up one day and said, "I hate these steps; I don't like saying them." Another woman brought out a copy of the Ms. article she had with her and they had a discussion. They agreed to read both the twelve steps and the sixteen steps in their group.

13. Clients or staff have taken "We Gather Together" and the sixteen steps to treatment programs and given them to staff.

14. A therapist started two therapy groups for people in recovery/uncovery from addiction using the sixteen steps combined with a group process. One group typified phase one, maintaining sobriety; the other was a phase two group. They would discuss a step each week, and participants would keep journals and open up the next meeting talking about insights they had gained throughout the week. Then they would discuss the next step.

15. A woman who teaches in a high school for recovering/uncovering chemically dependent adolescents said she took the steps to her staff. They have incorporated them as part of their philosophy and use them for their own consciousness-raising to look at their attitudes toward power and empowerment.

She also said that when she took them to referring agencies to see if they would support her using them, most the responses were off the record. "People were terrified at the idea of empowerment. They'd say things like, 'I'm intrigued; I haven't gone to AA in two years, but I'd get in trouble if I said I support you.' " So she decided to use them as part of a class on empowerment. She emphasized that it's a process, and it feels right to go slowly, but it has made a difference with the staff.

16. A woman's treatment program took the monograph I wrote on this subject and started making it available for women in their program. They started by having women read my discussion of the steps (similar to chapter 13) and lists of other people's steps, and then reword them. The counselor said, "We had to be quiet about it at first, but over a three-year period there has been more acceptance." She said there was still the stress of walking the fine line between doing what she believed was most empowering for her clients and not getting in trouble with their administration.

Another possibility is to use these steps for personal growth. Get some friends together and go through them, spending one or two weeks on each step.

GUIDELINES FOR GROUPS

It is important for people to be clear on group policy. The main thing is that the group reaches a consensus so that all people feel they can live with the ground rules.

Some common group guidelines are:

1. Define the purpose of the group, what the format will be, and the length of the meetings, as well as whether it is time-limited or ongoing.

2. Define how time will be divided between people.

3. Decide on a moderator, who will say, "Let's start now," "Let's end now." This could be shared or left to the moderator of the week. Members should alternate being the moderator periodically so no one is seen as a leader.

4. Develop a language to keep the group on track. For example, members could agree to interrupt if someone is going on at length, saying, "I'm aware of the time, and others still need to talk." Someone could be timekeeper, or mention when there is fifteen minutes of group time left.

5. If there are dues, have someone volunteer as a treasurer. Agree on how the dues should be spent.

6. Maintain confidentiality: People can talk about what they are learning in a group, but they are not to talk about other people. This should be underscored. The level of trust in the group depends on it.

7. Meet at the same place and the same time weekly. (Moving around adds stress for people, and increases resistance because it means change and trouble to find different places. On the other hand it sometimes works.)

8. Some groups ask for a six-week starting commitment for new members. While this can't be rigidly enforced, it prevents lots of people from just dropping in.

9. Start and end on time. Even if two people are there, start on time. People tend to like something they can count on.

10. Don't interrupt the flow of the group if a new person comes in with severe problems. Let them join the group, but not take control by having everyone shift the focus onto them. It is important that the one in distress realize the group boundaries and limitations so they can get help elsewhere and not make unrealistic demands on the group.

11. Suggest that people give at least two weeks' notice if they are leaving so people will have a chance to say goodbye.

12. Don't spend a lot of time trying to stop someone from leaving. We're on a journey and we get to choose our path. People instinctively know if a group is within their comfort level. Have your feelings, but don't guilt a person for leaving, and, if possible, support them in making the decision that feels best for them.

This is not a finite list. Some of these common ground rules will fit and some won't, and you may have others that apply to a group you will be in. One of my favorite lines from the twelve-step approach is to take what you like and leave the rest behind. Always, and forever.

In interviews and questionnaires, *many people* talked about their irritation in twelve-step groups of always closing with the Lord's Prayer. One woman said, "I mentioned that this prayer doesn't fit for me and I would like to use something else." The responses were typical, fear-based responses: "We've always done it that way"; "If it's not broke don't fix it."

An expression of a life-loving, creative spirituality would be for people to bring favorite poems, readings, and sayings to group and take turns reading them. As I said in the last chapter, I'm planning to put together a sixteen-step workbook and I would like to include a section on closings. If you have a favorite poem, saying, or reading you would like to have included, please send it to me with a reference so I can get permission to use it. Full instructions are in the back of the book.

Let's weave together, creating a form and a process that builds a foundation for positive change. Instead of one linear model, we can have many circles with many ways, all working toward growth, empowerment, and an ability to appreciate life.

16

A Return to the Circle:
Moving Beyond Hierarchy and Addiction

To move beyond addiction we must create a social system that values life and cares for all its people and all our natural resources. To do this we must leave our hierarchical ways of thinking and operating, and return to a circular kind of consciousness where all life is seen as interrelated and love is the highest value. In other words, we need a life-loving/creative spirituality, not one based on sin and redemption.

In the summer of 1989, when I visited the Blue Bay Healing Center on the Flathead Indian reservation in Montana, I saw a poster by Sam English with the words, "A Return to the Circle," announcing the first Native American Conference on Adult Children of Alcoholics. I was mesmerized by the poster's beauty—the power of the words and the image of a white eagle, its wings encircling a group of Native Americans. It conveyed comfort, coming together, and hope.

For many Native Americans, returning to the circle means stopping their abuse of alcohol and returning to their ways of child-rearing, their rich symbolic heritage, and their indigenous spirituality, which is closely tied to the earth, the seasons, and the interwoven nature of all life. Many of their rituals are done in a circle—sweat lodges, talking circles, and pipe ceremonies.

A circle suggests connections, motion, strength, and power. When we stand in a circle, arms linked, we can all see each other. If one person falls, we all see and feel the impact. Each person's survival depends on supporting everyone else in the circle and staying connected. In the linear images of our hierarchical society, it's as if we are all standing in a row, shoulder to shoulder, so no one sees anyone else. If someone falls down, few people notice or feel the impact.

PREVENTION, PREVENTION, PREVENTION

In *Women, Sex, and Addiction: A Search for Love and Power*, I included a chapter called "Rx for the Culture." It outlines numerous examples of social change that need to happen to alleviate addiction. In over 125 radio and TV interviews only two or three people referred to that chapter and it was never mentioned in reviews. People are just not drawn to talk about prevention—it doesn't sell.

As we end the socially bleak decade of the eighties in the United States, we are feeling the impact of our linear, hierarchical culture in blatant and insidious ways that are harming us all: increasing crime and violence, poverty, homelessness, addiction, depression, anxiety, psychic numbing, incest, battering, sexual harassment, dependent relationships, cancer, satanic ritual abuse, immunological diseases, apathy, increased learning disorders, illiteracy, fetal alcohol syndrome, racism, sexism, prejudice, high school dropouts, alienation, isolation, teenage suicide, and children who murder.

Hunger, which was nearly eradicated in the seventies, is back with a vengeance, creating spiritual, psychological and physical problems such as learning disabilities that will lead to more violence, desperation, gangs, and addiction. A Public Broadcasting Service television show on children made the point that if there was a drug for children that increased brain size, helped prevent learning disabilities, raised IQ, developed healthy bones and muscles, and helped physical development, that everyone would be interested. But when we say that the miracle drug exists and it's called *food*, no one is interested. On another PBS program on aging, a frustrated doctor talked about the fact that insurance companies or Medicaid won't fund $250 shoes that prevent diabetic people from having leg amputations, but will fund thousands of dollars for amputations, which are physically and emotionally debilitating.

* * *

The addicted person needs a crisis to realize he or she is in serious trouble. Our addictive culture is crisis-oriented as well. We seem to need a disaster to wake us up, pull us together, and get things done. Like an addicted person, we get high on rescue scenes, heroic acts, inventiveness, and making up exotic cures for rare diseases. But we are dismal when it comes to the idea of prevention—a sober approach which is often inexpensive, simple, and mundane, involving unglamorous things such as food, jobs, parenting classes, shoes, housing, immunizations, Head Start programs, and access to education.

It is not a question of money or techniques, because it has been demonstrated repeatedly that prevention is far cheaper than repairing the problem later, and we have had programs that have worked. The only hard thing about prevention is that it takes planning, awareness, generosity, consciousness, compassion, and love, as opposed to greed, self-centeredness, and complacency. In other words, it's a nonaddictive approach with no heroics or heroes and it doesn't lead to bombastic political rhetoric. It's a matter of including everyone in the circle.

How does this relate to addiction? Very directly. Take a child and give him insufficient food and care. The child develops slowly, causing learning problems. This leads to low self-esteem and hostility. Teachers and parents are frustrated, and the child starts to fail at school and then feels bad about himself or herself and starts acting out, eventually getting involved with a street gang, or having a baby, or getting into drugs, violence or a dependent, abusive relationship. When the heart and soul are left hungry, the survivor reaches for whatever promises relief.

In a very insidious way, our addictive approach to social problems relates to sin and redemption, because suffering is readily accepted and people who suffer are seen as deserving it or as heroes. For women, suffering is glorified. At our local children's theater, *The Little Match Girl*, the story of a bright little girl dying of starvation on the streets, is always shown at Christmastime. Why do we see this as a charming Christmas story?

In many ways, we are a degenerating society, with addiction as a primary symptom along with increasing neglect of people's basic needs. As a society, we are becoming spiritually bereft. When we blind ourselves to the suffering around us, we blind ourselves to our spirits and our ability to love. What has happened to the Christian teachings, "Love thy neighbor as thyself," "Thou shalt not kill," or "As you do unto the least of these, so you do it unto me?" It has become commonplace to hear the phrase, "We don't really know about Christianity because it hasn't been tried yet."

PSYCHIC NUMBING AND DISSOCIATION

From our circle image—a life-loving spirituality—we believe that all people deserve food, shelter, respect, and work, not just a privileged few. To return to the circle we re-member (a Mary Daly term), restore and reconnect.

To conquer people, the warrior patriarchs constantly "broke people's circles." For example, they attacked women's circles—their rituals surrounding birth, aging, and death. Endemic to establishing western patriarchal medicine was the elimination of nurse midwives, healers, herbalists, and natural forms of healing that connected us to the earth. As mentioned earlier, an estimated nine million people—predominantly women, who were healers and wise women—were burned to death over a period of three hundred years, accused of witchcraft. This holocaust is rarely mentioned in basic history books and seldom with an analysis of the true intent, but the legacy lives on in the form of a deep-seated fear many women carry in their unconscious about being wise, powerful, or successful.

Slave traders broke tribal circles in Africa. They took people from their homelands, their customs and rituals that gave their life meaning. They separated wife from husband, mother from child, brother from sister. They took away language, customs, heritage, and knowledge. (It was illegal to teach a "slave" to read.) Currently, in nearly every measure of social well-being in the United States, people of color have less access to the potential benefits of our culture. Thus they are more likely to be poor, have birth defects, learning problems, go to prison, or die young. Many lack access to health care, education, and meaningful work. It has been shown that simply going to buy something takes more energy because people of color are given slower, less courteous service and are more often the subject for surveillance or harassment as potential shoplifters.

One of the most atrocious examples of breaking people's circles with mass genocide was when Columbus invaded (sometimes called discovered) America, coming upon the Arawak people who had resided peacefully in the Caribbean since 8 B.C. According to an article "Rediscovering Christopher Columbus" by Joanna Kadi that appeared in the January 3rd, 1992, issue of *Equal Time*, within fifty years all but two hundred of approximately three million Arawaks were dead. Up to sixty-five million native people have died in this five-hundred-year holocaust, often carried out in the guise of progress or Christianity, but really because Europeans wanted to own land and have slaves. The genocide that started with guns and swords continued by taking away land, breaking up people's families, and forcing assimilation through degrading traditions, language, rituals, and spirituality. The onslaught continues to this day through economic deprivation and racism resulting in suicide and alcoholism. Fortunately, the five-hundredth anniversary of Columbus's accidental arrival is being seen by many from the viewpoint of the people who suffered at Columbus's hands, and the Europeans who followed.

Once we understand that patriarchy survives by breaking the circles of oppressed peoples and always women, it helps us see why, the recent backlash to women in terms of rape, incest, battering, controlling reproductive rights, and the feminization of poverty are forms of social control. The sad truth is that the backlash has extended to all vulnerable people in the United States. Thus in the late seventies and eighties, funding for programs to empower women and people of color has been greatly reduced, and tacit approval of racism and sexism has been supported by our leaders. Children are the ultimate victims—25 percent of whom now live in poverty in the United States.

Men who support change away from patriarchy and hierarchy also become targets of patriarchal wrath. A recent blatant example was the yearlong silencing by the Pope of Matthew Fox, a Catholic priest and creation theologist, who, after being investigated for several years, was accused of being a "fervent feminist." At least that's putting the sexism out where you can see it.

MOVING BEYOND OUR ADDICTIVE SYSTEM

As stated in the outset of this chapter, to move beyond our addiction-permeated culture, we must move to a circle that embraces life; a model that values nonviolence, cooperation, empathy, understanding, and creativity. We must symbolically link hands as equals and work cooperatively with reverence for all of life—people, plants, and animals.

I spoke earlier about our culture as the macrocosm of a multiple personality. We need to integrate that personality, and find a way for all the parts to hear one another. In circle consciousness, we stay open, we feel, we do not turn away from suffering—ours or that of other people. And, finally, we take action to bring people into the circle.

EQUALITY BETWEEN MEN AND WOMEN

We return to the circle by creating equality between men and women. Just recently when I asked my neighbor Kerry how she was, she exploded with rage about the group home she works in. For three years, a male resident had been threatening and intimidating other women, and Kerry had reported him on numerous occasions. "It's horrible being there with him and the residents are so upset around him. And he's tried to hit me several times."

Her words went unheeded, resulting in continued frustration. "Then," Kerry continued, "he hauled off and punched a *male* staff member, and he was removed from the group home within three hours. I was so mad I couldn't sleep, and I'm still mad." What Kerry described was a typical scenario taking place in a myriad of forms, draining women's energy. It is part and parcel of oppression to make people's lives stressful so they can't function optimally.

I couldn't take away her frustration, but I could listen and respond: "What a rip, what a frustration, how exhausting." I could be available to her and not minimize her frustration. As we help each other feel and validate the reality of the affronts to our lives, we gather power. We strengthen the circle.

In a linear model, we go from point A to point X, or from the bottom to the top. In a circle image, there is no bottom or top, and though we keep coming back to the same situations, we have a new perspective. The goal is to keep the circle connected. We do this by giving to others. They take what we have given, add their own wisdom, and in turn they give back to us. Like a weaving, the giving and receiving become intertwined, and almost indistinguishable as the tapestry takes form.

I believe all small acts of connecting, noticing, caring for others help change the atmosphere. Have you ever made a mistake or been upset and had a person stay relaxed and smile at you or help you out? Have you ever had someone scream at you as if you were a total jerk because you made a mistake? Both responses send out vibrations into the atmosphere—one is nurturing; the other, toxic.

A PERSONAL RETURN TO THE CIRCLE

The interactions between myself and Kelly formed a circle as we gave back and forth to each other. In March of 1991, I was nearly through with radiation treatments, tired, and struggling to stave off a deep-seated fear of never regaining the concentration and energy I needed to finish this book. I had continued writing, but could only hear my inner voice for fleeting moments, now and then. I felt so lonely for this connection to myself. Then Kelly invited me to come to her sixteen-step meeting to celebrate her sixth year of sobriety. I was touched and pleased to go. It had been five years since I had attended my last twelve-step group, and I looked forward to connecting with women committed to their healing. I was also curious what it would be like to be in a group using the steps I had written.

On a late Saturday afternoon, feeling weary, I arrived at the somewhat scruffy meeting room, furnished with torn plastic chairs and worn-out couches—a familiar setting for support groups. As the women filtered in, I felt a sense of relief—like a forgotten emptiness inside being filled up. My tiredness took away my defenses and I felt a peaceful, relaxing sort of vulnerability.

I felt a quiver of energy inside when I saw a stack of lavender sheets with the sixteen steps on a couch across the room. I knew they'd be there, but seeing them brought home the reality—people were using these steps. A woman passed out the sheets. She didn't know I'd written the steps and I appreciated the anonymity because I wanted to take in the meeting for myself.

When the women went around in a circle reading the steps, I felt both discomfort and a sense of wonder. It was actually happening—those words I had put together had taken on a life of their own.

After the women read the steps, Kelly told her history. The sun was setting, and the room with a single candle burning became dim. But no one got up to turn on a light. Kelly's history of being abandoned, alone, desperate for comfort, lost in her drug use, was no surprise to the women gathered in the room.

When Kelly was through, someone asked, "Who would you like to have give you your medallion?" When she said "Charlotte, would you give it to me?" I came close to tears. I felt honored. I don't remember anything I said to her, but I remember the words flowing easily. At the end, I hugged her and felt less weary. What I had given out was all coming back to me. The circle had come 'round.

As the women took turns sharing about their lives, one said, "I'm so glad there's a woman out there who wrote these steps down, especially the one about accepting the ups and downs of life." I wanted to say "That woman isn't out there, she's right in here with you, needing you as much as you need her," but I said nothing until afterwards.

I can't say there was a miraculous resurgence of energy, or that I rushed home and was filled with inspiration, but there was a shift deep inside. I had the thought, "You will have energy; people will help you; it's going to be all right."

A Return to the Circle: Valuing and Caring For Children

If I had the opportunity to stand on a mountain and make my voice heard across this land, I would yell, Take care of all our children. They are the future, they are sacred, they deserve our care. Whatever we don't spend on them in terms of care, opportunity, and love will haunt the next generation in terms of more violence, sickness, and apathy. And it will haunt us all on a spiritual level, because allowing children to starve and go without education and immunizations is a crime of the spirit.

One of the greatest connections we need to make is between the care we give our children and their ability to be productive, socially conscious adults. I can't stress enough that the seeds of addiction are planted during the first critical years of life. If addiction is being in denial, then the most addictive part of our culture is the way we deprive children of care and love—and then act surprised when they get into drugs, become violent, or have babies to fill up the emptiness. The cost to society is staggering, and the prognosis for the children of these children is terrifying. Yet we massively deny the needs of infants and young children, move them around and ignore all the research on the importance of early bonding and consistent care with loving and competent caregivers.

A Return to the Circle: Positive Sexuality

There are many ways we need to return to a circular way of thinking. Sexuality needs to be tied to a life-loving/creative spirituality, a circular energy where people give and receive, listen and understand and feel connected. Images of sexuality in the United States are closely tied into our sin-and-redemption, necrophilic system that worships violence and death. A common expression of these negative attitudes toward sex and women is in pornography, and reach their natural extreme in "snuff" movies, where a woman is actually killed when a man has orgasm.

All our cultural rules about sexuality come from the first three levels of faithing—external control. Sex is fine if you are married and heterosexual, even if a man is violent and rapes his wife or if sex is angry, violent, kinky, selfish or coerced through manipulation. It's also acceptable if a man goes to a woman in prostitution and pays for the use of her body, even though she may have been abducted, sold, or coerced to participate. On the other hand, sex is considered sinful if expressed by two women or two men, even though they may love and care deeply for each other. It's all backwards.

In a life-loving sexuality, we turn inside and ask: Does our sexuality express love and care for our partner? Are we being emotionally present and honest? Sex is associated with tenderness, warmth, love, and passion. In such a view, there would not be room for pornography because images of degradation are not in keeping with honoring everyone in the circle.

A Return to the Circle: Being Connected to the Earth

Children are brought up without an understanding of the circular energy system that exists. Children and adults alike need to create images in their minds that link manufactured products, food, water, and electricity to the resources of the earth. Meat doesn't grow in a package, wood doesn't come from a lumber yard, water doesn't just come out of a tap, electricity doesn't just pop on all by itself and trash doesn't just disappear into a garbage truck. We need to be conscious that paper comes from a supply of trees, water from rivers, and our food from the earth and that our leftovers take up space somewhere. How we treat the earth and her resources is tied to our spirituality, because it is about truly perceiving and being integrated.

A Return to the Circle: Life Cycles

We live in a culture that glorifies the young, rich and beautiful. We need to return to a circle of understanding all the phases of life from birth to death as an integral part of the life circle. All phases have important tasks to accomplish and have potential for meaning. We need to honor all times of life including death. If we regard people as important natural resources then we can become creative in nurturing these resources. For example, some child care centers have encouraged the elderly to be there to read to children and tell them stories. There are all kinds of possibilities once we make the consciousness change and value life from beginning to end.

A Return to the Circle: Honoring Women's Natural Bodies

A return to the circle means that we start restoring balance—balance within people and balance among people. One of the ways women have been knocked off balance is with unrealistic images of beauty which stress thinness.

Thus, one circle we need to return to is an acceptance and love for women's natural, round bodies—their bellies, hips, thighs, and breasts. We need to affirm that women come in many shapes and sizes, and that setting a norm is a form of oppression. I think of the many Goddess images with large round bellies, hips, and breasts, honoring women's capacity to create life.

The most cruel patriarchal switch, resulting in unimaginable collective self-hatred, has been to denigrate the natural woman's body by replacing it with models created in the image of adolescent boys—thin and lanky with no hips and tiny breasts. The images where women have breasts and fuller bodies are usually pornographic, pairing control, violence, and domination with sexuality. Thus, the symbols of fertility have been denigrated and shamed, and women waste their precious energy worrying about how they look rather than mobilizing their strength to create a life with purpose and happiness.

Chronic dieting, compulsive eating, bulimia, anorexia, and concern with weight and appearance are a massive expression of internalized oppression. To put the emphasis on how you look rather than on how you feel is to objectify your body and become separate from your spiritual roots.

A patriarchal switch back would be for women to stop holding in their bellies, stop chronic dieting, and create their own image of what it is to be a beautiful woman—hopefully, an image that has to do with being alive, passionate, natural, at home in one's body, and accepting hair, blemishes, and different sizes. Imagine the collective energy that would be released, and the shift in our collective consciousness, if women moved from worrying about their weight and appearance to examining the roots of their oppression.

How about creating groups for *giving up dieting, accepting our bodies as they are,* and taking action to improve our lives.

Naomi Wolf, in *The Beauty Myth,* a book that would be a wonderful starting point for group study of the patriarchal switch, writes: "There is a secret 'underlife' poisoning our freedom; infused with notions of beauty, it is a dark vein of self-hatred, physical obsessions, terror of aging, and dread of lost control." Wolf sees women getting drawn into the beauty myth as part of a violent backlash against feminism. On the book jacket the backlash is referred to as "a relentless cult of female beauty—anti-erotic, averse to love, and increasingly savage—[used] as a political weapon against women's recent advances, placing women in more danger today than ever before." According to Wolf, beauty is a currency system like the gold standard, which is not about women at all. "It is about men's institutions and institutional power."

Circle Images: A Return to the Goddess

For many people, returning to the Goddess signifies a return to feminine spirituality that centers on celebration of life and oneness with nature. It is essentially what I have been calling a life-loving/creative spirituality. The Reverend M. Susan Milnor, a minister in Minneapolis, gave a sermon titled "Unfold My Life and Weave Within," which brought home a beautiful image of female spirituality.

She told of her feelings when, as an adult, she came across a tattered old quilt her grandmother had made for her. In touching the cloth and seeing the many pieces of fabric, she felt a strong connection with her mother and grandmother that transcended the difficulties of their relationships. It was connected to feminine spirituality, which is grounded in an integration of the pieces of everyday life. She writes:

> Spirit means breath. Spirituality is the way we breathe life into ourselves, in the best and worst of times, and the way we breathe ourselves into life. . . . Historically, in our culture, certain things have very much been associated with spirituality. One is a radical distinction between the body and soul, matter and spirit. "The spiritual" had to do with the soul, with heaven, with another world, and thus with death. If anything, the emotions and activities of earth formed an obstacle. Similarly the spiritual was connected to extraordinary experiences; extreme isolation, bodily denial, out of body experiences, visions.
>
> We have begun to realize, however, that this kind of spirituality is not universal. It's certainly not that of primal or tribal peoples. Furthermore, women have begun to claim a spiritual heritage much more centered in life and creation.
>
> If there is any one truth about women's spirituality which determines all the other truths, it is this. Women's spirituality is rooted in the earth, at one with it, nurtured by it . . . this earth

centeredness is found in ancient as well as contemporary writings of women.

We human beings are not caught on the earth, alone, alienated, waiting for a more perfect world, a more perfect life, union with a distant God. We are at home here. We are at home as creatures who are born and die, creatures who love and fear. Our pain is here. Our ecstasy is here.

Women's spirituality lives in the things of the earth . . . in the relatedness of human beings to each other and to the rest of creation. Thus, it assumes and celebrates a unity of spirit and matter. The spirit is the body; the body becomes holy."

Notice all the words suggesting unity, relatedness, simplicity, integration: all of the words that go with a circular image. We don't transcend life. We value and become at one with it. Thus, unlike the patriarchal system of valuing that which is scarce—like gold—women's spirituality values that which is abundant and life-giving like air, earth, and water. Therefore, clean air is more important than gold; clean water is more important than expensive wine, an earth restored is more important than an excess of possessions, and happy children are more important than military might.

TURNING POINTS FOR PEOPLE IN DISCOVERY: CONNECTING

Turning points in general are a way we connect more deeply to ourselves and our purpose. At a personal level returning to the circle means connecting with our inner world—our feelings, hopes, dreams, and sense of essential worth. Often the first step is to connect with the pain that led us to the addictive use of substances or relationships. In the addiction field, bottoming is when people connect with the devastation in their lives and realize they are on a destructive path.

Drawing from the questionnaires, here are some experiences of the initial connections to pain, often called bottoming out:

"In 1976, when I couldn't pick up my first-born grandchild because I was shaking so badly, I realized I was in disastrously bad shape."

"I hit bottom in a mutually destructive relationship with a violent alcoholic. By the end, I was a hundred pounds overweight, no longer employed, sleeping much of most days, not seeing friends, [and had] minimal contact with family. . . . I was afraid of dying or being killed by him."

When we're lost in addiction individually and collectively, our capacity for denial becomes immense. As a culture we need to experience collectively what jolted these individuals into realizing they were in dire straits. In other words, the grandmother who couldn't pick up her grandchild because she was shaking so much is a metaphor for our treatment of children.

Is our culture bottoming out? It is easy to feel disheartened at the moment, but I believe the move to the extreme right in the 1980s and early 1990s is a backlash against the consciousness that has been steadily rising since the sixties and seventies, when this wave of feminism started to change the balance between men and women and steps were made to address the other "isms." While things look pretty grim if your values include the alleviation of human suffering, there is a huge grassroots movement of people who understand that we are in need of fundamental changes in our social structure.

Connecting with Other People

People wrote about connections with others that jarred them out of their denial about addiction and gave them hope or a feeling of being valued.

The grandmother who couldn't pick up her grandchild wrote,

"When I called AA and two women came to my door and picked me up in a car, I felt so rescued."

Other responses were:

"After going from one expensive weight-loss program to another, I met a nurse who asked about stress in my life—when seeing the extent of it, she said, 'I can't help you, you need to go to a recovery program.' I had not reached bottom. Then my parents died in their addictions. Finally I am accepting that I must trust this program or die an early death as well."

"When my brother confronted me with my drinking problem, I accepted the reality that I needed to quit drinking—the right time, right place, and a person who cared and loved me. He told me our friendship was over unless I quit drinking."

"When I read Melody Beattie's list of codependent behaviors in relationships, particularly the part about addictive rituals, I realized I had a problem."

"A therapist would not help me unless I went to AA or treatment."

"When I had about two years of sobriety, I hit my bottom emotionally—suicide was a daily thought. With the help and guidance of a friend/mentor, I got into therapy which lasted about two years and I believe turned my life around."

"It was coming out as a lesbian and going to a women's outpatient treatment center and talking about my childhood and hearing other women talk about what they'd been through, and seeing strong, capable, survivor lesbians."

"So many new, wonderful women have come into my life during this journey—sober beautiful lesbians, beautiful straight women—what a gift and major turning point—to surround myself with loving, caring souls."

"Meeting medicine people."

Connections—a loving brother who took a tough stand, a treatment program that empowered women, a nurse who had the courage to say "I can't help you." We can make a difference in each other's lives. While I have spoken at length about the importance of refraining from giving lots of unsolicited advice so that people can find their own path, this needs to be balanced with the knowledge that we are our sisters' and brothers' keepers. It is up to all of us to say, "Hey, no driving, you've been drinking," and "I don't want to hear any more stories of what other people did to you, but I'm glad to hear about ways you are taking care of yourself." It is a matter of timing, trust, and speaking from the heart, and even then there is no guarantee of the outcome. But interventions of this type are like building blocks. If a person hears something enough times, it might start to sink in. That's why self-help books sell so well. We need to hear the same thing over and over to counteract all our original programming.

The other part of the connecting that was extremely important for people was reflected in the last two quotes—being with understanding, caring people, telling one's history, and finding role models both in one's minority group and outside of one's minority group.

Connecting to New Beliefs and Having Insights

Another way we reintegrate our splintered personalities is to gain insight. In the lists of turning points, people wrote about coming to have a new perspective or new beliefs about themselves and life that helped externalize the shame and pain they had felt. People also talked about learning from books, therapists, friends, and others in their support and therapy groups.

"Being able to apply stuff from books. Example: *After the Tears* discusses 'spiraling.' I was able to see how my mother did this, and that it wasn't me who was defective—enormously freeing."

"I started realizing that I deserve unconditional love, and how unloved and worthless I had felt."

"I had a sexual physical experience with a man in the program while I was in recovery. I had thought since I wasn't drinking/drugging anymore, I wouldn't be promiscuous. . . . It took a long time to realize 'alcohol is only a symptom.' I immediately entered one-on-one therapy and agreed to my first experiential group for 'sexual dysfunction.' A wonderful turning point."

"A woman lover in 1978 said she was terminating a relationship. I fell apart emotionally and began therapy. Around the same time in graduate school I saw the film *Elm Street*, about a little girl and an alcoholic—I knew then I wasn't alone."

"In an incest survivor group, the two leaders and women made me aware that it isn't just the act of sex on a child which creates the damage, but the family's denial of the pain, lack of privacy, blaming, etc., which sets the child up for long-term psychological problems."

"I got the idea of living from the inside out instead of the outside in, and eventually came to find a balance between the two—how to let people affect me but always having a choice to make my own decisions."

Strengthening the Circle: Taking Action Leading to Life Changes and Spiritual Growth

After people realize they are suffering, and gain new insights that bring hope, the next step is taking action. In the turning points section people wrote about major changes that improved their lives:

"Leaving my husband, going to Al-Anon, returning to college, getting a job."

"Going to Sundance and sweat lodge."

"I had my novel bought and published and started being recognized as a 'real' writer."

"Going to ACA."

"I became active in the 'Up and Out of Poverty' movement."

SHIFTING OUR PERSPECTIVES

Most of all, a return to the circle requires that we change our values and the ways we think. The first step is to realize how culture-bound our perspective really is.

One of the wonderful potentials of addiction support groups is that people cross over barriers and bridge differences. As you speak from the heart, you often start to care for others in a special way. You feel the commonalities, and often the judgments slip away as you see people owning up to their own problems and pushing against their limits to expand their self concept. It doesn't mean you necessarily want to be friends or have contact outside the group. But that's not the issue. Expanding one's perspective, dropping stereotypes, listening, connecting, and caring open up our spiritual journeys and help us learn that while we travel many roads, at the core there is really one journey.

A PARADIGM SHIFT: FROM MECHANISTIC TO WHOLISTIC

A paradigm shift is when we change our whole reference point and ways of perception. Returning to the circle is a paradigm shift that requires new language, new perceptions, and new values. It requires that we leave our mechanistic view that people and the universe operate like a machine with removable, changeable parts, for a view that sees all life as a dynamic, indivisible whole. We need to apply this knowledge to every aspect of our lives.

We also need to realize that life is a mystery beyond comprehension and that a sign of greatness is to cast off the pretense of knowing and controlling everything and stand back and look at our world with awe and appreciation.

We need to go through a process similar to the one physicists experienced when they began studying the atomic and subatomic world. They were faced with phenomena they had no language to describe. Fritjof Capra writes in *The Turning Point*, "It shattered the foundations of their world view and forced them to think in entirely new ways. . . . Every time they asked nature a question in an atomic experiment, nature answered with a paradox. In their struggle to grasp this new reality, scientists became painfully aware that their basic concepts, their language, and their whole way of thinking were inadequate to describe atomic phenomena. The new physics necessitated profound changes in concepts of space, time, matter, object, and cause and effect."

Eventually it was found that everything existed in relationship to all else, and it was impossible to define anything as separate. Thus complementarity became an essential concept. Capra quotes Heisenberg: " 'The world thus appears as a complicated tissue of events, in which connections of different kinds alternate or overlap or combine and thereby determine the texture of the whole.' "

The process was difficult and created emotional upheaval. Capra writes, "The exploration of the atomic and subatomic world brought them [the physicists] in contact with a strange and unexpected reality that seemed to defy any coherent description. Their problems were not merely intellectual but amounted to an intense emotional and, one could say, even existential crisis. It took them a long time to overcome this crisis, but in the end they were rewarded with deep insights into the nature of matter and its relationship to the human mind."

A RETURN TO LOTS OF CIRCLES

My hope is that the shift in the physicist's understanding of the world as an indivisible whole with all things moving in relationship to each other becomes the foundation for our approach to childrearing, education, human relations, and our connection to earth. As we shift from valuing things, death, control, and power to valuing life, breath, air, love, connectedness, and beauty, we are going through a great struggle; yet, ultimately, we too will be deeply rewarded.

So, as we come to the close of this book, I would like to leave you an image to carry with you that reflects some of those suggestions.

My sister Lenore Davis and I have created an image of lots of little circles that symbolize some of those necessary social changes. Many of the people we saw in the hierarchy drawing are here.

Starting from the left, we see people picnicking by the river and building a sand castle. This suggests that we need to take time to be together with friends and family in beautiful places that renew the spirit. We need to come in touch with the earth and feel the nurturing it affords us. We need to provide pleasurable experiences to our children to instill a sense of wonder, develop their creativity and give them warm memories to carry into adulthood, memories that can be pulled out on difficult days as resources for comfort. Without happy childhood experiences, our inner world becomes a frightening place and we are likely to fend off buried pain with addictions or violence.

On the upper left, we see the school for living simply. This is a metaphor for changing our values from loving objects and requiring constant entertainment to loving life and loving people. Simplicity takes us back to ourselves. When we take away the external junk, we meet our internal world.

Don Aslett writes in *Clutter's Last Stand*: "Anything that crowds

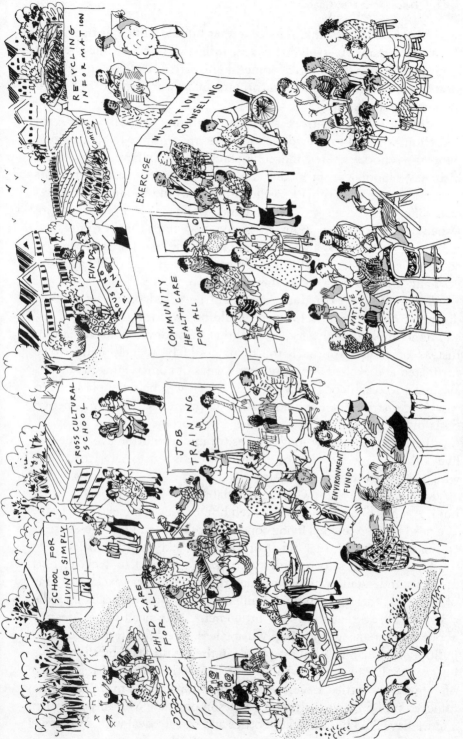

A Return to the Circle

the life out of you is junk. Anything that builds, edifies, enriches our spirit—that makes us truly happy, regardless of how worthless it may be in cash terms—isn't junk. Something worth $100,000 can be pure clutter to you if it causes discomfort and anxiety or insulates you from love or a relationship."

Moving to the right, we see a cross-cultural school. To prevent addiction, we need to provide schools that are sensitive to all races and peoples—schools where children are taught to learn from each other's histories, schools that provide a community meeting place for parents to connect with each other as well. Children would be taught to appreciate different people's ways which would build everyone's self-esteem. When people feel cared about, respected, have hope for the future, and strong connections to others, they are not likely to want or depend on addictive substances. And if they do get addicted, they will have support and a reason to give up their addiction.

The foundation of education would be based on understanding diversity, cooperation, self-esteem building, exploring human values, and noncompetitive physical activity that helps develop coordination. Instead of a rigid approach the focus could be to help children be fascinated and excited about the many ways of approaching problems. We need to teach consensus process, which will help people learn to work together and sometimes make compromises. The fundamental basis of consensus is that everyone is important and that we work together, no matter how long it takes, to find a solution everyone can live with. No one feels left out, thus no one is left to salve their hurt with addictive escapes.

Moving to the right, we have affordable, low-income housing being built. Again, children and adults need homes they can feel good about. We need to see wretched living conditions, slums, and homelessness as an unacceptable spiritual blight on our so-called civilized society.

The recycling information symbolizes our need to recycle, but, more, to understand ways to use materials wisely. I was excited to hear of architects' designing houses built with used tires and cans into the side of a hill so that they used little energy. We need to get creative about using, reusing, and simply using less. We could teach people to multiply their habits by all the people in the country and by all the days in the year. For example, if half the people in the country cut their use of canned or bottled beverages by one a day, that's more than one hundred million fewer cans and bottles in one day. Multiply it by 365 and we have 36.5 billion fewer bottles and cans to deal with. When we start thinking that way we get in touch with the enormous effect our daily habits have and how one small step by lots of people can make tremendous differences.

Next, as we go around the circle, we see community health care, exercise, and nutrition counseling for all. We absolutely must ensure health care for all people. Sick, tired children don't learn or concentrate well. As we return to the circle and to viewing all things as interconnected, health care will be a lot cheaper because people will use natural foods, and will exercise, relax more, have less stress, and be sick less often. The man getting up from the wheel chair was in the patriarchy drawing. He's greatly reduced the medications that wiped him out, and he's going to an exercise class at the nursing home.

In the two circles at the bottom of the page, we see diverse groups of children and adults getting together to tell their histories and learn from each other. This is crucial to our consciousness change. We can change laws, but we have to change at a spiritual level as well, or laws only result in backlash and violence. It's wonderful to see children in a preschool setting, free from prejudice and so willing to learn about others before they get indoctrinated into our multiple-personality system with different slots for different peoples.

Naturally, as we move on, we have environmental funds to preserve our beautiful land and work toward clean air, water, and soil, which will be easier when we lower consumption and live more simply. If we put our technological genius to work and do mass education, there are many things people could do daily to conserve energy and use many forms of energy we have only begun to explore. In the sixties, when the government gave tax write-offs for solar heating, lots of people used solar heating. It's not that we can't change things. Environmental protection needs to be a cooperative understanding of how to use renewable resources wisely and efficiently. Again, central to change is to massively educate people that we live on a finite planet. Our current approach to exploitation of the environment is like the addict's destroying his or her life before bottoming out and going for help. Unfortunately, some people die before they hit bottom. I hope we will do better than that.

Moving upwards, we see a group talking about job training. This is an obvious need if we are going to prevent addiction. If people have access to education and jobs, they are less likely to end up anesthetizing their lives with addiction and violence. We have had programs to create jobs for teenagers and adults. While they weren't perfect, they did a lot of good for a lot of people.

On the lower left we see a family making pasta together. This family is talking together and cooperating, and the little boy is feeling a sense of warmth and belonging he will always connect with preparing food, being together, and working cooperatively. If we give children more rich experiences, we give them the most precious commodity that exists—a sense of warmth and security within, ways of coping when the going gets rough, memories of being secure and loved. For too many people, thinking back brings pain, sorrow, and unhappiness, or a bleak landscape. Children want to belong and like to be useful if it is fun.

In the remaining two images, we see child care for all. If we look at where our values lie in relationship to what we spend, we see how little we value children. Many wonderful people want to work with children but simply can't live on $5.50 or $6 an hour—typical pay in many child care institutions. Even more important is that people who work with young children be carefully trained and well paid. That seems obvious, but in patriarchy we often see that things are upside down. We wouldn't hire a college professor to teach geography without being trained in geography, but we hire people with little or no training to care for children in their most important, vulnerable stages of development.

The stories of children being abused in child care facilities or being warehoused daily in dull, unstimulating environments represents the greatest part of our collective denial. If the media would devote as much time to the needs of children as they do to war, violent death, murders, fires, and robberies, it would facilitate a much quicker consciousness raising of the general public.

And speaking of what is left out of the media, one rarely reads about the problems of population growth on the planet. Even with careful planning, the earth will not be able to support the predicted doubling of the population in the next several decades. Unless we do something to slow down the growth, the mass starvation we are seeing now will be far greater, and the depletion of the earth's resources will be accelerated.

All our little circles in the illustration interrelate in terms of changing our value system and preventing addiction. Getting strength from nature supposes there is unpolluted nature available. Having jobs, housing, dignity, connectedness with others, and pride in one's heritage gives us the human bonds that are the antidote to addiction.

What is cost-effective is also the most humane and empowering. Child care is cheaper than group homes for teenagers, job training cheaper than prison, low-income housing cheaper than welfare, and paid maternity leave is cheaper than having damaged children or mothers on welfare. We have the resources to take care of all our people if we change from our authoritarian hierarchical stance to one of empowering people and fostering equality. The problem is not money. It's consciousness. We must come to value life.

I'll close by returning to where we began this book: embracing diversity, pushing through fear, and finding our own voice.

Adrienne, a Native American friend, agreed to take a group of Caucasian women in a therapy group to a sweat lodge as part of a healing weekend retreat. For all but myself, it was their first sweat lodge, and while all were eager for the experience, some of the women were quite fearful. We drove out to the country where the sweat lodge stands in a woods near a small lake.

The sweat lodge is a low, dome-shaped structure big enough for eight or ten people to sit in a circle with hot stones in the middle. It signifies going back into the earth, back into the womb, and connecting with the deepest parts of oneself. The sweat lodge we used was made from short poles and tree branches, and it was covered with an assortment of blankets and plastic tarps.

When we arrived, the fire outside was still burning from a previous sweat lodge ceremony, so we needed only to build it up and put in the rocks. While the rocks were heating, we made strings of prayer bags. Typically, each person makes about twenty, sometimes more, sometimes less. Taking little squares of cloth, you put a pinch of tobacco (considered sacred by Native Americans) on each one and say a prayer, and tie them to a string. The prayers can be for yourself, a friend, the family, or for peace. As we made the prayer bags, the women were alternately concentrating and getting giddy and joking, a way to relieve the anxiety.

Adrienne then led us through the ritual of crawling into the sweat lodge and hanging up our prayer bags. After we were all sitting in the circle, the helper brought in the red-hot rocks and put them in the center of the room. When Adrienne reached up and pulled down the heavy covering over the door, creating total darkness and a lot of heat, one of the women, Elaine, panicked. "Aren't we going to have the door open? Can I leave?"

I was worried about what would happen.

"No," said Adrienne, with total kindness yet conviction. "You can't leave. *You cannot break the circle with your sisters. They're all depending on you to be here. Just start praying and you'll be all right.*"

Elaine said, "But I'm afraid."

"Just start praying, and you'll be all right," Adrienne repeated with calm conviction.

The assuredness of Adrienne's words was stunning to me. As therapists, we learn to let people go at their own pace. So telling someone they can't leave when they're afraid would not be a typical approach. But there was a complete rightness to what Adrienne said. "No, you can't break the circle with your sisters." Sometimes we need to stay in when we are afraid, to push through, so we keep the energy flowing for our collective healing.

The sweat lodge got hot, and we went around the circle and everyone said their prayers out loud. It took nearly an hour. When we were all through, Adrienne opened the door, and then lit the pipe to pass around. After that, leaving our prayer bags hanging on the ceiling of the sweat lodge, we crawled out one at a time saying "all our relatives" to signify our connection to all people. Everyone looked invigorated and open when we left.

Later, when we talked about the experience, Elaine laughed and said, "That was terrible. I felt so afraid I reached out and grabbed Mary's hand and held on through the whole ceremony."

"I think that was pretty wonderful," Lou said.

"That I was afraid?" Elaine asked, puzzled.

"No! That you took someone's hand."

A big, warm grin came over Elaine's face. She blushed and looked for a moment like a child. As someone who had walked the path alone, admitting to fear and taking someone's hand to help her through was a monumental step. She had walked through fear. A month later, she reported that she hadn't had a cigarette ever since the sweat lodge, a habit she had been trying to break (the second time) for many months. Pushing through fear became a metaphor for Elaine's tendency to say, "But I'm afraid." By pushing through a very big fear, she had the confidence to start facing other fears.

When I talked later with Adrienne, she said, "Elaine's experience was not uncommon. . . . When people enter the sweat lodge, or when it becomes dark, they get afraid and want to run. It's a lot like entering treatment. You're going to have to face yourself, and you want to run away. People do everything to avoid their fear of facing their feelings of being unloved or hurt or having grief.

"The most human feelings come out in the sweat lodge; all of a sudden people cry or come out with what's making them afraid. That's what the medicine does. You create a circle that enables you to face God, yourself, and your feelings. And people always feel better afterwards."

Afterword

For several weeks I've been waiting for some inspiring thoughts to use as a closing for this book. After wondering why no great words of wisdom or lofty ideas graced my mind, I realized it was because at the moment I'm not interested in pondering anything of great significance. As I anticipate sending this book to the printer, I look forward to time for simple things, time for just being.

Last week when my mind went to mush while editing this manuscript, I decided to take a couple of days off just for pleasure. I went down to Calhoun Square, a pretty, small, enclosed shopping center with bookstores, delis, and clothing shops. I picked up some free local newspapers, got some soup and bread at a deli, and sat at their rather good imitation of a sidewalk cafe. (It's January in Minnesota.) How delicious it all was. Time. Eating slowly, reading, sitting, watching people. No plans, no pressure.

Sitting there brought back memories of my grandmother, Charlotte Pickett Davis, who used to take my sister and me on outings to art galleries and museums when we lived near Washington, D.C., as young children. I have no memory of hurrying. We would take the bus—or were they trolley cars?—for the trip into the city. During the day, if we got tired and wanted to sit down, we would find a bench or a cafeteria. Invariably, she would reach in her purse, pull out a book, and offer to read to us. I remember her reading to me in a shelter at a rose garden on a rainy day, in the Smithsonian Institution, and many other places. Remembering these sojourns stirs within me feelings of warmth, happiness, and security.

As I sat in Calhoun Square having my leisurely lunch, I also thought about the many people I interviewed who talked about stress and an almost desperate need for a break, for life to slow down. Time to relax or do simple tasks at a leisurely pace has become a scarcity in our so-called modern society. It is a paradox that the Native people, the Arawaks who inhabited the Guanahani Island that Christopher Columbus happened upon, worked cooperatively to feed all their people and had considerable time for leisure.

To me, particularly now that I have had a bout with cancer, time has become a most precious commodity. While the prognosis looks good, I no longer take life for granted. With the book completed, I have images of a leisurely lunch with friends, taking a drawing class, longer walks, playing the piano daily, trying some new recipes, writing letters, and a Saturday afternoon snuggled up with a quilt and a good novel. Most of all I think of slowing down everything I do from cutting up veggies to reading the mail.

I returned home thinking more and more about my grandmother. I dug out an old photograph album and looked at pictures of her. The one in her bedroom with a sewing basket on a table brought back memories of her showing me how she darned socks with the same meticulous energy she gave to reading or preparing a report for her book chat club. Nothing was ever rushed around her and everything was approached with the idea of dong a careful job.

More important about my grandmother was that she had an inquisitive mind and changed her opinions on the Bible, religion, and life until the day she died. We talked together about ideas from the time I was a young child and she always took my questions seriously. If one of us kids would come into the house with some bug she would get out the encyclopedia and look it up. Proud of her college degree in Botany, class of 1896, she would tell us the names of plants and flowers whenever we went to the woods for a hike.

Throughout this book I have talked about paired learning responses that create associations between events and emotions. For example, if your early experiences learning the times tables are paired with someone smacking your hand or calling you stupid when you make a mistake, your mind associates pain with math which can result in a lifetime of feeling anxious every time you start to deal with numbers. I was lucky that reading, questioning, and inquisitiveness were paired with being held, loved, and appreciated by my grandmother. Those paired associations got me through a lot of boring classes, sham-

Charlotte Pickett Davis, who loved me and taught me to question.
Charlotte Davis at about ten years of age in Missoula, Montana.

ing teachers, and dull books, because I knew inside me that learning was wonderful.

I hope we will take seriously the need for children to pair self-esteem and good feelings with reading, learning, questioning, cooperation, creativity, and a capacity to find pleasure in nature. These are the inner resources, the antidotes to violence and addiction they will need for the incredible job of restoring and preserving the earth and finding more humane ways to balance the earth's resources among all people. This crucial job requires vision and the kind of inner conviction that comes from being valued and cared for.

Sometimes people have said it was courageous for me to question the twelve-step institution, but I never experienced it as courageous. My grandmother was standing beside me all the time.

Appendix I

✖

Yeast Questionnaire

Adult

Answering these questions and adding up the scores will help you decide if yeasts contribute to your health problems. Yet you will not obtain an automatic "yes" or "no" answer.

For each "yes" answer in Section A, circle the Point Score in that section. Total your score and record it in the box at the end of the section. Then move on to Sections B and C and score as indicated.

Add the total of your scores to get your *Grand Total Score.*

SECTION A: HISTORY   Point Score

1. Have you taken tetracyclines (Sumycin®, Panmycin®, Vibramycin®, Minocin®, etc.) or other antibiotics for acne for 1 month (or longer)?_____   35
2. Have you, at any time in your life, taken other "broad spectrum" antibiotics* for respiratory, urinary or other infections (for 2 months or longer, or in shorter courses 4 or more times in a 1-year period?)_____   35
3. Have you taken a broad spectrum antibiotic drug*—even a single course?_____   6

*Including Keflex®, ampicillin, amoxicillin, Ceclor®, Bactrim® and Septra®. Such antibiotics kill off "good germs" while they're killing off those which cause infection.

4. Have you, at any time in your life, been bothered by persistent prostatitis, vaginitis or other problems affecting your reproductive organs?_____ 25

5. Have you been pregnant . . . 2 or more times?_____ 5
   1 time?_____ 3

6. Have you taken birth control pills . . . For more than 2 years? _____ 15
   For 6 months to 2 years?_____ 8

7. Have you taken prednisone, Decadron® or other cortisone-type drugs . . .
   For more than 2 weeks?_____ 15
   For 2 weeks or less?_____ 6

8. Does exposure to perfumes, insecticides, fabric shop odors and other chemicals provoke . . .
   Moderate to severe symptoms?_____ 20
   Mild symptoms?_____ 5

9. Are your symptoms worse on damp, muggy days or in moldy places?_____ 20

10. Have you had athlete's foot, ringworm, "jock itch" or other chronic fungous infections of the skin or nails? Have such infections been . . .
    Severe or persistent?_____ 20
    Mild to moderate?_____ 10

11. Do you crave sugar?_____ 10

12. Do you crave breads?_____ 10

13. Do you crave alcoholic beverages?_____ 10

14. Does tobacco smoke *really* bother you?_____ 10
    Total Score, Section A . . . . _86_

SECTION B: MAJOR SYMPTOMS:

For each of your symptoms, enter the appropriate figure in the Point Score column:

If a symptom is *occasional or mild*	score 3 points
If a symptom is *frequent and/or moderately severe*	score 6 points
If a symptom is *severe and/or disabling*	score 9 points

Add total score and record it in the box at the end of this section.

Point Score

1. Fatigue or lethargy_____ 6
2. Feeling of being "drained"_____ 3
3. Poor memory_____ 3
4. Feeling "spacey" or "unreal"_____
5. Depression _____ 9
6. Numbness, burning or tingling_____ 6
7. Muscle aches_____ 6

8. Muscle weakness or paralysis _____ _____
9. Joint pain _____ 6 _____
10. Abdominal pain _____ 3 _____
11. Constipation _____ 9 _____
12. Diarrhea _____ 3 _____
13. Bloating _____ 8 _____
14. Troublesome vaginal discharge _____ 3 _____
15. Persistent vaginal burning or itching _____ 3 _____
16. Prostatitis _____ _____
17. Impotence _____ _____
18. Loss of sexual desire _____ _____
19. Endometriosis _____ 9 _____
20. Cramps and/or other menstrual irregularities _____ 3 _____
21. Premenstrual tension _____ _____
22. Spots in front of eyes _____ 6 _____
23. Erratic vision _____ _____
     Total Score, Section B 5 6

SECTION C: OTHER SYMPTOMS:*

For each of your symptoms, enter the appropriate figure in the Point Score column:

If a symptom is *occasional or mild* . . . . . score 1 point

If a symptom is *frequent and/or moderately severe*   score 2 points

If a symptom is *severe and/or disabling* . . . . score 3 points

Add total score and record it in the box at the end of this section.

Point Score

1. Drowsiness _____ 1 _____
2. Irritability or jitteriness _____ 1 _____
3. Incoordination _____ _____
4. Inability to concentrate _____ 2 _____
5. Frequent mood swings _____ 2 _____
6. Headache _____ 2 _____
7. Dizziness/loss of balance _____ 1 _____
8. Pressure above ears . . . feeling of head swelling
   & tingling _____ 2 _____
9. Itching _____ 3 _____
10. Other rashes _____ 3 _____
11. Heartburn _____ 1 _____
12. Indigestion _____ _____
13. Belching and intestinal gas _____ 1 _____
14. Mucus in stools _____ _____

*While the symptoms in this section commonly occur in people with yeast-connected illness they are also found in other individuals.

15. Hemorrhoids _____ 3
16. Dry mouth _____ 2
17. Rash or blisters in mouth _____
18. Bad breath _____ 3
19. Joint swelling or arthritis _____ 3
20. Nasal congestion or discharge _____
21. Postnasal drip _____
22. Nasal itching _____
23. Sore or dry throat _____
24. Cough _____
25. Pain or tightness in chest _____
26. Wheezing or shortness of breath _____ 3
27. Urgency or urinary frequency _____
28. Burning on urination _____
29. Failing vision _____
30. Burning or tearing of eyes _____
31. Recurrent infections or fluid in ears _____
32. Ear pain or deafness _____
     Total Score, Section C 86
     Total Score, Section A 56
     Total Score, Section B 33

GRAND TOTAL SCORE . . . . _____

The Grand Total Score will help you and your physician decide if your health problems are yeast connected. Scores in women will run higher as 7 items in the questionnaire apply exclusively to women, while only 2 apply exclusively to men. Yeast-connected health problems are almost certainly present in women with scores *over 180,* and in men with scores *over 140.*

Yeast-connected health problems are probably present in women with scores *over 120* and in men with scores *over 90.*

Yeast-connected health problems are possibly present in women with scores *over 60* and in men with scores *over 40.*

With scores of less than 60 in women and 40 in men, yeasts are less apt to cause health problems.

Appendix II

Discovery Mandala

Directions: Fill in the sections with aspects of your growth.
Indicate how much progress you have made in various areas.

Appendix III

Resource List

Rational Recovery Systems
Jack Trimpey, LCSW
Box 100
Lotus, CA 95651
Telephone: (916) 621-4374

Save Ourselves or Secular Sobriety (SOS)
James Christopher
P.O. Box 5
Buffalo, NY 14215-0005
Telephone: (716) 834-2921

Women for Sobriety and Men for Sobriety
P.O. Box 618
Quakertown, PA 18951
Telephone: (215) 536-8026

Alcoholics Anonymous
P.O. Box 454
Grand Central Station
New York, NY 10017
Telephone: (212) 686-1100

National Council on Alcoholism and Drug Dependence, Inc. (NCADD)
12 West 21st Street

New York, NY 10010
Telephone: 1 (800) 475-HOPE (Help Line)
        1 (212) 206-6770 (General Information)

National Clearinghouse for Alcohol and Drug Information (NCADI)
P.O. Box 2345
Rockville, MD 20852
Telephone: 1 (301) 468-2600
        1 (800) 729-6686

Schick Shadel Hospital for Aversion Treatment
Dr. P. Joseph Frawley, M.D.
45 E. Alamar Avenue
Santa Barbara, CA 93105
Telephone: (805) 687-2411

HOW TO CONTACT THE PEOPLE WHO CONTRIBUTED TO THIS BOOK

Lenore Davis
Illustrator, soft sculptor, surface design
Workshop leader and illustrator
Box 47
Newport, KY 41072

Pat Rouse
Graphic designer and illustrator
420 N. 5th Street Suite 950
Minneapolis, MN 55401

Charlotte Kasl, Ph.D.
Workshops, trainings, organizational consulting, or you would
simply like to respond to this book

NOTE: If you would like announcements of workshops and trainings,
please send a self-addressed stamped legal size (preferably) envelope.

I read all the letters I receive and love to hear from people but I cannot
always respond personally and I do *not* have references for therapists around
the country.

Until July 1, 1992
Castle Consulting Inc.
Box 7073
Minneapolis, MN 55407

After July 1, 1992
Many Roads One Journey
Box 1302
Lolo, MT 59847

Appendix IV

❦

Guidelines for Input on
How You Used This Book

If you would like to give input for a follow-up guide related to the material in this book, I would very much appreciate your response. The following questions can be used as a guide, but feel free to add questions of your own.

Please be as specific as possible, and send your input to the address on page 406.

1. Did you use any of the sixteen steps in your personal life (whether or not you were in a specific group)?
   1b. Which ones? How did you use them and did they help?
2. If you started a group using the sixteen steps (or a modified version), or used this book as a resource to start your own type of group
   a. How did it happen? What was said?
   b. How was it initiated?
   c. Describe the focus of the group (for addiction in general, empowerment, substance abuse, incest, etc.).
   d. How has it gone?
3. Any advice or support you would like to give others attempting to start a group?
4. If you modified these steps I would love to have a copy, or if you developed a process for people writing their own, I would like to know what it was.

GROUP INTRODUCTION

1. Did you use the introduction suggested on page＿＿＿ (Chapter 14)?
   Did you change it in any way? If so please include a copy of what you wrote.

GENERAL RESPONSE

Any other ways this book was helpful to you? (helped you feel stronger, make a decision, improve your life, etc.)

CLOSINGS

I would love to put together a booklet including many possible closings for groups. It can be from any religion, culture, ethnic background and include poetry, literature, sayings, or it can be one you create yourself.

If you include a suggested closing please include the following:

1. A copy of the closing
2. Source: title of book, song, etc.
3. Publisher and address
4. If it is one you wrote, include your name and address and indicate if you would give permission to use it.

Bibliography

Al-Anon's Twelve Steps and Twelve Traditions. New York: Al-Anon Family Group Headquarters, Inc., 1989.

Alcoholics Anonymous Comes of Age: A Brief History of A.A. New York: Alcoholics Anonymous World Services, Inc, 1957.

Alcoholics Anonymous: Third Edition of the Big Book, the Basic Text for Alcoholics Anonymous. New York: Alcoholics Anonymous World Services, Inc., 1976.

American Heritage Dictionary: The Second College Edition. Boston: Houghton Mifflin Co., 1982.

American Psychiatric Association. *Diagnostic and Statistical Manual of Mental Disorders*. 3rd ed. Washington, D.C.: The American Psychiatric Association, 1980.

Andrews, Lynn V. *Flight of the Seventh Moon*. San Francisco: Harper & Row, 1984.

———. *Medicine Woman*. San Francisco: Harper & Row, 1981.

Aslett, Don. *Clutter's Last Stand*. Cincinnati: Writer's Digest Books, 1984.

Augustine Fellowship, The. *Sex and Love Addicts Anonymous*. Boston: The Augustine Fellowship, Fellowship-Wide Services, Inc., 1986.

Bailey, Joseph V. *The Serenity Principle: Finding Inner Peace in Recovery*. San Francisco: Harper & Row, 1990.

Beattie, Melody. *Beyond Codependency and Getting Better All the Time*. San Francisco: Harper & Row, 1989.

———. *Codependent No More*. San Francisco: Harper & Row, 1987.

Bepko, Claudia, and Krestan, Jo-Ann. *Too Good for Her Own Good: Breaking*

Free from the Burden of Female Responsibility. New York: Harper & Row, 1990.

Bly, Robert. *The Kabir Book*. Boston: Beacon Press, 1977.

Boesing, Martha. *Junkie*. At The Foot of the Mountain Theatre, 1981.

Bolen, Jean Shinoda, M.D. *Goddesses in Everywoman: A New Psychology of Women*. San Francisco: Harper & Row, 1984.

Bowlby, John. *A Secure Base: Parent-Child Attachment and Healthy Human Development*. New York: Basic Books, 1988.

Burns, David D., M.D. *Feeling Good: The New Mood Therapy*. New York: William Morrow & Co., 1980.

Caldicott, Helen. *Missile Envy: The Arms Race and Nuclear War*. New York, NY: William Morrow, 1984.

Cameron, Anne. *Daughters of Copper Woman*. Vancouver, B.C.: Press Gang Publishers, 1981.

Capra, Fritjof. *The Turning Point: Science, Society, and the Rising Culture*. New York: Simon & Schuster, 1982.

Carter, Steven, and Sokol, Julia. *Men Who Can't Love*. New York: Berkley Books, 1987.

Castaneda, Carlos. *A Separate Reality: Further Conversations with Don Juan*. New York: Simon & Schuster, 1971.

Cermak, Timmen L., M.D. *Diagnosing and Treating Co-Dependence*. Minneapolis: Johnson Institute Books, 1986.

Chesler, Phyllis. *About Men*. New York: Simon & Schuster, 1978.

———. *Women, Money, and Power*. New York: William Morrow & Co., 1976.

Christopher D. Smithers Foundation, The. *Understanding Alcoholism: For the Patient, the Family, and the Employer*. New York: Charles Scribner's Sons, 1968.

Christopher, James. *How to Stay Sober: Recovery Without Religion*. Buffalo, N.Y.: Prometheus Books, 1988.

———. *Unhooked: Staying Sober and Drug-Free*. Buffalo, N.Y.: Prometheus Books, 1989.

Colbin, Annemarie. *Food and Healing*. New York: Ballantine Books, 1986.

Common Boundary May/June 1990. "Why Spiritual Groups Go Awry." Edited by Joanne Sanders.

Crook, William G., M.D. *Chronic Fatigue Syndrome*. Jackson, Tenn.: Professional Books, 1992.

———. *The Yeast Connection: A Medical Breakthrough*, 3rd ed. Jackson, Tenn.: Professional Books, 1986.

Daly, Mary. *Gyn/Ecology: The Metaethics of Radical Feminism*. Boston: Beacon Press, 1978.

———. *Pure Lust*. Boston: Beacon Press, 1984.

———, with Jane Caputi. *Webster's First New Intergalactic Wickedary of the English Language*. Boston: Beacon Press, 1987.

Dass, Ram or Gordon, James S., "Why Spiritual Groups Go Awry," in *Common Boundary*, May/June 1990.

———. *Grist for the Mill.* Santa Cruz, Calif.: Unity Press, 1977.

———. *The Only Dance There Is.* Garden City, N.Y.: Doubleday & Co., Anchor Books, 1974.

Dass, Ram, and Paul Gorman. *How Can I Help?* New York: Alfred A. Knopf, 1985.

Davis, Angela Y. *Women, Race, and Class.* New York: Random House, Vintage Books, 1983.

Diamond, Harvey, and Marilyn Diamond. *Fit for Life.* New York: Warner Books, 1985.

———. *Fit for Life II: Living Health.* New York: Warner Books, 1987.

Dufty, William. *Sugar Blues.* New York: Warner Books, 1975.

Du Plessix Gray, Francine. "Women's Rites," in The *Utne Reader.* November/December 1987.

Each Day a New Beginning. Center City, Minn.: Hazelden Foundation, 1982.

Easwaran, Eknath, trans. *The Bhagavad Gita.* Petaluma, Calif.: Nilgiri Press, 1985.

Eisler, Riane. *The Chalice and the Blade.* San Francisco: Harper & Row, 1987.

Ellis, Albert, Ph.D., and Robert A. Harper, Ph.D. *A New Guide to Rational Living.* North Hollywood, Calif.: Wilshire Book Company, 1975.

Ettorre, E. M. *Lesbians, Women, and Society.* Boston: Routledge & Kegan Paul, 1980.

Ferguson, Marilyn. *The Aquarian Conspiracy: Personal and Social Transformation in the 1980s.* Los Angeles: Jeremy P. Tarcher, 1980.

Forward, Dr. Susan, and Joan Torres. *Men Who Hate Women and the Women Who Love Them.* New York: Bantam Books, 1986.

Fowler, James W. *Stages of Faith.* San Francisco: Harper & Row, 1981.

Frawley, P. Joseph, M.D. *Addiction: Who Is in Control?* Studio City, Calif.: Schick Laboratories, Inc., 1988.

Freire, Paulo. *Pedagogy of the Oppressed.* New York: Herder & Herder, 1972.

Fulani, Lenora, Ph.D. *The Psychopathology of Everyday Racism and Sexism.* New York and London: Harrington Park Press, 1987.

Gandhi, Mohandas K. *An Autobiography: The Story of My Experiments With Truth.* Boston: Beacon Press, 1957.

Gazda, George M. *Basic Approaches to Group Psychotherapy and Group Counseling.* 2nd ed. Springfield, Ill.: Charles C. Thomas, 1968, 1975.

Gilligan, Carol. *In a Different Voice: Psychological Theory and Women's Development.* Cambridge, Mass.: Harvard University Press, 1982.

———. *Making Connections: The Relational Worlds of Adolescent Girls of Emma Willard School.* Cambridge, Mass.: Harvard University Press, 1990.

Hallie, Philip. *Lest Innocent Blood Be Shed: The Story of the Village of Le Chambon and How Goodness Happened There.* New York: Harper & Row, 1979.

Hansen, James C., Richard W. Warner, and Elsie M. Smith. *Group Counseling: Theory and Process.* Chicago: Rand McNally College Publishing Company, 1976.

Havel, Vaclav. *Living in Truth.* Harlow, Essex: Faber & Faber, 1987.

Hazelden News & Professional Update, May 1991 article by Jeanne Engelmann "America Ignores Its No. 1 Drug Problem—Alcohol." Published by Hazelden Foundation, Minneapolis, Minn.

Hite, Shere. *Women and Love: A Cultural Revolution in Progress.* New York: Alfred A. Knopf, 1987.

Hoffman, Elizabeth Hanson. *The Smoking Papers: Recovery from Nicotine Addiction.* Center City, Minnesota, Hazelden, 1991.

Holy Bible, The (King James Version). London: Oxford University Press, 1965.

Humes, Alison. "The Culting of Codependency." In *Self-Help–7 Days,* November 1, 1989.

Johnson, Sonia. *Wildfire: Igniting the She/Volution.* Albuquerque, N.Mex.: Wildfire Books, 1989.

Johnson, Vernon E. *Intervention: How to Help Someone Who Doesn't Want Help.* Minneapolis: Johnson Institute Books, 1986.

Judith, Anodea. *Wheels of Life.* St. Paul, Minn.: Llewellyn Publications, 1987.

Kadi, Joanna, "Rediscovering Christopher Columbus," in *Equal Time,* January 3–January 17, 1992. Issue 254

Kantner, Rosabeth Moss, with Barry A. Stein. *A Tale of "O": On Being Different in an Organization.* New York: Harper & Row, 1980.

Kaplan, Louise J., Ph.D. *Oneness and Separateness: From Infant to Individual.* New York: Simon & Schuster, 1978.

Kasl, Charlotte Davis. *Women, Sex, and Addiction: A Search for Love and Power.* New York: Ticknor & Fields, 1989.

———. *"Dear Therapist: Through the Voices of Survivors."* Unpublished article, March 1986.

———. *"Psychotherapy Outcome of Lesbian Women as Related to Therapist Attitude Toward and Knowledge of Lesbianism."* Ph.D. diss., Ohio University, 1982.

———. "Female Perpetrators of Sexual Abuse: A Feminist View" from *The Sexually Abused Male.* Edited by Mic Hunter. Lexington, Mass: Lexington Books, 1990.

Katz, Judy H. *White Awareness.* Norman, Okla.: University of Oklahoma Press, 1978.

Kelberer, Michael. "Codependency: The More You Know, the Less You Are." In *The Phoenix,* May 1990.

Keyes, Ken, Jr. *Handbook to Higher Consciousness.* St. Mary, Ky.: Living Love Publications, 1975.

———. *The Methods Work . . . If You Do!* St. Mary, Ky.: Living Love Publications, 1978.

———. *Prescriptions for Happiness.* St. Mary, Ky.: Living Love Publications, n.d.

Kirkpatrick, Jean, Ph.D. *Goodbye Hangovers, Hello Life.* New York: Ballantine Books, 1986.

———. *The Program Booklet.* Quakertown, Pa.: Women for Sobriety, 1976.

———. *Turnabout: New Help for the Woman Alcoholic.* New York: Bantam Books, 1990.

Kurtz, Ernest. *Not-God: A History of Alcoholics Anonymous.* Center City, Minn.: Hazelden, 1979.

Kushi, Michio. *The Cancer Prevention Diet: Michio Kushi's Nutritional Blueprint for the Relief and Prevention of Disease.* New York: St. Martin's Press, 1983.

Larson, Earnie. *Stage II Recovery: Life Beyond Addiction.* San Francisco: Harper & Row, 1985.

Larson, Joan Matthews. *Breakthrough.* New York, NY: Villard, 1992.

Lazare, Daniel. in *The Village Voice* (January 22, 1990).

Lerner, Gerda. *The Creation of Patriarchy.* London: Oxford University Press, 1986.

Lerner, Harriet Goldhor, Ph.D. *The Dance of Anger.* New York: Harper & Row, 1985.

Magid, Dr. Ken, and Carole A. McKelvey. *High Risk: Children Without a Conscience.* New York: Bantam Books, 1987.

McAuliffe, Robert M., Ph.D., and Mary Boesen McAuliffe, Ph.D. *Essentials for the Diagnosis of Chemical Dependency. Vols. 1 and 2.* Minneapolis: The American Chemical Dependency Society, 1975.

————. *The Essentials of Chemical Dependency. Vol. 1.* Minneapolis: The American Chemical Dependency Society, 1975.

Meeker-Lowry, Susan. *Economics As If the Earth Really Mattered: A Catalyst Guide to Socially Conscious Investing.* Santa Cruz, Calif.: New Society Publishers, 1988.

Milam, Dr. James R., and Katherine Ketcham. *Under the Influence: A Guide to the Myths and Realities of Alcoholism.* New York: Bantam Books, 1983.

Miller, Alice. *For Your Own Good: Hidden Cruelty in Child-Rearing and the Roots of Violence.* New York, NY: Farrar, Strauss & Giroux, 1990.

————. *Thou Shalt Not Be Aware: Society's Betrayal of the Child.* New York: New American Library, 1984.

Miller, Jean Baker, M.D. *Toward a New Psychology of Women.* Boston: Beacon Press, 1976.

Miller, Saul, with Jo Anne Miller. *Food for Thought: A New Look at Food and Behavior.* Englewood Cliffs, N.J.: Prentice-Hall, 1979.

Mussen, Paul Henry, et al. *Child Development and Personality.* 4th ed. New York: Harper & Row, 1974.

Nakken, Craig. *The Addictive Personality: Roots, Rituals, and Recovery.* Center City, Minn.: New York: Harper & Row, 1988.

Nilsen, Mary Ylvisaker. *When a Bough Breaks: Mending the Family Tree.* Center City, Minn.: The Hazelden Foundation, 1985.

"No Gain, No Pain" (interview with Oprah Winfrey). In *People* magazine, January 14, 1991.

Norwood, Robin. *Women Who Love Too Much.* Los Angeles: Jeremy P. Tarcher, 1985.

One Day at a Time in Al-Anon. New York: Al-Anon Family Group Headquarters, Inc., 1978.

Pass It On: The Story of Bill Wilson and How the A.A. Message Reached the World. New York: Alcoholics Anonymous World Services, Inc, 1984.

Pearce, Joseph Chilton. *Magical Child*. New York: Bantam New Age Books, 1981.

Peele, Stanton. *Diseasing of America: Addiction Treatment Out of Control*. Lexington, Mass.: Lexington Books, 1989.

———. *Love and Addiction*. New York: New American Library, 1975.

Pharr, Suzanne. *Homophobia: A Weapon of Sexism*. Inverness, Calif.: Chardon Press, 1988.

Presnall, Lewis F. *The Search for Serenity and How to Achieve It*. Salt Lake City, Utah: U.A.F., 1959.

Putnam, Frank W. *Diagnosis and Treatment of Multiple Personality Disorder*. New York: The Guilford Press, 1989.

Rahula, Walpola. *What the Buddha Taught*. New York: Grove Press, 1959.

Restak, Richard, M.D. *The Brain*. New York: Bantam Books, 1984.

Rich, Adrienne. *Of Woman Born: Motherhood as Experience and Institution*. New York: W. W. Norton & Co., 1976.

Robbins, Anthony. *Unlimited Power*. New York: Ballantine Books, 1986.

Robinson, James M., gen. ed. *The Nag Hammadi Library*. San Francisco: Harper & Row, 1981.

Rodegast, Pat, and Judith Stanton. *Emmanuel's Book*. New York: Bantam New Age Books, 1985.

———. *Emmanuel's Book II: The Choice for Love*. New York: Bantam New Age Books, 1989.

Rush, Anne Kent. *Moon, Moon*. New York and Berkeley: Random House, Moon Books, 1976.

Scarf, Maggie. *Unfinished Business: Pressure Points in the Lives of Women*. Garden City, N.Y.: Doubleday & Co., 1980.

Schaef, Anne Wilson. *Co-Dependence: Misunderstood—Mistreated*. San Francisco: Harper & Row, 1986.

———. *Women's Reality*. Minneapolis: Winston Press, 1981.

Schaeffer, Brenda. *Is It Love or Is It Addiction?* Center City, Minn.: Hazelden Educational Materials, 1987.

Slater, Philip. *The Pursuit of Loneliness: American Culture at the Breaking Point*. Boston: Beacon Press, 1970.

Smith, Barbara. *Home Girls: A Black Feminist Anthology*. New York: Kitchen Table/Women of Color Press, 1983.

Smith, Wilfred Cantell. *Faith and Belief*. Princeton, N.J.: Princeton University Press, 1979.

———. *The Meaning & End of Religion*. New York: Viking Press, 1976.

Star Tribune, Minneapolis, Minn. May 31, 1991.

Starhawk. *Truth or Dare: Encounters with Power, Authority, and Mystery*. San Francisco: Harper & Row, 1987.

Stokes, Kenneth. *Faith Is a Verb: The Dynamics of Adult Faith Development*. Mystic, Conn.: Twenty-Third Publications, 1989.

Subby, Robert and Friel, John. "Co-Dependency: A Paradoxical Dependency." in *Co-Dependency: An Emerging Issue*. Pompano Beach, Fla.: Health Communications, 1984.

Suzuki, Shunryu. *Zen Mind, Beginner's Mind.* Tokyo: Weatherhill, 1970.

Swan, Bonita L. *Thirteen Steps: An Empowerment Process for Women.* San Francisco: spinsters/aunt lute, 1989.

Thomsen, Robert. *Bill W.* New York: Harper & Row, 1975.

Trimpey, Jack, LCSW. *Rational Recovery from Alcoholism: The Small Book.* California: Lotus Press, 1989.

Truss, C. Orian, M.D. *The Missing Diagnosis.* 1982. Available by writing to The Missing Diagnosis, P.O. Box 26508, Birmingham, AL 35226.

Twelve Steps and Twelve Traditions. New York: Alcoholics Anonymous World Services, Inc., 1952.

Twelve Steps for Everyone . . . Who Really Wants Them. Minneapolis, CompCare Publications, 1975.

Vaillant, George E. *The Natural History of Alcoholism: Causes, Patterns, and Paths to Recovery.* Cambridge, Mass.: Harvard University Press, 1983.

Wachtel, Paul L. *The Poverty of Affluence: A Psychological Portrait of the American Way of Life.* Philadelphia and Santa Cruz: New Society Publishers, 1989.

Walker, Lenore E. *The Battered Woman.* New York: Harper & Row, 1979.

Weatherford, Jack McIver. *Porn Row.* New York: Arbor House, 1986.

Wegscheider, Sharon. *Another Chance: Hope and Health for the Alcoholic Family.* Palo Alto, Calif.: Science and Behavior Books, 1981.

Wegscheider-Cruse, Sharon. *Choicemaking: For Co-Dependents, Adult Children and Spirituality Seekers.* Pompano Beach, Fla.: Health Communications, 1985.

Wholey, Dennis, et al. *The Courage to Change.* Boston: Houghton-Mifflin Co., 1984.

Wilson, Lois. *Lois Remembers.* New York: Al-Anon Family Group Headquarters, Inc., 1987.

Woititz, Janet Geringer, Ed.D. *Adult Children of Alcoholics.* Florida: Health Communications, 1983.

Wolf, Naomi. *The Beauty Myth.* New York: William Morrow & Co., 1991.

Yalom, Irvin D. *The Theory and Practice of Group Psychotherapy.* New York: Basic Books, 1975.

Copyright Acknowledgments

Index

419